Becoming Brazilians

This book traces the rise and decline of Gilberto Freyre's vision of racial and cultural mixture (*mestiçagem* – or race mixing) as the defining feature of Brazilian culture in the twentieth century. Eakin traces how *mestiçagem* moved from a conversation among a small group of intellectuals to become the dominant feature of Brazilian national identity, demonstrating how diverse Brazilians embraced *mestiçagem*, via popular music, film and television, literature, soccer, and protest movements. The Freyrean vision of the unity of Brazilians built on *mestiçagem* begins a gradual decline in the 1980s with the emergence of an identity politics stressing racial differences and multiculturalism. The book combines intellectual history, sociological and anthropological field work, political science, and cultural studies for a wide-ranging analysis of how Brazilians – across social classes – became Brazilians.

Marshall C. Eakin is Professor of History at Vanderbilt University. A specialist in modern Brazilian history, he is the author of four books including *The History of Latin America: Collision of Cultures*. He coedited *Envisioning Brazil: A Guide to Brazilian Studies in the United States*, with Paulo Roberto de Almeida.

New Approaches to the Americas

Edited by

Stuart Schwartz, *Yale University*

Becoming Brazilians

*Race and National Identity in
Twentieth-Century Brazil*

MARSHALL C. EAKIN

Vanderbilt University

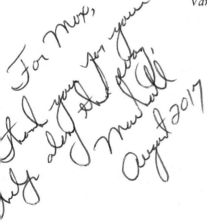

CAMBRIDGE
UNIVERSITY PRESS

CAMBRIDGE
UNIVERSITY PRESS

University Printing House, Cambridge CB2 8BS, United Kingdom

One Liberty Plaza, 20th Floor, New York, NY 10006, USA

477 Williamstown Road, Port Melbourne, VIC 3207, Australia

4843/24, 2nd Floor, Ansari Road, Daryaganj, Delhi – 110002, India

79 Anson Road, #06–04/06, Singapore 079906

Cambridge University Press is part of the University of Cambridge.

It furthers the University's mission by disseminating knowledge in the pursuit of education, learning, and research at the highest international levels of excellence.

www.cambridge.org
Information on this title: www.cambridge.org/9781107175761
DOI: 10.1017/9781316800058

First published 2017

Printed in the United States of America by Sheridan Books, Inc.

A catalogue record for this publication is available from the British Library.

ISBN 978-1-107-17576-1 Hardback
ISBN 978-1-316-62600-9 Paperback

aos meus amigos brasileiros e brasilianistas

Every Brazilian, even the light-skinned fair-haired one, carries with him in his soul, when not in body and soul ... the shadow, or at least the birthmark, of the Indian or the Negro.[1]

Gilberto Freyre

NOTE

1. "Todo brasileiro, mesmo o alvo, de cabelo louro, traz na alma, quando não na alma e no corpo ... a sombra ou pelo menos a pinta, do indígena ou do negro." Gilberto Freyre, *Casa-grande e senzala: formação da família brasileira sob o regime da economia patriarcal*, 49ª. edn. (São Paulo: Global Editora, 2003), 343. The translation is mine, slightly altered from Gilberto Freyre, *The Masters and the Slaves* [*Casa-grande e senzala*]: *A Study in the Development of Brazilian Civilization*, trans. Samuel Putnam, 2nd edn. rev. (New York: Alfred A. Knopf, 1970), 278. Unless otherwise noted, all translations are mine.

Contents

Figures

Acknowledgments

This book has had a very long gestation, and it has been nurtured along the way by numerous people across several continents, many of them without knowing it. The first book I ever read about Brazil was Gilberto Freyre's *The Masters and the Slaves*. I vividly remember reading Freyre one scorching summer (1972) in a tiny one-room apartment (without air-conditioning) in Lawrence, Kansas, in between my freshman and sophomore years in college. Little did I realize that summer in the middle of North America that this thick volume was one of the most important books about Brazil, and that it would become one of the most important in my life. Enthralled, during those torrid Kansas summer days I slowly sweated my way through this brilliant, eccentric essay. Looking back, I realize that I barely had begun to understand what Freyre was saying. My lack of comprehension was countered by the enthusiasm the book generated in me for this "new world in the tropics." Although I would take a very indirect path (through Central America), over the next decade I gradually became a historian of Brazil. Although my first writing and publications were on race and identity in early twentieth-century Brazil, for more than twenty years – from the 1970s to the 1990s – I studied and wrote primarily about the economic history of Brazil. Periodically, I would come back to my ruminations about Freyre and Brazilian culture, but it was not until recently that I finally returned to where I began. Over the years, as I researched, taught, and lectured about Brazil, I became intrigued at how the ideas and work of Gilberto Freyre became the central mythology that propelled the formation of Brazilian national identity in the twentieth century.

Long ago and far away in Kansas, Betsy Kuznesof helped get me started as a historian of Brazil. In Los Angeles, Brad Burns taught me to see the big picture and to try to speak beyond the narrow confines of academia. Many years in Belo Horizonte and my good friends in Minas Gerais persuaded me to see Brazil from inside out and not from the coast inward. In 1983, at a time when my academic career appeared to be stillborn, the History Department at Vanderbilt University took a chance on me, changing the trajectory of my life. I will be forever grateful to my colleagues in the department, then and now. I have benefited enormously by working at an outstanding university with even more outstanding programs in Brazilian and Latin American studies.

I am very fortunate to have received generous funding from a Fulbright-Hays Faculty Research Abroad Award (2009–2010) and a National Endowment for the Humanities Fellowship (2015) to spend long periods writing intensely while living in Brazil. Sabbaticals are one of the great privileges and luxuries of the life of a professor at a major research university. Longstanding and ongoing financial support from Vanderbilt University has been crucial throughout my career and especially in the work on this project over the past eight years. I am particularly grateful to former provost Richard McCarty for his support. Eight years ago he asked me to become the faculty director of the Ingram Scholarship Program. I began writing the first pages of this book at the same moment I joined the program, and I am writing the closing lines as I finish my time as director. In many ways unrelated to Brazil and Gilberto Freyre, the socially and civically engaged students in the program have pushed me to think deeply about my own worldview, beliefs, and assumptions. They have taught me a great deal, and this book and the Ingram Scholars have been equally important focal points in my life for the past eight years. I am especially indebted to my two exceptional program coordinators, Anne Gordon and Bryn Sierra, for all their support and for helping me balance my teaching, research, and administrative work.

I have been very fortunate to have worked at Vanderbilt University for more than three decades with a wonderful group of colleagues. The Center for Latin American Studies and the History Department are vibrant intellectual communities that have shaped my life as a scholar and teacher. The strength of the Brazilian studies program has constantly enriched my life and made it possible for me to grow. The late Alex Severino, Margo Milleret, Earl Fitz, Emanuelle Oliveira-Monte, Ben Legg, and Marcio Bahia all in their own ways helped me think and rethink *cultura brasileira*. Our program in Latin American history includes a truly wonderful and collegial group, including more than thirty graduate students over the last two decades. Jane Landers, Eddie Wright-Rios, Celso Castilho, Frank Robinson, and the late Simon Collier have been exceptional colleagues and friends. A special thanks to Joel Harrington for his support over the years, at home and abroad.

While I mentored Courtney Campbell, Max Pendergraph, Tiago Maranhão, and David LaFevor in their graduate training they also pushed me to think harder about my notions of nationalism, regionalism, and identity. Graduate and undergraduate students from various departments and programs took my classes on Latin America and seminars on race, nationalism, and nation-building, and they made me think more about the comparative picture, and even read and critiqued parts of my manuscript. Yoshi Igarashi, Gary Gerstle, Paul Kramer, Michael Bess, and Helmut Smith shared their own writing and research on nationalism and national identity with the seminars on nationalism. The graduate students in the interdisciplinary Brazilian Studies Reading Group also gave me valuable criticisms of the manuscript. From 2001 to 2015, Jane Landers, Celso Castilho, and I codirected a series of FIPSE-CAPSE student exchange grants on race and inequalities in Brazil and the United States in collaboration with the Universidade de São Paulo, the Universidade Federal da Bahia, the Universidade Federal do Rio Grande do Sul, the Universidade Federal de Pernambuco, Howard University, Fisk University, and the University of Florida. The three dozen students from Vanderbilt who attended our Brazilian partner institutions and the three dozen undergraduate students from Brazil who spent a semester at Vanderbilt, in many different ways, made me reflect often on the complexities of race and national identity.

A special thanks to Paula Covington, the incredible Latin American bibliographer at Vanderbilt. Due to Paula's work and that of her predecessors we have one of the great collections on Brazil in our library. For many years Paula has helped me with my research and taught me to be a better researcher. Mona Frederick has made enormous contributions to the intellectual life of Vanderbilt as the executive director of the Robert Penn Warren Center for the Humanities. I spent much of my last sabbatical at the Warren Center in a year-long seminar on public scholarship with a great group of fellow faculty and had the enormous luxury of a beautiful office where I could hide, read, write, and move this book closer to completion. Thank you, Mona.

As will be evident in the text, but especially in the endnotes, I could not have written this book without the vast and excellent scholarship across many disciplines, especially among those who study Brazil. For seven years (2004–2011) I served as the executive director of the Brazilian Studies Association and organized three international congresses for BRASA during that period. I cannot imagine what this book would look like, if it would even exist, had I not spent so much time collaborating in so many ways with Brazilians and Brazilianists during my time with BRASA. *Um obrigado muito especial* for my hardworking colleagues in leadership and support roles during those years, especially Jim Green, Tim Power, Jan French, Ken Serbin, Susan Quinlan, Peggy Sharpe, Jon Tolman, Cecilia Grespan, and Carolina Castellanos. A special thanks to Paulo Roberto de Almeida for asking me to coedit a survey of Brazilian studies in the United States that educated me extensively and resulted in two books.

Talks at a number of institutions helped me formulate, reformulate, and sharpen my arguments. Thanks to Mariza Soares at the Universidade Federal Fluminense; Jurandir Malerba and the Department of History at the Pontifícia Universidade Cátolica, Rio Grande do Sul; Ondina Fachel Leal and the Department of Anthropology at the Universidade Federal do Rio Grande do Sul; the Fundação Casa Rui Barbosa; Paula Barreto, the Centro de Estudos Afro-Orientais and the Universidade Federal da Bahia; colleagues at the Universidade de São Paulo in the departments of history, economics, and business; Parry Scott and the Department of Anthropology at the Universidade Federal de Pernambuco; Russell Walker and his students at the Kellogg School at Northwestern University; the Race Relations Institute at Fisk University; my colleagues and their students at the Owen Graduate School of Management, and the Osher Lifelong Learning Institute at Vanderbilt University. Some of my colleagues have been kind enough to read and comment on parts of this manuscript including Scott Ickes, Roger Kittleson, Jason Borge, and Bianca Freire-Medeiros. Chris Dunn, Bryan McCann, and Celso Castilho read the entire manuscript and provided me with very valuable feedback, helping make this a better book than it was in manuscript form. Over the past two years I have benefited from working with Liz Zechmeister, Tim Sterling, Fred Pereira, Heather Ewing, and Guilherme Russo on a healthcare study in Rio de Janeiro funded by Vanderbilt University. My colleagues in Brazil and at Vanderbilt in the project on "Building a Multi-disciplinary Approach to the Assessment of the Quality of Healthcare in Brazil" have provided me entirely new angles on race and national identity in Brazil. Kara

Schultz and Jeff Crosby facilitated the cover art, and my editorial team at Cambridge University Press skillfully guided me through the production process.

Finally, thank you Michelle for putting up with my long absences in Brazil and in Nashville hiding in my office working on this book. I could not have done this without your understanding, love, and support. *Um obrigado muito especial para o grande amor da minha vida.*

MAP 1 Map of Brazil and Its Regions
Source: Beth Robertson, Mapping Specialists Limited

INTRODUCTION

Creating a People and a Nation

[N]ations are constituted largely by the claims [they make for] themselves, by the way of talking and thinking and acting that relies on these sorts of claims to produce collective identity, to mobilize people for collective projects, and to evaluate peoples and practices.[1]

Craig Calhoun

GILBERTO FREYRE AND THE MYTH OF *MESTIÇAGEM*

The history of nationalism and national identities is a history of myth-making. This book reconstructs the story of how one myth of national identity became history. Brazilian national identity, like many other national identities, was constructed from local society up as well as from the State down. The combined and often conflicting efforts of the powerful and the less powerful forge peoples and nations over decades and centuries. Elites who wish to construct nations consciously seek to create a cohesive sense of national identity, solidarity, and allegiance to an articulated set of myths, rituals, and symbols. They pursue progress through order, and that order and progress hinge on the success of their attempts to impose homogeneity and uniformity. Despite their best efforts – and their power – often the plans of the nation-builders fail, either in part or in whole. The less powerful – especially the so-called masses (*o povo*) – quite often without setting out to do so create and shape their own myths, rituals, and symbols that sometimes reach a wide audience resonating with hundreds of thousands – even millions – of persons they have never met nor seen. This complex and dialectical process of the conscious and unconscious construction of peoples and nations through the emergence and evolution of a shared set of myths,

rituals, and symbols is the focus of this book. A generation ago, Benedict
Anderson brilliantly described this process as the creation of "imagined
communities."[2] *Becoming Brazilians* charts the emergence of an "imagined community" – what Brazilian intellectuals would call an *imaginário
nacional* (national imaginary/collective imagination) – the creation of
a people, and a nation, in twentieth-century Brazil.[3]

Since the 1930s, the most important national myth that has bound
people together in Brazil is what the anthropologist Roberto DaMatta
has called the "*fábula das três raças.*" This fable of the three races – what
I call the myth of *mestiçagem* (miscegenation) – asserts that Brazilians
share a common history of racial *and* cultural mixing of Native
Americans, Africans, and Europeans.[4] Although he did not invent this
myth, Gilberto Freyre's exuberant and optimistic vision of *mestiçagem*
has been its most potent and influential version. As Peter Fry has
concisely noted, Freyre declared that all Brazilians "whatever their
genealogical affiliation, were *culturally* Africans, Amerindians and
Europeans."[5] Even those Brazilians who are not biologically *mestiços*
are cultural hybrids. In Freyre's own oft-quoted words, "Every
Brazilian, even the light-skinned fair-haired one, carries with him in
his soul, when not in body and soul … the shadow, or at least the
birthmark, of the Indian or the Negro."[6] All Brazilians, regardless of
the color of their skin, carry with them shadows in their souls, traces of
Europe, Africa, and the Americas in their cultural, if not their biological,
DNA.[7] This is the essence of the Freyrean vision of Brazil, *brasilidade*
(Brazilianness), and Brazilian national identity in the twentieth
century. This book is a sort of cultural history of the Freyrean myth of
mestiçagem.

Before the publication of Freyre's monumental *The Masters and the
Slaves* (*Casa-grande e senzala* in the Portuguese original) in 1933, many
Brazilian and foreign intellectuals had recognized this mixing, but very
few viewed this *mestiçagem* favorably.[8] By the 1970s and 1980s, nearly
all Brazilians, at some level, shared this belief – it had become something
of a "master narrative of Brazilian culture."[9] When queried about race or
ancestry for surveys, most Brazilians tell the questioners they are
"Brazilian."[10] Today, when 200 million Brazilians enjoy the music of
Ivete Sangalo or participate in *carnaval*, or experience the exhilaration
of their national team (*seleção*) winning (or losing) a World Cup, they
resonate with some of the fundamental markers of Brazilian national
identity – ones that are all profoundly shaped by the Freyrean vision
of *mestiçagem*.

FIGURE I.I Gilberto Freyre, 1967
Source: Photo By Jack Riddle/*The Denver Post* via Getty Images

GILBERTO FREYRE AND *CASA-GRANDE E SENZALA*

Sophisticated social science research has shown that this cultural mixing in Brazil has been widespread and deep.[11] People of all skin colors take part in cultural practices and activities that emerged out of European, Native American, and African societies. Perhaps most visible are the profound African influences that permeate the cultural lives of Brazilians of all hues – from *candomblé* to *capoeira* and *carnaval*. In the words of one writer, "some Euro-Brazilians are more culturally Afro-Brazilian than some Afro-Brazilians." African influences pervade all facets of Brazilian culture and society, leading one scholar to observe that the dominant narrative in Brazil is that no one is really white![12] As Edward Telles has shown with sophisticated statistical and analytical rigor, miscegenation is not "mere ideology" in Brazil. Race mixture has been taking place for centuries, and continues, and represents a significant reality in the daily lives of Brazilians.[13] The influence of Freyre permeates nearly every nook and corner of contemporary Brazilian culture. Even those who vehemently reject Freyre's ideas must grapple with ways to contend with their power and influence. This book traces the emergence, maturation, and then (partial) decline of this Freyrean vision of *mestiço* nationalism, this imagined community of *mestiçagem*, of racial mixture and cultural convergence, from the 1930s to the 1990s. This book is a brief history of the most powerful narrative of Brazilian identity in the twentieth century.

Decades of sustained and devastating critiques of Freyre's notion of "racial democracy" offer paradoxical testimony to his continuing power and influence on Brazilian identity.[14] The vast literature attacking racial democracy has rarely been accompanied by a rejection of Freyre's most important assertion – that the essence of Brazil and Brazilians is this mixture of races and cultures.[15] In the decades following the publication of *Casa-grande e senzala*, Freyre gradually made stronger and more sweeping claims that the widespread mixing of races and cultures had provided Brazil with a form of racial democracy, a society without the racial prejudice and discrimination sanctioned by law and custom in the United States and South Africa (for example).[16] Ironically, Freyre did not create the term "racial democracy," and it apparently does not even come into use until the late 1940s and the 1950s.[17] Since the 1950s, this Freyrean view of racial democracy has been repeatedly attacked by scholars in multiple fields of study. While many have argued that racial democracy is some sort of false consciousness or a smoke screen fabricated by the elite to hide the racism in Brazilian society, I agree with those who have shown that few Brazilians (especially those who are darker and poorer) believe that Brazil is a racial democracy. They are fully aware of the racism they confront in their own lives, but cling to racial democracy as an ideal to aspire to – for all Brazilians.[18] At the same time, the most sophisticated sociological surveys demonstrate that a majority of Brazilians cling to the Freyrean vision of *mestiçagem*.[19] While Freyre's vision of *mestiçagem* and racial democracy are interconnected, the former does not inevitably lead to the latter (although many, many writers conflate the two in their critiques of Freyre). One may fully embrace the notion of mixing without believing it produces racial democracy.[20] I agree with Hermano Vianna's observation: "I never believed that to value *mestiçagem* was synonymous with defending the idea that we live in a racial democracy."[21] This book is *not* about what I see as Freyre's naïve and untenable claims about racial democracy in Brazil, but rather about how the "fable of three races" becomes so deeply embedded in popular culture and the *imaginário nacional*.[22] The myth of *mestiçagem* has been more powerful, widespread, and enduring than the myth of racial democracy.

Mestiçagem, however, is a protean concept.[23] It allows those who wish to emphasize the cultural and racial diversity of Brazilian identity to highlight the contributions of the African and Indian to Brazilian culture. Brazilian music, cuisine, arts, language, and even sports offer for them daily evidence of the importance of non-European peoples and cultures to the formation of Brazilian society. At the same time, *mestiçagem* can also provide a means for those who wish to de-emphasize the African and Indian heritage of Brazilians by highlighting the waves of European immigrants as an even more powerful contributor to the cultural and racial mix that is Brazil today. In this version, mixing becomes the means for whitening (*embranquecimento*) Brazilian culture and biology. This vision of *mestiçagem*, combined with racial democracy, has been a powerful alternative to the blatant expressions of white supremacist ideology that became so potent in other societies such as the United States.[24] In a sense, these two very different visions are two sides of the same coin of *mestiçagem*. As the following chapters show, these two very different visions, both accepting *mestiçagem* as central to the national narrative, are reshaped by different regions of Brazil for their own purposes. In effect, one sees *mestiçagem* as whitening while the other sees it as darkening Brazil.

In the following chapters, I analyze how and why the tens of millions living within the political boundaries of Brazil (and many more residing beyond those borders) in the twentieth century gradually come to see themselves not only as *brasileiros*, but *brasileiros* a la Freyre.[25] I argue that only in recent decades has Brazil finally become a nation, that is, a people within a defined set of political borders bound together by their attachment to a common set of myths, rituals, and symbols.[26] For much of the twentieth century, Brazilians forged "a culture in search of nation."[27] The rise of the new technologies of radio, film, and television – the emergence of new visual and aural cultures – made possible the creation of this "imagined community" in twentieth-century Brazil (and in other nations as well). The following chapters dissect the ongoing and constantly evolving process of "becoming Brazilians" in the twentieth century. At the heart of this analysis is the very notion of what it means to be "Brazilian" and how that identity evolves and shifts across most of the twentieth century – and continues to shift in the twenty-first. Gilberto Freyre's work provides the framework for the conceptualization of the Brazilians as a singular people who compose their own nation.

I do not pretend to demonstrate definitively the many ways in which the technologies of mass communication have fostered the enormous reach and power of the myth of *mestiçagem*. In this long, interpretive essay, I lay out what I believe are the key features and processes in the creation, diffusion, success, and eventual decline of this vision of Brazilian identity. The principal goals of this essay are to offer an interpretation of twentieth-century Brazil and stimulate others to discuss, debate, challenge, and engage in much more detailed studies of the many facets of the historical trajectory I describe in this book. I am certainly not the first to notice the importance of the new technologies for the emergence of popular culture in twentieth-century societies. Latin Americans, especially Brazilians, have not only created dynamic music, art, literature, film, and television, but they also generated a very stimulating and innovative body of work about popular culture. Scholars in many countries over the past thirty years have produced a large literature on nationalism and national identity, and a seemingly endless number of books and articles have discussed Brazilian identity in the twentieth century. In more recent decades, a vibrant group of writers have shown how central citizenship, in its many facets, is to contemporary societies and to efforts to cultivate democratic politics – in Brazil, or elsewhere in the world. In this book, I bring these diverse stories together to show how the consolidation of a vibrant cultural nationalism constructed around the myth of *mestiçagem* from the 1930s to the 1980s set the stage for the rise of a dynamic civic nationalism that has fostered among tens of millions of Brazilians a vital conversation about their origins, who they are today, what they would like to become, and where they will go in the twenty-first century.

CONSTRUCTING MYTHS, RITUALS, AND SYMBOLS

Brazilians built an extraordinary narrative unity around an exceptionally flexible sense of identity. The construction of this narrative took place over many decades across two centuries. In 1822, Pedro I's famous "Cry of Ipiranga" announced the creation of an independent Brazil free of Portuguese colonial rule. Much of the story of Brazilian history – and the Brazilian people – in the nearly two centuries after Pedro's cry (*grito*) is the long (and never-ending) struggle to create a people and a nation out of an idea – to make real the newly proclaimed nation in that cry for independence.[28] The great challenge for the State in constructing the Brazilian nation from the early nineteenth century to the mid-twentieth century was in many ways geographical and technological – how to reach all those peoples living within the enormous, fluid, and ill-defined political boundaries of Brazil.[29] Before becoming Brazilian, one must first become aware of the very notion of something called Brazil. The challenge for all Brazilian nationalists was not only to create myths, rituals, and symbols, but also to make the millions of peoples of African, Native American, and European descent – and their descendants – aware of those myths, rituals, and symbols. In the terminology of Ernest Gellner, the State had to foster the nationalism that precedes the creation of the nation. Even more so than most nations, Brazil faced the daunting challenge of scale in a country of truly continental dimensions.[30] I believe that the process of the creation of this set of shared myths, rituals, and symbols does not reach full fruition until the second half of the twentieth century *after* the emergence and expansion of the technologies of mass communication – radio, film, and television. As Eric Hobsbawm once observed, "The common culture of any late twentieth-century urbanized country was based on the mass entertainment industry – cinema, radio, television, pop music."[31]

The 1930s have long been seen as a critical turning point in modern Brazilian history with the rise of Getúlio Vargas and the increasing ability of the Brazilian State to extend its power into the vast interior of the country. At the same time, the central government begins systematically to create school curricula, museums, holidays, and national symbols to overcome the long history of regionalism and fragmentation that had characterized Brazilian society, culture, and politics since (at least) independence.[32] The rise of radio in the 1930s, and then film in the 1940s and 1950s, produces a powerful shift with the emergence of popular culture, especially popular music (samba, in particular), *carnaval*, and soccer (*futebol*) as shared national experiences.[33] Post-1930 Brazil is a fascinating mix of the efforts of the State to impose an increasingly unified vision of "Brazilianness" (*brasilidade*) as a diverse set of regional symbols, music, dance, and popular culture is eventually broadcast and spread across more than 8.5 million square kilometers of national territory. The expanding mass media bring the local and the regional into the national arena – and into regular contact with each other. New technologies produced (and continue to produce) an accelerating interactive intensity of people, places, and symbols from 1920s to the present.

An expanding scholarship over the past twenty years has persuasively argued that region and nation are mutually constitutive, and Brazil is an excellent example of these processes of interaction and mutual construction.[34] A history of nation-building is more than the story of centralizing authority and the State; it involves a complex process of constant integration and differentiation among regions and nation. Instability and contingency characterize an ongoing and never-ending process, a constant shape shifting if you will. The imaginings of the people who at some point in time see themselves as part of a community – regional or national – are never completely fixed or static. Region and nation, in these terms, are "cognitive arenas of struggle." Rather than just fixed spaces, they are "landscapes of action, of meaning, and of experience."[35] Rather than antagonistic and exclusive, the region-nation-building process in Brazil has largely been mutually reinforcing and interdependent. The emergence of regions in Brazil "was not just parallel with the new nationalist sentiment, but a reaction to it and another face of it."[36] Eventually, a relatively select set of myths, symbols, and rituals comes to be seen and experienced as defining features not of particular regions, but of Brazil as a whole. In many ways, the regional narratives that emerged in the early twentieth century offered competing visions of Brazil, visions that made claims to authenticity, power, and hierarchy.[37]

As new technologies (telegraphy, telephony, radio, cinema, television) draw more and more locales into an ever larger community, the interplay among the local, regional, national, and international intensify. Earlier generations of writers often portrayed this process as largely unidirectional – the top-down imposition (beginning with Vargas) of the State dominated by elites who sought to force the Freyrean vision of Brazil on the masses. The influence and agency of the majority of Brazilians disappear in many of these accounts.[38] I argue that this process of nation-building was not entirely State directed, nor driven simply by the desires and choices of individuals or groups.[39] The result, as with all complex cultures, is a constantly evolving mix of cultural traits that are always "hybrid," to use the terminology of cultural studies.[40] The focus of this book is on how a select group of defining features that became emblematic of national identity in the twentieth century emerged, flourished, and then were powerfully questioned and challenged. Their emergence was not foreordained or completely imposed from above, but arose out of a complex, protracted, highly contingent, and constant process of exchanges and conflicts among constituencies from all sectors of Brazilian society (and beyond).[41] As Prasenjit Duara has observed, nationalism "marks the site where different representations of the nation contest and negotiate with each other." He goes on to assert that "we find a polyphony of voices, contradictory and ambiguous, opposing, affirming, and negotiating their views of the nation."[42] State power and voices "from below" are constantly in a conflictual and evolving relationship that continually refines and reshapes notions of identity – local, regional, and national.[43] As in many countries, this polyphony of voices created an ongoing and unending conversation about the nature of Brazilian identity. Gilberto Freyre's portrayal of *mestiçagem* gradually became the dominant narrative (the dominant voice) among the contending narratives in this conversation. Intellectuals, like Freyre, frequently played the role of cultural mediators in this process.[44]

The emergence of radio and samba from the 1930s to the 1950s initiated the creation of what has been called a "culture industry" in Brazil creating for the first time a shared national popular culture. The Modernists in the 1920s and 1930s played a central role in this technological and cultural shift. The so-called folkloric, popular culture of pre-twentieth-century Brazil and the supposed erudite, cosmopolitan culture of the elites had never been separate, yet they blended and reconfigured in increasingly creative and powerful ways with the rise of mass media technologies. "The symbioses between radio and literature, cinema and theater, and theater and television," as Renato Ortiz has argued, "were constants." As he has also written, the idea of traditional cultures that defined the "popular classes" gave way to products, images, and festivities associated with cultural industries and the "masses."[45] The intervention of the State into the cultural arena in the same decades stimulated the creation of a "mass culture" (*cultura de massas*) in Brazil, but it was not until the 1960s and 1970s that a truly national community became possible. The conversation and debate about Brazilian national identity has been a long struggle over the very nature of what is deemed Brazilian culture.[46] First with film and then, more importantly, with the emergence of television after 1970, the technology was in place that truly stitched together the pieces of the national territory and Brazilian society to create the quilted mosaic that is Brazil today in the midst of this ongoing and never-ending conversation.[47]

Brian Owensby has argued that in a society that largely excluded Brazilians from civic citizenship and full political participation, popular culture offered sites of "unofficial citizenship" where "people could avoid entanglements with a politics that so often excluded them." Through samba, *carnaval*, and *futebol* (among other sites), to "be Brazilian ... is to rise to a moral plane above the pettiness, corruptions, and exclusions of politics."[48] Brazilians, in this sense, confront the negatives of politics and its flaws with the positives of participation in popular culture. In effect, Brazilians have forged an increasingly rich cultural citizenship over decades in the absence of a strong civic citizenship.[49] From the 1930s to the 1970s, this growing and vibrant popular culture spawned contending forms of cultural nationalism and identity. The 1970s, largely because of opposition to the military regime that took power in 1964 and instituted brutal repressive measures, mark a turning point in the emergence of a civic nationalism and a struggle for citizenship in Brazil. These two powerful forces – civic and cultural – converge in the 1970s and 1980s, with television, *futebol*, and popular music as the principal vehicles facilitating the convergence. The process of becoming Brazilians – of creating one people and one nation – reaches its climax under the military regime in the 1970s and 1980s, culminating with the mass mobilization of Brazilians through the process of re-democratization, national elections in 1989, and the impeachment of President Fernando Collor in 1992. In the "direct elections now" campaign (*diretas já*) in 1984, and the impeachment of President Fernando Collor in 1992, tens of millions of Brazilians rallied around "their" flag, national anthem, and other national symbols to claim their "rights" as Brazilians.[50] They fully and forcefully assumed their civic *and* cultural identity as Brazilians.[51] Nation and State finally converged more than a century and a half after Pedro's declaration of independence in 1822.

In the 1960s and 1970s, the military regime put into place many of the conditions for the consolidation of a shared national culture (extending State power and mass communications effectively across all of the national territory), and the climax of this sense of national belonging comes, ironically, with the massive mobilization of millions of Brazilians *against* the military regime in the 1980s. In one of ironies of Brazilian history, at the very moment that this modernizing project to create a sense of national identity finally experiences its greatest success in the 1970s and 1980s, intellectuals and activists had already begun to deconstruct the meaning of identity, nation, nationalism, and modernity, and they began to proclaim the very *impossibility* of the modernizing project and the very notion of this version of *a* national identity.[52] Many of them announced the death of the Freyrean vision of Brazil at the moment of its greatest influence.

KEY THEMES

This book brings together a series of fundamental themes in Brazilian, Latin American, and world history – identity, nation, nationalism, modernity, citizenship, and the State. An early historiographical tradition in Latin America produced a large literature on these themes and the creation of new nations in the nineteenth century. Much of this literature served the European and Europeanized elites in the newly independent nations of Latin America in their struggle to assert control over territories largely populated by non-European peoples – Indians, Africans, and the racially mixed.[53] Liberal and Conservative historiography in the nineteenth century (typified by classic works such as Domingo F. Sarmiento's *Facundo* and José Enrique Rodó's *Ariel*) sought to justify nation-building as a modernizing project aimed at transforming the peoples of Latin America into neo-Europeans.[54] In recent decades, an entirely new wave of scholarly works has returned to the nationalism and nation-building projects of the nineteenth century to show that many peoples, not just the elites, participated in and shaped the debates, language, and processes of nation-building and nationalism. This new literature has emphasized the multiplicity of understandings – among various groups within a given country – of the foundational concepts of nation-building, liberalism, citizenship, and civic culture. The works of Florencia Mallon on Mexico and Peru, Sarah Chambers and Mark Thurner on Peru, Peter Guardino on Mexico, and Greg Grandin on Guatemala (to cite a few examples) probe the multiple meanings of nation-building and nationalism among nonelite groups.[55] They have brought to the forefront of the discussion of nation-building and nationalism the importance of diverse groups within civil society and across regions within nations all playing a role in a growing conversation about ideas and ideologies. This is important work, but it has largely focused on the nineteenth century, and the nation-building projects in Latin America in the century after independence largely failed, became twisted beyond recognition, or died stillborn.

As Miguel Angel Centeno has eloquently argued, the elites who triumphed in the wars for independence "had no desire to imagine a national community" and "the inclusion and integration of the masses was the last thing on their mind." In most of Latin America, the Europeanizing projects of elites eradicated, persecuted, and stigmatized non-European cultures and peoples. By their very nature, the projects were incapable of forging unified nations filled with peoples of very diverse ethnic, racial, and cultural traditions. When faced with the question, "*que hacer con el pueblo?*" (what to do with the people?), elites chose exclusion and persecution over the inclusion and mobilization necessary for creating national communities.[56] Even in Argentina and Uruguay, the two most ethnically "European" countries in Latin America, the modernizing projects to build nations often ignored peoples within their own borders who did not fit into the elitist narratives of nationhood.[57]

At the dawn of the twentieth century, contrary to the classic arguments of Benedict Anderson, the "Creole Pioneers" of nineteenth-century Latin America had largely failed to forge imagined communities that even remotely coincided with their supposed national political boundaries. In Brazil, and much of Latin America, it is in the decades *after* World War I and the Great Depression that some of the many nation-building projects originally imagined in the nineteenth century finally came to fruition.[58] The dream of many of those nineteenth-century Liberals and Conservatives – to create a shared culture that spanned the national territory – did not become a reality until well into the twentieth century – and in ways that would probably have appalled most of them.[59] The many voices converge around a set of shared symbols and myths that come to define many Latin American nations – from Mexico to Brazil. Ironically, the foundational myth of many of these nations was the very racial and cultural mixture (*mestizaje/mestiçagem*) that the Creole Pioneers (such as Sarmiento) had attempted to annihilate and eradicate with their European visions of cultural modernity.[60]

The great touchstone of discussion about nation-building and nationalism for the past three decades has been Benedict Anderson's *Imagined Communities* (1983), one of the most widely read academic books of all time. Historians of Latin America have been both pleased and perplexed by Anderson's work. The Creole Pioneer elites who led the wars for independence and the creation of the new nations in the nineteenth century serve as the centerpiece of his argument bringing Latin America to the forefront of discussions of nationalism – discussions that for too long have been dominated by the European experience. Nevertheless, as many scholars of Latin America have pointed out, Anderson's (mis)understanding of the Creoles was largely based on a few very traditional and dated sources.[61] Ironically, Anderson's analysis of this group situated at the core of his argument has been seriously critiqued by historians of Latin America even while many still embrace the gist of his notion of "imagined communities." Anderson's work places great emphasis on the creation of a literate, print culture and Creoles as the precursor of these imagined communities in the nineteenth century.[62] I argue that in Brazil, and much of Latin America, the creation of these imagined communities does not occur through *print culture* in the nineteenth century (except among a small group of European elites and groups most closely connected to them), but rather these communities emerge in the mid-twentieth century out of *visual and aural cultures.*[63] Territories, argues Muniz de Albuquerque, are image based. "They arrive to us in channels – the media, education, social contacts, habits – cultural channels that encourage an abstraction of the real. In this way, history resembles theater, on which actors, historical agents, may create their forms of identity only through the markers of the past, through accepted and recognized roles, old masks that are forever updated."[64] It is the rise of radio, film, and television that make possible the creation of a "community" of tens of millions of Brazilians and eventually allows them to "imagine" themselves as part of *a* Brazilian people and *a* Brazilian nation.[65] Nationalism in Latin America provides peoples with an "idiom of identity," but this idiom is more aural and visual than print.[66]

Over the last thirty years or so, nationalism and nation-building have generated a substantial and stimulating literature. Much of this work grapples with how to define State, nation, nationalism, modernity, citizenship, and identity.[67] The rise of subaltern studies and a dynamic group of South Asian scholars has also provoked a move away from the Eurocentrism of much of the earlier work on nationalism.[68] As this literature has proliferated, the central concepts have become even less clear and more contested. Without going into a prolonged discussion of this literature, let me simply set out what I mean by the concepts that are central to this book.

As the sociologist Craig Calhoun has pointed out, there is no generally accepted definition of something as fundamental to the contemporary world as "nation."[69] Scholars such as Anthony D. Smith, Ernest Gellner, and E. J. Hobsbawm (to cite three of the classics) each have their own list of features. In this book, I define a nation as a people within a defined set of political borders bound together by their attachment to a common set of myths, rituals, and symbols. That shared culture – of myths, rituals, and symbols – forms the core of their identity as a people and a nation. As these people leave the national territory, they also carry with them their attachment to this identity, even as they add others. This imagined community is constantly changing, evolving, with moments of cohesion as well as conflict. Nothing is preordained (or primordial) about these communities, and their creation as well as their survival over time is contingent on many factors. In the case of Brazil, the State precedes the nation and the "fit" between the two is always complex and fraught with conflict.[70]

The vibrant literature that has appeared over the last thirty years emphasizes, as I will, that nations are cultural constructs that make claims to a collective identity, social solidarity, and the integration of the individual into membership in the whole. "Nationalism has become," in the words of Lloyd Kramer, "the most widespread, influential political and cultural idea in the modern world because it gives people powerful stories to help them explain the meaning of their lives."[71] Nationalism, as Calhoun writes, is a discourse, a project, and an "ethical imperative." The discourse seeks to frame a version of identity, the project strives to mobilize the population around that shared identity, and the imperative heightens the sense of national identity versus the "other." In twentieth-century Brazil, the Freyrean version of Brazilian identity becomes the dominant and "official" project. Although this identity clearly distinguishes the Brazilians from other peoples and nations, the lack of strong xenophobia in this project is striking. Nationalism, as I use it in my analysis, is an "expression of the desire among people who believe they have a common ancestry and a common destiny to govern themselves in a place peculiarly identified with their history and its fulfillment."[72]

Prior to the emergence of the Brazilian nation, or other nations, people understood themselves and their lives in relation to their family, kin, villages, and locales. Scholars of nationalism continue to debate whether nationalism is a product of the modern world (or, in fact, created the modern world), but most place its emergence in the "age of revolutions" in the Atlantic world in the late eighteenth and early nineteenth centuries.[73] Much ink has been spilt over whether nations and nationalism are constructs of the modern world or not and over ethnic versus civic nationalism. I will not enter into this debate, largely because it seems to me irrelevant in the case of Brazil (and for that matter, most of the Americas). Unlike so many peoples of the Old World (or even Mexico), Brazilians lay no claims to some ancient ethnic identity. Brazil's cultural nationalism has been intimately connected with the construction of a new "ethnic" identity forged in the Americas since 1500 rather than an appeal to an ancient one rooted in the Old World (or the New).[74] The dominant form of nationalism that emerges in twentieth-century Brazil is cultural rather than civic (until the very late twentieth century). As Renato Ortiz has pointed out, "The inability of Brazilian society to create national civic myths was due to a lack of a consciousness of citizenship."[75] While the great mass of Brazilians struggled throughout the nineteenth and early twentieth century to make claims to citizenship, their efforts in the civic arena were much less successful than in the cultural arena. Through their shared popular culture, Brazilians participate in the idea of the nation.[76] As Chapter 1 explains, this was especially true in the first half of the twentieth century. I argue (in Chapter 7) that in the last quarter of the century, cultural nationalism and an emerging civic nationalism converge in ways that transform Brazilians' sense of their own identity. The flawed nature of citizenship in contemporary Brazil, however, remains a serious problem in what is now the world's fourth largest democracy.

The debates over Brazilian national identity in the twentieth century are bound up intimately with notions of modernity. In the nineteenth century, Brazilian (and other Latin American) elites strove to remake their new countries in the image of Europe. For these elites, "modern" equaled "European."[77] Argentina and Uruguay offer the most telling versions of this striving for modernity (a la Europe). Both Sarmiento and Rodó are emblematic of generations of Eurocentric "Creoles" who self-consciously strove to remake their American societies into their idealized visions of Europe (especially France and England): educated, urban, industrial, technologically sophisticated, and white. It is no coincidence that these two iconic "Latin American" intellectuals lived and wrote in the two countries of the region most profoundly shaped by postcolonial European immigration. Their intellectual counterparts in Mexico, Central America, the Caribbean, the Andes, and Brazil lived and wrote in strikingly different, much more *mestiço* societies.

For Brazilian intellectuals, modernity and Modernism carry complex meanings.[78] By World War I, a Brazilian form of Modernism had emerged that consciously rejected the Eurocentric Modernism of Rodó and other Spanish American writers. In the 1920s, Brazilian Modernism emerged as a movement that explicitly and loudly proclaimed Brazil's cultural independence from Europe.[79] A "modern" Brazil, for these *avant-garde* artists and writers, was a nation that recognized and

FIGURE I.2 Candido Portinari, "Entry into the Forest," Mural, Hispanic Reading Room, Library of Congress
Source: Photo by Hart Preston/The LIFE Picture Collection/Getty Images

celebrated its mixed indigenous, African, and European heritage, but was also technologically, scientifically, and industrially advanced. This modernist movement became the crucible of the emergence of the dominant narrative of Brazilian national identity in the twentieth century. Many of these Modernists were the children of the political and economic elites. Initially the critics of the mainstream Brazilian cultural elite, by the 1940s many of the Modernists had become key figures in the government and the "official" arbiters of national culture. They had become functionaries of the State.[80]

The multiplicity of meanings and plasticity of "modernity" in Brazil is striking. The Modernists of the early twentieth century sought modernity in a "return" to the "traditional" and "authentic" in their own society. Their search took them to the traditions and customs of the popular classes, in particular, those of African and *mestiço* descent. As Florencia Garramuño has brilliantly argued, for the Brazilian Modernists, "primitivism functioned as a kind of bridge between copying the European avant-garde and discovering Brazil."[81] While the elites of the nineteenth century sought to create myths of nationhood by turning to the heroes and events of the wars for independence, the Modernists found the essence of Brazilian identity and nationalism in the cultural and social processes of the colonial era, especially the indigenous and African past. They sought to "recover" the "authentic" customs of the past to transform them into the foundations of national identity in the modern world. Throughout the twentieth century, many Brazilian intellectuals have marveled at the capacity of their society to blend the modern and the traditional, at the creation of a popular culture that draws on both. In the words of Ruben George Oliven, a "peculiarity of Brazilian society lies precisely in its capacity to take on those aspects of modernity that are of interest to it and to transform them into something suited to its own needs, in which the modern interacts with the traditional."[82]

MODERNISM

The Brazilian Modernists of the early twentieth century saw themselves as participants in the latest and most advanced stage of Western history. They were, after all, an avant-garde. Like the nation-builders of nineteenth-century Latin America, they admired and respected the cultural, political, and economic accomplishments of the Europeans – especially the French, English, and Germans. Unlike their predecessors, they explicitly rejected the slavish Eurocentrism and "bourgeois" worldview of their parents' and grandparents' generations. They aspired to be modern, but modern Brazilians, not modern Europeans. They embraced the fruits of economic and political modernization while sharing with European Modernists skepticism about the values of bourgeois culture. Many of these Modernists eventually became the cultural managers of the State by the 1930s and 1940s, and like their nineteenth-century precursors, they sought to craft a modern State and nation using the tools produced by economic modernization.[83] They became cultural engineers of Brazilian nation-building.

A contemporary of the Modernists, but more closely allied with the cause of the so-called Regionalists, Gilberto Freyre turned to the folkways of the Northeast.[84] While the Modernists were more closely identified with Brazil's Southeast (especially Rio de Janeiro, São Paulo, and Minas Gerais), the Regionalists were most notably from the Northeast (especially Pernambuco and Bahia). Although there was overlap and cross-fertilization between the Modernists and Regionalists, the latter group had a much more conservative and backward-looking vision. Much like their contemporaries in the U.S. South, these Northeastern intellectuals wished to define their region within the nation and to emphasize its heritage and traditions.[85] They produced poetry, novels, plays, and essays that (much like Southern U.S. literature during the same period) energized and enriched Brazilian literature. The tensions and interactions among these two movements stretched across the rest of the twentieth century and reflected the dynamic tensions among the multiple narratives of regional and national identity.[86]

Paradoxically, regionalism and nationalism emerged in the 1920s and 1930s in an ongoing dance of symbols, or in a series of "symbolic battles," to quote Pierre Bourdieu.[87] The regions that have become so stereotypical in Brazil, even to the point of official sanctification by government agencies at the state and national level, took shape most notably in the Northeast (especially Recife and Salvador), Rio Grande do Sul, Minas Gerais, Rio de Janeiro, and São Paulo. Just as at the national level, multiple narratives competed at the regional level. Was the "Northeast" the vision of those in Recife, Salvador, the backlands, Ceará? Who would define *gaúcho* identity in the South? At the same time, *paulistas, mineiros,* and *cariocas* grappled with just what distinguished them from other Brazilians. Lúcia Lippi Oliveira has shown how these contending and contested regional narratives took shape and provide a variety of alternatives for those seeking to define Brazilian national identity. Although the central State under Getúlio Vargas attempted after 1930 to determine the outcome of the struggle among narratives, once again, the process was much more nuanced and complex than the once dominant interpretation of top-down, hegemonic control asserted in the past. Lippi Oliveira shows that each one of these regional identities contributed to the national conversation and the formation of national identities.[88]

As much of the literature on nation-building and nationalism asserts, in Brazil, the State precedes the nation.[89] Out of the collapse of the colonial Iberian regimes in the 1810s and 1820s, the Creole elites seized control of the remnants of Bourbon and Braganza imperial political authority and labored to reshape that power to support national regimes and institutions in what would become some seventeen new countries by the 1850s. Those remnants of the imperial regime formed the core of the most basic functions of any State – the administration of public goods and a claim to a legitimate monopoly on violence. Nearly all the new Latin American countries struggled with reasserting the authority of the State in the aftermath of the destruction of the old bonds of imperial, monarchical authority. The power of the State in the nineteenth century rarely extended very far beyond the hinterlands of the main cities and towns, and when it did, it was often exercised by powerful landowners and their kinship networks. One of the great challenges in constructing Brazil was to make the State and the nation visible for the millions within the country's presumed political borders.[90] In contrast to the popular view that the State in Latin America has long been powerful and dominating, I agree with Miguel Centeno's assessment that States in Latin America have historically been large, ineffective, and unable physically to integrate society until well into the twentieth century. These States have often been despotic in relation to civil society, yet weak in their institutional capacity and ability to implement decisions. Their power has been "shallow and contested" for much of the past two centuries.[91] In Brazil, the "permanent institutional core of political authority" takes shape during three centuries of Portuguese colonialism and the leaders of the independence movement seize control of the State apparatus in the 1820s. Unlike their Spanish American counterparts, the Brazilian elites had the advantage of an independence transition led by the Braganza crown prince, and then his son.[92] However weak the State in Brazil, it was committed to the preservation and expansion of slavery and the maintenance of a profoundly unequal social hierarchy as two of the principal pillars of the new nation.[93]

The challenge, as with all nation-builders, was to use the power of the State to create a nation out of a national project – to construct a nation-state. As Gellner points out, two persons are of "the same nation if and only if they share the same culture, where culture in turn means a system of ideas and signs and associations and ways of behaving and communicating."[94] Nationalism is the political program to create the nation. This requires the ability to construct a social framework to project and attempt to inculcate into the targeted population a common set of myths, rituals, and symbols – a form of secular religion.[95] Ultimately, the objective is to create "a socially integrated body."[96] Elites attempt to do this through the power of the State to educate, conscript, and imprison, and through control of the media (to cite some of the most obvious instruments). I will emphasize in this interpretation that while the efforts of the State are fundamental, they are also sometimes ineffectual and, at other times, reshaped by unanticipated movements in various sectors of society and "from below."[97] The State is not simply an autonomous apparatus of power controlled by the elites to subject the masses. In the twentieth century, the State and popular culture are interpenetrating, interconnected, and inseparable. While those with great power may hold more cards than those large numbers of peoples with little power, their lives and destinies affect each other and the influence does not flow one way. The shaping of Brazilian identity is a multidimensional and multifoci process that cannot be simplified (as it was so often in the past) to State or cultural hegemony.[98] Throughout the twentieth century, State and nation have shaped and reshaped each other in Brazil operating in parallel, both reinforcing and, at times, undermining each other.[99]

As the sections on television show, in particular, new media of mass communication completely alter our notions of "cultural hegemony," "cultural imperialism," and unidirectional shaping of culture. The State and powerful firms that control mass communications cannot, and do not, simply shape ideas and identities. The creation and diffusion of the Freyrean vision of Brazilian identity from the 1930s to the 1990s was an increasingly interactive and intense process made possible by the rise of mass media.[100] The State, as Prasenjit Duara has noted, is never able to eliminate alternative constructions of the nation.[101] The end goal of nationalism, quite explicitly, is to create homogeneity and the submission of the individual to the collective. It is the effort to impose a single narrative over all other competing narratives of region and nation. In twentieth-century Brazil, this nationalist project ultimately becomes the creation of a particular version of the "*povo brasileiro*," the Brazilian people. This *povo* – this new ethnicity created out of the collision of three peoples – are the inhabitants of the Brazilian nation.[102]

The reemergence of nationalism and studies of national identity since the 1970s has provoked something of an intellectual countercurrent of scholars contesting the very notions of nationality and national identity. The emergence of Atlantic world history, the field of African diaspora studies, and a growing emphasis on transnational work have all led to sustained criticisms of the focus on nations and the national focus.[103] While I appreciate these critiques, I see no reason to abandon the nation as a unit of analysis, studies of national identity, or nationalism. Each is a different lens offering views into the human experience and they are not necessarily mutually exclusive. As this book clearly demonstrates, Brazilian nationalism and identity have always been forged out of influences emerging within the political boundaries of Brazil and from outside – from North America, Europe, Africa, and even Asia. To separate the "national" and the "transnational" as competing analytical approaches is both unproductive and unnecessary.

Amartya Sen has eloquently pointed out that everyone has multiple, multilayered identities – as citizens of nations, states, regions, kinship groups, genders, sexualities, and organizations, just to cite a few of the possibilities. "Socially," Serge Gruzinski reminds us, "a person constantly deals with a galaxy of individuals, each of whom has multiple identities."[104] Communities are dynamic and constantly in flux composed simultaneously of coherence, integration, contradictions, divisions, and ambivalence. To be Brazilian does not mean one cannot also see oneself as a *carioca, paulista, gaúcho, mineiro*, or a citizen of other nations simultaneously.[105] Unlike personal identity, collective identities are "constructed out of a synchronic web of affiliations and sentiments," and they express "individuals' sense of belonging within a society or community."[106] As this book shows, one of the great paradoxes of recent Brazilian nationalism (and other nationalisms as well) is the resurgence of regional identity formation parallel and in conjunction with the powerful centralizing push of the Brazilian State to forge a single national identity.[107] As the conversation about national identity develops after the 1930s, other conversations about regional identities also take shape. As those from Minas Gerais forge a strong sense of *mineiridade*, those from Rio Grande do Sul become *gaúchos, paulista* identity emerges in São Paulo, and *nordestino* (northeasterner) identity takes shape, all of these various regional narratives are contested and contest national narratives.[108] These regional identities take shape in a complex interaction with narratives of national identity and their "architects resided at the periphery as much as at the center."[109] As Barbara Weinstein has noted, Brazil in the early twentieth century "provides a compelling historical example of a period that witnessed both resurgent regionalism and emergent nationalism."[110]

Being Brazilian is one of many identities, at times the most important of those identities, but not to the exclusion of the others. In the words of an eminent U.S. historian, David Potter, loyalty to the nation "flourishes not by challenging and overpowering all other loyalties, but by subsuming them all and keeping them in a reciprocally supportive relationship to one another."[111] National identity is constantly contested and reconstructed over generations. As Stuart Hall has argued, identity "is always constructed through memory, fantasy, narrative and myth. Cultural identities are ... the unstable points of identification or suture, which are made within the discourses of history and culture. Not an essence but a *positioning*."[112] In this book, I am not trying to "define" Brazilian identity, rather I am examining how a constellation of rituals and symbols that most Brazilians see as quintessentially Brazilian (a collective solidarity) have come to be seen that way.[113] I show how, over decades, what it means to be Brazilian emerges, evolves, and is constructed and reconstructed – how this identity is created out of contesting myths, rituals, and symbols.

A set of beliefs – myths, to use the anthropological terminology – undergirds these rituals and symbols. Saying they are myths does not imply that they are not "true." I use this term in the anthropological sense – as ordered systems of social thought that embody the fundamental perceptions of a people about their social life.[114] They are beliefs that most citizens, at some level, see as defining the nation and its people. As Brian Owensby has put it, "the nation has represented a kind of sacred space premised on the incorporation and neutralization of historical time." Our myths are "true stories" located outside of historical time.[115] In the United States, for example, the belief in liberty, equality, and opportunity for all is one of the most cherished national myths. Although most in the United States firmly adhere to this belief, we know that not *all* are free, nor treated equally, and opportunity does not come for everyone. Yet, these beliefs remain at the core of what it means to be an American. Myths "can also be used to valorize the discontinuity between present and past, making the idea of history more plausible and appealing."[116] In this sense, myths are not only our beliefs, but also our dreams, aspirations, and ideals.[117]

The construction of Brazilian identity in the twentieth century, like the construction of identity in other nations, is not only a process of constructing myths, but also of what Ernst Renan called a process of "selective forgetting."[118] Perhaps the most notorious example of this cultural amnesia is Freyre's version of *mestiçagem*, an interpretation of Brazilian history that downplays the violence, struggle, and pain millions of people experienced in centuries of racial and cultural mixing in a society built on slavery, the slave trade, the subjugation of indigenous peoples, and the repression that kept powerful landowners and merchants in control of a society composed overwhelmingly of poor, rural peoples. The distinguished historian Edmund Morgan eloquently observed in his study of the formation of the United States, "Government requires make-believe. Make believe that the king is divine, make believe that he can do no wrong or make believe that the voice of the people is the voice of God ... Make believe that all men are equal or make believe that they are not." He goes on to argue that, "The political world of make-believe mingles with the real world in strange ways, for the make believe world may often mold the real one. In order to be viable, in order to serve its purpose, whatever that purpose may be, a fiction must bear some resemblance to fact." The success of governments in Brazil, as in the United States, "requires the acceptance of fictions, requires the willing suspension of disbelief."[119] As Gilberto Freyre's origin myth of Brazilian society became the dominant narrative of Brazilian identity in the mid-twentieth century, a succession of Brazilian governments strove to persuade all Brazilians that this fiction depicted Brazilian reality.

DECLINE OF THE FREYREAN VISION

Ironically, at the very moment of the greatest success of the Freyrean vision of Brazil, as this central mythology had become so deeply entwined in the very fabric of thought in all sectors and all social classes within Brazil, the vision's hold on many Brazilians began to erode and decline. The assault on this vision comes principally from two prominent directions – an intellectual elite and increasingly vocal groups within civil society organized around black (*negro*) and Afro-Brazilian identity.[120] Although black consciousness movements (*movimento negro*) had started to appear in Brazil in the nineteenth century and achieved substantial visibility in the 1940s and 1950s, a more sustained and growing movement began to take shape in the 1970s and 1980s.[121] The crystallizing moment, in many ways, was the centenary of the abolition of slavery in 1988, a moment of celebration (from the point of view of the Brazilian government) and a moment for reconsideration (from the point of view of many of these Afro-Brazilian groups). While the government promoted a multitude of conferences, commemorations, and events, black consciousness groups advocated and promoted something of a counter-commemoration. (This moment in Brazil bears strong resemblance to the 1992 quincentennial commemorations/counter-commemorations in the United States of the landmark voyage of Christopher Columbus as well as Modern Art Week in Brazil in 1922.)[122]

Over the past thirty years, the push for black consciousness (*conciência negra*) and the forceful critique of Brazil as a racially blended society have produced a sustained challenge to the Freyrean vision of Brazil as a society with one ethnicity, one people – of all Brazilians as *mestiços*. In a sense, this is a fictive ethnicity, one that for many, if not most, Brazilians is not genetic or biological. They do not have to carry the genes of indigenous and African peoples in their bodies. They carry the shadows of these peoples in their souls. The late nineteenth-century conception of race as a biological entity, however, experienced an ironic resurgence in the late twentieth century. The white and black races that were essentialized by the spurious science of the late nineteenth century condemning the latter to inferiority and glorifying the former as the rulers of the earth has reemerged in novel ways in the last generation. Rather than moving away from these essential categories of race, many black activists have returned to them as a means to build solidary movements. They employ what might be called a "strategic essentialism." Increasingly, the black consciousness groups from civil society have argued that Brazil is not a complex color continuum, but rather simply a bipolar society – of those who are "white" and those who are not. For these groups, Gilberto Freyre does not represent the affirmation of the African contribution to Brazilian culture. To the contrary, for them, Freyre annihilates "African" identity in Brazil and incorporates it into mainstream "white" culture. In affirming their black, African ancestry, these groups reject the myth of a "*povo brasileiro*," of a single Brazilian ethnicity. They return to the biological notion that any person with "African" ancestry is black.[123] The most visible example of this struggle in the past two decades has been the intense debate in Brazil over affirmative action, a debate that goes to the heart of what it means to be Brazilian.[124] What this debate over "race" has too often failed to grasp is that the essence of Freyre's vision was not simply biology and phenotype, but rather culture (shadows in the soul). The fluidity of phenotype may be fundamental to Brazilian society, but Freyre's most important contribution to the narrative of national identity was his assertion that all Brazilians, regardless of the color of their skin, carry with them the cultural *mestiçagem* that defines the formation of the nation. For Freyre, culture trumps biology.[125]

The other major challenge to the Freyrean vision comes from intellectual and cultural elites. On a global scale, at the very moment that nationalism reemerged with a vengeance in the late twentieth century, intellectuals around the world had already begun to deconstruct "nation" and "nationalism."[126] From South Asia to Europe to the Americas, powerful critiques have taken apart the "narratives" of nationalism and nation. The very notion of national identity has come under systematic and relentless criticism. With the rise of transnational history, globalization, and interdisciplinarity within the academy, the very notion that one can write about nations and national identities is now considered suspect.[127] Brazilians and Brazilianists over the past two decades have (like their intellectual counterparts in other areas of the world) systematically attacked the very notion of national identity and the existence of a Brazilian identity.

What this interpretive book attempts is not to claim that there is some "essence" of Brazilian national identity that we can identify and delineate.[128] Rather I seek to recover (to historicize in the language of cultural studies) how people in twentieth-century Brazil develop a consciousness of Brazilianness (*brasilidade*) and how that consciousness is principally defined (in their eyes) by the Freyrean mythology. We can see this consciousness in what I call the "national conversation" about *brasilidade* across the twentieth century. Many voices from all sectors of society participate in this conversation. By the middle of the century, the dominant voices in this conversation invoke the myths, symbols, and rituals associated with Freyre's visions of *mestiçagem*. While it is the dominant voice and narrative, it is never the view of every single individual in Brazil, yet it is for much of the second half of the century the most powerful and pervasive narrative of Brazilian identity across regions and social classes. Its power and dominance are very much in question at the beginning of the twenty-first century. By historicizing this dominant narrative of Brazilian identity, we see how such identity narratives are transitory and ephemeral, even if able to endure for long periods. In Brazil, as in many nations, there are many competing narratives of national identity and however dominant any one of them, no narrative ever achieves universal resonance. The great dream of nation-builders to homogenize and completely integrate all its inhabitants into one people is ultimately a utopian chimera.

Numerous authors have argued that Freyre "invented Brazil."[129] This is an old argument. This essay argues that Freyre invented *one* vision of Brazil, a powerful narrative that gradually triumphed over all others as the dominant perception of *brasilidade*. What I try to show in this book is how a sense of Brazilian culture emerges that is widespread, pervasive, and powerful, but transitory. As Renato Ortiz has also noted, one of the striking features of Brazilian society has been the longstanding intermingling of "erudite" ("high") and "popular" ("low") culture.[130] This cultural intermingling is at the heart of this book. Moreover, culture is never static; it is always shifting and changing. The myths, rituals, and symbols that are so foundational for the Freyrean vision – *mestiçagem* as a cultural positive, samba, the classic *carnaval* of Rio de Janeiro, *futebol* – did not exist in 1880. They begin to blossom by the 1930s. The Freyrean vision takes off in the 1930s, gains power in the 1940s and 1950s, is ascendant in the 1960s and 1970s, and then begins its decline in the 1980s onward. This is the story of the rise and relative decline of one version of national identity, one that become enormously influential and pervasive, even dominant (for a time). Defining Brazilian identity in the middle of the twenty-first century, no doubt, will involve another set of myths, rituals, and symbols.

The rise and relative fall of Gilberto Freyre's vision accompanies the larger, structural changes across twentieth-century Brazilian history. Modernism, cultural nationalism, and the Freyrean vision all emerge in the 1920s and 1930s as a "modern" Brazil emerged out of a rural society, a coffee economy, and an intellectual discourse dominated by scientific racism. The upheavals of the 1920s – the *tenente* revolts, the emergence of socialism, an urban labor movement, Modernism – and the Revolution of 1930 mark the pivotal "moment" in the birth of modern Brazil. By the 1940s and 1950s, the emergence of an intelligentsia committed to national development (from the ideological left to the right), and a State that increasingly intervened to promote industrialization, helped produce an increasingly urban, industrial, and integrated nation. In the 1960s and 1970s, this developmental nationalism reached its limits under an authoritarian, military regime that officially endorsed Freyre's vision of *mestiçagem* and his claims that Brazil was a racial democracy. In the last two decades of the twentieth century, the emergence of the neoliberal economic wave, globalization, and the critiques of the Freyrean vision all converged to mark the end of the developmental nationalism that had emerged in the era of Getúlio Vargas and blossomed in the postwar decades. By the 1990s, an increasingly fragmented intelligentsia, a growing and restive civil society, and a weakened nation-state marked the end of a historical period when the creation of a national identity constructed around a dominant narrative not only seemed possible, but close to realization.[131] The last decade of the twentieth century also marks the emergence of a new technological era – of the Internet and global digital communications – that make the 1990s the logical terminus for my analysis.

AN OVERVIEW OF THE BOOK

This book is an interpretive essay that aims to stimulate further research on the many aspects of Brazilian national identity, nationalism, citizenship, and media that I bring together in my analysis. Rather than a comprehensive case for the argument, this book brings together work from a wide variety of fields and disciplines in ways that suggest new angles on Brazilian identity. The essay consists of nine parts: an introduction, seven chapters, and an epilogue. Chapter 1, "From the 'Spectacle of Races' to 'Luso-Tropical Civilization,'" lays out for the reader the context of Brazilian history from independence to the early twentieth century focusing on the role of the State, regionalism, patrimonialism, and politics. At the core of the chapter is an overview of social thought in Brazil from the late nineteenth to the early twentieth century, in particular, a discussion about race and national identity. The final section introduces the work of Gilberto Freyre, his vision of *mestiçagem*, and the debates over race and identity in the 1930s. The following chapter, "Communicating and Understanding *Mestiçagem*: Radio, Samba, and *Carnaval*," turns to the first stage in the popularization of Freyre's vision with the rise of radio, samba, and "domestication" of *carnaval* in Rio de Janeiro. I explore the emerging tension and dynamic between the planned efforts of the State (especially under Getúlio Vargas) to construct a coherent and hegemonic vision of *brasilidade* and the unplanned, constantly shifting tides of popular culture and tastes. This creative and dynamic tension can be seen in the emergence of samba and its consecration as an "authentic" and "national" form of music and the gradual reshaping of *carnaval* in Rio de Janeiro.

Chapter 3, "Visualizing *Mestiçagem*: Literature, Film, and the *Mulata*," focuses on the rise of popular cinema and how it functions as the second wave of mass communication as a vehicle for the national conversation about Brazilian identity from the 1930s to the 1980s. While radio provides the aural culture for this conversation, film contributes a very powerful visual culture, in particular, for the communication of the Freyrean vision via the novels of Jorge Amado and their film incarnations. At the heart of this vision of Freyre and Amado is the sensual *mulata*. Ironically, Carmen Miranda (in the 1930s and 1940s) and Sonia Braga (in the 1970s and 1980s) – two light-skinned women – became the iconic images of the blending of African and Portuguese cultures that Freyre placed at the center of *mestiçagem*. Chapter 4, "'Globo-lizing' Brazil: Televising Identity," moves to the third wave of technological transformation, the emergence and proliferation of television broadcasting, in a period dominated by Rede Globo. With its ability to connect with virtually all the inhabitants of Brazil, Globo became the most powerful force in the shaping of a shared set of national myths, rituals, and symbols after 1970. In close collaboration with the military regime, Globo wielded an enormous power in communicating the regime's official version of the Freyrean vision. The focus of this chapter is the *Jornal Nacional* (Globo's evening news broadcast), *telenovelas*, and *futebol* beginning in the late 1960s. As with radio and film, we see the ongoing tension and dynamic as the State (and its instrument) attempts to impose a hegemonic vision on all Brazilians, yet it is never able to control or direct the rich and creative movements that emerge out of popular culture. Television became central to the lives of nearly all Brazilians by the 1980s and served as a powerful creator and mediator of popular culture.

Given the importance of *futebol* (especially as shown on television after 1970), Chapter 5, "The Beautiful Game: Performing the Freyrean Vision," departs from the technological waves of the previous three chapters (radio, film, television) to delve more deeply into what has been perhaps the most potent instrument of identity formation in twentieth-century Brazil. The success and appeal of *futebol*, and Brazil's unprecedented triumphs in the international arena, provided an extraordinary stage for performing the Freyrean vision. Many Brazilians (and foreigners) saw in the faces of the players and their style of play, especially those on the national team, the living imprint of Freyre's claims. The phenomenal success of Brazil – World Cup victories in 1958, 1962, 1970 – and the roles of players such as Garrincha and Pelé, seemed to confirm that Brazil *was* the land of racial and cultural mixture and that *mestiçagem* produced results that confirmed the nation's exuberance and greatness. As Roberto DaMatta has so eloquently written, *futebol* also became the vehicle for the convergence of cultural *and* civic nationalisms in late-twentieth-century Brazil. Chapter 6, "The Sounds of Cultural Citizenship," returns to popular music to show how (along with *futebol*) it offers the most important forum for the conversation about national identity in Brazil in the second half of the century. Popular music in the decades after 1960 both reflects and shapes the multiple narratives about Brazilian identity on a truly national scale and plays a central role in the emergence of cultural and political citizenship by the 1970s and 1980s. Chapter 7, "Culture, Identity, and Citizenship," brings the arc of the Freyrean vision to its downward turn by the 1980s and 1990s as intellectuals declared any national identity as illusory, and as they and many emerging Afro-Brazilian groups denounced the Freyrean vision as racist and false. The recent struggle for affirmative action in Brazil vividly illustrates the weakening of the Freyrean vision and its relative decline as the dominant narrative of national identity. Ironically, this critique of Freyre emerges just as the transition from dictatorship to democracy mobilizes tens of millions of Brazilians to rally consciously around a sense of *brasilidade*, but one based not only a cultural identity, but also a civic identity built around access to civic and political rights and citizenship. I argue that the decades of cultural nationalism constructed around the Freyrean vision helped make possible the emergence of a powerful civic nationalism by the 1970s and 1980s. Ironically, with the florescence of civic nationalism and civil society among the multiple voices are many that challenge the

Freyrean narrative. At the very moment that the technology of mass communications finally made it possible to create (quite literally) a national community, the dream of uniting all the inhabitants in Brazil around a shared set of myths, rituals, and symbols began to slip away.

Finally, in the Epilogue, "Nation, Modernity, and Identity in the Twentieth and the Twenty-First Centuries," I return to the central arguments and ideas in this essay. I emphasize the power and diffusion of the Freyrean vision through popular culture and its constant interaction with State power. Beginning in the 1990s, and with the rise of the latest technological wave (the Internet), the meaning of national identity, whatever the narrative, has now become even more complicated and diffuse than ever. This new technology of mass communication and the emergence of a dynamic and divisive civil society in Brazil in the 1990s mark the end of an era. The dream of constructing nation-states in Latin America built around an imagined community bound together by a single narrative of national identity, as it turns out, is most likely an illusion even in the age of increasingly powerful States. What was an impossible dream of nation-builders in the nineteenth century seemed entirely possible to their successors in the mid-twentieth century, but now appears impossible in the twenty-first century. In retrospect, the lack of technologies of mass communication made the dreams unachievable in the nineteenth century, the dramatic expansion of these technologies in the twentieth century helped create the illusion of complete national cultural integration, and the global, digital technologies of the twenty-first century have made that integration difficult, if not impossible. Brazil's experience with culture, technology, and identity in the twentieth century is not unique and should compel us to reflect on the same processes in the rest of Latin America and, indeed, the rest of the world.

NOTES

1. Craig Calhoun, *Nationalism* (Minneapolis: University of Minnesota Press, 1997), 5.
2. Benedict Anderson, *Imagined Communities: Reflections on the Origin and Spread of Nationalism*, rev. edn. (New York: Verso, 2006) [originally published in 1983].
3. The Brazilians, like the French, envision "the imaginary (*imaginaire*) as a constructed landscape of collection aspirations." Arjun Appadurai, *Modernity at Large: Cultural Dimensions of Globalization* (Minneapolis: University of Minnesota Press, 1996), 31.

4. Roberto DaMatta, "Digressão: a fábula das três raças, ou o problema do racismo à brasileira," in *Relativizando, introdução à antropologia social* (Rio de Janeiro: Rocco, 1990), 58–87. I use the extremely complicated term race to mean culturally constructed categories defined by heredity, physical appearance, cultural characteristics, or essences. See, for example, Peter Wade, Carlos López Beltrán, Eduardo Restrepo, and Ricardo Ventura Santos, eds., *Mestizo Genomics: Race Mixture, Nation, and Science in Latin America* (Durham, NC: Duke University Press, 2014), 4.

5. Peter Fry, *A persistência da raça: ensaios antropológicos sobre o Brasil e a África austral* (Rio de Janeiro: Civilização Brasileira, 2005), 215.

6. Freyre, *Casa-grande e senzala*, 343; and Freyre, *The Masters and the Slaves*, 278.

7. Recent genetic testing has shown that 87 percent of Brazilians have in their DNA genes that are at least 10 percent African in origin, and nearly half of this population self-classifies as white (*branco*) on the national census. Sérgio D. J. Pena e Maria Cátira Bortolini, "Pode a genética definir quem deve se beneficiar das cotas universitárias e demais ações afirmativas?" *Estudos Avançados*, 18:50 (January–April 2004), 43. In a recent study of the descendants of runaway slave communities (*quilombolas*) in the state of São Paulo, 40 percent of the genetic material was of African origin, 39 percent European, and 21 percent indigenous peoples. Reinaldo José Lopes, "Quilombola é 40% europeu, mostra DNA," *Folha de São Paulo*, 18 setembro 2013.

8. Gilberto Freyre transforma a negatividade do mestiço em positividade, o que permite completar definitivamente os contornos de uma identidade que há muito vinha sendo desenhada ... O mito das três raças torna-se então plausível e pode-se atualizar como ritual. A ideologia da mestiçagem, que estava aprisionada nas ambiguidades das teorias racistas, ao ser reelaborada pode difundir-se socialmente e se tornar senso comum, ritualmente celebrado nas relações do cotidiano, ou nos grandes eventos como o carnaval e o futebol. O que era mestiço torna-se nacional.

Renato Ortiz, *Cultura brasileira e identidade nacional* (São Paulo: Brasiliense, 2006), 41.

9. "[N]enhum brasileiro despertou tantas paixões, pró e contra, quanto Gilberto Freyre." Vamireh Chacon, *A construção da brasilidade (Gilberto Freyre e sua geração)* (Brasília: Paralelo 15 Editores, 2001), 14. The quote comes from Robin E. Sheriff, *Dreaming Equality: Color, Race, and Racism in Urban Brazil* (New Brunswick, NJ: Rutgers University Press, 2001), 5.

10. "The high level of recognition of particularist ancestries seems to speak to the idea of the formation of a Freyrean-type metarace or racial fusion. Ethnic and racial boundaries appear blurred in the popular mindset in favor of a more inclusive nationalist category of Brazilianness." Stanley R. Bailey, *Legacies of Race: Identities, Attitudes, and Politics in Brazil* (Stanford, CA: Stanford University Press, 2009), 82–83.

11. "Like racial democracy had been in previous decades, a belief in the positive value of miscegenation remains relatively uncontested, a sort of common-sense truth that continues to represent beliefs about Brazilian race relations. Ideas about racial hybridity and syncretism continue to predominate in popular culture." Edward E. Telles, *Race in Another America: The*

Significance of Skin Color in Brazil (Princeton: Princeton University Press, 2004), 77.

12. Quote is from Sheila S. Walker, "Africanity vs. Blackness: Race, Class and Culture in Brazil," *NACLA Report on the Americas*, 35:6 (2002), 20. Bailey, *Legacies of Race*, 80–83; Liv Rebecca Sovik, *Aqui ninguém é branco* (Rio de Janeiro: Aeroplano, 2009).

13. "Brazil's miscegenation is real and indicates relatively widespread interracial sociability." Telles, *Race in Another America*, 192 and 223.

14. "The racial democracy thesis ... insists that the disproportionate impoverishment of blacks and their absence among elites is due to class discrimination and the legacy of slavery, and that the absence of state-sponsored segregation, a history of miscegenation, and social recognition of intermediate racial categories have upheld a unique racial order." Mala Htun, "From 'Racial Democracy' to Affirmative Action: Changing State Policy on Race in Brazil," *Latin American Research Review*, 39:1 (February 2004), 64.

15. Sueann Caulfield, drawing on the work of Reid Andrews, Peter Fry, Hebe Castro, and Robin Sheriff (among others) sees the power of the myth of *mestiçagem* as far back as the 1920s and concludes that the myths of racial democracy and *mestiçagem*, of racial ideals and persistent racism, "might have developed through social and intellectual interaction rather than a one-way dissemination of elite ideology." *In Defense of Honor: Sexual Morality, Modernity, and Nation in Early-Twentieth-Century Brazil* (Durham, NC: Duke University Press, 2000), 147–53; quote from 153.

16. Antonio Sérgio Guimarães traces the emergence and usage of the infamous term "racial democracy" in "Democracia Racial: O Ideal, o Pacto e o Mito," in *Classes, raças e democracia* (São Paulo: Editora 34, 2002), 137–68.

17. Hermano Vianna, "A Meta Mitológica da Democracia Racial," in Joaquim Falcão e Rosa Maria Barboza de Araújo, orgs., *O imperador das idéias: Gilberto Freyre em questão* (Rio de Janeiro: Fundação Roberto Marinho/ Topbooks, 2001), 215–21; Paulina L. Alberto, "Of Sentiment, Science and Myth: Shifting Metaphors of Racial Inclusion in Twentieth-Century Brazil," *Social History*, 37:3 (August 2012), 261–96.

18. The most persuasive arguments for this view are Donna M. Goldstein, *Laughter Out of Place: Race, Class, Violence, and Sexuality in a Rio Shantytown* (Berkeley: University of California Press, 2003), esp. 108; Sheriff, *Dreaming Equality* and Bailey, *Legacies of Race*, esp. 218. "Far from being a legitimizing myth, racial democracy might best be understood, then, as a collective predisposition; as a set of values, interests, and experiences embraced by the masses; as a principled idea of a society in opposition to the United States and its formalized racial divides." Bailey, 115.

19. For an impressive and sophisticated analysis of the data on attitudes toward race and racial democracy, see Bailey, *Legacies of Race*, esp. 81, 115, 139, and 218. See also, Cleusa Turra e Gustavo Venturi, orgs., Folha de São Paulo/ Datafolha, *Racismo cordial: a mais complete análise sobre o preconceito de cor no Brasil* (São Paulo: Editora Ática, 1995).

20. For a recent example of scholars unable to distinguish between Freyre's claims about racial democracy and his thesis on racial mixture, see Bernd Reiter and

Gladys L. Mitchell, eds., *Brazil's New Racial Politics* (Boulder: Lynne Rienner, 2010), especially chapters 1 and 12. Reiter and Mitchell also depict a simplistic view of the State imposing Freyre's views on the Brazilian masses (depriving them of any agency).

21. Quoted in Christopher Dunn, "A retomada freyreana," in Joshua Lund e Malcolm McNee, eds., *Gilberto Freyre e os estudos latino-americanos* (Pittsburgh, PA: Instituto Internacional de Literatura Iberoamericana, Universidade de Pittsburgh, 2006), 45.

22. "Mas, acima de tudo, boa parte de suas [Freyre's] intepretações do Brasil naturalizou-se a tal ponto que passou a fazer parte do imaginário nacional." Enrique Rodríguez Larreta e Guillermo Giucci, *Gilberto Freyre: uma biografia cultural: a formação de um intelectual brasileiro: 1900–1936*, trad. Josely Vianna Baptista (Rio de Janeiro: Civilização Brasileira, 2007), 9.

23. "In Brazil, the existence of a mulatto category is both cause and consequence of an ideology of miscegenation and not an automatic result of the actual biological process of race mixture." Telles, *Race in Another America*, 218.

24. I would like to thank my colleague, Celso Castilho, for pointing this out to me.

25. This imagined community, eventually, will also extend far beyond Brazil's political borders to substantial communities of Brazilians overseas, especially in North America. See Maxine Margolis, *Goodbye Brazil: Emigres from the Land of Soccer and Samba* (Madison, WI: University of Wisconsin Press, 2013) and *Invisible Minority: Brazilians in New York City*, rev. edn. (Gainesville: University of Florida Press, 2009); H. B. Cavalcanti, *Almost Home: A Brazilian American's Reflections on Faith, Culture, and Immigration* (Madison: University of Wisconsin Press, 2012).

26. For a list of attributes that are often associated with definitions of "nation," see Calhoun, 4–5.

27. Quote is from David Levering Lewis, *W. E. B. DuBois, 1868–1919: Biography of a Race* (New York: Macmillan, 1994), 136.

28. "[N]ationalism has something inescapably paradoxical about it. It makes political claims which take the nation's existence wholly for granted, yet it proposes programs which treat the nation as something yet unbuilt." David Bell, *The Cult of the Nation in France: Inventing Nationalism, 1680–1800* (Cambridge, MA: Harvard University Press, 2001), 5. For a concise overview of "imagined nations" in Brazil from independence to the mid-twentieth century, see José Murilo de Carvalho, "Brasil: nações imaginadas," in *Pontos e bordados: escritos de história e política*, 2ª. edn. (Belo Horizonte: Editora UFMG, 2005), 233–68.

29. Throughout this book I will use "State" to refer to the central state in classical political terms, and "state" when I referred to the political subunits of the Brazil after 1889.

30. For a fine example of one part of this effort see, Todd A. Diacon, *Stringing Together a Nation: Cândido Mariano da Silva Rondon and the Construction of a Modern Brazil, 1906–1930* (Durham, NC: Duke University Press, 2004).

31. Eric Hobsbawm, *The Age of Extremes: A History of the World, 1914–1991* (New York: Vintage Books, 1996), 509.

32. See, for example, Daryle Williams, *Culture Wars: The First Vargas Regime, 1930–1945* (Durham, NC: Duke University Press, 2001).
33. The literature on the history of music and dance in this period is rich: Hermano Vianna, *O mistério do samba* (Rio de Janeiro: Zahar, 1995); Bryan McCann, *Hello, Hello Brazil: Popular Music in the Making of Modern Brazil* (Durham, NC: Duke University Press, 2004); John Charles Chasteen, *National Rhythms, African Roots: The Deep History of Latin American Popular Dance* (Albuquerque: University of New Mexico Press, 2004).
34. My thinking on this topic has been significantly shaped by Celia Applegate, "A Europe of Regions: Reflections on the Historiography of Sub-national Places in Modern Times," *American Historical Review*, 104:4 (October 1999), 1157–82.
35. The cognitive terminology is from Rogers Brubaker. Applegate, 1175 and 1182.
36. Durval Muniz de Albuquerque Jr., *The Invention of the Brazilian Northeast*, trans. Jerry Dennis Metz (Durham, NC: Duke University Press, 2014), 37. See also, Seth Garfield, *In Search of the Amazon: Brazil, the United States, and the Nature of a Region* (Durham, NC: Duke University Press, 2013), 28–29.
37. Barbara Weinstein, *The Color of Modernity: São Paulo and the Making of Race and Nation in Brazil* (Durham, NC: Duke University Press, 2015), 9. "[T]he relations do not tend to be egalitarian but it is clear that the power and construction of the event are a consequence of a complex and decentered fabric of reformulated traditions and modern interchanges, of multiple actors acting in combination." Néstor García Canclini, *Hybrid Cultures: Strategies for Entering and Leaving Modernity*, trans. Christopher L. Chiappari and Silvia L. López (Minneapolis: University of Minnesota Press, 1995), 189.
38. Some examples of this top-down view of the State and its power are such classic works as Raymundo Faoro, *Os donos do poder: formação do patronato politico brasileiro*, 3ª. edn. (Porto Alegre: Editora Globo, 1976) and Simon Schwartzman, *Bases do autoritarismo brasileiro* (Rio de Janeiro: Campus, 1982). As Nicola Miller has pointed out, much of the literature on nationalism in Latin America has been divided between those who have studied it "as a manifestation of political power, focusing on the state, and those who have worked on national identity as a cultural community, focusing on society." Nicola Miller, "The Historiography of Nationalism and National Identity in Latin America," *Nations and Nationalism*, 12:2 (2006), 212. In this book, I have tried to bridge this divide.
39. I differ here, quite dramatically, from the perspective of those such as Gellner who see nationalism as imposed from above. Ernest Gellner, *Nations and Nationalism* (Ithaca, NY: Cornell University Press, 1983), esp. 57. I agree with Peter Sahlins's analysis: "state formation and nation building were two-way processes ... States did not simply impose their values and boundaries on local society. Rather, local society was a motive force in the formation and consolidation of nationhood and the territorial state." Peter Sahlins, *Boundaries: The Making of France and Spain in the Pyrenees* (Berkeley: University of California Press, 1989), 8.

40. For a classic statement on cultural hybridity and Latin America, see, García Canclini, *Hybrid Cultures*. In the words of one of the founding figures of U.S. anthropology, Alfred Kroeber, "cultures can blend to almost any degree and not only thrive but perpetuate themselves." A. L. Kroeber, *Culture Patterns and Processes* (New York: Harcourt Brace and World, 1963), 67

41. Another example of this process is the emergence of Afro-Brazilian religions in Brazil. As Peter Fry has noted, "Os candomblés, as macumbas, os espritismos contemporâneos são o resultado de embates e negociações entre elite e povo, brancos e negros, letrados e iletrados ao longo dos anos." Fry, *A persistência da raça*, 162.

42. Prasenjit Duara, *Rescuing History from the Nation: Questioning Narratives of Modern China* (Chicago: University of Chicago Press, 1995), 8 and 10.

   Counter-narratives of the nation that continually evoke and erase its totalizing boundaries – both actual and conceptual – disturb those ideological manoeuvres through which "imagined communities" are given essentialist identities. For the political unity of the nation consists in a continual displacement of the anxiety of its irredeemably plural modern space – representing the nation's modern territoriality is turned into the archaic, atavistic temporality of Traditionalism. The difference of space returns as the Sameness of time, turning Territory into Tradition, turning the People into One.

   Homi K. Bhabha, *The Location of Culture* (London: Routledge, 1994), 213.

43. Gilbert M. Joseph and Daniel Nugent, eds., *Everyday Forms of State Formation: Revolution and the Negotiation of Rule in Modern Mexico* (Durham, NC: Duke University Press, 1994), esp. their introduction, "Popular Culture and State Formation in Revolutionary Mexico," 3–23.

44. See, for example, Ortiz, *Cultura brasileira e identidade nacional*; Nicola Miller, *In the Shadow of the State: Intellectuals and the Quest for National Identity in Twentieth-Century Spanish America* (London: Verso, 1999).

45. Renato Ortiz, "Culture and Society," in Ignacy Sachs, Jorge Wilheim, and Sérgio Paulo Pinheiro, eds., *Brazil: A Century of Change*, trans. Robert N. Anderson (Chapel Hill: University of North Carolina Press, 2009), 123 and 135.

46. The debate over identity is and has been "a struggle about culture, not a struggle between cultures." Frederick Cooper, *Colonialism in Question: Theory, Knowledge, History* (Berkeley: University of California Press, 2005), 87.

47. For an astute analysis of the rise of a *sociedade de massas* in Brazil, see Renato Ortiz, *A moderna tradição brasileira: cultura brasileira e indústria cultural* (São Paulo: Editora Brasiliense, 1988).

48. Brian Owensby, "Toward a History of Brazil's 'Cordial Racism': Race beyond Liberalism," *Comparative Studies in Society and History*, 47:2 (April 2005), 339 and 342. I am indebted to Owensby's essay for helping me clarify a number of points in my larger argument.

49. In contrast to the work of John Breuilly, who emphasizes the politics of nationalism over "culture, ideology, identity," I see politics, culture, and power as inseparable. John Breuilly, *Nationalism and the State*, 2nd. edn. (Chicago: University of Chicago Press, 1993), esp. 1.

50. For recent coverage of how the flag has been claimed by all Brazilians for their various causes, see Fabio Sexto e Joana Dale, "Em Progresso," *Revista O Globo* (14 July 2013), 24–29.

51. In both state formation and independence movements, the discourse of nationalism prompts the attempt to secure a satisfactory fit between nation and state. This is made especially important by the political ideologies emphasizing citizenship, for the participation of citizens demands a kind of lateral connection to each other and a kind of exclusive loyalty to the state not required by empires and other older forms of polity.
    Calhoun, 124.

52. For a recent argument against the notion of national identities, see Micol Seigel, *Uneven Encounters: Making Race and Nation in Brazil and the United States* (Durham, NC: Duke University Press, 2009), esp. the Preface and Introduction.

53. E. Bradford Burns, *The Poverty of Progress: Latin America in the Nineteenth Century* (Berkeley: University of California Press, 1980); Doris Sommer, *Foundational Fictions: The National Romances of Latin America* (Berkeley: University of California Press, 1991).

54. Domingo Faustino Sarmiento, *Facundo: civilización y barbarie, vida de Juan Facundo Quiroga*, 7ª. edn. (México: Editorial Porrúa, 1989) [first published in 1845]; José Enrique Rodó, *Ariel* (Madrid: Cáthedra, 2000) [originally published in 1900].

55. Sarah C. Chambers, *From Subjects to Citizens: Honor, Gender, and Politics in Arequipa, Peru, 1780–1854* (University Park: Pennsylvania State University Press, 1999); Greg Grandin, *The Blood of Guatemala: A History of Race and Nation* (Durham, NC: Duke University Press, 2000); Peter Guardino, *Peasants, Politics and the Formation of Mexico's National State, Guerrero, 1800–1857* (Stanford, CA: Stanford University Press, 1996); Florencia Mallon, *Peasant and Nation: The Making of Postcolonial Mexico and Peru* (Berkeley: University of California Press, 1995); Mark Thurner, *From Two Republics to One Divided: Contradictions of Postcolonial Nationmaking in Andean Peru* (Durham, NC: Duke University Press, 1997).

56. Miguel Angel Centeno, *Blood and Debt: War and the Nation-State in Latin America* (University Park, PA: The Pennsylvania State University Press, 2002), 173 and 175.

57. See, for example, George Reid Andrews, *Blackness in the White Nation: A History of Afro-Uruguay* (Chapel Hill: University of North Carolina Press, 2010) and *The Afro-Argentines of Buenos Aires, 1800–1900* (Madison: University of Wisconsin Press, 1980).

58. "Only in the mid-twentieth century, runs the Latin Americanist consensus, did mass political participation make nations compelling communities in the imagination of most Latin Americans." John Charles Chasteen, "Introduction: Beyond Imagined Communities," in Sara Castro Klarén and John Charles Chasteen, eds., *Beyond Imagined Communities: Reading and Writing the Nation in Nineteenth-Century Latin America* (Washington, DC: Woodrow Wilson Center Press; Baltimore, MD: Johns Hopkins University Press, 2003), xix.

59. "If a nation is a 'materially and morally integrated society' characterized by the 'mental … and cultural unity of its inhabitants' then few even mid-twentieth-century Latin American countries would qualify." Centeno, *Blood and Debt*, 171.

60. See, for example, Marilyn Grace Miller, *Rise and Fall of the Cosmic Race: The Cult of Mestizaje in Latin America* (Austin: University of Texas Press, 2004); Edward Telles and Denia Garcia, "*Mestizaje* and Public Opinion in Latin America," *Latin American Research Review*, 48:3 (2013), 130–52. "The ideology of *mestizaje* is still today the dominant ideology of national identity in Latin America." Eduardo P. Archetti, *Masculinities: Football, Polo and the Tango in Argentina* (New York: Berg, 1999), 29.

61. See, in particular, Sara Castro Klarén and John Charles Chasteen, eds., *Beyond Imagined Communities: Reading and Writing the Nation in Nineteenth-Century Latin America* (Washington, DC: Woodrow Wilson Center Press; Baltimore, MD: Johns Hopkins University Press, 2003); Michiel Baud, "Beyond Benedict Anderson: Nation-Building and Popular Democracy in Latin America," *International Review of Social History*, 50 (2005), 485–98.

62. For a critique of Anderson's analysis of print culture and Creoles see the chapter by François-Xavier Guerra in Klarén and Chasteen. As Nicola Miller has noted, Anderson also says very little about the gender or race. Miller, "The Historiography of Nationalism and National Identity in Latin America," 210.

63. "[W]hat marked verbal tradition was not literacy but orality, a feature that persists somewhat today, reinforced now not so much by the absence of schools but the failure of the educational system and by the prominence of audiovisual media." Ortiz, "Culture and Society," 122.

64. Muniz de Albuquerque, *The Invention of the Brazilian Northeast*, 8.

65. In Anderson's words, "all communities larger than primordial villages of face-to-face contact (and perhaps even these) are imagined. Communities are to be distinguished, not by their falsity/genuineness, but by the style in which they are imagined." Anderson, *Imagined Communities*, 6.

66. Claudio Lomnitz, "Nationalism as a Practical System: Benedict Anderson's Theory of Nationalism from the Vantage Point of Spanish America," in Miguel Angel Centeno and Fernando López-Alves, eds., *The Other Mirror: Grand Theory Through the Lens of Latin America* (Princeton, NJ: Princeton University Press, 2001), 337.

67. See, for example, Anderson, *Imagined Communities*; Liah Greenfeld, *Nationalism: Five Roads to Modernity* (Cambridge, MA: Harvard Univ. Press, 1992); E. J. Hobsbawm, *Nations and Nationalism since 1780: Programme, Myth, Reality*, 2nd edn. (Cambridge: Cambridge University Press, 1992); Gellner, *Nations and Nationalism*; Anthony D. Smith, *The Nation in History: Historiographical Debates about Ethnicity and Nationalism* (Hanover, NH: University Press of New England, 2000); Eugen Weber, *Peasants into Frenchmen: The Modernization of Rural France, 1870–1914* (Stanford, CA: Stanford University Press, 1976).

68. See, for example, Partha Chatterjee, *The Nation and Its Fragments: Colonial and Postcolonial Histories* (Princeton, NJ: Princeton University Press, 1993); Prasenjit Duara, *Rescuing History from the Nation: Narratives of Modern China* (Chicago: University of Chicago Press, 1997).

69. The following discussion owes a great deal to my reading and reflection on the works cited in note 12 above as well as: Calhoun, *Nationalism* and Gellner, *Nations and Nationalism*.

70. I see nations as communities that share common cultural characteristics, i.e., a "substantial collectivity," in contrast to those who reject this perspective. See, for example, Rogers Brubaker, *Nationalism Reframed: Nationhood and the National Question in the New Europe* (Cambridge: Cambridge University Press, 1996), 13–22.

71. Lloyd Kramer, *Nationalism: Political Cultures in Europe and the Americas, 1775–1865* (New York: Twayne Publishers, 1998), 1.

72. Robert H. Wiebe, "Humanizing Nationalism," *World Policy Journal*, 13:4 (Winter 1996/1997), 81. See also, Robert H. Wiebe, *Who We Are: A History of Popular Nationalism* (Princeton, NJ: Princeton University Press, 2011).

73. For a brief summary of this debate, see Kramer, *Nationalism*, chapter 1. "In Brazil of the 1930s, love of nation does not seem to have been as deeply rooted a sentiment as love of work or family." Brodwyn Fischer, *A Poverty of Rights: Citizenship and Inequality in Twentieth-Century Rio de Janeiro* (Stanford, CA: Stanford University Press, 2008), 112.

74. Ethnicity is used here in the sense that is common in much of the literature on nationalism, as a people with a common heritage. In much of the European historiography, this is a racial as well as cultural heritage. Ethnicity is used in U.S. scholarly literature today more as a cultural category as opposed to race, which has more traditionally been seen as a more biological category. Peter Wade, *Race and Ethnicity in Latin America* (London: Pluto Press, 1997), esp. chapter 1, 5–24. See also, Andreas Wimmer, *Ethnic Boundary Making: Institutions, Power, Networks* (New York: Oxford University Press, 2013), 7.

75. Ortiz, "Culture and Society," *Brazil*, 129. See also, José Murilo de Carvalho, *Cidadania no Brasil: o longo caminho* (Rio de Janeiro: Civilização Brasileira, 2005).

76. T. S. Heise, *Remaking Brazil: Contested National Identities in Contemporary Brazilian Cinema* (Cardiff: University of Wales Press, 2012), 18.

77. James Sanders has made a persuasive argument that, for Spanish America, many nineteenth-century political leaders were not seeking to copy North Atlantic politics, but rather saw themselves as the vanguard of a new politics. While I am not entirely persuaded by his arguments, I believe it does not hold when turning to other areas of culture, society, and economics. James E. Sanders, *The Vanguard of the Atlantic World: Creating Modernity, Nation, and Democracy in Nineteenth-century Latin America* (Durham, NC: Duke University Press, 2014).

78. García-Canclini provides a useful set of distinctions following Habermas and Berman defining "*modernity* as historical stage, *modernization* as socio-economic process that tries to construct modernity, and *modernisms*, or the

cultural projects that renew symbolic practices with an experimental or critical sense." García-Canclini, *Hybrid Cultures*, 11. [emphasis in original]

79. Saulo Gouveia, *The Triumph of Brazilian Modernism: The Metanarrative of Emancipation and Counter-Narratives* (Chapel Hill: University of North Press, 2013). The cultural vanguards of Modernism in Europe also rewrote their national histories and identities in the early twentieth century. Hobsbawm, *Age of Extremes*, 184.

80. Sergio Miceli, *Intelectuais à brasileira* (São Paulo: Companhia das Letras, 2001); Lúcia Lippi Oliveira, *Cultura é patrimônio: um guia* (Rio de Janeiro: Editora da FGV, 2008), 77–79.

81. Florencia Garramuño, *Primitive Modernities: Tango, Samba, and Nation*, trans. Anna Kazumi Stahl (Stanford, CA: Stanford University Press, 2011), 135.

82. Ruben George Oliven, "Brazil: The Modern in the Tropics," in Vivian Schelling, ed., *Through the Kaleidoscope: The Experience of Modernity in Latin America* (London: Verso, 2007), 70. In the same volume, see also, José de Souza Martins, "The Hesitations of the Modern and the Contradictions of Modernity in Brazil." For a brilliant analysis of this blending of popular and elite culture in Brazilian society, see José Miguel Wisnik, "Entre o erudito e o popular," *Revista de História*, 157:2 (2007), 55–72.

83. My use of modernization here refers to processes generating institutional changes while modernity is both a historical moment and a mentality. For a recent discussion of the problematic concepts of modernization and modernity, see "AHR Roundtable: Historians and the Question of 'Modernity,'" *American Historical Review*, 116:3 (June 2011), 631–751.

84. Courtney Jeanette Campbell, "The Brazilian Northeast, Inside Out: Region, Nation, and Globalization (1926–1968)," Ph.D. Dissertation, Vanderbilt University, 2014, esp. chapter 1, 31–74; Ricardo Benzaquen de Araújo, *Guerra e paz: Casa-Grande & Senzala e a obra de Gilberto Freyre nos anos 30* (Rio de Janeiro: Editora 34, 1994), 21.

85. "Freyre offered only a profoundly reactionary mythology of the past." Jeffrey D. Needell, "Identity, Race, Gender and Modernity in the Origins of Gilberto Freyre's *Oeuvre*," *American Historical Review*, 100:1 (February 1995), 59–61, quote from 72; *I'll Take My Stand: The South and the Agrarian Tradition, by Twelve Southerners* (New York: Harper and Brothers, 1930).

86. Weinstein, *Color of Modernity*, 11–13.

87. Quoted in Oliven, *Tradition Matters*, 7.

88. Lúcia Lippi Oliveira, *A questão nacional na Primeira República* (São Paulo: Editora Brasiliense, 1990), 194–97.

89. See, for example, Centeno, *Blood and Debt*, chapter 1.

90. "The state is invisible; it must be personified before it can be seen, symbolized before it can be loved, imagined before it can be conceived." Michael Walzer, "On the Role of Symbolism in Political Thought," *Political Science Quarterly*, 82:2 (June 1967), 194.

91. For the purposes of this essay, I follow Centeno in defining the State as "the permanent institutional core of political authority on which regimes rest and depend." Centeno, *Blood and Debt*, 2.

92. For a classic work on this topic see, Faoro, *Os donos do poder.*
93. See, for example, Rafael de Bivar Marquese, *Administração & escravidão: idéias sobre a gestão da agricultura escravista brasileira* (São Paulo: Editora Hucitec, 1999).
94. Gellner, 7.
95. "This sense of communality is supported by a state-sponsored liturgy whose set of symbols and rituals support a form of secular religion in which the people worship themselves." Centeno, *Blood and Debt,* 170.
96. Calhoun, 77.
97. Most of the "constructivist" theorists of nationalism emphasize a top-down, imposed identity driven by the rise of the modern State and industrial society. "The one persistent feature of this style of nationalism was, and is, that it is *official* – i.e. something emanating from the state, and serving the interests of the state first and foremost." Anderson, *Imagined Communities,* 159. "Some traditions may fall flat and some nationalisms may never resonate." Centeno, *Blood and Debt,* 171.
98. For an example of a pioneering effort to develop a more sophisticated and nuanced approach to State and popular culture, see Joseph and Nugent, eds., *Everyday Forms of State Formation.*
99. Miller, "The Historiography of Nationalism and National Identity in Latin America," 212.
100. See, for example, the work of Appadurai, *Modernity at Large* and Cooper, *Colonialism in Question,* chapter 3, "Modernity," This will be discussed in greater detail in Chapter 4.
101. Duara, *Rescuing the Nation from History,* 9.
102. For a recent interpretation along these lines see, Darcy Ribeiro, *O povo brasileiro: a formação e o sentido do Brasil,* 2ª. edn. (São Paulo: Companhia das Letras, 1995).
103. For a strident critique of the "national" in favor of "transnational" studies, see Seigel, *Uneven Encounters.*
104. Serge Gruzinski, *The Mestizo Mind: The Intellectual Dynamics of Colonization and Globalization,* trans. Deke Dusinberre (New York: Routledge, 2002), 26.
105. Person from Rio de Janeiro, São Paulo, Rio Grande do Sul, or Minas Gerais. Amartya Sen, *Identity and Violence: The Illusions of Destiny* (New York: W. W. Norton, 2006), esp. chapter 2.
106. Charles S. Maier, "'Being There': Place, Territory, and Identity," in Seyla Benhabib, Ian Shapiro, and Danilo Petranovic, eds., *Identities, Affiliations, and Allegiances* (New York: Cambridge University Press, 2007), 67. Following Burdick, "I take *identity* to refer to a set of beliefs held by a person that focus on the idea that he or she possesses values, experiences, or essences that are salient and central in his or her life and are durable over time. Values, experiences, or essences of the person him- or herself, without reference to others, are the person's *individual identity;* values experiences, or essences held in common with some larger group of people are the person's *collection identity.* It is the salience, centrality, and durability of these values, experiences, or essences that render them definitive of the

person's identity." [emphasis in original] John Burdick, *The Color of Sound: Race, Religion, and Music in Brazil* (New York: New York University Press, 2013), 18.

107. For an excellent discussion of these parallel and paradoxical paths, see Ruben George Oliven, "National and Regional Identities in Brazil: Rio Grande do Sul and Its Peculiarities," *Nations and Nationalism*, 12:2 (2006), 303–20.

108. Some examples of work on regional identities are: Ruben Oliven, *Tradition Matters: Modern Gaúcho Identity in Brazil*, trans. Carmen Chaves Tesser (New York: Columbia University Press, 1996); Barbara Weinstein, "Racializing Regional Difference: São Paulo versus Brazil, 1932," in Nancy P. Appelbaum, Anne S. Macpherson, and Karin Alejandra Rosemblatt, eds., *Race and Nation in Modern Latin America* (Chapel Hill: University of North Carolina Press, 2003), 237–62; Weinstein, *Color of Modernity*; Nísia Trindade Lima, *Um sertão chamado Brasil: Intelectuais e representação geográfica da identidade nacional* (Rio de Janeiro: IUPERJ, 1999); Durval Muniz de Albuquerque Jr. *A invenção do nordeste e outras artes* (Recife: Fundação Joaquim Nabuco, Editora Massangana, 1999); Stanley E. Blake, *The Vigorous Core of Our Nationality: Race and Regional Identity in Northeastern Brazil* (Pittsburgh, PA: University of Pittsburgh Press, 2011).

109. Garfield, *In Search of the Amazon*, 29.

110. Weinstein, "Racializing Regional Difference," 240; and Weinstein, *Color of Modernity*.

111. Quoted in Kramer, *Nationalism*, 6.

112. Hall goes on to say, "The diaspora experience … is defined, not by essence or purity, but by the recognition of a necessary heterogeneity and diversity; by a conception of 'identity' which lives with and through, not despite difference; by *hybridity*." Quoted in Kramer, *Nationalism*, 8. Emphasis in both quotes in the original.

113. For excellent empirical work on Brazilians' perceptions of themselves, see Alberto Costa Almeida, *A cabeça do brasileiro* (Rio de Janeiro: Editora Record, 2007). For a scathing critique of the very notion of identity, see Frederick Cooper, *Colonialism in Question*, with Rogers Brubaker, chapter 3, "Identity," 59–90.

114. See, for example, Fry, *A persistência da raça*, 164 and 174–75. "Social myths, like religious myths, are not simply falsehoods. They are stories that societies tell and retell themselves, stories that therefore become crucial common ground for debate and negotiation even as the powerful deploy them to parry demands for social change." Paulina L. Alberto, *Terms of Inclusion: Black Intellectuals in Twentieth-Century Brazil* (Chapel Hill, NC: University of North Carolina Press, 2011), 301.

115. Owensby, "Toward a History of Brazil's 'Cordial Racism,'" 324.

116. Muniz de Albuquerque Jr., *The Invention of the Brazilian Northeast*, 139–40.

117. "The polysemous nature of myths renders them able to express – in a more effective way than elaborate ideologies – national interests, aspirations, and

fears." José Murilo de Carvalho, "Dreams Come Untrue," *Daedalus*, 129:2 (Spring 2000), 60.

118. "It is through the syntax of forgetting – or being obliged to forget – that the problematic identification of a national people becomes visible. The national subject is produced in that place where the daily plebiscite – the unitary number – circulates in the grand narrative of the will." Bhabha, *The Location of Culture*, 230.

119. Edmund S. Morgan, *Inventing the People* (New York: W. W. Norton, 1988), 13–14.

120. For an academic critique of racial categories and theories in Brazil, see Antonio Sérgio Alfredo Guimarães, "Preconceito de cor e racism no Brasil," *Revista de Antropologia*, 47:1 (2004), 9–43.

121. Following Burdick, I am using the term *movimento negro* here to "mean groups that place an explicit emphasis on struggling against racism and building a positive black identity." John Burdick, *Blessed Anastácia: Women, Race, and Popular Christianity in Brazil* (New York: Routledge, 1998), 3.

122. For a thoughtful critique of these movements and the push for affirmative action, see Fry, *A persistência da raça*. For examples of two typical reactions to affirmative action policies often found in the popular press, see, for example, Roberta Fragoso M. Kaufmann, "A farsa do país 'racista,'" *O Globo*, 25 de outubro de 2009, 7; and, Rodrigo Constantino, "Segregação racial," *O Globo*, 7.

123. For a clear discussion of these issues, see Kia Lilly Caldwell, *Negras in Brazil: Re-envisioning Black Women, Citizenship, and the Politics of Identity* (New Brunswick, NJ: Rutgers University Press, 2007).

124. For a recent survey of this movement within Brazilian civil society, see Ollie A. Johnson III, "Afro-Brazilian Politics: White Supremacy, Black Struggle, and Affirmative Action," in Peter R. Kingstone and Timothy J. Power, eds., *Democratic Brazil Revisited* (Pittsburgh, PA: University of Pittsburgh Press, 2008), 209–30.

125. For an impressive analysis of the culturalist impulse in Brazilian social thought, see Marcelo Paixão, *A lenda da modernidade encantada: por uma crítica ao pensamento social brasileiro sobre relações raciais e projeto de Estado-Nação* (Curitiba: Editora CRV, 2014).

126. For a powerful and beautifully written example of this resurgent nationalism, see Michael Ignatieff, *Blood and Belonging: Journeys into the New Nationalism* (New York: Farrar, Straus, and Giroux, 1994).

127. See, for example, Seigel, *Uneven Encounters*; Walter D. Mignolo, *The Idea of Latin America* (Oxford: Blackwell, 2005).

128. The literature on this topic is nearly endless! Some stimulating examples are: Roberto da Matta, *Carnavais, malandros e heróis: para uma sociologia do dilema brasileiro*, 4ª. edn. (Rio de Janeiro: Zahar Editores, 1983); Darcy Ribeiro, *O povo brasileiro: a formação e o sentido do Brasil* (São Paulo: Companhia das Letras, 1995). We should also remember that, "Essentialisms can be important to people's self-definitions, [and] should not be entirely discounted as irrelevant fictions." Thomas Turino,

Nationalists, Cosmopolitans, and Popular Music in Zimbabwe (Chicago: University of Chicago Press, 2000), 24.

129. See, for example, Roberto Cavalcanti de Albuquerque, *Gilberto Freyre e a invenção do Brasil* (Rio de Janeiro: Editora José Olympio, 2000).

130. Ortiz, "Culture and Society," *Brazil*, 123.

131. For a provocative analysis of the Brazilian intelligentsia, the developmental nationalist model, and the end of this era, see Luciano Martins, "A Inteligentsia em situação de mudança de referentes (da construção da nação à crise do estado-nação)," in Leslie Bethell, org., *Brasil: fardo do passado, promessa do futuro: dez ensaios sobre política e sociedade brasileira*, trad. Maria Beatriz de Medina (Rio de Janeiro: Civilização Brasileira, 2002), 305–22.

I

From the "Spectacle of Races" to "Luso-Tropical Civilization"

The first rule that we must follow is that of national character. Every people has, or must have, a character; if it lacks one, we must begin by endowing it with one.[1]

Jean-Jacques Rousseau

[T]his state is not a nationality, this country is not a society, the populace is not a people, our men are not citizens.[2]

Alberto Torres

CONSTRUCTING STATE AND NATION

As in most of Latin America, in Brazil the State emerges and functions long before the creation of the nation. The State – taken here at its simplest to mean the apparatus of power that asserts a monopoly on the legitimate exercise of violence – begins to emerge in Brazil in the coastal Portuguese enclaves in the late sixteenth century.[3] For nearly three centuries, the State in Brazil operated as an extension of the power of the Portuguese monarchy and its reach was largely restricted to towns, ports, and only minimally into the vast continental hinterland. The presence of that State apparatus became more direct and visible with the transfer of the royal family and court to Rio de Janeiro from 1808 to 1821.[4] With the declaration of independence in 1822, Crown Prince (and then Emperor) Pedro and his Portuguese and Brazilian-born allies asserted control over the State and all its (limited) powers. Their task, like that of many of their Spanish American contemporaries, was to use that State power to create a new nation – in the unusual case of Brazil, as a constitutional monarchy rather than a republic.[5]

It has often been pointed out that Brazil was very different from the rest of Latin America, managing to remain intact in contrast to the eventual fragmentation of the four Spanish American viceroyalties into fifteen new countries by 1850. This political unity was not pre-ordained, nor inevitable. Brazil in the 1820s was a series of coastal enclaves (plus the slightly inland Minas Gerais) – an archipelago of settlements – dominated by powerful local landowners and merchants.[6] The emergent Brazilian State under the guidance of Pedro I and his son, Pedro II, and their (especially military) allies eventually managed to suppress a wave of revolts across the length of Atlantic Brazil led by elites and nonelites from the 1820s to the 1840s. Only during the early years of the so-called Second Reign of Pedro II (1840–1889) was the State able to assert its authority over the major population centers of nearly 8,000 kilometers of coastline and the urban centers of Minas Gerais. The vast interior – potentially some 8 million square kilometers or more – remained largely outside of State control and, in effect, not under the control of any nation-state (fortunately for the many indigenous peoples living there).[7] In the words of Lilia Schwarcz, "There was country called Brazil, but there were absolutely no Brazilians."[8]

Under the "First Reign" of Pedro I (1822–1831) and the Interregnum (1831–1840) the survival of Brazil as the vast territory shown on most maps was continually in doubt.[9] With the defeat of the last substantive regional revolts in the 1840s, Brazil became a confederation of islands of powerful landowners who, in effect, were the State incarnate in the countryside. As Victor Nunes Leal, Raymundo Faoro, and others have shown, Brazil was a sprawling patrimonial system where powerful landowners (*coronéis*) dominated local life.[10] For Faoro, an aristocratic elite of lawyers and military officers provided the personnel who both administered the State and derived their status and power from it. They used the patrimony of the State to strengthen central government, reward allies, and resolve conflict.[11] The central government of Brazil, quite simply, did not have the means or the resources even to attempt to assert its control over this enormous area. In exchange for their obedience to provincial (later state) authorities the landowners were left largely alone to run local affairs. When disputes among these landowners or from the poor masses threatened the peace, the provincial/state government would step in with its resources to restore stability. At the national level, provincial authorities remained obedient to the central government in exchange for their own relative autonomy. When disputes at the level of the province/state became too pronounced, the central government would step in to restore order.[12]

This system became even more highly developed after the overthrow of Pedro II in 1889 and the creation of the First (or Old) Republic. The decentralized "United States of Brazil," in effect, was a federation of states dominated by powerful landowners (*os poderosos da terra*) who exercised impressive autonomy while maintaining loyalty to the central government. In the face of frequent uprisings and rebellions from the 1890s to the 1920s, the central government repeatedly intervened in nearly every Brazilian state (often multiple times) to insure the integrity of a system sometimes called the "politics of the governors."[13] The Brazilian State repeatedly acted to guarantee stability, order, and to impose unity on contentious local and regional elites. The need to act frequently offers impressive testimony to the continuing weakness of the Brazilian State in the early twentieth century.[14]

On the surface, Brazil was a constitutional monarchy from 1824 to 1889 with parliamentary politics self-consciously modeled on the English political system. Elections at the municipal and provincial levels took place regularly and (especially under Pedro II) the two major political "parties" – Liberals and Conservatives – alternated in power for decades.[15] Despite the façade of electoral representation, the Empire was built on the politics of exclusion. The rights of citizenship were extended to very few. Only about 10 percent of the population could vote and, especially at the local level, powerful landowners determined the outcome of elections through coercion, force, and alliances.[16] In the 1880s, electoral legislation further restricted the vote. The Constitution of 1891, although modeled on that of the United States, severely restricted voting with requirements of wealth and literacy (even more so than in the United States). More important, those who controlled local politics determined who voted, whatever the official legal requirements. In the 1930 election, the last of the "Old" Republic (1889–1930), less than 3 percent of the population voted.[17] From the perspective of Brazilian elites, the system functioned fairly well. From the 1840s to 1930, this elite political consensus provided Brazil with an impressive stability compared with the other countries of the Americas – including the United States. Local revolts threatened peace, but were always contained. The most serious challenge to the system, the overthrow of the monarchy in 1889 ushered in five years of serious political turmoil, but by 1894, the powerful elites had once again reestablished a political system that balanced local and regional autonomy with national unity – as a federative republic rather than a (nominally) centralized monarchy. As Aspásia Camargo has observed of this period, "[N]ational identity ... appeared to be more virtual and symbolic than real."[18]

Over the past thirty years, scholars across the Americas have produced a rich literature on the struggles of the less powerful to challenge elite efforts to construct nations in Latin America from the top down and through the restriction of the rights of citizenship to a minority. Studies for Mexico, Peru, and Guatemala (to cite a few examples) have completely revised our understanding of the discourses of nationalism, nation-building, and citizenship, especially in the decades after the wars of independence.[19] With the largest slave population in the Americas and a nonwhite majority into the early twentieth century, these studies have also reshaped and deepened our understanding of Brazil in the late nineteenth and early twentieth centuries. Much of the struggle for citizenship revolved around the language of racial equality. These works have shown that despite elite domination of politics and the growing power of the State, many subaltern groups across Brazil have carried on an intense struggle to claim the full rights of citizenship since at least the early nineteenth century.[20]

This conflict between the powerful and less powerful has been a constant in Brazilian history over the past two century – in politics, economics, society, and culture. The continually expanding scholarship on citizenship has enriched our understanding of politics and culture, in particular, yet it has also shown the persistent power of Brazil's elites. I argue throughout this book (and especially in Chapter 7) that the less powerful have had greater success in shaping the development of cultural citizenship than political citizenship until the 1980s. Despite the ongoing challenges to elite political power, civic nationalism developed more slowly than cultural nationalism, and civic identity has been more tentative than cultural identity. Through varying regimes since the 1890s Brazilian political elites have responded to the challenges from below, be it through an "oligarchical" republic, populism, or authoritarianism. The struggle for full citizenship for the vast majority of Brazilians has a long history with its most expressive chapter taking shape in the late twentieth century.

From the 1890s to 1930 a handful of powerful states dominated this federal system: São Paulo and Minas Gerais, and to a lesser extent, Rio de Janeiro and Rio Grande do Sul. As the heartland of the Brazilian gold and diamond rush of the eighteenth century, Minas Gerais had become the wealthiest and most populous captaincy in Brazil by 1750. Even with the end of the era of large-scale gold mining in the late eighteenth century, Minas continued to be an important agricultural region and home to one of the largest slave communities in the Americas. (Until the 1940s Minas Gerais did not have a major urban center comparable to Salvador, Rio de Janeiro, or São Paulo.) Coffee transformed the frontier city and state of São Paulo after 1870 and by 1900 it had become the most dynamic economic center in Brazil. By the 1920s the city of São Paulo would become the largest metropolis in the country and by the 1940s the most important industrial center in Latin America. Minas Gerais and São Paulo dominated the politics of the Old Republic with their huge populations (roughly one-third of all Brazilians) and economic might. The hinterland around the city of Rio de Janeiro (the Court as it was called until 1889) had been the initial focal point of the coffee economy and the city had long been the principal Brazilian city and port (for gold exports, slave imports, and then coffee exports). By the end of the nineteenth century, Rio mattered because it was the country's political center and its second largest industrial and economic metropolis (with a population over 1 million by 1914). The enormous metropolises of Rio de Janeiro and São Paulo (both with more than a million inhabitants by the 1920s) would dominate Brazil's cultural agenda throughout the twentieth century. Rio Grande do Sul became the stepchild of this group. As the southernmost state, and one that had fought tenaciously in the 1830s and 1840s to break away from Brazil, Rio Grande do Sul would be the contentious challenger, and sometimes partner, in this collective of states that dominated the Old Republic.[21]

State-level political machines dominated the politics of the period. The Republican Party of São Paulo (Partido Republicano) and the Republican Party of Minas Gerais, for example, controlled the political machinery in their states from the 1890s to 1930. Much like the Partido de la Revolución Institucional(PRI) in Mexico in the mid-twentieth century, any politician aspiring to influence had to become part of the Partido Republicano in Minas or São Paulo or Rio Grande do Sul and work his way up through the system. Although elections took place on a regular basis, the outcomes were rarely in doubt, at the local, state, or national levels. Although other states may not have liked this *mineiro-paulista* dominance, they rarely had the opportunity to challenge it in any serious fashion. Although the Northeast remained one of the most densely populated regions of Brazil, throughout this period, the other traditionally large and powerful states such as Bahia and Pernambuco had to settle for sharing power rather than exercising it at the national level. The continual economic surge of the Southeast with coffee exports, and then industrialization, further reinforced the weakness of the Northeastern states. From the 1890s to the 1930s, the economic, demographic, political, and cultural power of São Paulo steadily increased. Minas, with its large population and resources, mainly played the role of powerful partner and arbiter in national politics.

The city of Rio de Janeiro continued to be the second largest urban and economic center, and the country's cultural capital, although the city of São Paulo would eclipse Rio's cultural power by the late twentieth century. Brazil's major urban centers in the Old Republic – Salvador, Recife, Rio de Janeiro, and São Paulo – provided the principal venues for intellectual and cultural elites, and for elite discussions about national identity. Well into the twentieth century, Rio de Janeiro remained the cultural magnet and center of gravity for publishing and elite cultural production. The economic and political rise of the state of São Paulo during the Old Republic signaled its emergence as a cultural force with its most visible symbol, the *Semana de Arte Moderna* (Modern Art Week), and the Modernist Movement in the 1920s.

RACE AND NATIONAL IDENTITY

Brazilian social thought in the late nineteenth and early twentieth centuries has been well studied by both Brazilians and Brazilianists.[22] The decades from the 1870s to the 1930s are the crucible for the formation of modern Brazil and its culture. A lively, vigorous, and fascinating series of debates on political theory, economic development, social organization, and cultural values preoccupied the Brazilian intelligentsia and eventually all Brazilians. Race and the future of Brazil were at the core of nearly all these debates. In the end, these debates ultimately grappled with how Brazil could become a "modern" nation – if it *could* become a modern nation. An intense pessimism imbued much of the discourse. Few writers exhibited strong optimism. Most were somewhere in the muddled middle trying to find hope for their country in spite of their concerns about what they perceived as the negative impact of centuries of racial mixture and the profound impact of Africa on their society and culture, what Lilia Schwarcz has called the "spectacle of races."[23]

At the close of the nineteenth century, most of Brazil's 17 million inhabitants were nonwhite. The majority of them were "black" (*preto*) or "racially mixed" (*pardo*), according to the standard government census categories.[24] Brazil's historical demography has always shaped the context of any discussion of its future. The majority of those thinkers who pondered the future of Brazil yearned for modernity and that meant to emulate Europe (and to a lesser extent the United States). France provided the great cultural exemplar and England the icon of economic and political success. As always with the formation of imagined communities, some of the critical influences are not only domestic but also foreign. For the first century and a quarter after independence Brazil's most important interlocutor in this process of nation-building would be Europe, especially France and England. After World War II, it would be the United States. In both cases, Brazilians experienced a mix of both envy and loathing toward the foreign, and the discussion over "national" identity took shape in a complicated and complex exchange with the "foreign."[25]

Beginning in the late nineteenth century, this mix of foreign and domestic also had a South American component. As a rivalry emerged between Argentina and Brazil, the Brazilians were acutely conscious of Argentina's economic, political, and cultural successes. Although the Brazilian economy today is five times the size of Argentina's, and Brazil's international projection is much more important, in the early twentieth century it appeared that Argentina was the South American nation destined to become a global power. By World War I, Argentina was one of the wealthiest nations in the world, Buenos Aires styled itself as the "Paris of South America," and its political system looked more like that of Western Europe than its more northern Latin American neighbors. The rivalry between the two largest nations in South America was economic, political, and diplomatic (and even extended into sports by the 1930s). On one level, this competition took on a racial component as European (primarily Italian and Spanish) immigration transformed Argentina (and Uruguay) into the most "Caucasian" populations in Latin America.[26]

Brazilian elites in the early twentieth century were painfully aware that the population of their country (around 25 million in 1914) had been forged out of the collision of Portuguese, Africans, and Native Americans. This mixing of races, especially of Africans and Portuguese, had long characterized the population of the colony, the Empire, and then the republic. Having absorbed and digested the racist, European social thought of the late nineteenth and early twentieth centuries, intellectual and political elites agonized over their "tainted" racial and cultural heritage. The most pessimistic among them believed the country was doomed to failure because of this "mongrelization" of the population. The abolition of slavery in 1888 and the drive to attract European labor were propelled, to some degree, by the desire to "whiten" (*embranquecer*) the Brazilian population and to make it more European. Although probably 2 million southern and eastern Europeans arrived in Brazil between 1880 and 1920, the profound imprint of Africa on Brazil's biological and cultural makeup was clearly evident to everyone in the early twentieth century.[27]

Writers have commented on the mixing of Native Americans, Europeans, and Africans in Brazil since the sixteenth century. Commentators in the colonial period repeatedly remarked on the profound African influences on the colony and on the rainbow of peoples. One widely repeated refrain about colonial Brazil characterized the society as "a hell for blacks, purgatory for whites, and paradise for mulattoes."[28] As José Murilo de Carvalho has emphasized, the Europeanized elites of the early decades after independence sought to create an image of Brazilian identity that either ignored the masses or depicted an idealized view of them.[29] The Brazilian intellectual and cultural elites in these early years of independence were anxious (in the Romantic tradition) to build a sense of *brasilidade* and like their European counterparts sought ways to demonstrate the logic of nationhood. In 1844, the recently created Instituto Histórico e Geográfico Brasileiro (IHGB) promoted a contest for the best essay on "How to Write the History of Brazil." Ironically, a foreigner, the Bavarian naturalist Karl F. P. von Martius, submitted the winning essay – one that fit the ambitions of the IHGB's leaders, but not perfectly.

In this landmark essay, published in the journal of the Instituto in 1845, von Martius forcefully set out the argument for racial mixture as central to Brazil's historical evolution.[30] A botanist, von Martius had formed part of the entourage that accompanied the Austrian Archduchess and future Empress Leopoldina to Brazil in 1817. He traveled widely through Brazil (1817–1820) – from Rio de Janeiro to the Amazon – before returning to a successful career in Munich as the conservator of the botanical garden. In the essay, von Martius urged Brazilian nation-builders to use the country's history to provide the new country with stability, cohesion, and a sense of self. For von Martius, Portuguese traditions and monarchy would provide the central stabilizing forces and the bedrock of the nation's development. Although the Brazilian cultural elites no doubt were drawn to von Martius's appeal to nation-building, monarchy, and their Portuguese heritage, today we remember the essay more for what must not have pleased the elite readers – von Martius's emphasis on the mixing of Africans, Native Americans, and Europeans that so character-ized Brazil's history. In Brazil, he wrote, the "three races" had converged "in a very particular way."[31] Eventually, he argued, the influence of the African and Indian would fade away leaving the European to lead Brazil. It would be nearly four decades before others took up von Martius's call.[32]

The cultural elites of the 1840s and following decades chose largely to ignore von Martius's emphasis on the racial fusion of Africans and Portuguese and instead turned to the role of the Portuguese colonizer, and the Native American, in constructing their vision of national identity.[33] Under the influence of Romanticism, they constructed a vision of the national heritage around the idealized imagery of the Native American.[34] In the novels of José de Alencar (1829–1877) – to single out the best example – the noble savage and the Portuguese colonizer became the principal emblems of the country's past.[35] The Romantic movement in Latin America lasted roughly half a century, flourishing from independence to the 1870s. The novel was its principal vehicle, the tragic romance its standard plot. The so-called Indianist novel was common in many countries. Alencar, Brazil's greatest Romantic novelist, wrote the classic Brazilian Indianist novel, *Iracema* (an anagram of America, 1865). The story of the love between an Indian princess, Iracema, and a Portuguese soldier, Martim, the novel is written in the Portuguese of the Brazilians of the period rather than the language of the metropolis. Iracema dies, sacrificing herself for Martim, shortly after the birth of their child, Moacyr, who represents the blending of the two races.[36] This elite, idealized notion of the nation's past, however, would give way in the last third of the nineteenth century to the realities of the demography of race.

With the rise of republicanism, positivism, and abolitionism after 1870, Brazilian social thought became consumed with the legacy of *mestiçagem* as writers tried to come to grips with Brazil's past and the country's potential.[37] The intellectual currents of Social Darwinism, Lamarckism, and Spencerianism deeply influenced Brazilian intellectuals. The French philosopher Auguste Comte (1798–1857) and the English thinker Herbert Spencer (1820–1904) were the two European writers who most influenced the social thought of nineteenth-century Brazilian elites. Comte's positivism glorified reason and scientific knowledge and rejected traditional religious beliefs. He believed that humanity had begun to overcome the superstitions and religious beliefs of the past, and with the guidance of science (positive knowledge), would soon enter into a new age where technocrats and engineers would run an authoritarian republic achieving true progress. Comte summed up his beliefs in a catchy epigram: "Love as the base. Order as the means. Progress as the goal." Comte believed in what some might call the imperialism of the scientific world-view, the belief that science will ultimately resolve all significant questions and problems. He coined a new word to describe the scientific study of society – sociology. His views deeply influenced those seeking a modern, industrial, republican Brazil, in particular, officers in the Brazilian military. In Spencer, Brazilian elites found a sophisticated scheme of social evolution that not only glorified science and reason but also provided them with a positivistic rationale to justify their control of the "inferior" racially mixed lower classes. It was Spencer who coined the phrase "survival of the fittest" and what we usually call Social Darwinism would be more accurately described as Social Spencerianism. Spencer believed that human races and peoples had evolved unevenly leaving some inferior to others. He and his followers developed elaborate evolutionary theories showing that white Europeans were the apex of human evolution, with the "lesser" races of Asia, Africa, and Latin America as examples of inferior and less fit peoples.[38]

Under the influences of these currents in social thought, Brazilian intellectuals grappled with a way to deal with the obvious influences of "inferior" races in their own society and their desires to be modern, i.e., European. At one extreme was Raymundo Nina Rodrigues (1862–1906). A physician and anthropologist from Maranhão, Nina Rodrigues became a central figure in Bahia at the end of the nineteenth century – an area that stood out as the most Africanized region of Brazil. In this hotbed of discussion about race, culture, identity, and nation, Nina Rodrigues made some of the first major contributions to the study of Africans and African influences in Brazil.[39] Ironically, this ardent racial pessimist provided clear evidence of the importance of the African contribution to Brazilian culture and became one of the founders of serious anthropological studies in Brazil. Of racially mixed heritage himself, Nina Rodrigues eventually concluded that Brazil was doomed and would never achieve modernity *precisely* because of its long-standing and widespread racial mixture. "The Negro problem in Brazil," for Nina Rodrigues, was at the heart of his despair about Brazil's future. The long and widespread mixing of the black majority with the white minority had produced a "mongrel" race that could never become civilized.[40] In his pessimistic words, blacks "will always constitute the determinant factor in our inferiority as a people."[41]

Although Nina Rodrigues represents the most pessimistic assessment of any major social commentator in the period 1870–1930, nearly all of the major writers in this period had been seduced by Herbert Spencer and the Social Darwinist influences of the late nineteenth century. While Nina Rodrigues carried out the racist and pessimistic logic of Social Darwinism to its extremes in his analysis of Brazil, his contemporaries grappled mightily trying to find ways to escape his logic. The prolific and polemical literary critic Sílvio Romero engaged in an ongoing debate with Nina Rodrigues for nearly twenty years. From the small, Northeastern province/state of Sergipe, Romero epitomized the intellectual gymnastics of so many of the writers of this period. Profoundly influenced by Herbert Spencer and his form of social evolutionism, Romero struggled to find a way for Brazil – with its racially mixed culture – to advance along Spencer's hierarchy of civilization.[42] Like Nina Rodrigues, Romero pioneered Brazilian ethnology and folklore primarily through his collection of stories, songs, and oral culture. Like Nina Rodrigues, he believed the fundamental feature of Brazilian society was racial mixture.[43]

Through his ethnological work and prolific polemical writings, perhaps more than any other intellectual, Romero set the stage for Gilberto Freyre. In the words of the great literary critic Antônio Cândido, Romero "fatally wounded the illusion of whiteness" in Brazilian intellectual circles. He took up the legacy of von Martius. In one of his more famous quotes from his monumental *História da literatura brasileira* (1888), Romero asserted that "every Brazilian is a mestizo if not in his blood at least in his ideas."[44] "The mestizo is the historical, ethnic, and physiological product of Brazil; he is the form of our national distinctiveness."[45] Romero also anticipated Freyre's dialectic of the regional and the national. "National culture," he wrote, "to be authentic, must be regional ... We do not dream of a uniform, monotonous, heavy, indistinct, nullified Brazil given to a dictatorship of central regulator of ideas. Our progress should come from the competition of the diverse qualities of states."[46]

Romero oscillated between moments of optimism and pessimism about Brazil's future. His great hope for progress was based on the influence of Lamarck's theory of the "inheritance of acquired characteristics," the belief a people (in this case, the Brazilians) could transform their negative biological traits through environmental influences. (This Lamarckian strain would also course through the writings of Freyre.) In his most optimistic moments, Romero believed that the influences of environment and European immigration would eventually whiten Brazil and allow it to become a modern nation.[47] Like many of the writers of this period, the way forward for Brazil, and the answer to the social evolutionary racists, was to whiten the Brazilian population through European immigration. Sílvio Romero trumpeted the cause of Brazilian nationalism, one built on the recognition of *mestiçagem*. In his *História da literatura brasileira* (originally published in 1888 and republished multiple times throughout the past century), he proclaims, "The history of Brazilian literature, at its core, is no more than the description of the diverse forces of our people to produce and think for themselves . . . it is nothing more, in one word, than the solution to the vast problem of nationalism."[48]

In many ways the most striking figure of this period is Euclídes da Cunha (1866–1909). Trained as a military engineer, da Cunha worked as a journalist and witnessed the crushing of one of the great social uprisings in late nineteenth-century Brazil at Canudos in the backlands of Bahia. Led by a religious mystic, Antônio the Counselor, the thousands of inhabitants of Canudos fought with local authorities in a series of skirmishes that eventually escalated into a major uprising. The determination and tenacity of these backlanders (*sertanejos*) who wanted to be left alone proved too much for local and state authorities, and a tough test of the Brazilian army. A six-month siege and thousands of wounded and dead were the price to crush the rebellion and its leader. Da Cunha wrote an epic account of the uprising that combines journalism with social commentary and ruminations on the nature of Brazilian identity. Published in 1902, *Os sertões* (*Rebellion in the Backlands* in the English translation, 1944) is a window into the psyche of the Brazilian intelligentsia at the turn of the century as they grappled with how to reconcile their European fixation with their American and African heritage. Da Cunha has enormous admiration for the racially mixed people of the interior, and he recognizes that *they* are the true Brazilian, "the bedrock of our race." Yet, he desperately wants Brazil to be European, and that inevitably meant the gradual elimination of the racially mixed people of the backlands and their replacement with European immigrants. "We are condemned to civilization," he declared. "Either we shall progress or we shall perish. So much is certain, and our choice is clear." Da Cunha and other intellectuals were trapped in what seemed to be an inescapable dilemma: to be "progressive" and "modern" meant turning their backs on their own heritage, the *mestiçagem* that defined them, and to stop being Brazilian.[49]

The most remarkable figure in this period is Manuel Querino (1851–1923), an Afro-Brazilian in Bahia who worked on the margins of elite intellectual life. Deeply involved in Afro-Brazilian religion and culture in Bahia, Querino researched and produced excellent ethnological work on the culture and customs of the Northeast. Unlike any other figure of this period, he reveled in the richness and beauty of the "African contribution to Brazilian civilization." He worked for decades as a public servant and as a practitioner of *candomblé*. Decades later, his life and work would be fictionalized and immortalized in Jorge Amado's novel (and later film) *Tent of Miracles*.[50] An outsider, few major intellectual figures at the time took his writings seriously.

The tragic pessimism of Nina Rodrigues and the exuberant optimism of Querino formed the polar extremes of intellectual debates in the last decades of the nineteenth century and the first two decades of the twentieth century. Few Social Darwinists (or more accurately, Spencerians) in Brazil could bring themselves to accept the cruel logic of Nina Rodrigues, and fewer still could divorce themselves from the racist social evolutionary thought developed in Europe and the United States. Prior to the appearance of Gilberto Freyre on the intellectual scene, Manoel Bonfim (1868–1932), Edgard Roquette-Pinto (1884–1954), and Alberto Torres (1865–1917) were the most prominent defenders of a culturalist approach that was explicitly antiracist. Bonfim, a physician from Sergipe, openly attacked scientific racism and the pessimistic analyses of his compatriots as early as 1906.[51] Roquette-Pinto drew on the work of Franz Boas (also one of Freyre's major influences) and the efforts to divorce notions of biological race and culture. He spoke out against mainstream, racist thought. Born in Rio de Janeiro in 1884 and trained as a physician, Roquette-Pinto (like Nina Rodrigues) took the "anthropological turn" and did both archaeological work and ethnology.[52] In 1912, he accompanied the legendary Cândido Mariano da Silva Rondon on his mission through western Brazil and studied the Nambikwara, a group Claude Lévi-Strauss would bring to world attention some three decades later.[53] As the director of the National Museum in Rio de Janeiro and as President of the First Brazilian Congress on Eugenics (1929), Roquette-Pinto was a prominent voice, but a prophet not yet recognized in his own country filled with racist eugenics.[54] Alberto Torres, who died young, also took a more culturalist perspective rejecting the notion that the biological heritage of Brazilians doomed them to inferiority.[55] Although Bonfim,

Roquette-Pinto, Torres, and Querino offered alternatives to the overwhelming discourse of racist social evolutionism, the prevailing tone of social thought from the 1870s to the 1920s was pessimism engendered by a recognition of the "deleterious" effects of Brazil's African (and indigenous) ancestry.[56]

MODERNISM AND MODERNITY

By the 1920s, cultural, economic, and political upheaval foreshadowed the emergence of modern Brazil in the following decade. Although the 1930s are generally considered the watershed decade in the emergence of modern Brazil, great transformations had begun to emerge in the previous decade. The decentralized "politics of the governors" of the big states faced serious challenges that would lead to civil war in 1930. The most visible manifestation of these challenges was the *tenentes* (lieutenants) movement of young army officers who revolted in July 1922 and again in July 1924 challenging what they saw as a corrupt and stagnant coffee oligarchy holding back the modernization of the country.[57] The collapse of the western economic system in 1929 would produce the beginnings of massive State intervention and forced industrialization that would continue for the next half century. The rise of a Brazilian "counterculture" in the 1920s foreshadowed challenges to decades of European social and cultural influences and the emergence of new visions of Brazilian identity.[58]

From the perspective of nation-building, it is the emergence of the Modernist Movement in the 1920s that propelled the creation and florescence of a new Brazilian nationalism, the "rediscovery of Brazil," based on the search for the "authentically" Brazilian.[59] The Romantics in nineteenth-century Brazil had followed the European pattern and sought in the first decades after independence to establish the cultural institutions (e.g., IHGB, National Archives, National Library) that would generate the texts, images, maps, and narratives that would define the "spirit of the people." These "Creole Pioneers" – to use Anderson's term – produced an idealized vision of Brazil that had its roots in a Portuguese heritage that had gradually taken its own course distinct from the metropolis. From the 1870s to World War I, Realism and Naturalism dominated Brazilian high culture. The classic works of the historian João Capistrano de Abreu (1853–1927) reflect the shift from the Romantic style. From the northern province/state of Ceará, Capistrano de Abreu's work reflects the shifts in the emergence of the historical profession in the late nineteenth century –

the pursuit of ample documentation, an emphasis on climate and geography, structures, and a tendency (in his case) to seek patterns rather than focus on the heroic individuals of the Romantic historians. Arguably, he is the first great modern historian of Brazil.[60]

These European Modernist influences came late to Brazil and did not flourish until after World War I. Numerous children of the Brazilian elite, especially of the newly wealthy São Paulo coffee elite, made their pilgrimage to Europe, especially to Paris, as had their parents and grandparents. They admired the works of the Cubists and Impressionists, read James Joyce (or tried to!), and immersed themselves in bohemian culture in Paris. Eventually, they organized to raise awareness of Modernism within Brazil. Their coming-out party took place during the centennial of Brazilian political independence in 1922. Modern Art Week in February 1922, a series of events staged in São Paulo, was a self-proclaimed "counter-celebration" of the centennial of Brazil's independence from Portugal in 1822.[61] Artists, writers, and intellectuals exhibited their paintings, sculptures, and read their works. Led by the two (unrelated) Andrades, Oswald (1890–1954) and Mário (1893–1945), the Modernists proclaimed the cultural independence of Brazil – from Eurocentrism.[62] The Brazilian Modernists, like those in Europe, fervently rejected "bourgeois" culture and the "official" history of the country. Their works aimed to shock the Brazilian bourgeoisie into a new consciousness – in the Brazilian case, a consciousness of Brazil as an amalgam of three cultural flows, from Europe, Africa, and the indigenous peoples of the Americas. In what would become one of the most memorable images of the movement, Oswald de Andrade published the *"Manifesto Antropófago"* (Cannibalist Manifesto) declaring that Brazil was like a cannibal who consumed the influences of the many and remade these influences into something new, something distinctly Brazilian.[63] Mário de Andrade set as the Modernist goal "to make the Brazilian one hundred percent Brazilian, to nationalize a nation that is as yet so lacking in national characteristics."[64]

Paradoxically, the Modernist avant-garde embraced the primitive and the past. As Dain Borges has noted, they consciously rejected the racial purity discourse of the previous decades and celebrated the "polluted" and "impure" in Brazilian culture. For the Modernists, Brazil was unified and a fusion of differences and impurities.[65] This was true in their paintings, novels, poetry, and theater. Its greatest exemplar in music was the legendary Heitor Villa-Lobos. "He marks the moment," according to José Wisnik, "when the literate culture of a slaveowning country finally saw in the liberation of its repressed and obscure potential, long connected to miscegenation and cultural mixture, interspersed with desire, violence, abundance and misery, the possibility of affirming its destiny and of revealing itself through the union of the erudite and the popular."[66] Florencia Garramuño shows how this process of "civilizing the primitive" takes shape in both Argentina and Brazil in the early twentieth century using tango and samba as her exemplars. "For the avant-garde," she argues, "tango and samba are amphibious products representing both the local, national primitive and the sophisticated and modern quality of the European primitive concept." They become examples of "the condensation of modernization and nationalization."[67]

The Modernists engaged in "a collective intellectual psychoanalysis of national identity" and formed a bridge between the racist, social evolutionary thought of the 1870s–1920s and the great transformation of the post-1930 period – the emergence and dominance of *mestiçagem* as the *positive essence* of Brazilian identity.[68] They led the way in the construction of a "modern" Brazil that became intimately linked to the idea of *mestiçagem*.[69] Sílvio Romero's emphatic trumpeting of racial mixture as the defining feature of Brazil, the antiracist ideas of Bonfim and Roquette-Pinto, and the Modernist search for "authenticity" in Brazil's culturally mixed past all set the stage for the tectonic shift in social thought that Gilberto Freyre would lead. The publication of Gilberto Freyre's *The Masters and the Slaves* galvanized this profound national cultural transformation in the 1930s.

GILBERTO FREYRE AND THE CREATION OF THE MYTH OF *MESTIÇAGEM*

Freyre, like most Brazilian intellectuals, acknowledged that what made Brazilians distinct was centuries of biological and cultural mixing, in particular, of Africans and Portuguese. Unlike his pessimistic, racist predecessors, Freyre glorified this mixture (*mestiçagem* or *miscigenação*) and argued that it made Brazilians unique and exceptional among all other peoples and nations. What had long been seen as a stigma became the great virtue of Brazilians.[70] Freyre turned the racist social thought about *mestiçagem* on its head.[71] He saw mixing as an opportunity rather than as a problem. Between the 1930s and the 1980s – with government support and through many grassroots shifts in popular culture – the Freyrean vision of Brazil gradually became the most potent narrative of Brazilian nationalism.[72] Although not the first intellectual to place *mestiçagem* at the core of Brazilian identity, or even the first to see it in a positive light, he became the most famous advocate of the myth of *mestiçagem*.[73] *Casa-grande e senzala* sparked what Carlos Guilherme Mota has called the *"gilbertização do país"* in the 1930s.[74]

Gilberto Freyre's influence on Brazilian social thought and the formation of a sense of *brasilidade* are indisputable and universally recognized.[75] Oswald de Andrade called him "our totemic writer" (*nosso escritor totêmico*).[76] President Fernando Henrique Cardoso (1995–2003), a world-renowned sociologist in his own right, remarked that "Freyre captivated me ... because he had been capable of formulating a founding myth or quasi-myth."[77] Darcy Ribeiro, another of the great intellectual figures of twentieth-century Brazil, called *Casa-grande e senzala* "the greatest Brazilian book and the most Brazilian of the essays we have written."[78] Ribeiro also astutely points out that the key to understanding Freyre's brilliance and the ability to write *Casa-grande* was his ambiguity – in his life and his worldview.

Born in 1900 in Recife, Freyre loved to point out that he descended from the *senhores de engenho* (sugar planters). He was the quintessential Northeasterner from Pernambuco. Yet, at the same time, he was deeply imbued with the foreign – both the influence of the United States and, even more so, of England. He saw Brazil from the vantage point of his beloved Northeast, which he once described as the "the most Brazilian part of Brazil," and at the same time, from the perspective of the Victorian English gentleman schooled in the United States.[79] As a youngster, Freyre attended a Baptist private school in Recife along with his older brother who went off to Baylor University in Waco, Texas, the largest Southern Baptist college in the United States.[80] In 1917, Freyre followed his brother to Waco where he sprinted through his degree. Under the influence of a charismatic English professor Andrew J. Armstrong, who would become a renowned scholar of the works of Robert and Elizabeth Barrett Browning, Freyre read widely and deeply. He even converted to Protestantism for a brief period. He maintained a lifelong friendship and correspondence with Armstrong, and became a dedicated Anglophile.[81] Freyre must have been a driven and brilliant student. He finished his degree at Baylor in three and a half years, graduating in December 1920. His experience on the far western fringe of the U.S. South, and then a long friendship with the U.S. historian Francis Butler Simkins, provided Freyre with personal exposure to race relations in the Jim Crow South.[82]

When he left Waco in early 1921, Freyre headed for New York City to attend Columbia University where he considered completing a doctorate in political science. He attended lectures by Franklin Giddings (1855–1931) and Franz Boas (1858–1942), two of the giant founding figures of modern sociology and anthropology. Boas, in particular, would later be a fundamental influence on Freyre's worldview.[83] He wrote a Master's thesis on "Social Life in Brazil in the Middle of the Nineteenth Century" that would serve partly as the basis for his later work.[84] It was at Columbia that he began long friendships with Rüdiger Bilden and Simkins, both of whom would read and provide critiques of his work for decades, especially *Casa-grande*.[85] Although his family was pressed to finance his studies abroad, after he finished his M.A. at Columbia in 1922, he spent the next two years touring Europe and falling in love with university life at Oxford.

When he returned to Recife in 1923, he must have been quite the odd bird with his English tweeds and cosmopolitan airs. An exceptional group of young men formed his intellectual and social circle (among them were José Lins do Rego and Sylvio Rabello), and he soon became the private secretary of the State's governor, Estácio Coimbra.[86] In the aftermath of the 1930 Revolution, he chose to follow the governor into exile in Portugal. It was abroad, again, that he conceived and began to formulate his masterpiece.[87] In 1931, he gave a course in Brazilian history at Stanford University and began to research and write intensively. ("It was at Stanford University that my project for this book took shape.")[88] With Simkins and Bilden, he drove across the U.S. through the Southwest and South on his way to New York City. It is one of the great ironies (and ambiguities?) of this most Brazilian of all works that much of it was conceived and partly researched while Freyre was abroad in Portugal, Germany, and the United States.[89] When he returned to Brazil in 1932 he finished researching the book while living in Rio de Janeiro. He did most of his writing in 1933 after his return to Recife and then returned later that year to Rio to personally oversee the final editing and production of the book. With the help of the well-known poet, Augusto Frederico Schmidt, *Casa-grande e senzala: formação da família brasileira sob o regime de economia patriarcal* (Rio de Janeiro: Maia & Schmidt) appeared in December 1933.[90]

Casa-grande is a long, rambling, immensely rich, erudite, and personal work. As Dain Borges has pointed out, *Casa-grande* "is a provocatively dirty book, not only erotic but also obsessed with hygiene far beyond the conventions of naturalist literature."[91] Although divided into five chapters, the prose seems at times to wander aimlessly and the chapter divisions often seem arbitrary. The book, like all of Freyre's work, lacks any overarching theoretical framework.[92] "*Casa-grande e senzala*," Thomas

Skidmore has written, "had no story line, no dramatic events, no heroes and no villains. In fact, there were few identifiable individuals in its six hundred pages."[93] In many ways, it is visionary, anticipating various trends in cultural and social history that would come decades later in Europe and the United States: the history of private life, mentalities, history "from below," and an emphasis on "hybridity" that would characterize a good deal of postmodern theorizing nearly fifty years later.[94] Richly documented with authors from Brazil, Europe, the United States, anthropologists, sociologists, geographers, physicians, and scientists, the work anticipates the call in academia in recent decades for "interdisciplinarity." Although he focuses on the world of the planters and the plantation, Freyre massively demonstrates the profound contributions of the least powerful in society – Africans, Indians, and their descendants – to the formation of Brazilian culture. It is a deeply ethnographic work filled with a virtual grab bag of details about diet, housing, family life, social interactions, and sex – especially sex.[95]

Freyre's boldness in talking openly and explicitly about sex and sexuality was perhaps the most shocking feature of the book. Jeffrey Needell has perspicaciously pointed out that, in many ways, this was yet another facet of Freyre's personal life playing out in his epic work.[96] At the heart of his analysis of *mestiçagem* is a deeply gendered argument about the formation of all Brazilians. For Freyre, the male colonizers (through consent and force) had their way with the female Africans and Amerindians, and this intercourse – quite literally – gave birth to Brazilian civilization. Although he has been accused many times of an idealized version of this sexual conquest, he not only acknowledges rape and the use of force, he places them at the core of the formation of Brazilian society.[97] Clearly, he reveled in the notion of a colonial world of constant sexual interaction (both heterosexual and homosexual). At times, his discussion of the sexual initiation of the young sons of the *senhores de engenho* seemed to be highly personalized. As Needell cogently argues, "his life's work was an attempt to rehabilitate, or, better, re-create and celebrate the origins and nature of Brazil's unique national identity: the stable, patriarchal childhood he had forever lost."[98]

Casa-grande has also been criticized for presenting an idealized portrait of sugar plantation life in Pernambuco and imposing that specific regional historical experience on all of Brazil.[99] (Much like Proust, Freyre is often seen as someone in "search of things past," a view Freyre encouraged.) It is true that Freyre's vision of Brazil was deeply regional, a vision of the "most Brazilian region of all Brazil," as he liked to say.[100] He began his pursuit of the national through the regional. The global and national forces of modernization by the 1920s, especially the dramatic rise of São Paulo, disturbed Freyre and he worried that the equilibrium of the Brazilian archipelago would be shattered by the urban, industrial power of the Southeast and lead to the decline and disruption of the more authentic Brazil, the agrarian Northeast. (Once again, the parallel with the Southern Agrarians writing at the same moment is striking.) He was wary of the "modernity" of the Southeast and sought to defend the "big house" against the skyscraper, traditional agrarian society versus the bourgeois urban world of São Paulo.[101]

Freyre played a central role in a decisive moment in the 1920s and 1930s for the emergence of both regionalism and nationalism in Brazil.[102] "Within such an atmosphere of pressure to recognize the nation," says Muniz de Albuquerque, "– to form it and integrate it – diverse regional discourses clashed as they strove to make their own customs, beliefs, and social relations the model for the nation and thus expand their hegemony." As an increasingly powerful discourse of nationalism emerged, it was accompanied by multiple and more codified discourses of regionalism. These regionalisms, despite their differences, "converged in a heroic tradition of nationalism." Facing the increasing centralization and bureaucratization of power after 1930, as well as the growing impact of global influences hastened by new technologies of transportation and communication, regional discourses – as *gaúchos, mineiros, paulistas, cariocas* – gave them roots even as they became more rootless and mobile. For people of the Northeast, in particular, as they continued to move out of their home region by the millions, especially to the Southeast and Amazonia, the emergence of an identity as a *nordestino* "provided an origin story that could reconnect people facing a diffuse, uncertain present to an ostensibly shared past."[103]

Although with an eye on the traditions of the past, the Modernists (principally based in São Paulo and Rio de Janeiro) looked to the future of the newly emerging, industrial, urban, middle-class Brazil. Uneasy with this possible future course, Freyre looked squarely back into the past longing for a disappearing, agrarian, rural, aristocratic Brazil.[104] Freyre sought national identity via regional identity. The Modernists aspired to a universal identity through national identity.[105] They also embraced the image and language of *mestiçagem* but the *paulista* version highlighted the *bandeirante* and an increasingly whiter version of this Portuguese-Indian figure from the colonial past. The regional narrative of the booming São Paulo, as Barbara Weinstein has shown, took *mestiçagem* down the path of whitening rather than an emphasis on the Indian and the African heritage that Freyre made vital to the narrative of the Northeast.[106] Brazilian nationalism has long been a constant tension and interaction between regionalism and nationalism, in the emergence of a few iconic regional symbols as national ones.[107] In Weinstein's words, "not only is region *not* the antithesis of nation, but it is an indispensable site from which to imagine the nation."[108] In this sense, Freyre is one of (if not the most important) contributors to this national pantheon of regionalisms as national icons. Even while the portrait is an idealized, nostalgic vision of his grandparents' world, the reality of racial and cultural mixture is undeniable.

At the heart of Freyre's vision and writing was a powerful argument for hybridity and plasticity that built on more than a century of writings on *mestiçagem* – by Brazilians and others.[109] As a number of critics have pointed out, Freyre loved the dialectical interplay of opposites and antagonisms: the Big House and the slave quarters, mansions and shanties, black and white, to name a few examples.[110] The maddening looseness of Freyre's terms and his emphasis on their interplay, interpenetration, and the rise of new forms out of opposites also give his work a richness and durability as generations of critics and analysts have constantly interpreted and reinterpreted his enormous *oeuvre*.[111] Ricardo Benzaquen de Araújo has argued that Freyre revolutionized Brazilian social thought placing hybridity, plasticity, ambiguity, and heterogeneity at the core of national identity.[112] Freyre also built on the long tradition from von Martius to Romero to Roquette-Pinto and enshrined *mestiçagem* at the heart of Brazil's identity – of the identity of all Brazilians. Even those Brazilians who were not biologically *mestiços* were cultural hybrids, carrying within their souls the shadows of the Indian and the African.[113] Gilberto Freyre did not invent the idea of *mestiçagem*, nor was he the first to place it at the core of Brazilian identity. The power and influence of his writings, however, quickly made him its most famous and principal exponent.

In the 1920s and 1930s, intellectuals in other regions of Latin America had also begun to proclaim the power of *mestiçagem/mestizaje* as the core of national identities.[114] Drawing on influences across the Atlantic world, they rejected the constraints of the prevailing racist theories and made a cultural turn. Following the lead of Franz Boas at Columbia University, they liberated their people from the confines of racialism and turned to culture as their salvation and liberation.[115] In Mexico, José Vasconcelos declared Mexicans the "cosmic race" (*raza cósmica*), a blend of indigenous peoples and Spaniards. In the aftermath of the Mexican Revolution, *mestizaje* became the official ideology of the new regime with the Indian (especially the Aztec) as the iconic figure of national pride. The great Cuban anthropologist, Fernando Ortiz, developed his theory of transculturation to explain cultural mixture in Cuba and the Caribbean basin. José Martí, as early as the last decades of the nineteenth century, had anticipated the ethnographic work of Ortiz when he spoke of "our mestizo America" (*nuestra América mestiza*).[116] Ironically, in Mexico, the ongoing and powerful racism toward indigenous people and those of darker skin belied the official version of race relations. In Cuba, the official ideology became one of a raceless people in a society marked by pronounced racism. In Brazil, Freyre's narrative became the dominant and official view, along with his ideas about racial democracy. As I will argue in later chapters, despite the persistence of racism and prejudice in Brazil, *mestiçagem* became widely accepted as the dominant narrative of identity even as the vast majority of Brazilians recognized the persistence of racism in their own society.

The publication of *Casa-grande* was a transformative moment in Brazilian culture. The convergence of decades of intense intellectual debate on eugenics, social thought, and Brazil's relationship with Europe converged with a world economic crisis, a brief civil war, and the rise of Getúlio Vargas to power. Freyre synthesized, completed, and innovated in the long debate about Brazilian culture. The book is inconceivable without the decades of social debate that had produced a large base of documentation on cultural mixing in Brazil and in other areas of the Americas ("transculturation" to use the terminology of Fernando Ortiz).[117] Freyre is also deeply indebted to Sílvio Romero, Raymundo Nina Rodrigues, and Roquette-Pinto, among others. In many ways, *Casa-grande* is a thick encyclopedia of folklore and ethnographic work done over previous decades. Freyre puts all these pieces together to forge this interpretation of what he came to call "luso-tropical civilization" – Portuguese civilization in the tropics. His great originality is not in the recognition of *mestiçagem* but in his strikingly positive portrayal of its role in the formation of Brazilian society. Over centuries, the mixing of races and cultures produced a new people – Brazilians – who formed a new nation – Brazil.

Freyre's vision provides Brazilians with a powerful and positive form of cultural nationalism forged out of his experience in Brazil, the United States, and Europe. His was a nationalism that drew on his extensive readings in multiple languages and nations but became quintessentially

Brazilian.[118] The influences on the shaping of Freyre's thought highlight the arguments of the current proponents of transnational studies, analyses that seek to place the formation of nationalisms within their broader international contexts. Equally striking, especially in comparison with Europe, Africa, the Middle East, and South Asia, Freyre's vision evokes a powerful call to national identity but not one that arises out of conflict with another nation or people. In the words of Vamireh Chacon, it is, "A cultural nationalism without xenophobia but with self-criticism, passionate and therefore internationalist in its universalism."[119] For the cultural critic José Wisnik, Freyre liberated Brazilians to turn the "stigma" of colonization on its head. "The deep *violence of mixing*, once it is unveiled – and whose name, if spoken, would be a terrifying *loving rape* – is invested with a cathartic and redemptive power: a trauma or historical karma from which will be derived, paradoxically, a humanity open to differences."[120]

Freyre's book, in hindsight, was the most important of a series of foundational works produced in the two decades after the end of World War I, especially two others produced just a few years before and after *Casa-grande*. In stark opposition to Freyre's work were the deeply pessimistic interpretations of Brazil by Francisco José de Oliveira Vianna and Paulo Prado. Deeply influenced by the racial and geographic determinism of the European thinkers of the late nineteenth century, Oliveira Vianna's *Populações meridionais do Brasil: história, organização, psicologia* (1921) depicted a Brazil deeply flawed from its racial composition and its authoritarian traditions. Whitening the population and new forms of authoritarianism offered, to him, the path to progress for Brazil.[121] Prado's *Retrato do Brasil: ensaio sobre a tristeza brasileira* (1928) opens with a striking and dramatic statement, "In a radiant land lives a sad people."[122] Prado surveyed the cultural and political landscape and concluded that Brazil was fatally flawed. In a sense, his analysis is the Modernist version of earlier forms of cultural pessimism. Both authors were from generations who came of age at the beginning of the century. Prado, from an incredibly wealthy and influential coffee exporting family in São Paulo, was born in 1869 and Oliveira Vianna in 1883. The cultural pessimism in Prado and Oliveira Vianna offers a sharp contrast to Freyre's glowing optimism.

The third fundamental work in this series of foundational works on Brazilian identity is Sérgio Buarque de Holanda's *Raízes do Brasil* (*Roots of Brazil*, 1936).[123] Like Prado (and certainly unlike Freyre), Buarque de Holanda's book is a relatively short interpretive essay on

Brazilian society and culture. Although he also recognizes the mixing of cultures that made Brazil, especially the Portuguese cultural influence, Buarque de Holanda sees around him a Brazil in transformation – from agrarian to urban, from agricultural to industrial, from the old social relations of patriarchal society to the emerging social relations of industrial capitalism. While Freyre's fascination with the Northeastern planters leaves him nostalgic for the past, Buarque de Holanda's experience in the booming state of São Paulo moves him to look to the future. (No doubt Buarque de Holanda's experience living in Weimar Germany in the 1920s also shaped his worldview in ways very distinct from Freyre's U.S. experience.) This evocative and rich essay does not convey the extreme pessimism of Prado or the exuberant optimism of Freyre. Buarque de Holanda sees the negative legacies of Portuguese colonial culture – personalism, patrimonialism, patriarchy – and how they are adapted in the tropics. Most notably, he describes the formation of what he called the *"homem cordial"* (cordial man) – the Brazilian who prefers to solve problems of a public nature through personal relationships rather than bureaucratic means. He antici-pates what the anthropologist Roberto DaMatta would call the "web of personal relationships" that are so important for the functioning of Brazilian society.[124] While Freyre's vision led him to an increasing conser-vatism in the post-World War II years as he longed for the patriarchal, plantation past, Buarque de Holanda's analysis led him to increasing poli-tical dissidence – against the dictatorships of Vargas and then the military dictatorship after 1964, and ultimately as one of the founders of the *Partido dos Trabalhadores* (PT) in 1980.[125]

In a widely repeated quote from the renowned literary critic and historian Antonio Candido, he calls Freyre's *Casa-grande* (1933), Buarque de Holanda's *Raízes do Brasil* (1936), and Caio Prado Júnior's *Formação do Brasil contemporâneo: colônia* (1942) the three works that most shaped his generation's intellectual formation – those completing high school and attending university in the 1930s and 1940s.[126] Along with his *Evolução política do Brasil: colônia e império* (1933), Caio Prado's *Formação do Brasil contemporâneo: colônia* reinterpreted Brazilian history under the powerful influence of Marxist historical mate-rialism. In the following decades, Caio Prado's work would exert greater influence on historians, intellectuals, and radical students than his con-temporaries Freyre and Buarque de Holanda.[127]

Vibrancy and dynamism characterized the Brazilian intelligentsia in the 1920s and 1930s, as these pathbreaking interpretations demonstrate. The Modernists and their contemporaries in the two decades after

World War I launched a cultural transformation in the arts, literature, music, and discussions of Brazilian culture and identity as they sought to "rediscover Brazil." Although a contemporary of the Modernists, Freyre had already begun in the early 1930s to lament the passing of the society he nostalgically described in *Casa-grande*. He longed for the patriarchal, authoritarian society of the colony and Empire, traits that would become increasingly pronounced as the decades passed, and would eventually align him closely with the military regime after 1964. He would not share the fascination with modernization and modernity that drove the Brazilian Modernists.[128]

Although *Casa-grande* was a truly transformative work, its influence on Brazilian culture and identity formation across the twentieth century could not have been predicted in the 1930s. Freyre made *mestiçagem* a positive and fecund process for the creation of the Brazilian people rather than a negative and degenerative force. At the same time, this *mestiçagem* could (and would) be interpreted in vastly different ways. For Freyre himself, mixing inevitably led him to his rosy view of Brazilian racial democracy, a perspective adopted by politicians and governments as diverse as those of Getúlio Vargas, Juscelino Kubitschek, the military regime, and the New Republic. For those who lamented the African and indigenous contributions to Brazilian culture, the cultural and biological mixing provided a path to the modernization and whitening (*embranquecimento*) in what appeared to be less racist terms than those of the Old Republic. Freyre's most strident critics in Afro-Brazilian consciousness movements in the late twentieth century charged him with the formulation of a powerful ideology for the denial of racism in Brazil and the gradual elimination of the African features (biological and cultural) of Brazilian society.[129] These developments were decades in the future in the 1930s, and largely unforeseen. Along with the rich and provocative works of his fellow intellectuals of the period, Freyre had produced *a powerful narrative* of Brazilian identity, but it was *one of many competing narratives*. In particular, he challenged the long prevailing narrative of *mestiçagem* as degenerating, debilitating, and fatal to Brazil's future. The sweeping triumph of the Freyrean vision of *mestiçagem* was not inevitable and would come later, and that is what the rest of this book will explore.[130]

NOTES

1. Quoted in Smith, *The Nation in History*, 8.
2. Quoted in Owensby, "Toward a History of Brazil's 'Cordial Racism,'" 339.

3. See, for example, Richard Graham, "Constructing a Nation in Nineteenth-Century Brazil: Old and New Views on Class, Culture, and the State," *The Journal of the Historical Society*, 1:2–3 (Winter 2000), 17–56; Fernando Uricoechea, *O minotauro imperial: a burocratização do estado patrimonial brasileiro no século XIX* (Rio de Janeiro: Difel, 1978); Simon Schwartzman, *Bases do autoritarismo brasileiro* (Rio de Janeiro: Editora Campus, 1982). For a parallel example, see Simon Collier, *Chile, The Making of a Republic, 1830–1865: Politics and Ideas* (New York: Cambridge University Press, 2003).

4. Jurandir Malerba, *A corte no exílio: civilização e poder no Brasil às vésperas da Independência (1808 a 1821)* (São Paulo: Companhia das Letras, 2000).

5. In Brazil, "the nation began with a continental extension of sovereignty, inclusive and overarching, but one throughout which the state was unable to extend either its authority or knowledge. Simply put, the national state was nonexistent in the greater part of the national territory, just as the colonial administration before it." James Holston, *Insurgent Citizenship: Disjunctions of Democracy and Modernity in Brazil* (Princeton, NJ: Princeton University Press, 2008), 65.

6. For one of the most famous analyses of this "archipelago," see Francisco José de Oliveira Viana, *Problemas de política objetiva* (São Paulo: Companhia Editora Nacional, 1930).

7. For a brilliant synthesis of the problems of centralism and federalism in Brazil since independence, see Aspásia Camargo, "Federalism and National Identity," in Sachs et al., *Brazil*, 216–52.

8. "Havia um país chamado Brasil, mas absolutamente não havia brasileiros." Lilia Moritz Schwarcz, *As barbas do imperador: D. Pedro II, um monarco nos trópicos*, 3ª.edn. (São Paulo: Companhia das Letras, 1999), 35.

9. Roderick J. Barman, *Brazil: The Forging of a Nation, 1798–1852* (Stanford, CA: Stanford University Press, 1988); Jeffrey D. Needell, *The Party of Order: The Conservatives, the State, and Slavery in the Brazilian Monarchy, 1831–1871* (Stanford, CA: Stanford University Press, 2006); Emilia Viotti da Costa, *The Brazilian Empire: Myths and Histories*, rev. edn. (Chapel Hill: University of North Carolina Press, 2000); José Murilo de Carvalho, *Teatro de sombras: a política imperial* (Rio de Janeiro: IUPERJ/São Paulo: Vértice, 1988).

10. Victor Nunes Leal, *Coronelismo: The Municipality and Representative Government in Brazil*, trans. June Henfrey (New York: Cambridge University Press, 1977); Raymundo Faoro, *Os donos do poder*. For a more recent, and synthetic, overview of the evolution of State power across the twentieth century, see Luiz Carlos Bresser Pereira, "From the Patrimonial State to the Managerial State," in Sachs et al., *Brazil*, 141–73.

11. Sérgio Buarque de Holanda, *Raízes do Brasil* (Rio de Janeiro: Editora José Olympio, 1936) is a brilliant precursor to the works of Faoro and Leal.

12. Under the Empire (1822–1889) the captaincies of the colonial period became provinces. After 1889 the provinces became states. For an excellent analysis of efforts to forge a sense of national identity through civic festivities, see Hendrik Kraay, *Days of National Festivity in Rio de Janeiro, Brazil, 1823–1889* (Stanford, CA: Stanford University Press, 2013).

13. The most famous and serious of these revolts, in the backlands of the Northeast, was immortalized by Euclides da Cunha, *Os sertões (campanha de Canudos)*, Leopoldo Bernucci, ed., 2ª edn. (São Paulo: Ateliê Editorial, 2001).

14. "Without a doubt, the 'original sin' of Brazilian federalism was oligarchic regionalism, which ended up weakening through successive cycles of central government interventionism." Camargo, "Federalism and National Identity," 218.

15. Richard Graham, *Patronage and Politics in Nineteenth-Century Brazil* (Stanford, CA: Stanford University Press, 1990); Carvalho, *Teatro de sombras*; José Honório Rodrigues, *Conciliação e reforma no Brasil: um desafio histórico-cultural* (Rio de Janeiro: Editôra Civilização Brasileira, 1965).

16. [I]t is likely that approximately 10% of the total population, 12% of the free population, and 24% of the adult population were registered to vote in 1872. In other words, about 1.06 million Brazilian citizens were active (*votantes* and *eleitores*) and the remaining 7.4 million were passive, disqualified from voting for one reason or another. Of the active citizens, approximately twenty thousand were electors, amounting to 0.2% of the total population and 0.5% of the adult.

    Holston, Insurgent Citizenship, 91.

17. Leslie Bethell, "Politics in Brazil under Vargas, 1930–1945," in Leslie Bethell, ed., *Cambridge History of Latin America, Brazil since 1930*, v. IX, (Cambridge: Cambridge University Press, 2008), 3–86; and Graham, *Patronage and Politics*.

18. Camargo, "Federalism and National Identity," 226.

19. See, for example, Chambers, *From Subjects to Citizens*; Grandin, *The Blood of Guatemala*; Guardino, *Peasants, Politics and the Formation of Mexico's National State, Guerrero, 1800–1857*; Mallon, *Peasant and Nation*; Thurner, *From Two Republics to One Divided*.

20. See, for example, Celso Thomas Castilho, *Slave Emancipation and Transformations in Brazilian Political Citizenship* (Pittsburgh, PA: University of Pittsburgh Press, 2016); Flávio dos Santos Gomes e Olívia Maria Gomes da Cunha, *Quase-cidadão: histórias e antropologias da pós-emancipação no Brasil* (Rio de Janeiro: Editora FGV, 2007); Flávio dos Santos Gomes e Petrônio Domingues, *Da nitidez e invisibilidade: legados do pós-emancipação no Brasil* (Belo Horizonte: Fino Traço Editora, 2013); Kim Butler, *Freedoms Given, Freedoms Won: Afro-Brazilians in Post-Abolition, São Paulo and Salvador* (New Brunswick, NJ: Rutgers University Press, 1998). I owe a great deal to my colleague, Celso Castilho, for enlightening me on the literature on citizenship.

21. "The disfigured federalism that greeted the twentieth century was, therefore, a mere agent for the promotion and legitimization of regionalism, a variant of patrimonialism, according to which 'the regional actors accept the existence of the nation-state but seek economic favoritism and political sinecures from the larger political unit, even at the risk of putting in danger the political regime itself.'" Camargo, "Federalism and National Identity," 233–34.

22. The two most widely read syntheses are Lilia Moritz Schwarcz, *O espectáculo das raças: cientistas, instituições e questão racial no Brasil, 1870–1930* (São

Paulo: Companhia das Letras, 1993); Thomas E. Skidmore, *Black into White: Race and Nationality in Brazilian Thought* (New York: Oxford University Press, 1974).

23. Schwarcz, *O espectáculo das raças*.

24. Melissa Nobles, *Shades of Citizenship: Race and Census in Modern Politics* (New York: Cambridge University Press, 2000); Mara Loveman, *National Colors: Racial Classification and the State in Latin America* (New York: Oxford University Press, 2014); Mara Loveman, "The Race to Progress: Census Taking and Nation Making in Brazil (1870–1920)," *Hispanic American Historical Review*, 89:3 (2009), 435–70.

25. For an excellent recent and polemical study that examines this relationship with the United States, see Seigel, *Uneven Encounters*.

26. Luiz Alberto Moniz Bandeira, *Conflito e integração na América do Sul: Brasil, Argentina e Estados Unidos: da Tríplice Aliança ao Mercosul, 1870–2003*, 2ª. edn., rev. (Rio de Janeiro: Editora Revan, 2003); Boris Fausto e Fernando J. Devoto, *Brasil e Argentina: um ensaio de história comparada (1850–2002)*, trad. Sérgio Molina (São Paulo: Editora 34, 2004); Ori Preuss, *Bridging the Island: Brazilians' Views of Spanish America and Themselves, 1865–1912* (Madrid: Iberoamerican – Vervuert, 2011).

27. Schwarcz, *O espectáculo das raças*; Skidmore, *Black into White*. For an excellent synthesis of immigration history, see Jeffrey Lesser, *Immigration, Ethnicity, and National Identity in Brazil, 1808 to the Present* (New York: Cambridge University Press, 2013).

28. Quoted in Robert Edgar Conrad, ed., *Children of God's Fire: A Documentary History of Black Slavery in Brazil*, 2ª. edn. (University Park: Penn State Press, 1994), 56.

29. José Murilo de Carvalho, "Brasil: Nações Imaginadas," *Pontos e bordados: escritos de história e política* (Belo Horizonte: Editorial UFMG, 2005), 233–68.

30. Carl Friedrich Philipe von Martius, "Como se deve escrever a história do Brasil," *Revista do Instituto Histórico e Geográfico Brasileiro*, 6:24 (January 1845), 381–403.

31. Von Martius, "Como se deve escrever a história do Brasil," 389–90.

32. For an astute analysis of the essay, see Francisco Iglésias, *Historiadores do Brasil: capítulos de historiografia brasileira* (Rio de Janeiro: Nova Fronteira, 2000), 65–72.

33. For an analysis of nation-building projects under the monarchy and republic, see Jeffrey D. Needell, "The Domestic Civilizing Mission: The Cultural Role of the State in Brazil, 1808–1930," *Luso-Brazilian Review*, 36:1 (Summer 1999), 1–18.

34. For an excellent study of the elite incorporation of the Indian into national culture in Spanish America, see Rebecca Earle, *The Return of the Native: Indians and Myth-Making in Spanish America, 1810–1930* (Durham, NC: Duke University Press, 2007).

35. See Doris Sommer, "*O Guaraní* and *Iracema*: Brazil's Two-Faced Indigenism," in *Foundational Fictions: The National Romances of Latin America* (Berkeley: University of California Press, 1991), 138–71. "[The]

rhetorical relationship between heterosexual passion and hegemonic states functions as a mutual allegory, as if each discourse were grounded in the allegedly stable other." Sommer, *"O Guaraní* and *Iracema,"*31. Tracy Devine Guzmán, *Native and National in Brazil: Indigeneity after Independence* (Chapel Hill: University of North Carolina Press, 2013).

36. José de Alencar, *Iracema* (Rio de Janeiro: F. Alves, 1975).

37. See, for example, Carolina Vianna Dantas, *O Brasil café com leite: mestiçagem e identidade nacional em periódicos: Rio de Janeiro, 1903–1914* (Rio de Janeiro: Edições Casa de Rui Barbosa, 2010).

38. Marshall C. Eakin, "Race and Identity: Sílvio Romero, Science, and Social Thought in Late 19th Century Brazil," *Luso-Brazilian Review*, 22:2 (Winter 1985), 151–74.

39. Julyan Peard, *Race, Place and Medicine: The Idea of the Tropics in 19th Century Brazilian Medicine* (Durham, NC: Duke University Press, 2000); Dain Borges, "The Recognition of Afro-Brazilian Symbols and Ideas, 1890–1940," *Luso-Brazilian Review*, 32:2 (Winter 1995), 59–78.

40. Schwarcz, *O espectáculo das raças*, 207–13.

41. Quoted in Lilia Moritz Schwarcz, "Nina Rodrigues: um radical do pessimism," 90–103, in André Botelho e Lilia Moritz Schwarcz, orgs., *Um enigma chamado Brasil: 29 intérpretes e um país* (São Paulo: Companhia das Letras, 2009), 99.

42. Eakin, "Race and Identity."

43. Roberto Ventura, *Estilo tropical: história cultural e polêmicas literárias no Brasil, 1870–1914* (São Paulo: Companhia das Letras, 1991).

44. Schwarcz, "Nina Rodrigues," 96.

45. Sílvio Romero, *História da literatura brasileira*, 7ª.edn., 5 v. (Rio de Janeiro/Brasília: José Olympio/INL, 1980), 1:120, cited in Antonio Dimas, "O turbulento e fecundo Sílvio Romero," in Botelho e Schwarcz, 82.

46. Quote in Ricardo Luiz de Souza, *Identidade nacional e modernidade brasileira: o diálogo entre Sílvio Romero, Euclides da Cunha, Câmara Cascudo e Gilberto Freyre* (Belo Horizonte: Autêntica, 2007), 51.

47. Eakin, "Sílvio Romero," 164–68.

48. Romero, *História da literatura brasileira*, 2:406, cited in Dimas, 84.

49. Nísia Trindade Lima, "Euclides da Cunha: o Brasil como sertão," in Botelho e Schwarcz, 104–17. For a comprehensive analysis of the writer, the work, and its reception over time, see Regina Abreu, *O enigma de Os sertões* (Rio de Janeiro: Funarte: Rocco, 1998).

50. Jorge Amado, *Tenda dos Milagres; romance* (São Paulo: Martins, 1969). The novel was made into a film by Nelson Pereira dos Santos in 1977 and a miniseries on Rede Globo. Manuel Raimundo Querino, *The African Contribution to Brazilian Civilization*, E. Bradford Burns trans. and ed. (Tempe: Arizona State University, Center for Latin American Studies, Special Studies, No. 18, 1978).

51. *A América Latina: males de origem, o parasitismo social e evolução*, 4ª. edn. (Rio de Janeiro: Topbooks, 1993 [1905]). André Botelho, "Manoel Bonfim," in Botelho e Schwarcz, 118–31. For a discussion of the influence of Roquette-

Pinto on Freyre see, Maria Lúcia G. Pallares-Burke, *Gilberto Freyre: um vitoriano dos trópicos* (São Paulo: Editora UNESP, 2005), 332–45.

52. Ricardo Ventura Santos, Michael Kent, and Verlan Valle Gaspar Neto, "From Degeneration to Meeting Point: Historical Views on Race, Mixture, and the Biological Diversity of the Brazilian Population," in Wade et al., *Mestizo Genomics*, 42.

53. Claude Lévi-Strauss, *Tristes Tropiques*, trans. John and Doreen Weightman (New York: Penguin, 1992) [originally published in French in 1953].

54. Schwarcz, *O espectáculo das raças*, 96. Nancy Leys Stepan, *The Hour of Eugenics: Race, Gender, and Nation in Latin America* (Ithaca, NY: Cornell University Press, 1991); Luis de Castro Faria, *A contribuição de E. Roquette-Pinto para a antropologia brasileira* (Rio de Janeiro: Universidade do Brasil, Museu Nacional, 1959).

55. See, for example, Alberto Torres, *O problema nacional brasileiro* (São Paulo: Companhia Editora Nacional, 1914).

56. Another prominent exponent of *mestiçagem* as positive was paulista writer Eduardo Prado (1860–1901). Carlos Henrique Armani, *Discursos da nação: historicidade e identidade nacional no Brasil en fins do século XIX* (Porto Alegre: EDIPUCRS, 2010), esp. 131–37.

57. Edgard Carone, *O tenentismo: acontecimentos, personagens, programas* (São Paulo: Difel, 1975); Maria Cecília Spina Forjaz, *Tenentismo e Forças Armadas na Revolução de 30* (Rio de Janeiro: Forense Universitária, 1989).

58. Although this term is normally used to describe the 1960s and 1970s, I am using it here to show the parallels – rejection of bourgeois middle-class society and culture, rejection of the status quo, the turn to alternative cultural forms especially in art.

59. The best overview of the Modernists from a literary perspective is Alfredo Bosi, *História concisa da literatura brasileira*, 43ª. edn. (São Paulo: Editora Cultrix, 1994), 301–79.

60. Iglésias, *Historiadores do Brasil*, 117–25. "Capistrano foi a mais lúcida conciência da historiografia brasileira ... foi o primeiro historiador moderno e progressista do Brasil." José Honório Rodrigues, quoted in Iglésias, 125.

61. The literature on Brazilian Modernism is enormous. For one penetrating look at Modern Art Week in São Paulo, see Nicolau Sevcenko, *Orfeu extático na metrópole: São Paulo, sociedade e cultura nos frementes anos 20* (São Paulo: Companhia das Letras, 1992), esp. 223–308.

62. It is ironic here that a European intellectual and cultural movement spurs the declaration of Brazilian cultural independence. The Brazilian Modernists were following a pattern established by their European counterparts where "each country's cultural vanguard rewrote or revalued the past to fit in with contemporary requirements." Hobsbawm, *Age of Extremes*, 184.

63. Benedito Nunes, *Oswald Canibal* (São Paulo: Perspectiva, 1979). Interestingly, this manifesto and much of the Modernist imagery is much more focused on the Amerindian than the African role in Brazilian culture, probably a result of the *paulista* origins of the writings. As Chris Dunn notes, "During this period, key artists and intellectuals sought to explain the originality of Brazilian civilization in terms of its racial and cultural hybridity,

thereby establishing a paradigm for a *mestiço* national identity." Chris Dunn, *Brutality Garden: Tropicália and the Emergence of a Brazilian Counterculture* (Chapel Hill: University of North Carolina Press, 2001), 13.

64. Quoted in Moser, *Why This World*, 98.

65. Borges, "The Recognition of Afro-Brazilian Symbols and Ideas."

66. "Ele marca o momento en que a cultura letrada de um país escravocrata tardio enxergou na liberação de suas potencialidades mais obscuras e recalcadas, ligadas secularmente à mestiçagem e à mistura cultural, entremeadas de desejo, violência, abundância e miséria, a possibilidade de afirmar seu destino e de revelar-se através da união do erudito com o popular." Wisnik, "Entre o erudito e o popular," 61–62.

67. Garramuño, *Primitive Modernities*, 51, 75, and 141.

68. Quote is from Camargo, "Federalism and National Identity," 236. For an excellent analysis of the emergence of *mestiçagem* as a positive among the literati, see Tania Regina de Luca, A Revista do Brasil: *um diagnóstico para a (N)ação* (São Paulo: Fundação Editora da UNESP, 1999).

69. A "representação vitoriosa dos anos trinta, quando o mestiço transformou-se em ícone nacional, em um símbolo de nossa identidade cruzada no sangue, sincrética na cultura isto é: no samba, na capoeira, no candomblé e no futebol." Lilia Moritz Schwarcz, "Gilberto Freyre: adaptação, mestiçagem, trópicos e privacidade em Novo mundo nos trópicos," in Lund e McNee, *Gilberto Freyre e os estudos latino-americanos*, 305–34. Quote is on 310.

70. "Gilberto Freyre não somente modificou o diagnóstico, fazendo do estigma uma virtude." Enrique Rodríguez Larreta e Guillermo Giucci, "*Casa-grande & senzala*: os materiais da imaginação histórica," in Gilberto Freyre, *Casa-grande & senzala, edição crítica*, Guillermo Giucci, Enrique Rodríguez Larreta e Edson Nery da Fonseca, coords. (Madri: ALLCA XX, 2002), 732.

71. "In its day, the single most important statement made in CGS was its praise of miscegenation (*miscigenação, mestiçagem*), since to make this assertion was to turn conventional wisdom upside down." Peter Burke and Maria Lúcia G. Pallares-Burke, *Gilberto Freyre: Social Theory in the Tropics* (Oxford: Peter Lang, 2008), 61.

72. The most complete recent edition of Freyre's magnum opus is Gilberto Freyre, *Casa-grande & senzala: formação da família brasileira sob o regime da economia patriarcal*, 49ª. edn. (São Paulo: Global Editora, 2003). The first English-language edition is Gilberto Freyre, *The Masters and the Slaves: A Study in the Development of Brazilian Civilization*, trans. Samuel Putnam (New York: Alfred A. Knopf, 1946). See also, Enrique Rodríguez Larreta e Guillermo Giucci, *Gilberto Freyre, uma biografia cultural: a formação de um intelectual brasileiro: 1900–1936*, trad. Josely Vianna Baptista (Rio de Janeiro: Civilização Brasileira, 2007).

73. For a fine-grained discussion of the pessimism/optimism about *mestiçagem* in the 1910s and 1920s, see Tania Regina de Luca, A Revista do Brasil: *um diagnóstico para a (N)ação* (São Paulo: Fundação Editora da UNESP, 1999), esp. 160–75. For a discussion of positive images of racial mixture in popular music see Martha Abreu, "*Mulatas, Crioulos* and *Morenas*: Racial Hierarchy, Gender Relations, and National Identity in Postabolition Popular Song:

Southeastern Brazil, 1890–1920," in Pamela Scully and Diana Paton, eds., *Gender and Slave Emancipation in the Atlantic World* (Durham, NC: Duke University Press, 2005), 267–88.

74. Quoted in Carlos Fico, *Reinventando o otimismo: ditadura, propaganda e imaginário social no Brasil* (Rio de Janeiro: Editora Fundação Getúlio Vargas, 1997), 34.

75. The great Brazilian poet, Carlos Drummond de Andrade, wrote, "A casa-grande; a senzala/inda os remorsos mais vivos/–tudo resurge e me fala/grande Gilberto em teu livro." Quoted in Chacon, *A construção da brasilidade*, 18.

76. Quoted in Burke and Pallares-Burke, 16.

77. Burke and Pallares-Burke, 212.

78. Darcy Ribeiro, "Gilberto Freyre, uma introdução a *Casa-grande e senzala*," in Freyre, *Casa-grande & senzala*, 11–42. Quote is from p. 11.

79. Quote is from Burke and Pallares-Burke, 114. Ribeiro, "Gilberto Freyre," 20. In a poll in the mid-1990s, Brazil's most important weekly news magazine asked fifteen major Brazilian intellectuals (all male!) to list the twenty most representative books of Brazilian culture. All fifteen listed *Os sertões* and fourteen listed *Casa-grande e senzala*. The next highest on the list were João Guimarães Rosa's *Grande sertão: veredas* (1956) with thirteen votes, and Mário de Andrade's *Macunaíma* (1928) with eleven votes. "Biblioteca Nacional," *Veja*, 23 novembro 1994.

80. The literature on Freyre is also vast. Some fine examples are: Burke and Pallares-Burke, *Gilberto Freyre*; Ricardo Benzaquen de Araújo, *Guerra e paz: Casa-grande e senzala e a obra de Gilberto Freyre nos ano 30* (Rio de Janeiro: Editora, 34, 1994); Vamireh Chacon, *A construção da brasilidade* (Brasília, DF: Paralelo 15; São Paulo: Marco Zero, 2001); Rodríguez Larreta e Giucci, *Gilberto Freyre, uma biografia cultural*.

81. Armstrong was chair of the English Department at Baylor from 1912–1952 and brought a series of major intellectual figures (W. B. Yeats, John Masefield, and Robert Frost, among others) to this small Texas town on the edge of the U.S. South and the beginning of the West. He raised funds to build a special collections library for a major Browning collection. www.baylor.edu/abl/index.php?id=45920 [Consulted 13 August 2016]

82. Francis Butler Simkins (1897–1966) completed his doctorate in history at Columbia University in 1926, spent his entire academic career at Longwood College (Farmville, Virginia), and became a distinguished historian of the U.S. South. In the 1950s he served as president of the Southern Historical Association. Long perceived as a liberal historian of the South, in the final years of his career he became a staunch defender of Southern tradition. James S. Humphreys, *Francis Butler Simkins: A Life* (Gainesville: University Press of Florida, 2008).

83. "O que devemos reter sobre a herança acadêmica de Gilberto Freyre é a fonte boasista, tanto do seu ateoricismo como de sua propensão etnográfica." Ribeiro, "Gilberto Freyre," 23. The finest study of Freyre's early years is Pallares-Burke, *Gilberto Freyre*.

Foi o estudo de Antropologia sob a orientação do Professor Boas que primeiro me revelou o negro e o mulato no seu justo valor – separados dos traços de raça os efeitos do ambiente ou da experiência cultural. Aprendi a considerar fundamental a diferença entre raça e cultura; a discriminar entre os efeitos de relações puramente genéticas e os de influências sociais, de herança cultural e de meio.

From the preface to the first edition of *Casa-grande*, emphasis in original. Gilberto Freyre, *Casa-grande e senzala*, 44.

84. A condensed version of the thesis was published as "Social Life in Brazil in the Middle of the 19th Century," *Hispanic American Historical Review*, 5:4 (November 1922), 597–630.

85. Maria Lúcia Garcia Pallares-Burke, *O triunfo do fracasso: Rudiger Bilden, o amigo esquecido de Gilberto Freyre* (São Paulo: Editora UNESP, 2012).

86. Freyre's mother's cousin was married to Coimbra. Rodríguez Larreta e Giucci, 21.

87. Freyre offered his own version of the genesis of the book in Gilberto Freyre, "Como e porque escrevi *Casa-grande & senzala*," reprinted in Gilberto Freyre, *Casa-grande & senzala, edição crítica*, Guillermo Giucci, Enrique Rodríguez Larreta e Edson Nery da Fonseca, coords. (Madri: ALLCA XX, 2002), 701–21. Originally published in Gilberto Freyre, *Como e porque sou e não sou sociólogo* (Brasília: Editora da Universidade de Brasília, 1968), 115–43.

88. Freyre, "Como e porque escrevi *Casa-grande & senzala*," 711.

89. "A formação intelectual de Gilberto Freyre é de um viajante imóvel. As incessantes aventuras em diversas culturas, autores e disciplinas não o fastam de seu universo familiar." Enrique Rodríguez Larreta e Guillermo Giucci, "*Casa-grande & senzala*: os materiais da imaginação histórica," in Freyre, *Casa-grande & senzala, edição crítica*, 722.

90. The most detailed biographical reconstruction of this period is Rodríguez Larreta e Giucci, esp. 371–422. See also, Gilberto Freyre, "Augusto Frederico Schmidt, Poeta e Homem de Ação," in *Pessoas, coisas & animais*, 1a série (Rio de Janeiro: Editora Globo, 1980), 70–73.

91. Borges, "The Recognition of Afro-Brazilian Symbols and Ideas," 59. Nicolau Sevcenko called the myth of *mestiçagem* "Esse mito, erótico e holístico, de criação de uma nova raça." *Orfeu extático na metrópole*, 38.

92. "Em *Casa-Grande & Senzala* simplesmente não há método nenhum."Ribeiro, "Gilberto Freyre," 27.

93. Thomas E. Skidmore, "Raízes de Gilberto Freyre," *Journal of Latin American Studies*, 34:1 (2002), 13.

94. "A obra freyreana explicitamente trata de, ou implicitamente prefigura, tendências críticas e rumos de pesquisa aparentemente novos, tais como: a hibridez, o multiculturalismo, a heterogeneidade multi-temporal, as ficções fundacionais, a agência de sujeitos populares, a territorialidade e a desterritorialização, a colonialidade (no sentido atual), o Atlântico negro, a sexualidade como configuração do poder, a micro-história, o carnavalesco, etc." Joshua Lund e Malcolm K. McNee, "Gilberto Freyre e o sublime brasileiro," in Lund e McNee, *Gilberto Freyre e os estudos latino-americanos*, 8.

95. For a discussion of the role of food in Freyre's work, see Nil Castro da Silva, "Culinária e Alimentação em Gilberto Freyre: Raça, Identidade e Modernidade," *Latin American Research Review*, 49:3 (2014), 3–22.

96. Needell, "Identity, Race, Gender and Modernity in the Origins of Gilberto Freyre's *Oeuvre*," 51–77, and "The Foundations of Freyre's Work: Engagement and Disengagement in the Brazil of 1923–1933," *Portuguese Studies*, 27:1 (2011), 8–19.

97. In Freyre's case the model is surely comedy, or more exactly tragic-comedy, a story about conflict and suffering that produces a harmonious resolution. A central theme of the book is the way in which the violent actions of the Portuguese colonizers and plantation owners, taking and sometimes raping indigenous and African women, led to a miscegenation which would lead in its turn to a situation of relative harmony. In other words, the reader is offered a complex story about unintended consequences and not the simple story about good colonizers that the author has often been accused of writing.

    Burke and Pallares-Burke, 78–79. "For Freyre claimed that the sado-masochistic relationship integral to planters' relations with slave women was the key social relationship and metaphor for the society. Domination was simultaneously racial, sexual and social." Needell, "The Foundations of Freyre's Work," 18.

98. Needell, "The Foundations of Freyre's Work," 19. See also, Helena Bocayuva, *Erotismo à brasileira* (Rio de Janeiro: Garamond, 2001).

99. "[A] sua nostálgica visão de senhor de engenhos e de escravos que ele expressa, sentimentalmente, ao longo do livro." Ribeiro, "Gilberto Freyre," 25. For an excellent reflection on the changing fortunes of Freyre among academics, see Stuart Schwartz, "Gilberto Freyre e a história colonial: uma visão otimista do Brasil," em Falcão e Barboza de Araújo, *O imperador das idéias*, 101–17. "Pouco a pouco, cheguei à conclusão de que, apesar de suas deficiências, *Casa-grande & senzala* era uma obra profunda que eu, como estrangeiro que nunca pisou no massapê, não poderia superar, nem mesmo igualar." (101)

100. According to Freyre, "the good Brazilianism is the one which puts together various regionalisms." Burke and Pallares-Burke, 48. According to Freyre, "o Brasil é isto: combinação, fusão, mistura. E o Nordeste, talvez a principal bacia em que se vêm processando essas combinações, essa fusão, essa mistura de sangues e valores que ainda fervem." Gilberto Freyre, *Manifesto Regionalista de 1926* (Rio de Janeiro: Departamento de Imprensa Nacional, Os Cadernos da Cultura, 1955), 48.

101. Muniz de Albuquerque Jr., *The Invention of the Brazilian Northeast*, 61–72.

102. I have been most influenced in my thinking here by the brilliant work of Muniz de Albuquerque Jr., *The Invention of the Brazilian Northeast*.

103. *Ibid.*, 22–23, 45–46.

104. "[W]hile modernism is linked to the advancement and consolidation of an urban middle class, Gilberto Freyre represents the dimension of an aristocratic, rural power that sees itself threatened." Renato Ortiz quoted in Oliven, *Tradition Matters*, 23.

105. Oliven, *Tradition Matters*, 19–20.

106. Weinstein, *The Color of Modernity*.
107. Aspásia Camargo notes that the "disfigured federalism that greeted the twentieth century was, therefore, a mere agent for the promotion and legitimization of regionalism" and "on the one hand [fostered] a strong regional identity and on the other a strong commitment to national patriotism and identity." "Federalism and National Identity," 233–34.
108. Weinstein, *The Color of Modernity*, 9.
109. "Uma dos aspectos mais destacados nessa obra de Freyre é o caráter plástico da cultura brasileira e sua capacidade de adaptação." Schwarcz, "Gilberto Freyre," 317.
110. "The strength, or, better, the potential of Brazilian culture seems to us to reside wholly in the wealth of its balanced antagonisms." From *Casa-grande e senzala*, quoted in Needell, "Identity, Race, Gender," 68; Benzaquen de Araújo, *Guerra e paz*.
111. Através de suas centenas de páginas, Gilberto é sucessivamente senhorial, branco, cristão, adulto, maduro, sem deixar de ser o oposto em outros contextos, ao se vestir e sentir escravo, herege, índio, menino, mulher, efeminado. As dualidades não se esgotam aí mas se estendem nas de pai-e-filho, senhor-e-escravo, mulher-e-marido, devoto-e-santo, civilizado-e-selvagem, que Gilberto vai encarnando para mostrar-se pelo direito e pelo avesso, página após página, linha por linha.
   Ribeiro, "Gilberto Freyre," *14*.
112. Araújo, *Guerra e paz*, 43–57; Owensby, "Toward a History of Brazil's 'Cordial Racism,'" 328.
113. As Anadelia Romo has pointed out, the rejection of this racial hierarchy was replaced (for many) with a cultural hierarchy that valued Europe and whiteness over Africa and blackness. Anadelia A. Romo, "Rethinking Race and Culture in Brazil's First Afro-Brazilian Congress of 1934," *Journal of Latin American Studies*, 39 (2007), 31–54.
114. Mignolo argues that even the notion of "Latin" America "is the political project of Creole-Mestizo/a elites." Mignolo, *The Idea of Latin America*, 59.
115. Quoting Oswald Spengler, Freyre envisioned "race" as a "mysterious cosmic force that binds together in a single rhythm those who dwell in close proximity." José Amador, *Medicine and Nation Building in the Americas, 1890–1940* (Nashville, TN: Vanderbilt University Press, 2015), 146.
116. Muniz Sodré, *Claros e escuros*, 105.
117. Freyre's argument was only the culmination of stands already present in the intellectual climate – Monteiro Lobato's resurrection of Jeca Tatú; Alberto Torres's and Manuel Bonfim's national rejection of scientific racism; the public health doctor's crusades to apply science to disprove the determinist dogma that had condemned the Brazilian of the interior. *Casa Grande* was written – and received – more as a manifesto than as a tightly reasoned work of scholarship.
   Skidmore, "Raízes de Gilberto Freyre," *13*.
118. "Gilberto Freyre, em suas obras, empreendeu um esforço evidente em abandonar a aplicação de modelos externos e procurou sempre entender esse país sob o signo da diferença; da sua diferença. Aí está a modernidade de sua obra e, talvez, a atualidade de suas interpretações." Schwarcz, "Gilberto Freyre," 329.
119. Chacon, *A construção da brasilidade*, 53.

120. "A *violência mestiçante* de fundo, uma vez desvelada – e cujo nome, se dito, seria um aterrador *estupro amoroso* –, investe-se de um poder catártico e redentor: um trauma ou um carma histórico do qual terá derivado, para-doxalmente, uma humanidade aberta às diferenças." José Miguel Wisnik, *Veneno remédio: o futebol e o Brasil* (São Paulo: Companhia das Letras, 2008), 416. Emphasis in the original.

121. Francisco José Oliveira Vianna, *Populações meridionais do Brasil: história, organização, psicologia* (São Paulo: Monteiro Lobato, 1921). Jeffrey D. Needell, "History, Race, and the State in the Thought of Oliveira Viana," *Hispanic American Historical Review*, 75:1 (February 1995), 1–30.

122. Originally published by Oficinas Gráficas Duprat-Mayença (Reunidas) – São Paulo. Prado (1869–1943) came from one of the most influential and powerful coffee planter families in São Paulo.

123. Sérgio Buarque de Holanda, *Raízes do Brasil* (Rio de Janeiro: Editora José Olympio, 1936).

124. For the classic analysis of these webs of personal relationships see, Roberto DaMatta, *Carnavais, malandros e heróis: uma sociologia do dilema brasileiro*, 6ª. edn. (Rio de Janeiro: Rocco, 1997).

125. For a rich, creative, and erudite comparison of these two giants of twentieth-century Brazilian social thought see, Richard M. Morse, "Balancing Myth and Evidence: Freyre and Sérgio Buarque," *Luso-Brazilian Review*, 32:2 (Winter 1995), 47–57.

126. Antonio Candido, "O Sentido de *Raízes do Brasil*," in Sérgio Buarque de Holanda, *Raízes do Brasil*, 12ª.edn. (Rio de Janeiro: José Olympio, 1978). *Casa-grande* was translated into English in 1946, as*The Masters and the Slaves* and Prado's book was translated as *The Colonial Background of Brazil*, trans. Suzette Macedo (Berkeley: University of California Press, 1967). Oddly, *Raízes do Brasil* was not translated into English until very recently. *Roots of Brazil*, trans. G. Harvey Summ (South Bend, IN: University of Notre Dame Press, 2012).

127. For a very useful, brief survey of key writers and bibliography for this period, see Bernardo Ricupero, *Sete lições sobre as intepretações do Brasil*, 2ª. edn. (São Paulo: Alameda, 2008). Both Buarque de Holanda's *Raízes do Brasil* and Caio Prado's *Formação do Brasil contemporâneo* appear on *Veja*'s ranking of canonical Brazilian books (with *Raízes* getting eight votes and *Formação* getting four). "BibliotecaNacional," *Veja*, 23 novembro 1994.

128. "Freyre knits together the threads of race, miscegenation, and reactionary authoritarianism as essentially one cloth – the tapestry of what was essentially Brazilian." Needell, "The Foundations of Freyre's Work," 18.

129. Muniz Sodré, *Claros e escuros*, 103.

130. Thomas Skidmore cogently points out that, "In a 1944 volume containing the testimonies of 26 leading intellectuals who were asked to summarize the most important influences on the formation of their thought, only one contributor mentioned Freyre." Skidmore, "Raízes de Gilberto Freyre," 11.

2

Communicating and Understanding *Mestiçagem*

Radio, Samba, and Carnaval

Artists, authors, bureaucrats, popular composers, and, to a surprising degree, everyday Brazilians, shared in an investigation of Brazil's cultural roots and identity – an investigation that in itself became a process of reinvention and reconstruction.[1]

Bryan McCann

THE STATE, MEDIA, AND POPULAR CULTURE

Gilberto Freyre's *Casa-grande e senzala* sent seismic shock waves through the small world of Brazilian intellectual and literary circles from one end of Brazil to another in the 1930s – but probably not even a minor tremor among the vast majority of Brazilians. The central question in this book is deceptively simple: how does that intellectual revelation – the Freyrean manifesto – eventually become so widely shared and repeated by so many Brazilians from a typical Brazilian on the street to university-educated intellectuals? Writings about the intellectual history of Freyre's work would fill a small library. The topic has been written, and rewritten, by several generations over the last three-quarters of a century. My primary interest is not to return to this discussion of social thought among the *cognoscenti*, but rather to analyze how this vision eventually percolates throughout Brazilian society and culture reaching and resonating with virtually all Brazilians. The diffusion and widespread adoption of the view that Brazilians are basically one people – one race or ethnicity sharing the same key cultural traits – forged out of the collision of Native Americans, Europeans, and Africans is driven by three powerful, interacting, sometimes converging, and at times, conflicting forces – the State, media, and the people of Brazil.

The role of the State and, in particular, the role of Getúlio Vargas has been the focus of many studies; yet, the majority of this work has concentrated on the Vargas regimes (1930–1945) and has overemphasized the role of the State as a directing – sometimes hegemonic – force in the construction of Brazilian identity. Yet, the Vargas years are just the *beginning* of the process of the construction of this myth of *mestiçagem*. The role of the State under democracy (1945–1964) and dictatorship (1964–1985), and then democracy again (1985–present), has attracted far less attention. Throughout this book, I follow the role of the State in the decades before and after 1945 and I emphasize the equally powerful role of popular culture, the tastes and choices of millions of Brazilian producers and consumers of culture, in the diffusion of the Freyrean vision throughout Brazilian society by the late twentieth century. Mass media – especially radio and then television – provide the most important forum for what eventually becomes a national conversation about Brazilian identity. At the core of my analysis is the interaction among these powerful and complex forces – the State, media, and the people – in the communication and understanding of Freyre's myth of *mestiçagem*.

The role of media in the communication and understanding of *mestiçagem* has also been studied, in a wide variety of disciplines – sociology, anthropology, communication studies, film studies, to name a few. The larger patterns over the half-century or so from the 1930s to the 1990s are the rapid growth of the Brazilian population and its urbanization, the steadily expanding power of the State, and the emergence and florescence of mass media – especially of major corporations (both national and transnational). All three forces converge by the 1970s to produce a dynamic industry of mass consumption and popular culture. This triangle of forces is often difficult to disentangle. Rapid urbanization and population growth create a mass consumer market with complex desires, corporations attempt both to create and respond to consumers, and the State seeks to create a national culture and identity – through repression, censorship, propaganda, cooptation, and mediation. At times, the State tries to manage the corporations and their agenda, and at other times, the corporations seek to influence and even challenge the power of the State. In short, theories that emphasize cultural hegemony imposed by the State, the media, or both, are simplistic and mechanistic. All three forces interact, and despite the relatively weaker power position of the masses in Brazil, they are not powerless in shaping the forging of culture and identity.[2] Again, as a number of scholars have pointed out, intellectuals and producers (such as musicians) often served as the key cultural mediators in this interaction among the State, mass media, and the Brazilian people.[3]

To communicate the Freyrean vision of *mestiçagem* to everyone in Brazil in the 1930s was impossible. In the 1930s, Freyre's work was a manifesto (as many have noted), but it was not yet a movement. It would take decades of *technological* transformations to make it possible to create a community that could share, understand, accept, critique, or reject this myth of *mestiçagem*. The first great challenge, not only for the Freyrean vision but for any effort to communicate myths, rituals, and symbols with everyone in Brazil, was the limitation of print culture. Illiteracy in Brazil in the 1930s remained extremely high, about 70 percent of the population above the age of five.[4] (This figure was much higher in rural areas as compared to urban centers.) In the cities of São Paulo and Rio de Janeiro, the two major cultural and publishing centers in the country (each with a metropolitan population above 2 million), the average number of copies printed for a major book published in the 1930s was probably around 1,000.[5] *Casa-grande*, this most Northeastern of all interpretations of Brazil, written by a native of Recife, was published in Rio de Janeiro by a small press largely through the assistance of Freyre's friend Rodrigo Mello Franco de Andrade.[6] In a country still a fragmented archipelago of regions, lacking basic transportation networks, with a minimal public education system, and without true mass communications, Brazilian culture in the middle of the twentieth century was primarily aural and visual. Print literacy was less important than aural and visual literacies. The reach of a book published in Rio de Janeiro like *Casa-grande*, addressing an educated elite, was extremely limited.

Although many studies have shown the widespread influence of print media through public "readers," theater, and other performances, the vast reach of Brazil, its regional fragmentation, and the lack of truly national forms of communication in the early twentieth century made the passing of literate messages through oral and visual media fragmented, dispersed, and highly asynchronous. In the backlands of the Northeast, for example, the now well-studied *literatura de cordel* (chapbook literature) effectively functioned as a means to communicate ideas and connect communities across impressive distances. Yet, this "literature on a string" (or chapbooks) was largely a Northeastern phenomenon and did not have national reach.[7] Prior to the age of radio, perhaps the most important means of connecting up many communities across the vast Brazilian interior was circuses, which also, at times, served as theater troupes.[8] In many ways, the history of twentieth-century Brazil is the story of how roads, aviation, telephones, radio, film, and television gradually spread across more than eight million square kilometers to bind up the people and places of all Brazil into an integrated and dynamic community of producers and consumers of popular culture.

Public schooling has long been one of the most important means to promote the State's views on national identity, and after 1930 the cultural and intellectual managers in the State bureaucracy made very effective use of teacher training and public schools in their efforts to communicate what I am calling the Freyrean myth of *mestiçagem*. Jerry Dávila has shown in detail how the State consciously and consistently employed the public schools, especially elementary schools, after 1930 to teach students of all colors that there was a Brazilian race forged out of the collision of three people. This curriculum clearly conveyed the message that racial mixture defined Brazil and Brazilians, that it whitened the population over time, and through hard work, education, and good hygiene anyone could be white. This Brazilian version of *mestiçagem* recognized the importance of nonwhites to the formation of national identity while making the mixture incredibly elastic and flexible. Environment and culture took precedence over biology, but those values associated with whiteness stood out as the ones for students to emulate. Even the darkest child could learn to excel and eventually receive a "diploma of whiteness."[9]

This process of national integration moved in fits and starts across the length of the century and was not effectively complete (or close to completion) until the 1990s. (During the decades from the 1930s to the 1990s, the population of Brazil quadrupled from around 40 million to more than 170 million.) Even more so than the telegraph, telephone, roads, and aviation, advances in the technologies of mass communications eventually made this integration possible and, ironically, by the beginning of the twenty-first century, made the consolidation of any single narrative of national identity virtually impossible. The new technologies served for most of the twentieth century as homogenizing, centripetal forces for a society experiencing powerful centrifugal forces threatening to pull Brazil apart – abolition, immigration, industrialization, and urbanization. Too often in the study of nationalism and popular culture, this technological transformation is overlooked or underplayed. The creation over decades of a national radio network, then the extension of roads and air traffic, and the construction of a national television network by the 1970s were indispensable in the creation of an "imagined community" and an *imaginário nacional* within the vast stretches of Brazil's distant borders (and then beyond). The satellite technology that makes possible the immense multiplication of access to diverse providers of television programming, usage of the Internet, and now, cell phones, is the latest and the most sophisticated phase in this technological transformation, integration, and globalization of the Brazilian national territory.[10]

This process of national integration through modern technology begins in the nineteenth century with the telegraph, but slowly and primarily through the interconnection of the major urban centers. In 1900, Brazil remained "an archipelago of social practices, interests, and powers."[11] Although the telegraph first appeared in Brazil in the 1850s, and a direct link was established with Europe in the 1870s, it was not until the 1890s that all the state capitals had a direct telegraphic connection with the capital.[12] By the late 1880s all the major cities of the country were finally connected and the news of the passage of the Golden Law abolishing slavery in May 1888 was immediately telegraphed across the country. Abolition was likely the first major political event communicated nearly simultaneously across most of the urban space of Brazil, although the population of the country was more than 80 percent rural.[13] Unlike Europe, the United States, or Argentina, the railway has relatively little impact as an integrative force. The relatively small railway network constructed in Brazil at the end of the nineteenth century was primarily concentrated in the coffee zone of the Southeast and did virtually nothing to connect up the major regions of Brazil, even those along the Atlantic coast.[14] The absence of an integrated railway network in Brazil today remains a major obstacle to national development. Not until the 1920s did (minimally) functioning highways connect the three major cities of the most economically and politically dynamic region of Brazil – Rio de Janeiro to São Paulo and Belo Horizonte to Rio de Janeiro.[15] The highway between the old colonial capital of Bahia and the city of Rio de Janeiro was only completed in 1949.[16] The construction of Brasília in the late 1950s pushed the edge of the highway transportation network north of its old limits in Minas Gerais, but not until the 1970s did the Brazilian government (under military rule) finally push to build (barely) functional highways into the vast interiors of Brazil, the two-thirds of the country's landmass in the North and Center-West.[17] Not until the 1950s, for example, did regular commercial aviation reach Manaus, the major urban center in Amazonia. Until then, the only viable means of transportation was via waterways.[18]

RADIO AND THE CREATION OF SAMBA

The technology of radio broadcasting provided the first important instrument of the twentieth century in the integration of the nation and the ability (at least in theory) to connect all the peoples of Brazil into a single community.[19] Although radio was introduced into Brazil by 1922, it was not until the mid-1930s that commercial radio began to reach substantial areas of the country. Between the 1930s and the 1950s, radio became the single most important means of communicating with the vast majority of Brazilians and across all regions.[20] In 1931, there were just 20 radio stations in all Brazil. By 1950, there were 300. By the mid-1940s, more than eight out of ten households in Rio de Janeiro and São Paulo owned a radio and these two markets dominated broadcasting across the country.[21] By the 1930s, phonographs, records, and radios became affordable for large sectors of the Brazilian population.[22] Radio broadcasting, especially the influence of producers of programming in Rio de Janeiro, formed the first wave in the communication and understanding of the Freyrean vision of Brazil. The most important medium in this first wave was popular music and its first vehicle was samba.[23]

As Bryan McCann shows brilliantly in *Hello, Hello Brazil*, the expansion of radio broadcasting provided the means to communicate (eventually) with nearly everyone in Brazil, and popular music played on radio stations "emerged as a decisive forum for debate over national identity, and Brazilians began to view the exercise of musical preference in the cultural marketplace as an act of enormous consequences." Nearly everyone – artists, producers, writers, and consumers – consciously and unconsciously debated and helped create a sense of national identity.[24] They all participated in the creation and constant reformulation of Brazilian culture and identity.[25] Brazilian popular music has served as one of the most important venues over the last century "for the affirmation of this *mestiço* national identity."[26]

A combination of factors converged to produce this lively cultural debate and diffusion of key myths and symbols – the rise of commercial broadcasting, the emergence of a State that consciously strove to create a sense of national identity, and the role of artists, composers, producers, and intellectuals as cultural intermediaries. Radio broadcasters provided the first national forum. The State became a conscious force to create a sense of *brasilidade*. Composers, artists, producers, bureaucrats, and intellectuals played perhaps the most important role as the central intermediaries creating, translating, and conveying images and ideas between political, cultural, and economic elites, and the great masses of Brazilians – *o povo*.[27] As McCann, Marc Hertzman, and others have pointed out, this was not a clear-cut, directed, and predictable process. It was a messy, complicated, and an ongoing process of discussion of regionalism, nationalism, and identities. By the 1950s, this process had helped communicate a series of notions of identity across the length and breadth of Brazil, helping construct the first powerful wave of the mass cultural construction of the Freyrean vision. The most visible symbol constructed out of the emergence of radio and popular music from the 1930s to the 1950s was samba (the so-called "golden age" of samba).

McCann, Hertzman, Carlos Sandroni, and Hermano Vianna have skillfully and elegantly demonstrated how samba moved from its obscure role as the music of the *favelas* of Rio in the early twentieth century to a powerful symbol of Brazilian national identity by the 1940s.[28] The musicians who created samba struggled to assert control over the music they wrote and performed, and to define its meaning amidst hotly contested claims about race, gender, and national identity.[29] Vianna, an anthropologist by academic training, highlights how the emergence of samba as a national symbol was emblematic of a larger process taking place in the 1930s and 1940s as the modernity the elites desired began to threaten the traditions that had held together their world for so long. As the powerful faced challenges from emerging new actors and cultural transformations, this "inspired a backward gaze, a search for lost times, a return to roots." Nowhere else is this more evident than in the work of Gilberto Freyre. His form of regionalism as nationalism, observes Vianna, "did not represent a return to roots so much as an imaginative recreation of those roots."[30] The converging forces of a centralizing State under Vargas, the rapid expansion of popular music through the new medium of radio, and cultural mediators (such as Freyre and musicians) both gave rise to and reshaped samba into a national symbol. Samba formed a crucial part of the larger project to modernize Brazil and make it into a nation built on "ethnic integration."[31] It became the first powerful visual and aural symbol of *mestiçagem* to emerge across Brazil as the essence of *brasilidade*. As one black gospel samba singer explained to an American anthropologist in Rio recently, "Samba makes me proud to be Brazilian."[32]

The emergence of samba as a powerful symbol of Brazilian identity beautifully illustrates Hobsbawm and Ranger's "invention of tradition" in action.[33] By the 1940s, the language of discourse about samba had already become an intense debate over "authenticity," that is over which form of samba was the most Brazilian, which really meant the version most deeply shaped by "African" influence. Here was a musical genre that a few decades earlier had rarely been heard by the vast majority of the peoples within Brazil, yet, by mid-century, intellectuals hailed it as emblematic of a Brazilian culture forged out of centuries of African influence. Despite its recent emergence and diffusion across the airwaves of Brazil, samba had quickly become a symbol of centuries of cultural *mestiçagem*. As the idea of racial and cultural mixture became more deeply ingrained among Brazilians, they began to construct competing images of African, Native American, and European culture. The meaning of "African" influence has been debated throughout the twentieth century and into the twenty-first.[34] By the beginning of the twenty-first century, for many Brazilians, the story of the emergence of samba had become one of "exchange, cooperation, and creativity . . . a story of reciprocity" among the "three races."[35]

This invocation of the "national" and the "authentic" is ironic given the complex fusion of musical influences. The confluence of different musical styles from rural Brazil, urban Rio de Janeiro, jazz and swing from the United States, and direct contact through tours in Europe all played a role in the emergence of samba, the musicians, composers, and bands that wrote and performed the music. Perhaps the most famous of these groups, the Oito Batutas (Eight Aces, Pros, or Batons), who are often singled out as one of the pioneering bands, originally wore "folkloric *sertanejo* costumes," played various types of popular music, and then toured France. They were deeply influenced by jazz and one of their members, the legendary Pixinguinha (Alfredo da Rocha Viana), took up the saxophone. Over the next five decades, Pixinguinha became one of the most beloved and important musicians and composers in Brazilian music moving across a wide variety of genres and styles. A writer in the early 1920s saw in the Batutas's music the "loving flower of three sad races," the very core of Brazil's "racial soul." The Batutas – through their music – became crucial cultural mediators between Brazil's rural past and its urban future.[36] While the purists may see samba as quintessentially Brazilian, the samba that emerged in the mid-twentieth century as "authentically" Brazilian was forged out of musical influences from across the Atlantic world.[37]

Nevertheless, a powerful State intent on constructing a nation is not enough. At times, the heavy handed efforts of the State to shape and impose myths, rituals, and symbols on the people fail miserably. When the Vargas regime created the *Hora do Brasil* radio program in the 1930s, it was met with scorn and derision for decades. This unsubtle effort to promote a specific cultural and political agenda failed disastrously compared to the market-driven programming on commercial radio. By one estimate, in the 1950s, roughly half of the listeners simply switched off their radios when the program aired between eight and nine in the evenings (Monday through Saturday). The always clever Brazilian public referred to the program as the *Hora da fala sozinha* (hour of it talks to itself). The regime might have been able to co-opt or seize cultural trends and use them for the purposes of nation-building, but simply creating and imposing trends was another matter.[38]

A fascinating and paradoxical part of this process of creating a national identity was the creation and reinforcement of regionalism and regional identities. At the same time Vargas moved to centralize and nationalize, the regions of Brazil resisted and the growing presence of mass media made it possible to create strong regional (in many cases, state) identities. The new technologies not only made it possible to reach all those within a region of Brazil, but also to communicate those regional identities across the country. Even as these regional identities emerged, and at times even contradicted national narratives, they formed part of a national conversation about identities. Brazilians, just as other peoples, balanced multiple identities and that sometimes included regional and national identities with all their contradictions and convergences. As Ruben Oliven has shown for Rio Grande do Sul, *gaúcho* identity emerges parallel with Brazilian identity in the twentieth century. The same holds true for *mineiros, baianos, paulistas,* and the more wide reaching identity of the *nordestino* (to cite some of the best-known examples). As McCann shows in *Hello, Hello Brazil*, as samba emerges as national music we can also see the emergence of "Northeastern" music, most powerfully, in the personas of Dorival Caymmi and Luiz Gonzaga.

Caymmi (1914–2008), from Salvador, and Gonzaga (1912–1989), from the interior of Pernambuco, were contemporaries who built long and iconic careers on their regional roots expressed through music that had great appeal across Brazil beginning in the 1930s. As McCann says, "Caymmi and Gonzaga saved the essence of the fading Northeast and brought it in a usable format to the modernizing Southeast, and then to all of Brazil." Rather than exclusionary and separatist, their music and personas played into the construction of national identity. They linked region and nation, communicating "a crucial part – to the whole." With an Italian father and a Brazilian mother, Caymmi both embodied and projected the culturally mixed image in his life and music. According to

McCann, Caymmi "did as much to popularize a Freyrean understanding of race in Brazil as anyone."[39] Gonzaga, with his music and his *sertanejo* outfits, came to epitomize the essence of the *nordestino* in the decades of mass migration of his compatriots from the Northeast to the booming Southeast. In many ways, he virtually created the archetypal image of the *nordestino* for Brazilians just as Caymmi forged the image of the *baiano* for a national audience. As millions of *nordestinos* fled to the south and west of Brazil after 1930, they both created markets for this regional music across the country, and helped construct this regional identity as "foreigners" in their own country.[40] Each of them constructed very different Northeastern identities. Gonzaga played the role of the *sertanejo* (primarily a cultural and ethnic mix of Europeans and Indians) while Caymmi projected the image of the coastal region, especially Bahia and its Afro-Brazilian culture.

The emergent regional identities in the Northeast and São Paulo provide vivid and contrasting examples that highlight the simultaneous and interactive rise of regional and national identities in Brazil in the mid-twentieth century. Gilberto Freyre and Jorge Amado's beloved Northeast (Salvador and Recife) represented a regional vision claiming to represent the nation, one that looked back to *mestiçagem*, Africa, the indigenous, and the rural as the basis of regional and national identity. The music and images of Caymmi and Gonzaga provided the soundtrack for the rich cultural heritage of the Northeast. At the same time, these cultural mediators lauded this region known for its racial and cultural mixture, and its long-standing socioeconomic backwardness, the emerging industrial power of the Southeast, São Paulo, claimed another regional identity, one constructed out of economic dynamism and cultural modernity. The burgeoning metropolis of São Paulo, in particular, became the touchstone of this economic and cultural modernity.

Barbara Weinstein has beautifully demonstrated that the *paulistas* consciously built a regional identity in contrast to the *nordestinos*, emphasizing whiteness, industrialism, urban cosmopolitanism, and modernity in clear contrast to the racially mixed, decadent, rural, provincial, and backwards Northeast.[41] Ironically, each region turned to the rural pioneer as their symbol – the *sertanejo* in the Northeast, and the *bandeirante* in São Paulo. Although both emerged out of *mestiçagem* of the colonial period, Euclides da Cunha had portrayed the former as hardy but destined for annihilation, while the *bandeirante* became the precursor of the increasingly white, European São Paulo.

The *paulistas* lost out not only in their failed revolt against Vargas and the centralizing State in 1932; in the official battle for recognition, Freyre and his vision triumphed over the other regional contenders, including the white, modern, industrial vision of the *paulistas*. From Vargas onward, the official version of many (very diverse) Brazilian presidents and politicians would be Freyre's vision of *mestiçagem* and the key corollary that eventually emerged from it – racial democracy. Much as a group of social scientists in recent years have begun to dismantle the old notion that racial democracy serves as a hegemonic false consciousness that has masked prejudice and discrimination in Brazil, many others have shown the complex interplay between elites and masses, State and people, region and nation. To use the terminology of the Argentine anthropologist, Néstor García Canclini, they reveal how popular culture "is constructed through complex, hybrid processes, using elements from diverse classes and nations as signs of identification."[42] Samba, in this case, emerged through the unorganized, uncoordinated efforts of many individuals, groups, organizations, and official agencies. It was unplanned, unanticipated, and emblematic of the hybrid processes that create popular culture.[43] My argument in this book is that these same processes of negotiation, mediation, and the creation of hybridity characterize Brazilian popular culture across the twentieth century, and the formation of a national identity constructed around Freyrean *mestiçagem*.

SAMBA, *CARNAVAL*, AND GETÚLIO VARGAS

Much has been written about the role of the Vargas regime in the centralization of power, the consolidation of the State in twentieth-century Brazil, and its role in promoting a sense of Brazilian national identity. The Revolution of 1930 brought down the "coffee and cream" oligarchy dominated by São Paulo and Minas Gerais, and ushered in a new era of "conservative modernization" led by the central political figure in twentieth-century Brazil – Getúlio Vargas. In various guises – first as provisional president (1930–1934), then as indirectly elected president (1934–1937), then as the dictator of the authoritarian Estado Novo (1937–1945) – Vargas played the leading role in the transformation of the State, society, and culture in Brazil.[44] As in many countries of the Western world in the 1930s, the economic crisis led to increasing State intervention in all areas of life. Vargas expanded the role of the State creating a wide variety of new ministries (Education and Public Health; Labor, Industry, and Commerce, for example) and new departments and councils (such as the Department of the Administration of Public Service; Department of Press and Propaganda). The intervention into economic activities led to the emergence of the import-substitution industrialization (ISI) model that would dominate economic development policies until the 1960s and 1970s. From my perspective, just as important was the intervention of the State into cultural affairs, a topic that has been well studied.[45]

Vargas wisely and cleverly brought many of the major intellectual figures of the 1930s and 1940s into government in key roles in government agencies from education to propaganda to cultural patrimony. Many of the major figures of the Modernist Movement such as Mário de Andrade and Carlos Drummond de Andrade became "public functionaries" (*funcionários públicos*). Vargas sought to unify and integrate the Brazilian archipelago – economically, politically, and culturally.[46] These intellectuals were brought on board to craft cultural unity through the creation of a clear sense of Brazilian identity. As Daryle Williams has shown, they engaged in "culture wars" among themselves over exactly what that identity would be – in school curricula, museums, publications, and public events and rituals. In Williams's words, these intellectuals became "cultural managers."[47]

While samba became the symbol par excellence of *mestiçagem* in popular music, *carnaval* emerged in the 1930s and 1940s as the principal ritual showcasing the Freyrean vision. Samba and *carnaval* may be intimately connected, but their emergence as the principal symbol and primary ritual of *mestiço* nationalism took very different paths. Although at times promoted by the government, samba emerged in these decades largely because of its appeal across the length and breadth of Brazil – due to its resonance with the tastes of consumers. In short, it was "market driven." Radio broadcasters and record companies both stimulated and responded to the demand for samba. A Dorival Caymmi song sums it up: "Anyone who doesn't like samba is either sick in the head or crippled in the feet."[48] In contrast, the Brazilian State under Getúlio Vargas consciously and systematically appropriated a very specific version of this pre-Lenten festival – *carnaval* in Rio de Janeiro – and strove successfully to make it a showpiece for all Brazilians and for the international community. "Carnival," in the words of McCann, "became expressly a festival of civic instruction."[49] Vargas and his cultural managers constructed *carnaval* in Rio as an emblematic ritual for Brazilians, and exported the imagery. "*Carnaval* in Rio," declared Oswald de Andrade in his legendary "Brazilwood Manifesto," "is the religious event of our race."[50] During

FIGURE 2.1 *Carnaval* in Rio de Janeiro
Source: Getty Images

the various regimes of Getúlio Vargas, his cultural managers took this ostensibly religious event and turned it into one of the most sacred rituals of the secular nationalism of the mid-twentieth century. Alongside new school curricula, textbooks, museums, and holidays, *carnaval* in Rio became the most holy ritual of *mestiço* nationalism and the celebration of *mestiçagem.*[51]

Vargas helped usher in a new era in Brazilian politics that sought to manage the dramatic social and economic transformations pulsing across all of Brazil in the decades after World War I. The greatest of these transformations was doubly demographic – the explosion of the population of the country from around 30 million inhabitants in 1920 to 150 million by 1990, and the massive migration of rural people into cities of all sizes. In 1920, only about 25 percent of the population lived in urban areas, some 8 million souls. By 1990, 75 percent of the country lived in urban areas, more than 110 million Brazilians (a nearly fourteen-fold increase). This movement of tens of millions from countryside and villages to towns, cities, and teeming metropolises is one of the greatest social transformations of Latin America, and of the world, in the twentieth century.[52]

The half-century after 1930 witnessed the gradual and steady disappearance of the peasantry, the explosion of urban areas across all of Brazil, the consequent expansion of *favelas*, the rise of an urban working class, middle class, and an impoverished urban underclass of enormous dimensions. The technological waves in communications accompanied the rise of urban Brazil and Getúlio Vargas was the first major political figure in Brazil to grasp the beginnings of these social and technological shifts. Much like Franklin Delano Roosevelt, his contemporary, Vargas was a conservative modernizer who sought to co-opt and control these fundamental shifts through new political, social, and economic policies that his own social class generally viewed with horror. Especially after the imposition of the authoritarian Estado Novo (1937–1945), Vargas centralized the powers of the State at the expense of the old regional oligarchies to create, for the first time in Brazilian history, a semblance of central government control over the vast expanses of the country.[53]

Vargas embarked upon an ambitious and highly effective cultural policy to promote the centralization of power – and to create a sense of Brazilian national identity.[54] The most notorious display of this drive to central power took place shortly after the coup of November 1937 (that created the Estado Novo), when all of the state flags were burned in an elaborate ceremony in Rio de Janeiro.[55] The message was clear – the State would eradicate the long-standing power of the states and subordinate them to central authority. In this drive to create a single national identity, Vargas and his cultural managers chose to enshrine the Freyrean vision of *mestiçagem* at the core of this cultural policy.[56] As a number of scholars have shown, the 1930s mark a turning point for the intellectual and cultural elites. Vargas and his successors in the succeeding decades created what Sergio Miceli has called a "central market of public positions" (*mercado central de postos públicos*) that gave Brazilian intellectuals access to the halls of power and influence as opposed to the sinecures offered to them by the oligarchs of the Republic. In the post-1930 Brazil, intellectuals filled not only the mundane posts of *funcionários públicos* but also the possibility to create and shape national culture via the power of the State.[57]

As literary scholars have long pointed out, the Modernist Movement and the political vision of Vargas were both fraught with competing tensions – between cosmopolitanism and cultural nationalism ("contradictory modernity"), modernization and tradition.[58] The State expanded its influence, either directly or indirectly, into all areas of cultural production after 1930, and especially after 1937. The newly created Ministry of

Education under the strong leadership of Gustavo Capanema, in particular, played a leading role in setting an agenda of cultural nationalism. Capanema proved to be a very resilient and effective operator within the power structure of the Vargas regimes. He envisioned the school curriculum as "the cement of *brasilidade*."[59] A former small-town school teacher from Minas Gerais, Capanema brought two of his fellow *mineiros* with him to Rio – the great poet Carlos Drummond de Andrade, who served as Capanema's chief of staff (and intellectual alter ego), and Rodrigo Mello Franco de Andrade (who had helped Freyre find a publisher for *Casa-grande*), who headed the new Serviço de Patrimônio Histórico e Artístico Nacional (SPHAN) – and many, many other major intellectuals served in positions that shaped cultural production – from music to art to architecture. The convergence between the Modernist Movement, intellectuals, and the State under Vargas was crucial in the official consecration of the Freyrean vision of *mestiço* nationalism.[60]

Under Vargas, the State "domesticated" *carnaval*. For decades, political and cultural elites had derided, bemoaned, and suppressed the various forms of street celebrations, music, and dancing. Much of this derision arose from both class and color prejudices as the majority of the street revelers, no doubt, came from the lower classes and were darker skinned. The *blocos*, or neighborhood street bands, that took shape in the early twentieth century in Rio organized themselves in the 1920s and the city government eventually began to extend financial assistance in exchange for standardization and regulation. Vargas's Departamento de Imprensa e Propaganda (DIP, Department of Press and Propaganda) began to review song lyrics and promoted the ones that glorified Brazilian identity. The domestication of *carnaval* produced interesting tradeoffs. While it may have represented the "taming" of the more "African" and "uncivilized" side of the event for the conservatives, it officially enshrined African influences (via samba) as central to the performance of Brazilian identity.[61] According to one spokesperson for the DIP who sought to strip *carnaval* of its "pagan" and "sensual" side, "We recognize that all the illiterate, rude louts who live in our cities are frequently linked to civilization through music." He wanted the government to "combat" these negative traits "by 'dominating the barbarous impetus' of samba on the radio."[62]

In his nuanced study, *Making Samba*, Marc Hertzman dissects the "officialization" of *carnaval* showing the role of the State's cultural managers and the musicians creating the music. Although the symbolic starting point for samba has long been associated with the record *Pelo*

Telefone (1917), Hertzman (building on the scholarship of Carlos Sandroni) shows how what is now considered the classic sound of samba does not emerge until the late 1920s with what became known as the Estácio Sound associated with the Rio neighborhood of the same name. One of the great contributions of *Pelo Telefone* was to popularize the term samba and, in the public mind, to link it to the music associated with *carnaval* in Rio de Janeiro. In 1932, the popular publication *Mundo Sportivo* organized the first competition of the samba schools (during the *futebol* off-season). By the mid-1930s, the Rio city council had begun to offer cash prizes for the top finishers in the competition. With the formation of the Union of Samba Schools, the organizations, in effect, set in motion a process of negotiation and discussion with government officials who continually sought to standardize *carnaval* and impose regulations. Both samba school officials and the creators of the music constantly worked the system to move samba and *carnaval* in directions they desired rather than simply accepting government controls and regulations.[63]

For the creators of samba, the musicians, and composers, the State was "everywhere and nowhere." Many of these creative and influential individuals came from neither the poor nor the elite, but rather from the middle sectors of Brazilian society. In Hertzman's words, "they neither simply reproduced nor entirely rejected discourses handed down to them from above or pressed upon them from below. Rather, they engaged those discourses in such a way that allowed them to tweak them and incorporate them into their own identities and ideas." They represent for Hertzman (citing the work of Homi Bhabha) a process where elites alternately embrace and reject marginalized groups and their cultural forms. In short, neither the State nor any social group dictated the terms and forms of identity formation, national or otherwise. The emergence of samba and *carnaval* in its classic forms by the 1940s, in fact, beautifully illustrates the complexities, ambiguities, and contradictions of the processes of identity formation and nationalism.[64]

The differing ways *carnaval* and its celebration developed across Brazil also illustrate the subtle dynamics of regional and national identity formation. *Carnaval* in Rio became the iconic version of this Brazilian ritual – in particular several nights with tens of thousands seated in the *sambódromo* cheering on the top samba schools. Ruy Castro has called it "*Gone with the Wind* multiplied by *Ben-Hur*."[65] Bahia's version of *carnaval* also became one of the most famous regional versions, but with its own styles, music, and performances. From the 1930s to the 1950s, the poor and working classes of Salvador formed their own version of samba schools known as *batucadas*, heavy on percussion and crucial in the elaboration and celebration of African-Brazilian musical practices. Salvador's version of *carnaval* became central to the emergence of a Bahian identity emphasizing the African contributions to Brazilian culture. As with *carnaval* in Rio, the "officialization of carnival" emerged out of the efforts of elite groups and Afro-Brazilians from the lower classes, often with the support of the government (local, state, and federal). This Brazilian ritual also served as a quintessentially Bahian ritual reinforcing both a regional and a national identity, and drawing on support from many directions.[66]

In the years after 1930, all Brazilian governments attempted to export the image of *carnaval*, especially the Rio version, as the quintessential Brazilian ritual. Perhaps no other ritual has shaped the foreign view of Brazil in the twentieth century as profoundly as this ostensibly pre-Lenten festival. As samba spread across Brazil gaining acceptance through the tastes of consumers, cultural managers worked closely with the *escolas de samba* to codify and shape *carnaval* in Rio. From the 1930s to the 1960s, *carnaval* produced nearly 400 new songs each year, and the ones that became hits "became standards" and part of the permanent repertory of the annual event.[67] The lower classes that created and sustained the *escolas de samba* began a long struggle with the representatives of the State as each attempted to control and determine the direction of *carnaval* with samba at its center. Just as with the creation of "authentic" samba in the first half of the century, intense debates emerged over "authenticity" as *carnaval* in Rio became one of the principal rituals of *mestiço* nationalism. The people of Rio de Janeiro, who had faced persecution and repression periodically over the previous century as they attempted to express their own versions of *carnaval*, now became the central performers of perhaps the most famous export of Brazilian national identity.[68]

CARNAVAL, GENDER, THE *MALANDRO*, AND THE *MULATA*

Many of those observing the emergence of samba recognized this music as a prime example of the racial and cultural mixing that they saw as the essence of Brazil. Pixinguinha's brother, China, asserted, "Who brought samba into society? It was the *mulato*." Samba, in the view of these observers, "came from Africa, but it was only through *mulato* mediation that the music or 'African blood' could be appropriately incorporated into Brazil."[69] This cultural and racial *mestiçagem* gave birth to new symbols

FIGURE 2.2 The *Malandro*-Musician Look (date unknown)
Source: Heitor dos Prazeres Family Archive

associated with this emerging national ritual. At the center of *carnaval* in
Rio emerged two vivid symbols of the gendered nature of Freyre's vision
of *mestiçagem* – the *malandro* and the *mulata*. Although both figures pre-
dated both Freyre's work and the emergence of the iconic *carnaval* in Rio
in the 1930s, the *malandro* and the *mulata* became intimately associated
with samba and *carnaval*. The *malandro*, often translated as rogue or
rake, is one of the iconic figures in Brazilian popular culture. In the
words of Martha Abreu, he is "the symbolic antithesis of the disciplined
worker and the well-behaved citizen: idle, disrespectful of the law and
of good habits."[70] The *malandro*, clearly the result of *mestiçagem*, was
"good humored, good at soccer and samba, the rogue was the master of
a style summed up in the 1950s in the famous expression 'Brazilian
cleverness' (*jeitinho brasileiro*)."[71] He is a "culture hero" for the masses
and a nightmare for the authorities attempting to construct a model
citizen, one who is obedient, subservient, law-abiding, and respectful of
authority.[72] Eduardo das Neves, one of the first great sambistas, has been
recognized as the first great *malandro*, a flashy dressing hustler and an
Afro-Brazilian with a penchant for dating white women, a *trovador de
malandragem* (troubadour of roguery).[73]

THE *MALANDRO*

The Vargas regimes worked assiduously to construct a monolithic and authoritarian vision of nationality and citizenship in the 1930s and 1940s. The authorities strove to tame *carnaval* and turn it into a showcase for Brazilian culture and identity, yet the "untamed" side of samba and *carnaval*, epitomized by the *malandro*, constantly challenged their designs.[74] Those sambistas like Neves ran great risks as their style and music both captivated much of the Brazilian public and appalled many government officials. As the music industry and the samba schools became more organized, better funded, and regulated in the 1930s and 1940s, the presence of the *malandro* streak (*malandragem*) among some of the greatest and most popular sambistas created a potent and creative musical and artistic milieu. The *malandros* also made it impossible for the government simply to impose their vision of samba and *carnaval* on the producers and consumers of popular culture. As we see in Chapter 5, the iconic figure of the *malandro* and *malandragem* also created a powerful trope in Brazilian culture and society, one that also infused *futebol* as it emerged as a professional sport – as the professional sport – in Brazil during the same period. Some of the greatest stars of Brazilian *futebol* played the part of the *malandro*, and the creativity, improvisation, and roguishness of the *malandro* have also been seen by many to be at the core of the excellence and brilliance of Brazilian *futebol*.

While the emblematic male associated with samba is the *malandro* who embodies the qualities of improvisation, creativity, and skill, with a hint of danger, the emblematic female is the *mulata*, the object of male desire.[75] Freyre has been frequently and ferociously attacked by critics for the images he created of Indian and African women as often greeting the Portuguese males with open arms, and open thighs. Although Freyre describes in *Casa-grande* a world filled with oversexed Africans, Portuguese, and Native Americans (although the latter he viewed as the least sexually expressive), he does emphasize the sadism and power of the *senhor de engenho* (powerful landowner). The truth, he observed, "is that we were sadists; the active element in the corruption of family life; and kids and *mulatas* are the passive element."[76] Nonetheless, the Freyrean gaze is clearly that of the white male of the manor. The vision he portrays, one that continues to imbue contemporary sexual relations in Brazil, is that of the patriarchal, white male obsessed with females of color – in particular, the *mulata*.[77] Over the course of the twentieth century, the *mulata* has been enshrined, not only as the centerpiece of *carnaval* in Rio

FIGURE 2.3 The *Mulata* as the Centerpiece of *Carnaval*
Source: Getty Images

but also as the object of desire of the "Brazilian male." Samba became the
symbol of the cultural synthesis of Brazil's African and European music,
and the *mulata*'s body its biological synthesis.[78] By the late twentieth
century, the *mulata* had become the iconic sex symbol of Brazil,
a symbol exported to the rest of the world.

Two songs, one written and the other cowritten, by Lamartine Babo
epitomize the glorification of the *mulata* and her role in *carnaval*. Babo

(1904–1963) is one of the legendary figures of Brazilian popular music and one of Brazil's most prolific composers. Although originally composed by two brothers in Recife, *O Teu Cabelo Não Nega* (1932), the *marchinha* was slightly revised by Babo who was originally listed as the sole writer. This enormously successful hit begins with the verse, "Your hair doesn't hide it, *morena*/Because you are *mulata* in your skin color/But skin color doesn't pass from one to another/Girl, I want your love." Exalting her beauty the song goes on, "The envious moon is grimacing/Because the *mulata* is not from this planet." Another poignant example is Babo's 1939 composition, *Hino do Carnaval Brasileiro*, sung by the equally legendary Almirante in the original recording. "Save the *morena*/the brown color of a pleasurable Brazil," goes the first verse followed later by "Save the *mulata*/the color of cinnamon." The song ends with the refrain, "Save, save/your *carnaval*, Brazil." Although this is one of the best-known and most popular songs in this genre, the examples could be multiplied almost endlessly.[79]

Perhaps no other writer has captured the essence of this *mulata* symbolism better than the Mexican-American journalist Alma Guillermoprieto. Her analysis goes to the heart of the Freyrean vision of Brazilian sexuality, a vision that had become pervasive by the 1980s when Guillermoprieto spent a year with the Mangueira samba school in Rio de Janeiro.

Mulatas are glorified sex fetishes, sanitized representations of what whites viewed as the savage African sex urge, but they are also, of course, tribute and proof of the white male's power: his sexual power, and his economic power, which allowed him to wrest the *mulata*'s black mother away from her black partner. At the same time, the *mulata* serves to perpetuate one of the myths that Brazilians hold most dear, that there is no racism in Brazil, that miscegenation has been natural and pleasant for both parties, that white people really, sincerely, do like black people. In fact, the aesthetic superiority accorded to light-skinned black women – *mulatas* – underlines the perceived ugliness of blacks before they have been "improved" with white blood. The white skin also serves to lighten a sexual force that in undiluted state is not only threatening, but vaguely repulsive, and at the same time, the myth goes, irresistible.[80]

Freyre wrote from a "white male gaze" creating an image of *mestiçagem* that revealed little about what women might have thought about the Big House or the slave quarters, or their views of sexuality. His *mestiço* nationalism was one imbued with the patriarchal ethos of colonial Brazilian society.[81] For decades, this masculine vision of a seigneurial sexuality at the heart of this nationalist vision went unquestioned, and largely unanalyzed. Not until the last two decades of the century did Brazilians begin to examine seriously (through surveys, for example) what was the object of desire of women if the *mulata* was supposedly the sex fetish of males.

Although originally a festival from Europe, *carnaval* in the 1930s and 1940s became the quintessential *Brazilian* ritual and *national* festivity. The eminent historian and anthropologist Lilia Schwarcz has summed up the cultural transformations of this period. Through popular music and *carnaval*, she says, "the ideal of *mestiçagem* was transformed into the locus of national authenticity, and the category of *mulata*, into a site for this ideal. In this figure, clearly idealized and exoticized, resided the possibility of promoting a precarious equilibrium in which differences live together intensely and ambiguously."[82] Promoted quite consciously by Vargas and the State as his cultural mediators attempted to shape and sanitize its contours, the image of *carnaval* with its music (samba) and sexual symbol (the *mulata*) became the most powerful international images of Brazil. Always lurking in the background, however, the *malandro* served to continually disrupt and disturb this official imagery. By the mid-twentieth century, following Richard Parker, the Brazilians created a *carnaval* with "a uniquely Brazilian sexuality – a vision built up in the rhythms and movements of *samba*, the trickery and cunning of *malandragem*, and the voluptuous pleasures of the *mulata*."[83] Despite the top-down efforts of Vargas and the Brazilian State, this is not simply a story of elite manipulation. The music, dance, and festivities ultimately grow and thrive as a result of their immense popularity and appeal to the great masses of Brazilians. The State, cultural producers (such as musicians), and the *povo* converged around *carnaval* jointly forging the most powerful image of modern Brazil and one of its two most universally celebrated national rituals.

NOTES

1. McCann, *Hello, Hello Brazil*, 2.
2. Ortiz, *A moderna tradição brasileira* is a meditation on these issues. "Popular culture is obviously the hegemonic battlefield, but total hegemony is impossible to obtain." Thomas Tufte, *Living with the Rubbish Queen: Telenovelas, Culture and Modernity in Brazil* (Luton, UK: University of Luton Press, 2000), 19.
3. Owensby, "Toward a History of Brazil's 'Cordial Racism,'" 333.
4. The literacy rate in the 1920 national census was 25 percent. Leslie Bethell, "Politics in Brazil under Vargas, 1930–1945," in *Brazil since 1930*, 5.

5. "In 1920 in São Paulo, 209 titles and 900,000 copies of books and pamphlets were published. In the same decade in Rio de Janeiro, about 780 titles were edited per year, with total press runs of 2.2 million copies. The average printing of a novel reached 1,000 copies." Ortiz, "Culture and Society," in *Brazil*, 121.

6. In Portuguese alone, *Casa-grande* has gone through more than 40 editions. Gilberto Freyre, *Casa-grande & senzala: introdução à história da sociedade patriarcal no Brasil – 1*, 40ª.edn. (Rio de Janeiro: Editora Record, 2000).

7. Candice Slater, *Stories on a String: The Brazilian* Literatura de cordel (Berkeley: University of California Press, 1982); Mark J. Curran, *La literatura de cordel: antología bilingüe* (Madrid: Orígenes, 1991).

8. "Between the 1890s and the 1920s, traveling circuses were among Brazil's most important entertainment institutions and conduits, bringing music and theater performances from Rio and São Paulo to distant locations. Most of Rio's early recording stars spent time playing at or performing in the circus. Between 1919 and 1922, the city had at least thirty-five circus venues, with an average capacity of seventeen hundred people." Marc Hertzman, *Making Samba: A New History of Race and Music in Brazil* (Durham, NC: Duke University Press, 2013), 67.

9. Jerry Dávila, *Diploma of Whiteness: Race and Social Policy in Brazil, 1917–1945* (Durham, NC: Duke University Press, 2003), esp. 1–27.

10. For the latest stage, see André Lemos e Francisco Paulo Jamil Almeida Marques, "O plano nacional de banda larga brasileira: um estudo de seus limites e efeitos sociais e políticos," *Revista da Associação Nacional dos Programas de Pós-graduação em Comunicação, E-compos*, 15: 1 (jan.–abr. 2012), 1–36. My thanks to Courtney Campbell for calling my attention to this source.

11. Ortiz, "Culture and Society," 121.

12. Victor M. Berthold, *History of the Telephone and Telegraph in Brazil, 1851–1921* (New York: n.p., 1922), 16–30. The first submarine cables connecting Brazil with Europe went into operation in 1874 and to the United States in 1886. Berthold, 12–14. The first direct cable connecting Brazil and the U.S. operated via Valparaiso, Chile and Galveston, Texas. John A. Britton, *Cables, Crises, and the Press: The Geopolitics of the New International Information System in the Americas, 1866–1903* (Albuquerque: University of New Mexico Press, 2013), 85–86.

13. In 1888, "Havia, então, quase 11.000 km de linhas, com desenvolvimento de mais de 18.000 km de fios condutores, ligando 173 estações por todo o país." Eduardo Silva, "Integração, Globalização e Festa: A Abolição da Escravatura como História Cultural," in Marco Pamplona, org., *Escravidão, exclusão e cidadania* (Rio de Janeiro: Access, 2001), 107–18. Quote is from 109.

14. William Roderick Summerhill, *Order without Progress: Government, Foreign Investment, and Railroads in Brazil, 1854–1913* (Stanford, CA: Stanford University Press, 2003).

15. Joel Wolfe, *Autos and Progress: The Brazilian Search for Modernity* (New York: Oxford University Press, 2010), 53–54.

16. Paulo Fontes, " 'With a cardboard suitcase in my hand and a pannier on my back': Workers and Northeastern Migrations in the 1950s in São Paulo, Brazil," *Social History*, 36:1 (February 2011), 5.

17. Wolfe, *Autos and Progress*, 151–54.

18. Aldo Pereira, *Breve história da aviação comercial brasileira* (Rio de Janeiro: Europa, 1987).

19. As Eric Hobsbawm has observed, "For the first time in history people unknown to each other who met knew what each had in all probability heard (or, later, seen) the night before: the big game, the favourite comedy show, Winston Churchill's speech, the contents of a news bulletin." *Age of Extremes*, 196.

20. What made the "radio universal was the transistor, which made it both small and portable, and the long-life battery which made it independent of official (i.e. mainly urban) networks of electric power." Hobsbawm, *Age of Extremes*, 501.

21. McCann, *Hello, Hello Brazil*, 23–24.

22. Hertzman, *Making Samba*, 70.

23. "Robert Stam has argued that popular music has been more successful than any other area of Brazilian culture in generating syntheses that are simultaneously local and cosmopolitan, popular and experimental, pleasurable and political. In his view, Brazilian music 'has been the least colonized and the most Africanized branch of Brazilian popular culture, as well as the most successful in disseminating itself not only within Brazil but also around the world.' " Dunn, *Brutality Garden*, 10–11.

24. McCann, *Hello, Hello Brazil*, 5–6.

25. *Ibid.*, 2.

26. Dunn, *Brutality Garden*, 13.

27. A fine analysis that shows the role of the *povo* in the emergence of samba is Abreu, "*Mulatas, Crioulos* and *Morenas*: Racial Hierarchy, Gender Relations, and National Identity in Postabolition Popular Song: Southeastern Brazil, 1890–1920."

28. Carlos Sandroni, *Feitiço decente: transformações do samba no Rio de Janeiro, 1917–1933* (Rio de Janeiro: Jorge Zahar Editor, 2001); Hermano Vianna, *The Mystery of Samba: Popular Music and National Identity in Brazil*, ed. and trans. John Charles Chasteen (Chapel Hill: University of North Carolina Press, 1999) originally published as *O mistério do samba* (Rio de Janeiro: J. Zahar Editora/Universidade Federal do Rio de Janeiro, 1995).

29. Hertzman, *Making Samba*, esp. 116–17.

30. Vianna, *Mystery of Samba*, 41.

31. *Ibid.*, 51 and 92.

32. Burdick, *The Color of Sound*, 129.

33. Eric Hobsbawm and Terence Ranger, eds., *The Invention of Tradition* (New York: Cambridge University Press, 1992).

34. Hertzman, *Making Samba*.

35. There are many current examples of this in the informants for Burdick, *The Color of Sound*, e.g., 118.

36. Ironically, Pixinguinha had little interest in samba and preferred other musical genres. Hertzman, *Making Samba*, 105–8 and 158.

37. Vianna, *Mystery of Samba*, 81–84. As Hertzman shows, the Batutas and their manager, Arnoldo Guinle, consciously crafted their foreign tours as "research missions" to gather musical material. Hertzman, *Making Samba*, 105–6. For a fine article that delves deeply into the complexities of the creative process, the meanings of diaspora, Africa, transnational, national, and samba, see Marc Adam Hertzman, "A Brazilian Counterweight: Music, Intellectual Property and the African Diaspora in Rio de Janeiro (1910s–1930s)," *Journal of Latin American Studies*, 41 (2009), 695–722.

38. For a nice synopsis of the early experience of the *Hora do Brasil*, see McCann, *Hello, Hello Brazil*, 26–29.

39. McCann, *Hello, Hello Brazil*, 120, 121, and127.

40. For a fascinating look at the creation of *nordestino* enclaves in São Paulo, see Paulo Fontes, *Um nordeste em São Paulo: trabalhadores migrantes em São Miguel Paulista (1945–66)* (Rio de Janeiro: Editora FGV, 2008). "[D]espite their diversity, migrants from the Northeast and Minas Gerais state who arrived in São Paulo were all generally referred to as '*Baianos*' (born in Bahia state)." Paulo Fontes, " 'With a cardboard suitcase in my hand and a pannier on my back,' " 16.

41. Weinstein, "Racializing Regional Difference," 237–62.

42. Quoted in Vianna, 16. See also, Pierre Bourdieu, "The Field of Cultural Production, or: The Economic World Reversed," in *The Field of Cultural Production: Essays on Art and Literature*, ed. Randal Johnson (New York: Columbia University Press, 1993), 29–73.

43. Vianna argues that "the crystallization of the genre and its symbolic elevation were concurrent – not consecutive – processes. There never existed a well-defined, 'authentic' samba genre prior to its elaboration as a national music ... the whole process lacked coordinated direction." Vianna, *Mystery of Samba*, 112.

44. For the most recent synthesis and overview of the period, see Bethell, "Politics in Brazil under Vargas, 1930–1945," in *Brazil since 1930*, 3–86.

45. For just a couple of examples with very different perspectives: Sergio Miceli, *Intelectuais à brasileira* (São Paulo: Companhia das Letras, 2001), esp. 69–341; Daniel Pécaut, *Os intelectuais e política no Brasil (entre o povo e a nação)* (São Paulo: Ática, 1990).

46. Oliveira, *Cultura é patrimônio*, 97–111. An important facet of this cultural nationalism was the assimilation of the immigrants and children of the immigrant wave of the early twentieth century into Brazilian society. New legislation severely restricted the functioning of educational institutions in languages other than Portuguese. This was primarily aimed at the substantial German-speaking communities in southern Brazil, but also affected "international" schools that operated in English, French, and other languages. Bethell, "Politics in Brazil under Vargas, 1930–1945," 59.

47. Williams, *Culture Wars in Brazil*.

48. "Quem não gosta do samba bom sujeito não é/ou é ruim da cabeça ou doente do pé." www.letras.mus.br/dorival-caymmi/45588/ [accessed 19 May 2016]

English version from Larry Rohter, *Brazil on the Rise: The Story of a Country Transformed* (New York: Palgrave Macmillan, 2010), 111.

49. McCann, *Hello, Hello Brazil*, 67.

50. Dunn, *Brutality Garden*, 16.

51. "Pode-se dizer que a prefeitura do Distrito Federal funcionava como um laboratório de experiências, que, se bem sucedidas, eram estendidas ao país." Oliveira, *Cultura é patrimônio*, 106.

52. "The most dramatic and far-reaching social change of the second half of this century, and the one which cuts us off for ever from the world of the past, is the death of the peasantry." Hobsbawm, *The Age of Extremes*, 289. Between 1950 and 1980, nearly 40 million people left the countryside for the cities of Brazil. Fontes, " 'With a cardboard suitcase in my hand and a pannier on my back,'" 3.

53. Bethell, "Politics in Brazil under Vargas, 1930–1945."

54. "[T]he network of federal cultural policy-making institutions founded during the first Vargas regime built itself into the bedrock of Brazilian culture and state power. Even when these institutions acted as their own worst enemies, they helped the Vargas regime and all subsequent federal administrations lay claim to managing brasilidade." Williams, *Culture Wars in Brazil*, 53.

55. Bethell, "The Estado Novo, 1937–1945," 57; Oliven, "National and Regional Identities in Brazil," 305.

56. "é só com o Estado Novo que projetos oficiais são implementados no sentido de reconhecer na mestiçagem a verdadeira nacionalidade." Schwarcz, "Gilberto Freyre," 314.

57. Miceli writes, "These co-opted intellectuals defined themselves as spokespersons from all of society .... Seeing themselves as responsible for the administration of the nation's cultural assets, they placed themselves in a position to assume the work of preservation, diffusion, and manipulation of this heritage, working to celebrate authors and works which could be of use in this cause." Miceli, *Intelectuais à brasileira*, esp. "Os intelectuais e o Estado," 195–291. See also, Denis Rolland, "O Historiador, o Estado e a Fábrica dos Intelectuais," in Marcelo Ridenti, Elide Rugai Bastos e Denis Rolland, orgs., *Intelectuais e Estado* (Belo Horizonte: Editora UFMG, 2006), 95–120; Luciano Martins, "A Genese de uma Intelligentsia: Os Intelectuais e a Política no Brasil, 1920–1940," *Revista Brasileira de Ciências Sociais*, 2:4 (1987), 65–87.

58. Randal Johnson, "The Dynamics of the Brazilian Literary Field, 1930–1945," *Luso-Brazilian Review*, 31:2 (1994), 5–22. The term "contradictory modernity" comes from Daniel Pécaut, as cited in *Os intelectuais e política no Brasil*, 8. See also, Oliveira, *Cultura é patrimônio*, 78.

59. Bethell, "Politics in Brazil under Vargas, 1930–1945," 61.

60. Simon Schwartzman, Helena Maria Bosquet Bomeny, Vanda Maria Ribeiro Costa, *Tempos de Capanema*, 2ª.edn. (São Paulo: Paz e Terra/Fundação Getúlio Vargas, 2000); Oliveira, *Cultura é patrimônio*, 104–5.

61. Robert M. Levine, "Elite Intervention in Urban Popular Culture in Modern Brazil," *Luso-Brazilian Review*, 21:2 (Winter 1984), 9–22.

62. *Ibid.*, 15.

63. Hertzman, *Making Samba*, Chapter 8.

64. *Ibid.*, 246–49.

65. Ruy Castro, *Rio de Janeiro: Carnival Under Fire*, trans. John Gledson (London: Bloomsbury, 2004), 88–89.

66. Scott Ickes, *African-Brazilian Culture and Regional Identity in Bahia, Brazil* (Gainesville: University of Florida Press, 2013), chapter 5.

67. Castro, *Rio de Janeiro*, 88–89.

68. In the 1980s the Brazilian government constructed the *sambódromo* along the Rua Marquês de Sapucaí as the centerpiece of Rio's *carnaval*. Designed by Oscar Niemeyer, this 700-meter-wide street has concrete grandstands and luxury boxes on either side that hold 90,000 spectators. The parades of the *escolas de samba* now make their way down this corridor each year rather than disrupting traffic on the main thoroughfares of the central city. Chris McGowan and Ricardo Pessanha, *The Brazilian Sound: Samba, Bossa Nova, and the Popular Music of Brazil* (New York: Billboard Books, 1991), 39.

69. Hertzman, *Making Samba*, 153–55.

70. Abreu, "*Mulatas, Crioulos* and *Morenas*: Racial Hierarchy, Gender Relations, and National Identity in Postabolition Popular Song: Southeastern Brazil, 1890–1920," 279.

71. "bem-humorado, bom de bola e de samba, o malandro era mestre em um tipo de postura resumida, nos anos 1950, na famosa expressão 'jeitinho brasileiro.'" Lilia Moritz Schwarcz, *Nem preto nem branco, muito pelo contrário: cor e raça na sociabilidade brasileira* (São Paulo: Claro Enigma, 2012), 61.

72. *Malandragem* "is a way of surviving and of finding meaning and enjoyment in life – an affirmation of sensual pleasures in the face of the most severe difficulties. It is a style of life, a mode of being, that is defined as distinctly Brazilian, and that finds its fullest realization in the *carnaval*." Richard G. Parker, *Bodies, Pleasures, and Passions: Sexual Culture in Contemporary Brazil* (Nashville, TN: Vanderbilt University Press, 2009), 170–71.

73. Hertzman, *Making Samba*, 80–82 and Abreu, "*Mulatas, Crioulos* and *Morenas*," 277.

74. See, Ruben George Oliven, *Violência e cultura no Brasil*, 2ª. edn. (Petrópolis: Vozes, 1983), chapter 3, "A Malandragem na Música Popular Brasileira," 29–60.

75. "[I]n a national survey conducted in 1995, white men declared, by an order of three to one, that *mulatas* were 'better in bed' than *pretas*; for young white men the order was closer to five to one, and two out of three young *negros* were also of this opinion." Burdick, *Blessed Anastácia*, 31.

76. Freyre, *Casa-grande e senzala*, 430.

77. Freyre prominently repeated an old saying, "Branca para casar, mulata para f ..., negra para trabalhar." Freyre, *Casa-grande & senzala*, 40ª.edn., 85.

78. Burdick, *The Color of Sound*, 117.

79. "Salve a morena/A cor morena do Brasil fagueiro... Salve a mulata/Cor de canela ... Salve, salve/Teu carnaval, Brasil." www.letras.mus.br/marchinhas-de-carnaval/528848/[accessed 20 May 2016] For more on Babo and Almirante, see McCann, *Hello, Hello Brazil*, esp. 1–4. Babo was sued by

the brothers who composed the song and the publisher put their names on the credits although Babo's name is most associated with the composition.

80. Alma Guillermoprieto, *Samba* (New York: Knopf, 1990), 180. See, also, Natasha Pravaz, "Brazilian *Mulatice*: Performing Race, Gender, and the Nation," *Journal of Latin American Anthropology*, 8:1 (2003), 116–47.

81. Freyre was not alone in this emphasis on sexuality and mixing. The rise of the emphasis on *mestizaje* in many regions of Latin America in the early twentieth century produces other writers with similar views. "Mestizaje is a sexualized and gendered practice and ideology: it refers to sexual relations and reproduction between men and women perceived as belonging to different races, colors, or ethnicities." Wade et al., *Mestizo Genomics*, 19.

82. "o ideal de mestiçagem acabou se transformando no *locus* da autenticidade nacional, e a categoria *mulata*, em uma espécie de acerto desse ideal. Nessa figura, claramente idealizada e exotizada, residia a possibilidade de promover um precário equilíbrio, em que as diferenças conviveriam intensa e ambiguamente." Schwarcz, *Nem preto nem branco*, 68.

83. Parker, *Bodies, Pleasures, and Passions*, 173.

3

Visualizing *Mestiçagem*

Literature, Film, and the Mulata

In Brazil, popular cinema has acted as a source of collective identification in a modern, increasingly urban world in which the secular nation-state has replaced religion, village or region as the "imagined community."[1]

Stephanie Dennison and Lisa Shaw

A NEW VISUAL CULTURE AND THE FREYREAN *MULATA*

Film forged the second wave for communicating the myth of *mestiço* nationalism following on the first wave of radio and the rise of samba. Although the power and reach of radio continued into the 1960s (and beyond), it was film – the great cultural medium of the twentieth century – that became the second potent technological vehicle for the emerging national conversation around Brazilian identity.[2] From the 1930s to the 1980s, film increasingly functioned as an enormously powerful medium for the construction of mass popular culture – both through the communication of myths, symbols, and rituals meant to be quintessentially Brazilian, and through the circulation of a wide variety of voices and claims on national and regional identity. Film was one of the most powerful media in the creation of collective imaginaries in the twentieth century. Through film, the many competing symbols and discourses of regional and national identity became even more widespread and resonant even as they often clashed and conflicted.[3] With radio, samba emerged as the music most associated with Brazilian identity. In the case of film, two of the most potent images to emerge were those of *carnaval* and the *mulata*. Collectively, the impact of film provided Brazilians with an array of images that eventually became associated (at home and abroad) with

Brazilian culture. *Carnaval* took shape as one of the most powerful of these images and the *mulata* the most potent image of Brazilian sexuality and *mestiçagem* – imagery portrayed in a wide variety of films, genres, and directors. Although film brought a multitude of often conflicting images and ideas to the attention of nearly everyone across the vast reaches of Brazil, by the 1970s and 1980s the most influential (at home and abroad) Brazilian films consolidated Freyre's vision of *mestiçagem* as well as many of its most important symbols and rituals: *carnaval*, samba, and the African contribution to Brazilian civilization.[4]

Radio, film, and television were not simply new forms of technology for Brazilians; they also restructured social and cultural relations as their reach spread across the national territory. The print technologies of the nineteenth century made possible the circulation of newspapers, magazines, and pamphlets on a mass scale.[5] While telegraphy had expanded the great web of Brazilians who were instantly (or nearly) interconnected, telegraphers with their codes served as the gatekeepers or intermediaries in this increasingly national and global information flow. Radio brought a more direct connection through sound helping forge a national aural culture complete with shared events, products, styles, and language. As with Franklin Roosevelt's famous "fireside chats" in the United States, the radio set became a focal point for social encounters and interactions in Brazilian homes and businesses. Film revolutionized this experience by adding a new national visual culture that (by the 1930s) was also aural. Even more so than radio, film offered the promise of access to the products, styles, and ways of life of the modern world, especially to the tens of millions of poor Brazilians, both rural and urban.[6]

As with television in the last decades of the twentieth century, the medium of film permeated and interacted with Brazilian society very differently than radio. When a Brazilian consumer purchased a radio, for example, she – and often a large extended family and neighbors – gained access to new worlds of information at the touch of a switch. Access to films, however, required the consumer to attend a showing, be it in a movie theater or simply on the side of a building in a town plaza. As with vinyl records, one can track taste and response (to some extent) through the purchase of the "product" (be it a record or a movie ticket). Filmmakers, however, could not distribute their product as readily to millions of viewers as could radio by the 1950s. The reach and distribution of film was more fragmented and haphazard than radio (and even more skewed toward urban audiences).[7] Given the precarious nature of the Brazilian film industry over the decades from the 1930s to the 1980s, the creation and distribution of cultural products was more erratic than with record companies and radio stations.[8] Nevertheless, film became one of the most powerful and widespread media in Brazil in the second half of the twentieth century and a potent means to help create a truly national cultural conversation from Acre to Alagoas, from Roraima to Rio Grande do Sul.

While popular music forges a new language in aural culture, film creates and disseminates an equally powerful visual (as well as aural) culture. Musicians, instruments, and rhythms conveyed both explicitly and implicitly the message of cultural and racial mixture in Brazil, a message eventually picked up and supported by the State. From the 1930s to the 1980s, Brazilian film contributed to the creation of a national visual culture and one of the most potent symbols of Brazilian identity – the *mulata* as the epitome of Brazilian sexuality. In this chapter, I will focus on the *mulata*, sexuality, gender, and identity and how they become central to the *imaginário nacional* through film (as well as literature and television). Much like samba in the world of music, film brought these images to the attention of all Brazilians (and the international community) providing the visual references and evidence, and often the argument, for Gilberto Freyre's vision of Brazil.

The mythical *mulata* and her allure form a powerful and enduring symbol across centuries of Brazilian history, from the colonial era to the present.[9] From colonial writers, to nineteenth-century travel accounts, to the works of Gilberto Freyre in the mid-twentieth century, the supposed Brazilian male's preference for the *mulata* has been asserted, analyzed, and deconstructed. She is one of the most pervasive images in Brazilian culture, and in the twentieth century becomes the preeminent archetype of Brazilian female sexuality.[10] As Alma Guillermoprieto's quote at the end of the last chapter emphasized, the *mulata* has also come to symbolize the very essence of Brazil – *mestiçagem*. Gilberto Freyre did not create this powerful image of the *mulata*, but his vision of *mestiçagem* would thrust her to the center stage of the narrative of Brazilian identity.[11] The *mulata* would become one of the most prominent icons in Brazilian film in the twentieth century.

The very definition of *mulata* illustrates the fluidity and ambiguity of Brazilian color categories. In a society where all skin tones are in the eye of the beholder, the *mulata* may be of racially mixed heritage but she can range from dark to light. Some would argue that the iconic *mulata* is actually a *morena* (literally, brown), a lighter-skinned, tanned female with facial features and hair seen by many as only vaguely reminiscent of peoples of African descent.[12] In common speech and perceptions, the term *morena* often becomes a means of lightening one's skin tone and shifting one's status.[13] Recent ethnographic studies complicate the terminology even further showing not only how fluid the use of *morena* and *mulata* are in daily life, but also how even sun-tanned blonde women can be viewed as not "really white."[14] The very disagreement over the "ideal" *mulata* illustrates the fluidity of color categories and the genius of the myth of *mestiçagem* in its inclusiveness.[15]

In Freyre's gendered vision of *mestiçagem* with its profoundly male gaze, the *mulata* plays a central role. She is both the product of the sexual collision of people and the instigator of ongoing cultural and biological mixing. Her beauty and sensuality emerge out of this sexual fusion and they help generate ongoing *mestiçagem*. In one of Freyre's most frequently quoted passages from *Casa-grande*, he first praises the black wet-nurse, "Who suckled us. Who fed us, mashing our food with her own hands. The old black woman who told us our first tales of the boogeyman and ghosts [*bicho e mal-assombrado*]." He then goes on to say, "Of the *mulata* who relieved us of our first *bicho-de-pé* [flea embedded in foot], of a pruriency that was so enjoyable. Who initiated us into physical love and gave us, to the creaking of a canvas cot, the first complete sensation of being a man."[16] This fascination with the black nanny and the *mulata*, as some writers have suggested, no doubt reflects Freyre's own personal efforts to work through his own sexual development and history as he wrote a narrative of his own society's development.[17]

As with the other symbols, rituals, and beliefs surrounding the myth of *mestiçagem*, the image of the sensual *mulata* beauty is largely a creation of the mid-twentieth century.[18] Although the image appears much earlier in written sources, the image of the highly sexualized, beautiful, and alluring *mulata*, so often proclaimed as the epitome of Brazilian sexuality and sensuality, takes shapes with the emergence of Modernism and the work of Freyre. In his deeply male vision of *mestiçagem*, the *mulata* plays a pivotal role. The rise of the *mulata* as a sexual icon of Brazilian national identity is central to the ascent of Freyre's vision. Through Brazilian literature (especially in the work of Jorge Amado) and in film (especially the screen versions of Amado's novels), and as the sensual centerpiece of *carnaval* in Rio de Janeiro, the *mulata* became by the late twentieth century one of the most potent and pervasive images in Brazil and of Brazil.[19]

CARMEN MIRANDA: AN ICONIC CINEMATIC *MULATA*?

As with radio and popular music, the role of Rio de Janeiro as the cultural and political capital of Brazil in the early twentieth century profoundly shaped the emergence of film and the dominant motifs in popular cinema. From the origins of the production of film at the beginning of the twentieth century, until the rise of São Paulo in the postwar decades, the vast majority of Brazilian film production emerged out of Rio de Janeiro. Prior to the 1920s, the majority of films viewed in Brazil were locally produced. By the 1930s, the power of Hollywood and U.S. cinema had become a permanent feature of the cultural landscape. As with music, the constant interaction of the regional, national, and international shapes the images on Brazilian theater screens and the production of films in Brazil.[20] Although I will draw on international cinema in this chapter, especially to emphasize the conversation between the foreign and the national, my focus here is on the films and images produced in Brazil. In particular, I am interested in two iconic female figures at two moments I consider transformative to the construction of Brazilian identity: Carmen Miranda in the 1930s and 1940s and Sonia Braga in the 1970s and 1980s. Through their on-screen appeal and sensuality, both women came to embody *mestiço* nationalism via the blending of African and European cultures (and to a lesser extent, indigenous ones). Miranda achieved this synthesis through her music, costumes, and dance, at first in Brazil and then in Hollywood and the world stage that cinema offered. Braga became the premier visual image of *mestiço* nationalism through her portrayal of iconic *mulatas* in the cinema (and television) of the 1970s and 1980s. In some of the most important films, she brought to the screen the most emblematic figures of print culture – most prominently the best known *mulata* in Brazilian literary culture, Gabriela in Jorge Amado's classic novel, *Gabriela, Clove and Cinnamon.*[21]

In many ways, Carmen Miranda brought visually to the silver screen the very essence of the *mestiço* nationalism projected aurally in samba on the radio. As many have noted, it is a powerful irony that a very light-skinned woman, born in Portugal, came to epitomize for Brazilians, and even more so, the world, the "essence" of Brazilian identity. Miranda's singing, dancing, and costumes all adapted, synthesized, and transformed the most fundamental elements of samba, *carnaval*, and Afro-Brazilian culture (via the image of the *baiana*). At the very moment in the 1930s and 1940s when the elemental symbols, rituals, and beliefs that would form the core of Brazilian identity were emerging, Carmen Miranda became their most important intermediary and icon.[22] Gilberto Freyre even singled out Miranda's singing and dancing in *Sobrados e mucambos* (the follow-up in 1936 to *Casa-grande*), as emblematic of the fusion of African elements into the core of Brazilian popular culture.[23]

Just as the new technology of radio facilitated the emergence of samba as a national form of music, the florescence of the talking film in the 1930s and 1940s helped make Carmen Miranda a national icon, and consolidated samba, *carnaval*, and Afro-Brazilian culture as central to national identity. A new style of low-budget musical comedy, the *chanchada*, became the principal vehicle, "the basic narrative"[24] in Brazilian popular cinema, which would bring to all of Brazil the most salient images and sounds that would take shape in the *imaginário nacional*. Drawing on elements of the *teatros de revista* (a sort of burlesque music hall) in late nineteenth- and early twentieth-century Rio de Janeiro, the *chanchada* drew heavily on popular culture with its music, parody, satire, and comedy. *Malandragem* was a power ethos of many of the *chanchadas* and the sensual *mulata* was a recurring motif.[25] In the words of two historians of Brazilian cinema, "*Chanchadas* mixed the circus, *carnaval*, radio and theater in films that depicted the Brazilian *malandro*, the unemployed, landlords and maids, always trying to reach a larger public, with simple language coming from other artistic works that were already successful."[26] This film genre both imitated and diverged from the Hollywood musicals that flooded the Brazilian market in the 1930s and 1940s. According to Gustavo Dahl, the *chanchada* became "profoundly original, modern and Brazilian."[27] The *chanchadas* were cheap, easy to make, and a reliable source of revenue for the principal film studios.

Three studios dominated Brazilian film production in the 1930s and 1940s: Cinédia, Atlântida, and Vera Cruz – all based in Rio de Janeiro. Each, in its own way, took up national themes and crafted films that projected local customs and traditions to domestic audiences. Vera Cruz became known for its efforts to produce high-quality films that could compete with Hollywood. Atlântida became the principal producer of *chanchadas*. Through its close relationship with the most powerful chain of theaters in the country, those controlled by Luís Severiano Ribeiro, the studio guaranteed a wide distribution of its products. Cinédia concentrated on films with Brazilian themes such as *carnaval* and musicals. Carmen Miranda emerged as a star in the musicals of Cinédia in the 1930s.[28]

FIGURE 3.1 Carmen Miranda circa 1945
Source: Photo by NBC Television/Getty Images

One of the iconic figures of the twentieth century, Carmen Miranda is a woman whose image conjures up very different meanings in Brazil and the United States.[29] Born in a small village in northern Portugal in early 1909, Maria do Carmo Miranda da Cunha arrived in Brazil at the age of ten months with her immigrant family. Her father was a barber and she and her six siblings grew up in humble conditions in Rio de Janeiro, in the heart of the city. She went to work as a teenager as a seamstress and hatmaker, skills that would serve her well in designing and producing her own well-known costumes. By her early twenties she had secured a contract with Rádio Mayrink Veiga and began to appear in films. Mayrink Veiga's station had an enormous range covering the states of Rio de Janeiro, Minas Gerais, Espirito Santo, parts of São Paulo, and even reaching Bahia and Pernambuco and other areas in the Northeast.[30] In the early 1930s, Miranda rapidly became a major star, first on the radio and then on film. She benefitted from the florescence of the incredibly rich musical scene of the 1930s in Rio de Janeiro with its gifted composers and musicians. She would become the most prominent voice and image of popular music in the 1930s. Just as radio and cinema propelled the sounds and images of samba and *carnaval* into a national and international stage, Miranda emerged as the greatest star on those stages. In the age before the word became fashionable, she was a celebrity.

Within a few years in the early 1930s, Miranda constructed an image that would make her a superstar in Brazil, and then in Hollywood films. Very cleverly, she moved from the typical female singer to a charismatic performer who sang and danced her way to international fame by blending samba, *carnaval*, tropical imagery, and key elements of Afro-Brazilian culture. Most notably, she appropriated the image of the *baiana* – the traditional black woman from Bahia with her long skirts, turban, and jewelry.[31] In 1932 and 1933, she recorded a series of enormously successful sambas by some of the great composers of the period – Cartola, André Filho, Donga, Assis Valente, and others.[32] At the same time, her musical show increasingly drew on popular dance and she even claimed to have become a *sambista de favela* (samba dancer from the slums) – something she claims to have learned from *as mulatas dos morros* (the *mulatas* from the hills/slums). In the words of her most thorough biographer, Ruy Castro, Carmen Miranda was the first Brazilian woman "to create for herself a public personality – and to make a living from it."[33]

Robert Stam has pointed out that Miranda may have been the flamboyant and campy "Latin" bombshell to international audiences, but to Brazilian audiences she had created an identity and performance style that was deeply indebted to Afro-Brazilian culture. "This debt," he asserts, "is multidimensional, having to with her body language and kinetics, with her samba dance steps, with the use of her voice as an instrument, with her percussive approach to tongue-twisting lyrics (a distant cousin to 'scat' singing), with her talking-style singing (as in blues), and with her capacity for improvisation."[34] Miranda originally fashioned her famous "tutti-fruti" costume for her role in the 1939 *chanchada, Banana da terra* (Banana of the Land), where she sang the Dorival Caymmi composition, "*O que é que a baiana tem?*" (What Does the Baiana Have?).[35] Out of this collaboration, two powerful new icons of Brazilian national and regional identity would emerge over the next two decades. Caymmi's music and lyrics (indeed, even his costume advice) launched Miranda's new persona as a "white baiana," and Miranda's successful performance of Caymmi's composition helped launch this novice composer's long career as an icon of Northeastern music and identity.[36]

A musical comedy that self-consciously parodied Brazilian symbols and imagery, it also included a performance of the song "*A jardineira*" by one of the greatest samba singers of all time, Orlando Silva, and many scenes from *carnaval* in Rio. The very light-skinned Carmen Miranda adapted and adopted all these features of Afro-Brazilian culture and brought them to the heart of Brazilian cinema and the *imaginário nacional*.[37] According to one of her biographers, during *carnaval*, in the aftermath of the release of *Banana da terra*, "almost every man who participated in the parades along the streets of Rio wore a *baiana* – not quite the classic Bahian costume, but the new Miranda version. Even more striking was that the women, who generally kept away from the streets but participated in balls and contests, also had discovered the *baiana*."[38] In Salvador, the home of the *baianas*, Miranda's influence caused a "fashion craze" among middle-class and elite women in the 1940s and 1950s for jewelry "associated with African-Bahian women, as a fashion statement and status symbol."[39] As her biographers have noted, Carmen Miranda crystallized and catalyzed many of the symbols and images of Afro-Bahian culture that were already part of the *imaginário* of cariocas. She drew upon this rich set of images and traditions that had long been part of the culture of Rio and Salvador, and recast it – as Brazilian.[40]

No doubt, a dark-skinned Brazilian performer would never have been able to pull this off. She became the embodiment of the Freyrean argument that all Brazilians (even one born in Portugal!) carried with them the traces of Africa in their cultural heritage even if not in their genes. Much like Elvis Presley in the U.S. in the 1950s, Carmen Miranda learned music and dance from peoples of African descent, gave it her own personal interpretation, and helped make this music and dance more widely accepted than it had been previously.[41] The color line that Elvis crossed was clearly more defined and rigid, yet Miranda transited that much broader and blurred line in Brazil helping consolidate Afro-Brazilian cultural symbols and rituals as central to national identity. She was perhaps the most spectacular example of this cultural mediation (as was Elvis in the United States), but many others were moving Brazil in the same direction in the 1930s and 1940s. In those decades, the city of Salvador da Bahia and its rich Afro-Brazilian culture were emerging as elements of both regional and national identity as the "Mama Africa" of Brazil. Like Elvis, Carmen's timing and talent combined to make them into both superstars and powerful cultural mediators.[42]

The creation of Carmen Miranda's persona demonstrates the power of the new media – radio and film – as instruments of both national and regional identity formation. She had already established herself as one of Brazil's biggest radio performers, and as she transitioned to a film star she discovered the persona that would make her an international superstar, and she unwittingly became the vehicle for the consolidation of Afro-Bahian culture, both as the defining identity of a region and as a central element of Brazilian national identity. If Gilberto Freyre's *mestiçagem* made Brazil Brazil, the Northeast was its birthplace and Bahia the black mother (*mãe preta*) of all Brazilians. From the 1930s to the 1960s, as Brazilian identity crystallized around the myth of *mestiçagem*, other regional identities were taking shape in conversation with national identity and, just as in the national conversation, the regional conversations involved a complex process of negotiation, mediation, and filtering involving all sectors of society.[43]

Within months of the release of Miranda's iconic film, visiting American musical impresario Lee Shubert saw her perform "*O que é que a baiana tem?*" at the Urca Casino. For more than three years, Miranda had been performing at the casino, perfecting her act in front of live audiences. After Shubert saw her perform, he immediately issued an invitation to work for him in the U.S. and, within a few months, she was onstage in New York, and soon after on her way to Hollywood.[44] She would spend nearly the rest of her short life (until her death in 1955) in the U.S.[45] In the mid-1940s, Miranda became the biggest box office star in Hollywood (and the world) in musicals that displayed her singing and dancing skills with elaborate variations of her *baiana* costume. For Hollywood, she lost her Brazilianness and became a generic Latina, much to the chagrin of her Brazilian fans.[46]

CARNAVAL AND CINEMA

The full-blown emergence of the ritual of *carnaval* in Rio de Janeiro simultaneously with the arrival of cinema with sound proved a potent combination for the convergence of the aims of the State and the desires of the *povo*. *Carnaval* in the twentieth century, especially *carnaval* in Rio de Janeiro, has become perhaps the most striking ritual enactment of the Freyrean vision of *mestiçagem* with an array of images and symbolism, all distilled into a few days of national celebration. Along with *futebol*, this Catholic pre-Lenten festival with its bacchanalian revelry has become linked with the very "essence" of

Brazil. Despite its close association with contemporary Brazilian culture, *carnaval* has only emerged in its present form in the mid-twentieth century. *Carnaval* originated in the Christian world in the Middle Ages as several days of festivities prior to the beginning of Lent, the period of fasting and penitence prior to Easter. In Portugal, these activities were known as the *entrudo*. On both sides of the Atlantic, the Portuguese staged mock street battles in the days before Lent with opposing groups throwing eggs, water, and flour at each other. In nineteenth-century Brazil, these battles became so destructive and violent that the government attempted to ban them. Simultaneously, Africans and Afro-Brazilians had begun to celebrate by dancing and playing music in the streets. The white elites viewed these festivities with disdain and horror at the openly sexual overtones of the dances.[47]

Gradually, in the late nineteenth century, the music and dancing became widespread and accepted, and more ritualized. The musicians normally played drums, whistles, and rattles, and danced the *lundu* (of Angolan derivation), which gradually evolved into samba. In the first decades of the twentieth century in Rio de Janeiro, clubs of dancers and musicians began to take shape in the *favelas* and march through the streets as "schools" (*escolas*). The first legally recognized samba school was the legendary Estação Primeira de Mangueira, located in a neighborhood on the Estrada de Ferro Central running into the heart of the city. The samba schools and the street *carnaval* with its parades and music were dominated by Afro-Brazilians.[48] In the first half of the century this more Africanized street festival gradually overtook and swept aside the "paler" and more affluent *carnaval* of the middle and upper classes. The *carnaval* of the upper classes gave way to *carnaval pequeno* or *popular*. By the 1950s, the *carnaval do povo* had become the dominant form of what had become the most Brazilian of all rituals, and the *carioca* version had emerged as the supreme image and version in Brazil.[49] To play off the words of Ruy Castro, the celebration of the upper classes was "from the navel upwards" while *carnaval do povo* was from the navel downwards.[50]

During the early decades of silent film, *carnaval* provided the focus for dozens of films. With the advent of "talkies" it became possible to bring the full visual and aural force of *carnaval* to the silver screen. As some have pointed out, in the 1930s "the promotion of carnival music became the raison d'etre" for many films and the *chanchada* developed along with these "carnival" films. *Alô, alô, Brasil* (1935) set the basic formula with loosely connected scenes designed to showcase the musical talents of radio stars, in this particular case, Carmen Miranda and her younger sister,

Aurora. With the increasingly technical sophistication of sound, movie theaters became one of the principal venues for promoting *carnaval* as a national ritual, samba as the most Brazilian of music and dance, and Carmen Miranda as Brazil's biggest star.[51]

Just as the Brazilian studios made *carnaval* the backdrop for so many films (especially *chanchadas*) in the 1930s, the various regimes of Getúlio Vargas very astutely chose to appropriate Rio's version of *carnaval* as a showcase for Brazilian culture, especially to the rest of the world.[52] The convergence of emerging popular culture, film, and the State produced a powerful combination that propelled *carnaval* to the forefront of the narrative of Brazilian identity. The efforts of Getúlio Vargas to centralize power and create a nation spurred him to employ every tool available to create a single, unified Brazilian identity. As we saw in the previous chapter, Vargas recognized the emerging power of radio and tried to appropriate it for his own objectives. The *Hora do Brasil* remains one of the more vivid examples of the limits of the ability of the State to impose its cultural will. In a 1934 address to the Association of Brazilian Film Producers (*Associação Cinematográfica de Produtores Brasileiros*), Vargas proclaimed, "cinema will be the book of luminous images in which our coastal and rural populations will learn to love Brazil, increasing confidence in the Fatherland. For the mass of illiterates, it will be the most perfect, the easiest, and the most impressive pedagogical tool." He then went on to say,

Combining the cinema with radio and the rational cultivation of sports, the government will complete an articulated system of mental, moral, and hygienic education, endowing Brazil with the indispensable tools for the development of an enterprising, hardy, and virile people. And the people that comes into being in this way will be worthy of the enviable heritage it receives.[53]

Although Vargas and his cultural managers may have envisioned film as a tool for national development and the formation of national identity, like radio, the State could attempt to shape and guide the Brazilian population, but it could not dictate or impose unilaterally its vision of Brazil. The State and movie studios may have had the upper hand in providing the menu of choices for consumers but, in the end, the preferences and desires of the public determined which films succeeded or failed at the box office. As with samba on the radio, it was the collective response of hundreds of thousands, even millions, of the public who "voted" with their tickets for the songs, films, singers, and stars who would top the popularity charts. Complicating and multiplying the array of images, sounds, and choices on the screen was the decades-long competition among Brazilian and foreign-produced films.

As scholars of transnational studies have emphasized in recent years, the old categories of "foreign" and "national" are overly simplistic and rigid. As I emphasize throughout this book, the local, national, and foreign are always intertwined, interacting, and conversing. Filmmakers in Brazil, from the very beginning of the era of film, were in conversation with European and (to a lesser extent) with U.S. filmmakers. Whether it was new technology, new techniques, or innovative modes of storytelling, the emergence of Brazilian cinema has been since its inception part of a transatlantic community.[54] With the rise of studios in Brazil, the issue of "ownership" further illustrates this interaction of the "domestic" and the "foreign." While some studios were financed by local capital, others were a mix of Brazilian and foreign investors. One of the most successful Brazilian studios and directors in the 1930s and 1940s, Cinédia led by Adhemar Gonzaga, worked closely with the U.S. producer/director Wallace Downey to create a string of hits including the quintessential *chanchada, Alô, alô, Brasil.*[55]

Downey's relationship with Gonzaga speaks volumes to the intertwining of the foreign and the domestic. Arriving in Brazil in the late 1920s as a representative of Columbia Records, over the next two decades Downey became one of the principal entrepreneurs in Brazilian recording and filmmaking. Bringing with him not only foreign capital, but also access to the latest technology and techniques, Downey played an important role in the 1930s and 1940s in the florescence of radio and cinema. His first collaboration with Gonzaga, one of the great pioneers of Brazilian cinema, was the production of *Alô, alô, Brasil.* The method was simple and straightforward: string together a series of musical numbers performed by the biggest radio stars with a minimal script to hold (loosely) the numbers together. The objective was straightforward: attract the masses to theaters. *Carnaval* was a favorite setting.[56] Was this most Brazilian of Brazilian films, directed by an American, a Brazilian film? Much like *Casa-grande e senzala*, this film that becomes identified with the essence of Brazilian identity emerged out of the interaction and intermixing of the "domestic" and the "foreign."

This interaction became even more complex and transnational with the departure of Miranda for the United States in 1939. Over the next decade she would become one of the biggest box office stars in the world, a stardom built on the singing, costumes, and dancing she brought from Brazil, but adapted into a generically "Latin" style for international audiences.[57] Although quickly dubbed the "Brazilian Bombshell," Carmen Miranda's on-screen image blended her *baiana* persona along with scenes, music, and dance from a variety of Latin American countries. Most non-Brazilians probably saw her as "Latin" – a woman from somewhere in Latin America. For many Brazilians, Carmen Miranda's roles and performances in the 1940s appeared to be a betrayal of her *brasilidade*, a sell out to Hollywood style and marketing. When she returned to Rio in 1940, her sold out show in front of *carioca* high society was a disaster, one she never forgot.[58] She would not return to Brazil for another fourteen years. Miranda's status as a "true" Brazilian, and an international superstar indelibly imprinted the imagery of Afro-Brazilian culture in the *imaginário nacional* – samba, *carnaval*, the *baiana*.

MESTIÇO NATIONALISM, *CINEMA NOVO*, AND *BOSSA NOVA*

From the 1950s through the 1980s, the images of *mestiço* nationalism and the *mulata* became increasingly powerful and prevalent in print, aural, and visual culture amidst an ideological war between both the Right and the Left in Brazil. Throughout these Cold War decades, differing versions of nationalism clashed across the political spectrum, but both the Right and the Left converged on their imagery of Brazil as the result of a collision of peoples and cultures from the Americas, Africa, and Europe. By the 1960s, the Freyrean vision of *mestiçagem*, combined with the notion of racial democracy, became the official ideology of the right-wing military regime. In the hands of the best-known novelists and filmmakers, *mestiçagem* became a means to seek the authentic Brazil – in its people (*povo*) – and in the hands of the radical filmmakers of the *Cinema Novo*, to highlight the bankruptcy of the claims of racial democracy. While many scholars have been consumed with efforts to "debunk" and "unmask" the claims of racial democracy, they have too often lost sight of the more basic and widespread acceptance of the foundational myth of *mestiçagem*.

In many ways, the popular film and music of the 1960s and 1970s became the successors of the Modernists of the 1920s and 1930s. Just as Brazilian Modernism in the 1920s was a sort of a countercultural movement against "bourgeois" artistic orthodoxy, *Cinema Novo* in film and *Tropicalismo* in popular music formed a countercultural movement against the orthodoxy of the times. In both cases, these "rebels with a cause" would eventually become the icons of mainstream Brazilian culture. *Cinema Novo* returned to "the modernist problematic of discovering Brazil's identity through confronting its roots, and assessing the national unconscious through its archetypes."[59] Even while rejecting racial democracy, the myth of *mestiçagem* served as a powerful trope in the works of many of these radical filmmakers, testimony to the power of the myth even for the critics of Freyre.

Many of the directors of the *Cinema Novo* movement in the 1950s and 1960s sought to create a "national" and "popular" cinema that would be "a socially progressive cinema nourished by popular Brazilian traditions."[60] Much like the intellectuals who helped popularize samba, these filmmakers consciously saw themselves as intermediaries between elite and popular classes. Nelson Pereira dos Santos, Glauber Rocha, Ruy Guerra, and others created some of the most innovative films of the 1950s and 1960s, cinema that produced some of the most vivid and enduring images of Brazil for the rest of the world. Films such as Nelson Pereira dos Santos's stark portrayal of drought and death in the Northeast in *Vidas secas* (*Barren Lives*, 1963) and Glauber Rocha's *Deus e diabo na terra do sol* (*Black God, White Devil*, 1964) with its depiction of millenarianism in the backlands, delved deeply into the most pressing social issues of the times.[61] These directors brought poverty, prejudice, race, and class to the forefront in their films as they sought to expose the realities of Brazilian society and culture. In the process, they also reinforced the developing regional stereotypes, emphasized regional, class, and racial hierarchies, and often highlighted the cultural *mestiçagem* that had come to dominate the discourse on national identity by the 1960s.

As with many other facets of Brazilian identity, the most powerful cinematic influence (in Brazil and abroad) in these years arose out of a convergence of the regional, national, and international. The most spectacular example of these converging influences came not from *Cinema Novo* but from the Franco-Brazilian film *Black Orpheus* (1959), which "initiated millions of non-Brazilians into Brazilian culture, forging in the international consciousness a powerful association between three related concepts: Brazilianness, blackness, and carnival."[62] While hugely successful on the international film circuit, the film created controversy within Brazil as full of stereotypes and exoticism.[63] The French director, Marcel Camus, and his screenwriter, Jacques Viot, spent months in Rio de Janeiro and then filmed the movie with Brazilian actors, crew, and musicians. Their film is a screen adaptation of the 1956 play *Orfeu da conceição*, written by the great Brazilian poet and composer Vinícius de Morais.[64] Much like *Casa-grande*, the play develops out of many experiences and influences. A career diplomat who served all over the world, Vinícius later wrote that the embryo of the project took shape during an evening in Rio with the

American writer Waldo Frank. On a visit to the Praia do Pinto *favela* in Leblon, Frank marveled at the sensual dancing, remarking to the Brazilian poet that the *favelados* seemed like Greeks, before Greek culture developed. The first act of the script took shape during Rio's *carnaval* in 1942 when Vinícius's houseguest was Orson Welles, then filming his ill-fated *It's All True*.[65] He did not complete the play until many years later while living in Los Angeles. Based on the Greek myth of Orpheus and Eurydice, the story of their love, her death, and Orpheus's descent into the underworld (unsuccessfully) to retrieve her, Vinícius sets the tale amidst *carnaval* in Rio, a samba school, and Afro-Brazilian religious ceremonies.[66]

The soundtrack for the film featured the most innovative music of the late 1950s, an emerging style that came to be known as *bossa nova* (new wave). With songs by Luis Bonfá, Antônio Carlos Jobim, and João Gilberto, the film helped launch *bossa nova* as an international phenomenon.[67] Much like the music of Carmen Miranda, *bossa nova* helped incorporate Afro-Brazilian influences into national culture and world music although in ways that were very distinct from samba. In the hands of Jobim and Gilberto, the intense and frenetic samba became cool and a form of "counterpoint samba." Cool and sophisticated, *bossa nova* largely emerged out of the white, middle-class suburbs of the Zona Sul in Rio de Janeiro in the 1950s and early 1960s.[68] Much like jazz in the United States, *bossa nova* reinterpreted and reinvented African influences and blended with jazz as it became an international phenomenon. For some critics, this reinvention downplayed the more African influences in samba and made it "whiter," a powerful irony given the origins of the jazz that was now influencing samba. When Jobim and Gilberto (and his wife Astrud) came to New York in the early 1960s, they recorded with the stellar saxophonist Stan Getz to produce one of the greatest jazz albums ever. The recording of *The Girl from Ipanema* (written by Jobim and Morais), sung by Astrud Gilberto in English and Portuguese, became an international sensation.[69]

The film and its *bossa nova* soundtrack reflect the dual sides of the myth of *mestiçagem*. While the French filmmakers took the Brazilian play and heightened the Afro-Brazilian imagery making it even more Africanized, *bossa nova* provided the film with a more "whitened" sound. In the hands of the composers and musicians, samba became counterpoint samba – cooler, whiter, more middle class, and less African, less Afro-Brazilian. While both images and sound stay grounded in the dynamic discourse of cultural and racial mixture, the foreigners who made the film (unconsciously, no doubt) offer the imagery of *mestiçagem* as the darkening of

Brazil. The newly emerging music from the Zona Sul of Rio (again, unconsciously) produced the sound of *mestiçagem* in forms that many critics would argue is the whitening of Brazilian culture. Technically complex, filled with images of individual "love, smiles, and flowers," and associated with the affluent middle classes, *bossa nova* could not, however, compete for the hearts of the Brazilian *povo* on the same scale as samba and other forms of popular music.[70]

Cinema Novo and *bossa nova* both helped bring Brazil to international attention by the 1960s. Ironically, it was a French-produced and -directed film that emerged as the most visible international image of both these Brazilian cultural movements. In 1959 and 1960, *Black Orpheus* won the Palme d'Or at the Cannes Film Festival, the Academy Award for Best Foreign Language Film, and a Golden Globe for Best Foreign Film. In Europe and the United States, the film helped to make *carnaval* and *bossa nova* the unforgettable images of Brazil in the minds of the public. The international acclaim for the film also impressed upon Brazilians the importance of samba and *carnaval* as quintessentially Brazilian cultural artifacts. Arguably, Carmen Miranda introduced a first wave of samba to the world in the 1940s, *Black Orpheus* generated a second wave in the 1960s, paving the way for an "explosion of samba and axé music around the world in the 1980s and 1990s."[71]

CREATING THE ICONIC *MULATA*: JORGE AMADO AND SONIA BRAGA

Film and music may have propelled images and sounds of Brazil onto a global stage in the 1950s and 1960s, but it was the literature of Jorge Amado that provided the most powerful and enduring images of *mestiço* nationalism and the sensual *mulata* in the decades after 1950. The images Amado created in print were then translated to the screen and his literary image of the sensual *mulata* was brought to life in the work of the actress Sonia Braga on television and in film. A native of Ilhéus in southern Bahia, Jorge Amado published his first novel in 1932 at the age of 19. Nearly all of his novels (some two dozen) are set in the Northeast, often in the city of Salvador, where he lived for decades (until his death in 2001). Although his early work focused on the social issues and harsh realities of life in the Northeast, beginning in the 1950s his best-known works celebrated the exuberance and sensuality of life in Bahia, the most African and racially mixed of Brazil's large cities.[72] His work, in many ways, is a window into the *mulato* soul of Brazil. As Amado himself once said, "It's enough to see a mulata walk on the beach or down the street to understand the mysteries of *mestiçagem*, cultural syncretism, and a certain national specificity."[73]

While Gilberto Freyre's voluminous writings addressed a primarily elite, white, reading public, Amado's work takes the imagery of *mestiçagem* to a vast public in Brazil (and abroad), through his record-breaking book sales in the decades after 1958, and then through the medium of cinema (and later, television). In *Gabriela, cravo e canela* [*Gabriela, Clove and Cinnamon*] (1958), *Dona Flor e seus dois maridos* [*Dona Flor and Her Two Husbands*] (1966), and *Tenda dos milagres* [*Tent of Miracles*] (1969) – to cite the most notable examples – Amado paints a vision of Brazil that brings to life in fiction the very essence of the Freyrean vision of *mestiço* nationalism.[74] Freyre's Pernambuco formed the archetype of his Brazil with its delicious cuisine, sounds, and carnal sensuality. Amado's Bahia with its sights, sounds, smells, and tastes (and its sensuality) supplants Pernambuco as the most Brazilian of Brazilian regions. As Amado became the best-selling author in Brazilian publishing history (at home and abroad), his imagery – especially of the sensual *mulata* – became by the 1980s some of the most pervasive and potent imagery in both the *imaginário nacional* and *internacional*. The translation of *Gabriela* into many languages quickly made it the best-known Brazilian novel of all time.[75] In Brazil, the *telenovela* version of *Gabriela* (1975) consolidated the image of this sexy *mulata* at the center of Brazilian culture and Sonia Braga as the iconic symbol of the *mulata*. The film version of *Dona Flor* (1976), also starring Sonia Braga, became the biggest box office success in Brazilian film history, an achievement not eclipsed for thirty-five years.[76]

As numerous cultural critics have pointed out, *Gabriela* represents a major turning point in the literary career of Amado.[77] In the previous quarter-century, his work had largely focused on issues of social injustice, poverty, and inequities in the Brazilian society. With *Gabriela*, his writing retained its strong sense of the inequalities and injustices in Brazil, but the role of humor, exuberance, and the picaresque emerged prominently and these features would dominate his work for the rest of his life (more than four more decades). Set in Ilhéus in the 1920s, the novel tells the story of the young, beautiful *mulata*, Gabriela, who arrives in town with impoverished migrants from the backlands. An extraordinary cook, she is soon working for Nacib Saad, the Syrian immigrant owner of a local bar. The larger context of the story is the struggle between those who seek to modernize the port city and the traditionalists who have little interest in transforming their town. Like much of Amado's subsequent work, the novel is a luxuriating tour through the cuisine, customs, and traditions of the Northeast. At the center of the plot is the alluring, seductive, yet always elusive, Gabriela.[78] Sonia Braga brought Gabriela to life on both television and the cinema screen. She indelibly consolidated her role as the essence of the Brazilian *mulata* in her 1980 role in the film version of Amado's *Dona Flor and Her Two Husbands*.

Few films manage to capture and communicate images that sum up a nation's identity at a particular historical moment. Bruno Barreto's *Dona Flor and Her Two Husbands* brilliantly conveys Freyre's vision of Brazilian culture and identity at the very moment this vision's power peaks, and then begins to decline.[79] Through its phenomenal international box office success the film offers to the rest of the world this alluring and compelling vision. The film has been a very powerful influence shaping the way tens of millions of Brazilians and non-Brazilians "imagine" Brazil. Filmed on locations in Salvador, Barreto's cinematic version of Amado's 1966 novel portrays a Brazil profoundly shaped by centuries of *mestiçagem*, primarily of Portuguese and African people. The film and the novel brilliantly capture this vision of *mestiçagem* through Bahia's food, religions, *carnaval*, and race relations. At the center of this vision of Brazilian culture and identity is the *mulata*, the light-skinned, racially mixed beauty who (in this vision) epitomizes the luxuriance and sensuality of Brazilian *mestiçagem*. The film consolidated (especially for international audiences) the image of this sexy *mulata* at the center of Brazilian culture, and the actress Sonia Braga as the ultimate symbol of the Brazilian *mulata*.

As the film opens, Vadinho (José Wilker), the *bon vivant* husband of Flor, drops dead on the streets of Salvador surrounded by his fellow *carnaval* revelers. As Flor (played by Sonia Braga) grieves over the coffin of her departed husband, the *carnaval* festivities continue outside the wake on the streets of Salvador. Much of the first half of the film flashes back through their life together and we see how much Flor loved Vadinho's sensuality and lovemaking, but fought with him constantly over his gambling, womanizing, and drinking. Vadinho is the iconic *malandro* in Brazilian culture, the clever but always morally dubious rogue. In the second half of the film, the dull but respectable local pharmacist, Teodoro (Mauro Mendonça), courts and marries Dona Flor. The ghost of Vadinho appears, visible only to Flor (most of the time he is in the nude), and mocks the pathetic lovemaking of the tendentious and boring Teodoro. As she succumbs to the passionate sexual advances of the phantom Vadinho, Dona Flor eventually realizes that she has the best of both worlds, the sensual and torrid lovemaking of her (invisible)

FIGURE 3.2 Sonia Braga circa 1982
Source: Photo by Sonia Moskowitz/IMAGES/Getty Images

malandro first husband, and a bourgeois life as the wife of her bland yet respected (and visible) second husband. In the final scene, Dona Flor leaves her house and heads down the streets of Salvador with the elegantly dressed Teodoro on one arm, and the completely nude Vadinho on the other.

In retrospect, Barreto's film is something of the culmination of a decades-long process of projecting the power of Freyre's myth of *mestiçagem* aurally and visually across all of Brazil and overseas. Film and music propelled images and sounds of Brazil onto a global stage in the 1950s and 1960s bringing this vision of *mestiçagem* to all Brazilians and the world. Carmen Miranda in the 1940s and *bossa nova* in the late fifties and early sixties helped forge an international image of Brazil as an exotic and culturally rich land. The novels of Jorge Amado provided the most potent and enduring images of Freyre's myth of *mestiçagem* and the sensual *mulata* in the decades after 1950. The images Amado created in print were translated to the screen – small and large – and his literary image of the sensual *mulata* was brought to life in the work of the alluring Sonia Braga on television and in film.

Many critics have noted the profound irony of the impact of the small- and big-screen versions of *Gabriela* and *Dona Flor* and their star attraction. These films powerfully project the myth of *mestiçagem*, but they also show how that mixing can not only praise the African roots of Brazilian culture but also simultaneously whiten those roots. Much like Carmen Miranda in the 1930s and 1940s, Braga is very light-skinned. (Through her parents, Braga has both indigenous and black ancestors.) Through both makeup and tanning, Braga became a *mulata*, but a very light one, a *morena*.[80] The *mulata* may have become the ultimate male sex fantasy, but in the form of Sonia Braga she also became a very light version of racial mixture. While Miranda donned the traditional costume of the black Afro-Brazilian women of Bahia and made the sounds of samba a national and international pillar of Brazilian culture and identity, in the 1970s Braga darkened her skin through makeup and tanning and rose to international stardom as the emblematic Brazilian *mulata* (as *morena*). After viewing her performances, Jorge Amado himself declared her the living and breathing epitome of the Brazilian *mulata* and "*the* Brazilian muse" and Gilberto Freyre called her "the perfect example of a Brazilian woman."[81]

Amado published *Tenda dos milagres: romance* [*Tent of Miracles: A Novel*] in 1969 and the film version (released in 1977) was directed by Nelson Pereira dos Santos, one of the great figures of the *Cinema Novo*.[82] This novel is perhaps Amado's most exuberant and spirited depiction of *mestiçagem* as the very essence of Brazilian identity. Using humor and satire brilliantly, he constructs two parallel stories – contemporary efforts (led by a pompous American professor) to revive the memory of Pedro Archanjo as one of the early-twentieth-century heroes of Afro-Brazilian culture and letters, and flashbacks to tell the story of Archanjo's life. Probably based on a composite of historical figures, Amado's novel draws primarily on the life of Manuel Querino (1851–1923), a black Bahian who was one of the few early-twentieth-century intellectual figures to both research Afro-Brazilian culture, and to take pride in it. As we saw in the Introduction, he also carefully documented the fusion of cultures (African, European, and indigenous) that produced the rich cuisine, music, dance, and the art of Bahia.[83]

First in print, then on screen, Amado's rich and colorful portraits in some ways provide a bookend at the end of an era for Freyre's bookend at the beginning. The nonfiction, historical vision of *mestiçagem* in *Casa-grande e senzala* provided the intellectual spark that ignited decades of a gradually developing and constantly growing conversation about *mestiçagem* as the central myth of Brazilian society and culture. The enormous sales of his novels and their film versions provided a lush and attractive popular version of *mestiçagem* by the 1980s that helped the Freyrean vision achieve its apogee a half-century after the publication of *Casa-grande*. In the *imaginário nacional* the power of this vision probably reached its climax in the 1980s, in many respects due to the print and film versions of Amado's novels.

Film and television substantially amplified the power of Amado's writing and its influence reaching many more tens of millions in the 1970s and 1980s. They also provided the flesh-and-blood icon of the Brazilian *mulata*, Sonia Braga. In the 1980s, Braga created a screen persona that became for many Brazilians and for the rest of the world the epitome of Brazil's *mestiçagem*, and more specifically, the archetypal Brazilian *mulata*. As Gabriela (on television and in film), as Dona Flor, and in a series of films, Sonia Braga redefined the role of the beautiful, alluring, and sensual *mulata*. As with Carmen Miranda, the powerful irony here is that Braga is also light-skinned and had to resort to makeup and tanning to assume the appearance of *mestiçagem* for her key film roles. Both Miranda in the 1930s and 1940s, and Braga in the 1970s and 1980s, emerged as Brazilian superstars and international celebrities. Both helped to bring *mestiçagem* to the forefront of national popular culture, to make it a stronger mainstream presence, and to reinforce the profoundly gendered Freyrean vision of Brazilian identity.

The hold of Freyre's vision of *mestiçagem* peaked in the 1970s and 1980s and the novels of Jorge Amado as well as their film versions, in effect, crystallized this luxuriant, tropical, and sensual vision just before it began to come under powerful attacks from the emergence of Afro-Brazilian movements that rejected Freyre's vision as racist and wrong-headed, and intellectuals who declared any form of "national identity" an elusive fiction. As the debates over Brazilian identity have intensified and Brazilians in the early twenty-first century, it would be very hard today to produce a film comparable to *Dona Flor*, or a *telenovela* like *Gabriela*, in their ability to capture and communicate so effectively a single vision or narrative of national identity. Whatever one might think of the Freyrean vision of *mestiçagem*, Jorge Amado, Bruno Barreto, and Sonia Braga provide us with unforgettably sensual cinematic images of the most powerful myth of Brazilian identity in the twentieth century.

NOTES

1. Stephanie Dennison and Lisa Shaw, *Popular Cinema in Brazil* (Manchester: Manchester University Press, 2004), 6.
2. In 1946, roughly 50 percent of all Brazilians went to the movies at least once a month with the numbers higher for the poor and the middle class, and lower for the upper classes. Silvana Gontijo, *A voz do povo: IBOPE do Brasil* (Rio de Janeiro: Editora Objetiva, 1996), 83.
3. T. S. Heise, *Remaking Brazil: Contested National Identities in Contemporary Brazilian Cinema* (Cardiff: University of Wales Press, 2012), 1–2.
4. For a wide-ranging and impressive survey of race and Brazilian cinema, see Robert Stam, *Tropical Multiculturalism: A Comparative History of Race in Brazilian Cinema and Culture* (Durham, NC: Duke University Press, 1997).
5. "At the beginning of the twentieth century, the average press run for a daily newspaper in Rio de Janeiro did not exceed 3,000 copies, a number comparable to that in Paris at the beginning of the nineteenth century." Ortiz, "Culture and Society," 121.
6. For a discussion of this cinematic transformation, see Maite Conde, *Consuming Visions: Cinema, Writing, and Modernity in Rio de Janeiro* (Charlottesville: University of Virginia Press, 2012), 9–10.
7. For an example of the possibilities of film viewings in locations as remote as the Amazon, see Garfield, *In Search of the Amazon*, 35.
8. Some of the key studies of Brazilian cinema in English are: Randal Johnson and Robert Stam, eds., *Brazilian Cinema*, Expanded Edition (New York: Columbia University Press, 1995); Randal Johnson, *The Film Industry in Brazil: Culture and the State* (Pittsburgh: University of Pittsburgh Press, 1987); Lúcia Nagib, *Brazil on Screen: Cinema Novo, New Cinema, Utopia* (London: Palgrave Macmillan, 2007); Lisa Shaw and Stephanie Dennison, *Brazilian National Cinema* (London: Routledge, 2007).
9. See, for example, Raymond S. Sayers, *The Negro in Brazilian Literature* (New York: Hispanic Institute in the United States, 1956); Giorgio Marotti, *Black Characters in the Brazilian Novel*, trans. Maria O. Marotti and Harry Lawton (Los Angeles: Center for Afro-American Studies, University of California, Los Angeles, 1987); Russell G. Hamilton, "Gabriela Meets Olodum: Paradoxes of Hybridity, Racial Identity, and Black Consciousness in Contemporary Brazil," *Research in African Literatures*, 38:1 (Spring 2007), esp. 181–84; Abreu, "*Mulatas, Crioulos* and *Morenas*."

10. See, for example, Miller, *Rise and Fall of the Cosmic Race*, esp. chapter 4, "Showcasing Mixed Race in Northeast Brazil," 96–118 and Pravaz, "Brazilian *Mulatice.*" For the role of the *mulata* in Brazilian poetry, see Affonso Romano Sant'Anna, *O canibalismo amoroso* (São Paulo: Editora Brasiliense, 1984), esp. 41–44 and his discussion of "a mulata cordial." For the role of the *mulata* in popular theater in early twentieth-century Rio de Janeiro, see Antonio Herculano Lopes, "Inventing a Mestizo Identity: Musical Theater in Rio de Janeiro 1900–1922," Ph.D. diss., New York University, 2008, esp. chapter 5.

11. "Because the mulata is so much a product of a national ideology about both race and sexuality, it forms a particular set of images that is much more protected and even exalted as a positive reading of national identity, and not one that is criticized as an overly exoticized or overly sexualized image of black women." Goldstein, *Laughter Out of Place*, 112.

12. "The widespread use of moreno is remarkable when one considers that it has never been officially used in the more than one hundred years of Brazilian censuses. However, its centrality in the popular Brazilian classification may be due to its tie to the racial-democracy ideology because it downplays racial differences and emphasizes a common Brazilianness." Telles, *Race in Another America*, 83.

13. For discussions of these terms in contemporary speech, see Alexander Edmonds, *Pretty Modern: Beauty, Sex, and Plastic Surgery in Brazil* (Durham, NC: Duke University Press, 2010), 132–35; and, Kia Lilly Caldwell, *Negras in Brazil: Re-envisioning Black Women, Citizenship, and the Politics of Identity* (New Brunswick, NJ: Rutgers University Press, 2007), 62–63.

14. For a fascinating study of gender, sexuality, race, and aesthetics, see Edmonds, *Pretty Modern*. Citation is from 133.

15. For a discussion of the *morena/mulata* terminology by his informants, see Burdick, *Blessed Anastácia*, esp. 29–32.

16. "Que nos deu de comer, ela própria amolengando na mão o bolão de comida. Da negra velha que nos contou as primeiras histórias de bicho e mal-assombrado. Da mulata que nos tirou o primeiro bicho-de-pé de uma coceira tão boa. Da que nos iniciou no amor físico e nos transmitiu, ao ranger da cama-de-vento, a primeira sensação completa de homem." Freyre, *Casa-grande e senzala*, 343. Translation from Freyre, *The Masters and the Slaves*, 278, with my alterations.

17. On Freyre's own sexual identity, see Needell, "Identity, Race, Gender and Modernity in the Origins of Gilberto Freyre's *Oeuvre*," 51–77.

18. "Embodying an entire ideology, she becomes a representation of Brazil itself – of the Brazilian people, formed from the mixture of three races and cultures, somehow marginal and distant (beneath the equator) from the world's great centers of wealth and power, yet possessing a seductive charm that sets them apart from any other people anywhere on the face of the earth." Parker, *Bodies, Pleasures, and Passions*, 172.

19. For important sociological work on the image of the *mulata* among contemporary Brazilian female adolescents see, Jennifer J. Manthei, "The Brazilian

Mulata: A Wood for All Works," in Hendrik Kraay, ed., *Negotiating Identities in Modern Latin America*, (Calgary: University of Calgary Press, 2007), 189–211.

20. In the mid-1920s, of the more than 1,200 films reviewed by the police censors, a little over a 1,000 were produced in the U.S., followed by France (85), Brazil (52), Germany (24), Portugal (20), and Italy (19). Anita Simis, *Estado e cinema no Brasil* (São Paulo: Annablume/FAPESP, 1996), 74–75.

21. Jorge Amado, *Gabriela, cravo e canela* (São Paulo: Martins, 1958); *Gabriela, Clove and Cinnamon*, trans. James L. Taylor and William L. Grossman (New York: Knopf, 1962).

22. For two key treatments of this moment and Miranda see Stam, *Tropical Multiculturalism*, 80–85 and Dennison and Shaw, *Popular Cinema in Brazil*, 52.

23. "os passos do samba se arredondando na dança antes baiana do que africana, dançada hoje pela artista Carmen Miranda sob os aplausos de requintadas platéias internacionais; as sobrevivências do culto de Ogun e do culto de Alá dissolvendo-se em práticas marginalmente católicas." Gilberto Freyre, *Sobrados e mucambos*, 1951: 881–82.

24. Alice Gonzaga quoted in Dennison and Shaw, *Popular Cinema in Brazil*, 45.

25. Lisa Shaw, "Vargas on Film: From the Newsreel to the *chanchada*," in Jens R. Hentschke, ed., *Vargas and Brazil: New Perspectives* (New York: Palgrave Macmillan, 2006), 214; Dennison and Shaw, *Popular Cinema in Brazil*, 111.

26. "As chanchadas misturavam o circo, carnaval, o rádio e o teatro em filmes que retratavam o malandro brasileiro, desocupados, donos de pensão e empregadas domésticas, tentando sempre atingir um público mais amplo, com linguagem fácil e oriunda de outras manifestações artísticas que já faziam sucesso." Ricardo Wahrendorff Caldas e Tânia Montoro, coord., *A evolução do cinema brasileiro no século XX* (Brasília: Casa das Musas, 2006), 59–60.

27. Quoted in Dennison and Shaw, *Popular Cinema in Brazil*, 44–45.

28. Caldas e Montoro, *A evolução do cinema brasileiro no século XX*, 289–90.

29. For a recent biography that delves into the multiple images, see Lisa Shaw, *Carmen Miranda* (London: Palgrave Macmillan, 2013).

30. The most complete biography of Miranda in Portuguese is Ruy Castro, *Carmen: uma biografia* (São Paulo: Companhia das Letras, 2005). The early years are covered in chapters 1–4. The most complete biography in English is Martha Gil-Montero, *Brazilian Bombshell: The Biography of Carmen Miranda* (New York: Dutton, 1989). The most recent study of Miranda is Kathryn Bishop-Sanchez, *Creating Carmen Miranda: Race, Camp, and Transnational Stardom* (Nashville, TN: Vanderbilt University Press, 2016). For the range of Rádio Mayrink Veiga see Castro, p. 118.

31. For a discussion of Miranda's *baiana* costumes and jewelry (*balangandãs*) see Tânia da Costa Garcia, *O "it verde" de Carmen Miranda* (1930–1946) (São Paulo: Annablume; Fapesp, 2004), esp. 107–39; and, Simone Pereira de Sá, *Baiana internacional: as mediações culturais de Carmen Miranda* (Rio de Janeiro: MIS Editorial, 2002), 97–120.

32. Miranda recorded songs written by Ary Barroso (30), Joubert de Carvalho (28), Assis Valente (24), André Filho (21), Lamartine Babo (12),

Braguinha (9), Synval Silva (8), and Luiz Peixoto (8). Pereira de Sá, *Baiana internacional*, 51.

33. "a criar para si uma personalidade pública – e viver dela." Castro, *Carmen*, p. 92.

34. Stam, *Tropical Multiculturalism*, 84.

35. For an analysis of this pivotal moment and Miranda's appearance, see Shaw, *Carmen Miranda*, 24–37.

36. Pereira de Sá, *Baiana internacional*, 98–101; Aloysio de Oliveira, *De Banda pra lua* (Rio de Janeiro: Record, 1982), 63–64.

37. Darién J. Davis, *White Face, Black Mask: Africaneity and the Early Social History of Popular Music in Brazil* (East Lansing: Michigan State University Press, 2009), 79 and 136–39.

38. Gil-Montero, *Brazilian Bombshell*, 58.

39. Ickes, *African-Brazilian Culture*, 224.

40. Bishop-Sanchez, *Creating Carmen Miranda*, 68.

41. See, for example, Michael T. Bertrand, *Race, Rock, and Elvis* (Urbana: University of Illinois Press, 2000), esp. chapters 1 and 7; Bobbie Ann Mason, *Elvis Presley* (New York: Penguin, 2003), 6–7. For a very fine analysis of the intermingling of country and soul music, see Charles L. Hughes, *Country Soul: Making Music and Making Race* (Chapel Hill: University of North Carolina Press, 2015). Hughes calls the musical hybrids produced in this interaction "mulatto" music. Hughes, 5.

42. See, for example, Ickes, *African-Brazilian Culture*; Stefania Capone, *A busca da África no candomblé: tradição e poder no Brasil* (Rio de Janeiro: Pallas, 2005); Patricia de Santana Pinho, *Mama Africa: Reinventing Blackness in Brazil* (Durham, NC: Duke University Press, 2010); Anadelia Romo, *Brazil's Living Museum: Race, Reform, and Tradition in Bahia* (Chapel Hill: University of North Carolina Press, 2010).

43. For a sensitive analysis of these processes in Bahia, see Ickes, *African-Brazilian Culture*. Ickes argues that, of all the regional identities, "it was in Bahia that the idea of racial and especially cultural inclusivity was, discursively at least, taken the furthest." Ickes, 234.

44. Castro, *Carmen*, esp. chapter 10; Ana Rita Mendonça, *Carmen Miranda foi a Washington* (Rio de Janeiro: Editora Record, 1999), 15–22; Dennison and Shaw, *Popular Cinema in Brazil*, 52–53.

45. For an excellent documentary of her life, see *Carmen Miranda: Bananas Is My Business*, dir. Helena Solberg (Fox, 1995).

46. For a discussion of Miranda's time in Hollywood, see Darlene Sadlier, *Brazil Imagined: 1500 to the Present* (Austin: University of Texas Press, 2008), 227–33.

47. Maria Isaura Pereira de Queiroz, *Carnaval brasileiro: o vivido e o mito* (São Paulo: Editora Brasiliense, 1992) provides a fine synthetic overview of the history of *carnaval* in Brazil. See also, Maria Clementina Pereira Cunha, *Ecos da folia: uma história do Carnaval carioca entre 1880 e 1920* (São Paulo: Companhia das Letras, 2001) and Felipe Ferreira, *O livro de ouro do carnaval brasileiro* (Rio de Janeiro: Ediouro, 2004).

48. Pereira de Queiroz, *Carnaval brasileiro*, 93–94.

49. *Ibid.*, 58–59.

50. Castro, *Rio de Janeiro: Carnival Under Fire*, 69.

51. Dennison and Shaw, *Popular Cinema in Brazil*, 36.

52. Simis, *Estado e cinema no Brasil*, esp. Parte I.

53. Dennison and Shaw, *Popular Cinema in Brazil*, 33.

54. Caldas e Montoro, *A evolução do cinema brasileiro no século XX*, Capítulo I, "O Cinema Carioca e os Ciclos Regionais (1898–1930)"; Campbell, "The Brazilian Northeast, Inside Out."

55. Castro, *Carmen Miranda*, 116–120.

56. *Ibid.*, 116–120.

57. For an analysis of Miranda and the treatment of Rio in several Hollywood films, see Bianca Freire-Medeiros, "Hollywood Musicals and the Invention of Rio de Janeiro, 1933–1953," *Cinema Journal*, 41:4 (Summer 2002), 52–67.

58. Some Brazilian critics later reacted in similar fashion to *bossa nova*. For a description of the negative reaction to the now famous *bossa nova* show at Carnegie Hall in 1962, see Ruy Castro, *Chega de saudade: a história e as histórias da bossa nova* (São Paulo: Companhia das Letras, 1990), 329–31. Carlos Lyra's "Influência do jazz" is a response to these criticisms.www.yo utube.com/watch?v=SjMSvuASw7E [accessed 31 May 2016]

59. Muniz de Albuquerque, *The Invention of the Brazilian Northeast*, 201. See also, Eliska Altmann, "Cinema Novo," in Louis Bayman and Natália Pinazza, eds., *Directory of World Cinema: Brazil*, v. 21 (Bristol, UK: Intellect Books, 2013), 58–63.

60. Stam, *Tropical Multiculturalism*, 157.

61. Mauro Rovai, "Barren Lives," and Mariana AC da Cunha, "Black God, White Devil," in Bayman and Pinazza, *Directory of World Cinema: Brazil*, 64–66 and 87–89.

62. Stam, *Tropical Multiculturalism*, 167.

63. For the furious reaction of Vinícius de Moraes to the film adaptation of his play, see Stam, *Tropical Multiculturalism*, 172.

64. José Castello, *Vinícius de Moraes: o poeta da paixão, uma biografia* (São Paulo: Companhia das Letras, 1994), 111 and 180–83; Waldo Frank, *South American Journey* (New York: Duell, Sloan and Pearce, 1943), 26–44.

65. Lúcia Nagib, *Brazil on Screen: Cinema Novo, New Cinema, Utopia* (London: I. B. Tauris, 2007), 88–89; Catherine Benamou, *It's All True: Orson Welles's Pan-American Odyssey* (Berkeley: University of California Press, 2007).

66. Stam, *Tropical Multiculturalism*, 166–73; Scott Jordan Harris, "Black Orpheus," in Bayman and Pinazza, eds., *Directory of World Cinema: Brazil*, 112–14.

67. "Jazz artists Herbie Mann, Paul Winter, Cannonball Adderley, and others helped globally popularize the new sound, which had a breezy syncopation, progressive harmony, and a deceptive simplicity." McGowan and Pessanha, *The Brazilian Sound*, 13.

68. *Bossa nova* had an "aesthetic of subdued, subtle, and polished expression." Charles A. Perrone, *Masters of Contemporary Brazilian Song: MPB 1965–1985* (Austin: University of Texas Press, 1989), xxiii.

69. *Getz/Gilberto*, Verve, 1963. Castro, *Chega de saudade*, esp. 335–37. "Bossa nova is a sacred form of music for many Brazilians. It's political and nationalistic and poetic. It's a form of high modernist art that somehow became one of the most popular musics on earth." Caetano Veloso quoted in John Lewis, "Why Bossa Nova Is 'The Highest Flowering of Brazilian Culture' ,"*The Guardian*, 1 October 2013, www.theguardian.com/music/20 13/oct/01/bossa-nova-highest-culture-brazil [accessed 27 November 2013].

70. For a fine analysis of *bossa nova* within the competition of musical styles in the 1960s, see David Treece, "Guns and Roses: Bossa Nova and Brazil's Music of Popular Protest, 1958–1968," *Popular Music*, 16:1 (January 1997), 1–29. I would like to thank Chris Dunn for bringing this article to my attention.

71. Stam, *Tropical Multiculturalism*, 177. Axé is a style of music that emerges out of Bahia in the 1980s and 1990s fusing several genres including reggae, calypso, and frevo, among others. Daniela Mercury's 1992 multimillion selling album *Canto da cidade* (Epic/Sony) moves axé music into the mainstream of Brazilian culture.

72. For an analysis of the shift in Amado's writing beginning with *Gabriela*, see Joanna Courteau, "*Gabriela, Clove and Cinnamon*: Rewriting the Discourse of the Native," in Keith H. Brower, Earl E. Fitz, and Enrique Martínez-Vidal, eds., *Jorge Amado: New Critical Essays* (New York: Routledge, 2001), 43–56. "Amado strove to capture the essence of Brazilian cultural identity through the recuperation of its popular character and popular roots." Muniz de Albuquerque, *The Invention of the Brazilian Northeast*, 155.

73. Sergio Marras, *América Latina: marca registrada* (Buenos Aires: Grupo Editorial Zeta, 1992), 168.

74. Jorge Amado, *Gabriela, cravo e canela, crônica de uma cidade do interior; romance* (São Paulo: Martins, 1958); *Dona Flor e seus dois maridos: história de moral e amor: romance* (São Paulo: Martins, 1966); *Tenda dos milagres; romance* (São Paulo: Martins, 1969); *Gabriela, Clove and Cinnamon*, trans. James L. Taylor and William Grossman (New York: A. A. Knopf, 1962); *Dona Flor and Her Two Husbands: A Moral and Amorous Tale*, trans. Harriet de Onís (New York: 1969); *Tent of Miracles*, trans. Barbara Shelby (New York: A. A. Knopf, 1971).

75. The English translation first appeared in 1962, *Gabriela, Clove and Cinnamon*, trans. James L. Taylor and William Grossman (New York: Avon Books, 1962). The novel has been translated into more than thirty languages and gone through nearly 100 editions!

76. *Dona Flor e seus dois maridos*, directed by Bruno Barreto (Embrafilme, 1976). *Tropa de elite* (2007) and *Tropa de elite 2* (2010), by José Padilha both easily surpassed the earning of *Dona Flor*. Heise, *Remaking Brazil*, 122; Benjamin Legg, "The Bicultural Sex Symbol: Sônia Braga in Brazilian and North American Popular Culture," in Kathryn Bishop-Sanchez and Severino João Medeiros Albuquerque, eds., *Performing Brazil: Essays on Culture, Identity, and the Performing Arts* (Madison: University of Wisconsin Press, 2015), 202–23.

77. For a succinct analysis of Gabriela as the novelization of the Freyrean myth of Brazilian origins, see Laura Moutinho, *Razão, "cor" e desejo: uma análise comparativa sobre relacionamentos afetivo-sexuais "inter-raciais" no Brasil e na África do Sul* (São Paulo: Unesp, 2004), 147–48.

78. See, for example, Bobby J. Chamberlain, *Jorge Amado* (Boston: Twayne Publishers, 1990), Chapter 3, "*Gabriela, cravo e canela*: A Chronicle of Cacao, Love, and Liberation," 29–49.

79. Dário Borim Jr, "Dona Flor and Her Two Husbands," in Bayman and Pinazza, eds., *Directory of World Cinema: Brazil*, 116–18.

80. For a discussion of the *morena/mulata* category, especially in relation to Sonia Braga, see Shaw and Dennison, *Brazilian National Cinema*, 163.

81. Shaw and Dennison, *Brazilian National Cinema*, 164 and 175.

82. Cecília Mello, "Tent of Miracles," in Bayman and Pinazza, eds., *Directory of World Cinema: Brazil*, 221–22.

83. For a detailed analysis of Amado as a proponent of *mestiçagem*, in particular, through *Tenda dos milagres*, see Miller, *Rise and Fall of the Cosmic Race*, chapter 4, "Showcasing Mixed Race in Northeast Brazil," 96–118.

4

"Globo-lizing" Brazil

Televising Identity

Television has thus become the most significant shaper of the image of Brazilian national identity, both internally and externally.[1]

Robert Stam, João Luiz Vieira, and Ismael Xavier

The programs had an enormous audience. For the first time, a child in Copacabana could see that the buffalo that lived in the flooded fields of the Amazon were part of his country; at the same time, the Indian in Belém do Pará could see via television the tall buildings of Rio de Janeiro. *The idea of the nation began to be understood.*[2] [emphasis added]

Joe Wallach

I saw a Brazil on TV.[3]

Chico Buarque de Holanda, *Bye Bye Brasil*

THE TELEVISION REVOLUTION AND THE RISE OF THE GLOBO EMPIRE

The technologies of radio and film initiated a cultural transformation in the 1930s facilitating the emergence of the aural and visual cultures that made possible the creation of a truly *national* conversation about Brazilian identity.[4] Beginning in the 1960s, the technology of television completed the process and finally made possible a shared national culture across the length and breadth of Brazil's territory.[5] Although television broadcasting augments the power of the State to shape the creation of a dominant narrative of nationalism and national identity, it also reveals the impossibility of achieving the dream of all nation-states – to homogenize national culture producing a hegemonic, universal narrative of national identity. Despite the enormous power of the Brazilian military regime and Rede Globo, they were not able to impose a single vision of Brazilian identity on all Brazilians. Ironically, the decades of dictatorship witnessed the greatest power and reach of the Freyrean vision of *mestiçagem*, as well as the onset of its decline. The technology of mass communications, paradoxically, provided both the means to reach and communicate – to stay on message – with virtually every inhabitant of the Brazilian national territory while, at the same time, it would lead to an endlessly proliferating cacophony of voices offering many, many narratives of national identity (and other identities). In many ways, the emergence of television multiplied the complexity of layered and shared identities.[6] In addition to the local, regional, and national identities at play, the new technologies of the 1990s – cable and satellite television, and the Internet – also exposed Brazilians to local, regional, national, and transnational identities from around the globe. Globo's enormous power declined within Brazil with the advent of these new technologies, the seemingly endless proliferation of viewing options, and the astonishing range of sounds and images available to the majority of Brazilians by the beginning of the twenty-first century.[7]

In the 1970s and 1980s, a technological consumer revolution in Brazil made television the most pervasive and influential of all mass media in the country.[8] In 1970, less than a quarter of Brazilian households owned a television set. By 1990, "95 percent of all Brazilians affirmed that they watched television on a regular basis." By the late 1990s, that figure had reached 99 percent![9] More than 90 percent of Brazil's households had a television set, a figure surpassing the number of households with radios. A 2005 survey revealed that Brazilians spent nearly five hours per day watching television, much of it national programming. Unlike most "developing" countries, Brazil produces more than 85 percent of broadcast content, and Globo is one of the largest media producers in the world.[10] According to the anthropologist Conrad Kottak, "Brazil's Globo network plays each night to the world's largest and most devoted audience."[11] The power of television, and the *telenovela*, is further magnified by the printed press, which produces a flood of magazines, daily articles, and commentaries on the nightly *novelas* and their stars.[12]

Since the late 1960s, television has played a central (if not the central) role in the rural to urban shift of tens of millions of Brazilians, and in connecting the remaining rural inhabitants of the country into the nation and national culture. Television in these decades became the principal gateway into the regional, national, and global villages.[13] Studies of the viewing and reception of Brazilian television have shown class and regional differences among viewers, in particular, the greater connection of the middle and upper classes to global cultural influences and knowledge. Despite these differences, it is clear that the medium has engaged Brazilians of all social classes and facilitated the creation of national cultural capital.[14] Conrad Kottak's deep and long-term ethnographic fieldwork has shown a "mass, democratizing, common knowledge," especially through *telenovelas, futebol,* and *carnaval*. First through radio, and then through television, poor and rural Brazilians have "learned to feel comfortable with other Brazilians and with being Brazilian." They become aware of national holidays, as well as "foods, sports, and music, which gradually begin to supplement traditional local activities and consumption."[15]

In this chapter, I look at the emergence of a national telecommunications network in Brazil beginning in the 1960s and 1970s, in particular the role of Rede Globo and its founder, Roberto Marinho. Although I emphasize the power and influence of Globo to shape an "official" narrative of nationalism and national identity, I also stress the limitations of this power and the importance of many, many voices challenging, contesting, and reshaping this vision. I agree with those in media studies that show that while "television may not tell us what to think, it is very successful in telling us what to think about."[16] The power of the government and corporations to set the agenda is enormous and shapes the conversation more than any other factor in the national conversation. Nevertheless, as in the chapters on radio and film, I want to emphasize the constantly contested symbols, rituals, and beliefs at the center of national conversation about Brazilian identity and nationalism, and the role of the mass public in shaping the conversation.

Although nearly all Brazilians share an awareness of these symbols, rituals, and beliefs, they are not fully embraced by everyone in the same fashion. Indeed, they are bitterly rejected by significant groups. What is important for the formation of a national imaginary is that everyone is aware of those symbols, rituals, and beliefs – that they resonate – not that everyone embraces them with the same intensity and understanding. By the 1990s, the *telenovela, carnaval*, and *futebol* had become the most powerful and resonant symbols and rituals of Brazilian identity. Each, in its own way, helped communicate the myth of *mestiçagem* to all Brazilians, and to the rest of the world. The military regime and Rede Globo helped bring the Freyrean vision to its moment of greatest influence and reach while attempting to suppress or ignore alternative visions. Their efforts demonstrate both the power and the limits of State and mass media to consolidate and impose a single narrative of nationhood on Brazilians, or any other people. At the same time, I argue that the power and reach of the Freyrean vision of *mestiçagem* increases in the 1970s due to the impact of television and Rede Globo, before the challenges from activists and intellectuals begin to weaken their hold in the 1980s and beyond.

Just as roads and waterways gradually began to connect up the various regions of Brazil in the nineteenth century, and as radio waves eventually washed across the national territory in the 1930s and 1940s, television finally stitched together all of the major regions of Brazil in the 1970s and 1980s. The development of television broadcasting took shape in the uneasy postwar decades of Brazil's "experiment in democracy" and emerged full blown under the military dictatorship in the 1960s and 1970s. Getúlio Vargas had played a crucial role in centralizing State power and nation-building after the Revolution of 1930, and then imposing the Estado Novo in 1937. He and his technocrats had consciously sought to harness and channel the power of radio and popular music as one of their tools in constructing a cultural nationalism that drew on Freyre's vision of *mestiçagem*. After Vargas was forced from power in 1945, populism and nationalism dominated Brazilian politics for the next two decades as millions of Brazilians experienced mass, democratic politics for the first time. The Constitution of 1946 gave the vote to all Brazilians over the age of 18 (except illiterates, who were perhaps a third of the population). During this period of rapid population growth (from 40 million in 1940 to more than 80 million by the mid-1960s), a massive shift of people from the countryside to the cities, and an industrial surge (especially under President Juscelino Kubitschek, 1956–1961), Brazilian politics was vibrant, highly charged, and constantly unstable. At this moment of Cold War politics and revolutionary upheaval across Latin America, Brazil's electoral democracy was on the verge of collapse repeatedly in the 1950s and early 1960s.

The culture industries and popular culture also grew dramatically and flourished in the postwar decades. In many ways, the period from 1945 to 1985 is the moment when Brazil truly emerges as a nation, and as an imagined community defined by myths, rituals, and symbols that resonate across the national territory and social classes. Politicians, policy makers, and intellectuals in the postwar decades across much of the ideological spectrum promoted nationalism and development. Especially on the Left, but for many on the Right, the construction of a strong nation was both an economic and a cultural project. Indeed, much of the bitter ideological struggle in the 1950s and 1960s was generated by differing views of this economic and cultural project. The military regime's jingoistic brand of nationalism can be seen as a right-wing response to the vibrant left-wing cultural projects of the postwar period.[17]

Facing high inflation, economic stagnation, and intense ideological battles, Brazilian democracy collapsed in 1964 when the military deposed President João Goulart (1961–1964). The Brazilian coup was the first in a wave of military coups and dictatorship across Latin America over the next two decades. Much to the surprise of nearly all civilian politicians (especially the Right who had called vociferously for military intervention), the armed forces remained in power and attempted to transform the country through a brutal repression of dissent (especially, but not exclusively, on the Left) and a massive national economic development project. Hundreds "disappeared" and thousands were jailed and tortured. The generals (and admirals) ruthlessly eradicated any Leftist threat, and dramatically accelerated industrialization through massive government intervention. Although never completely shutting down politics, the military "purged" all branches of government and created two political parties: the Aliança Renovadora Nacional (National Renewal Alliance, or ARENA) as the government party, and the Movimento Democrático Brasileiro (Brazilian Democratic Movement, or MDB) as the official party of the opposition. The repression did not begin to ease until the late 1970s, and the transition back to civilian democracy spanned nearly the entire 1980s.

Roberto Marinho and Rede Globo seized the opportunities presented by a close alliance with the military regime and the drive for development and national integration. The turning point in the creation of a truly national broadcasting came in 1969–1970. In late 1969, Globo debuted the *Jornal Nacional* (*JN*), in 1970, *Irmãos Coragem* became the first nationally broadcast *novela*, and the World Cup was shown live for the first time across all of Brazil.[18] Similar to the television revolution in U.S. society in the 1950s, the expansion of telecommunications technology in the 1970s revolutionized Brazilian culture.[19] For the first time in the history of Brazil, the State and cultural producers had the ability to reach virtually every inhabitant within the country's borders – and beyond. By the 1990s, this technology had made possible a national conversation in "real" time about issues in Brazilian society, and beyond. In a decade or so – from the mid-1960s to the early 1980s – telecommunications technology transformed the country.[20] Television, even more so than cinema, demonstrates the power of aural and visual cultures in the creation of imagined communities in Latin America in the twentieth century rather than through print culture in the nineteenth century. (Daily newspaper circulation in Brazil, for example, in the early 1980s was 2 million in a country of 120 million inhabitants with 70 million regular television viewers.)[21] Globo, and other networks, promoted a vision of Brazil that was modern, urban, and industrial – a country on the move. More so than any other medium of communications in the past, television projected modernity and urban life as the goal and future of Brazil.[22]

Although television broadcasting began in Brazil as early as 1950, its impact remained overwhelmingly local and restricted to a very small group of the well off in major urban centers who could afford television sets.[23] Two inextricably intertwined processes combined to transform television broadcasting in Brazil – the military coup of 1964 and the rise of Roberto Marinho's Rede Globo beginning in the late 1960s. In 1965, Brazil had a rapidly growing population of 85 million, with fewer than 2 million vehicles, 1 million telephones, and 4 million television sets. Television stations were largely locally owned, often by families who controlled local radio stations or newspapers, and the majority of broadcasting was local. As numerous writers have pointed out, the government's granting of broadcasting licenses (radio and television) has long been an important form of political patronage in Brazil that reinforces the power of the local and regional *coronéis* (colonels, or powerbrokers) and their alliances with national governments.[24] Although there were no true networks, some powerful media figures controlled multiple television and radio stations as well as major newspapers. The most infamous of these early media magnates was Francisco Assis Chateaubriand whose TV Tupi represented the most important competitor for Roberto Marinho until the 1980s.[25]

Marinho purchased his first television station, in Rio de Janeiro, in 1957, and a second in Brasília in 1962. (In 1965, there were five stations in Rio de Janeiro and four in São Paulo.)[26] He forged a highly controversial alliance with the U.S.-based multinational corporation Time-Life in the 1960s to secure external financing for his incipient telecommunications business. In an era of intense nationalism (on both the Left and Right), Marinho's dealings with Time-Life faced intense questioning and scrutiny, including a congressional investigation during the early years of the military regime.[27] The pivotal moment for Globo and Brazilian television was 1969. Intent on developing the country, the military constructed the foundations of a nationwide microwave broadcasting system, primarily for telephone service.[28] Globo arranged to transmit its signal through this microwave network in an agreement with the State monopoly that controlled this system – Embratel. Marinho and his key executives not only had their key alliance with the military regime (for which they have been regularly denounced), but they also had the great foresight to seize this emerging opportunity to construct the first – and the most successful – national television network in Brazil.[29] Political influence and business acumen converged.

On 1 September 1969, Globo's evening news broadcast, *JN*, initiated national broadcasting in Brazil. At around the same time (1970), Marinho ended his relationship with Time-Life allowing Globo to determine its own destiny free of the wishes and desires of its foreign associates in New York. In the first phase of the expansion of national broadcasting (in the 1970s), Globo and its competitors had to overcome enormous obstacles. At the beginning of the decade, only half of all homes in Brazil had electricity and just a quarter had a television set. In this first phase of national broadcasting – especially in the small cities and towns of the countryside – viewing was often communal, and a novelty, around the television set in a neighborhood bar or the home of one of the few locals to own one.[30] In the 1970s and 1980s, television had saturated urban Brazilian communities, and the medium had become "a powerful national agent of *mass enculturation.*"[31] By the early 1990s, Brazil had 30 million television sets, or one for every five Brazilians.[32] Seventy-five percent of all Brazilian homes had a television set. By the beginning of this century, 87 percent of households had at least one television set, more than 39 million homes.[33] By the late 1980s, Globo reached 98 percent of the national territory with its 86 stations (*emissoras*), and on an average captured 56 percent of viewers. Globo's now legendary *JN* alone had a nightly audience of 50 million viewers.[34] Globo's *telenovelas*, especially in the most heavily watched time slot (8:30 p.m.), regularly captured 70–80 percent of viewers, and at times reached 100 percent![35]

The power and reach of Roberto Marinho and Globo have generated a substantial literature, much of it negative, especially by those on the Left of the political spectrum.[36] While a debate has raged over whether Globo and Marinho have been a force for good or evil in Brazil, across the ideological spectrum there is widespread agreement on their power and influence, on their ability to broadcast their images and words to more Brazilians and more widely across Brazil than any other person or institution in the history of the country. The rise of the "Globo-lization" of Brazil in the 1970s and 1980s simultaneously integrated the nation through mass communications and helped reshape the decades-long

FIGURE 4.1 Television Reaches the Amazon (Gurupá, Pará)
Source: Photograph by Annie Pace

conversation on national identity through a new and more powerful medium than even radio or film. Globo's phenomenal audience share also made it possible to focus the conversation more than at any other time since the emergence of the Brazilian State. The goals of the Brazilian State and Globo may have converged powerfully, but we must remember that each had very different objectives. Globo, like all commercial broadcasting networks, is a capitalist enterprise seeking to make a profit. The means to that profit is creating more and more consumers while attracting advertisers to sell products to these consumers.[37] The creation of programming, then, ultimately aims to create an audience and the programming changes over time to respond to audience shifts and interests. The State seeks the creation of a unified nation – in the case of Brazil a modern, consumer society constructed around a powerful narrative of national identity. Globo and the Brazilian State generally converged in their efforts, if not their motivations. Globo was not simply a lackey of the Brazilian State and the company's management were (and are) deeply sensitive to the shifting sands of politics, society, and culture in Brazil. My analysis of the power of Globo diverges from much of the traditional Leftist critique of the power of Globo to impose a single, hegemonic vision on the Brazilian public. The State, Globo, and Brazilians have long been engaged in a complex conversation and negotiation (albeit a very unequal one) about the nature and directions of Brazilian society, culture, and politics. While Globo may have been dominant and oligopolistic in the world of broadcasting in the 1970s and 1980s, and the State a constant, powerful interventor, both audiences and producers shaped the conversation just as they had with the rise of radio and film.[38]

MODERNITY, IDENTITY, AND THE *JORNAL NACIONAL*

Globo's rise to media dominance required the assistance of powerful allies in the military regime, financial support from Time-Life, and a management team with great creativity and brilliance. As those connected with Globo love to emphasize, the network set a standard of excellence (*padrão Globo de qualidade* [Globo standard of quality]) that effectively became the standard for all Brazilian networks (and would-be networks).[39] Management initially built programming on three pillars: news, *telenovelas*, and humor/variety shows. By the 1990s, sports programming had become an additional pillar of programming.[40] *Telenovelas* and the *JN*, in particular, became the driving forces of the programming genius that established Globo as the superpower of Brazilian television.[41] (Both genres are also highly lucrative, ultimately, the primary force that drives commercial television.)[42]

Roberto Marinho envisioned Globo as a powerful force for the transformation of Brazil into a modern nation – one integrated by telecommunications and drawing together all the locales and regions of Brazil into a national consumer culture. This vision of modernity aspired to emulate Western Europe and the United States with their capitalist, consumerist, urban, industrial societies. In many ways, this modernizing vision represented the latest version of the Eurocentric, elite vision of modernity in the nineteenth century. Marinho's aspirations and vision coincided perfectly with the leadership of the military regime in their pursuit of a modern, industrial Brazil constructed around a clear and coherent nationalism – and anticommunism.[43] Much like Getúlio Vargas in the 1930s and 1940s, the generals in the 1960s and 1970s saw the State as an instrument for national cohesion and the formation of a hegemonic narrative of nationalism and national identity.[44] Globo and the generals became a formidable – if not always harmonious – couple.[45] The generals provided the technological infrastructure for national integration, and Globo the cultural intermediary. In the terminology of information technology, the generals constructed the hardware and Globo, the software for facilitating and shaping the national conversation on Brazilian identity.

The *JN*, along with *telenovelas*, formed the principal means to capture and consolidate viewer dominance in prime time (*horário nobre*) – 6 to 11 p.m. The strategy from its inception was to sandwich the news broadcast between the 7 p.m. and the 8 p.m. *novelas* – the first a lighter fare, and the latter the principal dramatic *novela* of the night. In its early years, the broadcast began at 7:50 p.m. and ran for just 15 minutes. (As the *JN* became more established, the broadcast was moved to 8 p.m. and lengthened.)[46] As Carlos Eduardo Lins da Silva noted long ago, *JN* set a new standard for Brazilian news broadcasting, not simply as the first truly national news journal. In a style that has become even more emphatic today in the age of 24-hour cable news, *JN* offered viewers seemingly immediate ("breaking") news, in a cool and "objective" style, with reporters from all corners of the country and abroad. The style of its anchors, especially the legendary Cid Moreira, reflected the influence of anchors like Walter Cronkite in the U.S. – to project an aura of complete confidence and credibility. One of the greatest achievements of Globo in the 1970s was to move first and quickly to establish a virtual monopoly on national and international reporting, produced with high quality, giving the Brazilian viewer an appearance of being completely authoritative and true.[47]

Many critics have pointed out that the close relationship between Roberto Marinho and the military regime shaped the images and content in all Globo's programming, but in none more important than the *JN*. As with all Brazilian media, Globo dealt with the censors, but none dealt more directly with the most powerful figures in the regime. All those who worked with Globo in these years recount episodes of censors altering or suppressing programming – most famously, perhaps, the banning of the *telenovela Roque Santeiro* (1975), not yet on the air, but with some three dozen episodes already filmed. Perhaps no greater evidence of the close relationship of this media giant and the military regime are the phone calls Marinho would receive during (and after) evening news broadcasts from the military presidents or their advisors. Between Marinho's own interventions and directives to his underlings, and the direct intervention of generals and censors, the news Brazilians received from the *JN* in the 1970s presented a Brazil free of torture, violent conflicts, economic crises, and authoritarianism. In a widely repeated quote from an interview on the program in 1973, President Emílio Médici – known for his tough, hard-line repressive measures – waxed expansive, unknowingly revealing the disconnect between Brazilian reality and television news: "It makes me happy, every night, when I turn on the television to watch the news. While there is news of strikes, disturbances, attacks and conflicts in various parts of the world, Brazil moves peacefully towards development. It is as if I had taken a tranquilizer after a day of work."[48]

As Globo worked to integrate the nation through telecommunications, it simultaneously strove to forge a sense of national unity and development. Leaving the local reporting to its affiliates, the focus of *JN* is the national and international. As with *telenovelas*, the image that dominates is the forging of modern, urban, industrial, consumerist, and capitalist Brazil. Ironically, in stressing the role of Brazilians to be good citizens of the nation, Globo was both serving the military regime and, ultimately, helping prepare the way for all Brazilians to demand the rights of citizenship.[49] As the regime went through a long and slow process of *abertura* (political opening) in the late 1970s and early 1980s, Globo walked a complex path seeking to remain loyal to the generals who made their very existence and spectacular success possible, and recognizing that the regime would eventually have to return power to civilians. The news editors understood this gradual transformation. As one editor noted, the *JN* could not continue simply to serve as a mouthpiece of the regime, "In the train of the political opening, Globo Network is the last car and the *JN* is the last seat. But, even when arriving late, we will also arrive in the same station as the locomotive."[50]

As discussed in Chapter 7, Globo's shifting role in the long process from hard-line military regime (pre-1975) to *abertura* (post-1975) to the demands for direct elections (*diretas já*) was fundamental not only to the success of the long process of re-democratization, but also in the final stages of consolidating an intense cultural nationalism and the early stages of a new era of civic nationalism. The power of the *JN* was (and is) impressive, but not determinant. It provides perhaps the most important instrument in the consolidation of a truly national community of active participants in Brazilian culture and politics, but it does not unify and homogenize opinions and beliefs. As Lins da Silva pointed out in his classic study of the *JN* and the Brazilian working class, the workers were not ignorant and alienated masses, but active and engaged participants in society. Globo and the *JN* may have provided the messages and the medium, but the workers, and all other Brazilians, reacted to and discussed this information in a multitude of ways.[51] After 1970, Brazilians increasingly relied on television (especially *JN* and Globo) for exposure to the most important forum on discussions about the nation and national culture.[52] *JN* and Globo provided the framework for the national conversation, with all of its constraints and limitations, but tens of millions of Brazilians complicated that conversation especially as the military regime gave way to civilian, democratic politics in the 1980s.

TELENOVELAS AND NATIONAL IDENTITY

Telenovelas have a long ancestry in Brazil and they are much more than "soap operas" a la U.S. television. The *novelas* harken back to the *literatura de cordel* of the backlands, traveling circuses, *revistas de teatro*, and the radio *novelas* in the 1930s and 1940s. Much like the serial publications of the nineteenth century (such as Charles Dickens's novels), the *telenovela* develops in chapters or episodes. A film or a play might unfold over an hour and a half or two hours, but a successful *novela* develops in six segments per week over many months. The media critic Artur da Távola has called the *telenovela* an "electronic serial."[53] The first *telenovelas* appeared in the 1950s with the modern form appearing in the 1960s. Globo took up this genre in the 1960s and 1970s, perfected it, and rode the ratings to dominance of the Brazilian airwaves. Globo's creative and managerial leadership gradually realized that placing their *novelas* in Brazilian locales focusing on contemporary issues provided a powerful appeal to viewers. As Joseph Straubhaar has put it, "Globo transformed the Brazilian *telenovela* into a forum for the discussion of Brazilian reality ... [*Telenovelas*] have created a space to discuss the nation. They have become the way the nation is currently imagined." Globo's creative personnel effectively forged a genre that became quintessentially Brazilian and, at the same time, became one of the most important venues for the national conversation on Brazilian identity.[54] By the 1980s, viewing the nightly *novelas* became one of the most important rituals in Brazilian culture.[55]

Despite spirited debates about the content of *novelas*, their portrayal of race, and their impact on Brazilians, critics generally agree that they have provided the most important forum for the conversation about national identity since the 1960s. The analysis of Maria Rita Kehl, a staunch critic of Rede Globo, sums up the consensus view on the reach of the *novelas* and their impact on the discussion of national identity:

The *telenovela*, daily and domestic, transforms itself during this period into the principal form for producing the ideal image of the Brazilian. More specifically, Globo's 8 p.m. *novelas*, the most wide-ranging and most viewed on Brazilian television, served in the 1970s ... the role of offering to the uprooted Brazilian who had lost his cultural identity a glamorous mirror, closer to desired reality than the reality of life, and for this reason *functioned as a conformist element for a new identity, a Brazilian identity, an identity-as-Brazilians, perhaps the closest to a national identity that this country has had.*[56] [emphasis added]

Nelson Pereira dos Santos, one of the greatest filmmakers of the *Cinema Novo* era, recognized the special power of television and the *telenovela* and its ability to reach the public much more effectively and powerfully than film and theatre:

The television *novela* contributed massively to Brazilian dramaturgy. It put on video what Brazilian cinema had already placed on the screen: the colonel, the rural drama. Through this the people became accustomed to see themselves, to have their own mirror. Until this moment, the guy who lived in the favela had only seen films of lords, fazendeiros, "upscale people." Then, the *telenovela* arrived and did what cinema had already done, without having been able to reach the public because of the monopoly of theaters. Globo produces its own novels and brings them into the home. There are no intermediaries and this is a great advantage.[57]

The enormous success of the *telenovelas* produced by Globo powered its rise to dominance in Brazilian television. Viewers of the *novelas* became loyal viewers of Globo's other programming. The management was well aware of the appeal of the *telenovelas* and their central role in capturing and keeping an audience. In the words of Walter Clark, the director general of Globo in its formative years, "Without the *novela* the station cannot live; because the *novela* provides a fixed audience. The foundation of television is the *novela*."[58] While the *JN* offered Brazilians the news in what seemed to be an objective and authoritative style, the *telenovelas* sought to move Brazilians' passions and emotions. Each, in its own way, provided virtually all Brazilians with a vision of Brazil and its place in the world.

In Brazil, and other areas of Latin America, television and *telenovelas* have helped move the region from rural, oral-based cultures to urban, electronic culture. With about 20 percent of the population still classified as illiterate at the beginning of the 1990s, the visual and aural culture of radio, film, and (especially) television played a central role in the everyday life of most Brazilians.[59] The power of television, in particular, to reach into the most remote areas of Latin America has led some scholars to argue that media and mass communications do not just influence everyday life, "they are everyday life." An emerging movement in cultural studies over the past generation has shifted away from previous theories that cast mass communications as simply a means of "cultural imperialism" to recognize that the *interactions* among individuals and mass communications are complex and that consumers of culture are also producers of culture.[60] In the words of two of the most prominent analysts of mass communications as cultural mediation, "television is the **means** not only in the instrumental sense – measurable in the effects that it produces – but also in the most profoundly cultural sense of **mediation** between reality and desire, between what we live and what we dream."[61] As in the case of radio, consumers shape the directions and influence of cultural trends and movements. This pattern is clearly visible in the structure and development of Brazilian *telenovelas*.[62]

The *telenovela* in Brazil had its "Golden Age" in the 1970s and 1980s, an era dominated by Rede Globo. The genre had an astonishing ability to attract viewers across region, class, color, age, and gender.[63] Unlike the soap operas of U.S. television, Brazilian *telenovelas* have a beginning and end, and generally run anywhere from a few months to more than a year. Broadcast in prime evening hours, a *telenovela* is on the air six nights a week (Monday through Saturday) and is a "work in progress" (*uma obra semi-aberta*).[64] The longest running *novelas* have reached up to 200 "chapters" (episodes), but the filming is rarely more than 20 chapters ahead of the broadcasts. Since the late 1960s, Globo has done extensive, ongoing viewer surveys to determine which plot lines and characters are garnering the strongest reactions, and the writers then adjust their plots and character development in reaction to these surveys.[65] Quite literally, viewers shape the unfolding of the *telenovelas* in a process Jesús Martín-Barbero would call "mediation."[66] The authors of the *novelas*, as others have pointed out, are in an ongoing, critical dialogue with Brazilian reality, and with the millions viewing the programs.[67]

The power and influence of these *telenovelas* to shape and project popular culture is impressive and striking, in particular in the 1970s and 1980s – before the rise of cable, satellite, and the Internet.[68] When the *novela* format took off in the 1960s, a phase often labeled "romantic" by critics, the dominant figure (first at TV Tupi and then at Globo) was the Cuban exile Gloria Magadan who staged productions with exotic themes and in foreign locales. Often the plots and storylines for the *novelas* were imported from Cuba or Argentina.[69] Esther Hamburger, one of Brazil's foremost experts on television and *telenovelas*, argues that prior to 1968, the *novelas* had storylines that owed more to "*fantasia*" than daily realities. From 1968 to 1990, in what she characterizes as the "national-popular" phase, the *novelas* had "plots in contemporaneous time, successively updated, and in geographical spaces, urban or rural, easily recognizable, much like the conventions of documentaries, they constructed a credible universe, recognized as the national territory."[70] Filming on the city streets (especially of Rio de Janeiro) and weaving into the plots contemporary issues, language, and events helped draw the viewer into the stories as they were able to see themselves within clearly local, regional, and national settings.[71]

In the 1970s and 1980s, the *telenovela* format was effectively Brazilianized and nationalized achieving phenomenal reception and success across all of Brazil and all social classes.[72] *Beto Rockefeller* (TV Tupi, 1968–1969) is frequently singled out as the *novela* that began a new era in Brazilian television. *Beto Rockefeller* became the model for future *novelas*, the melodrama focusing on contemporary themes, daily life, colloquial language, popular music for the sound track, and a type of realism in dealing with the issues of Brazilian society.[73] The "antihero," Beto, was a middle-class shoe salesman who managed to pass himself off as a millionaire in various social settings using his wit and charm (shades of the *malandro!*).[74] Globo's first great success was *Irmãos Coragem* (1970), authored by Janete Clair, one of the legendary writers of the genre over the next generation. Her husband, Dias Gomes, was equally successful in the genre.[75] *Irmãos Coragem* began Globo's domination of the genre over the succeeding decades. With a compelling mixture of social issues, politics, and *futebol*, Clair pulled in an enormous audience, male and female, and across social classes. Eventually reaching 328 episodes, it is the second-longest *novela* in Globo's history.[76] Janete Clair's *Selva de Pedra* (1972–1973) was arguably the most popular *novela* of all time in Brazil achieving an astounding 100 percent of all viewers in one dramatic episode where the central female protagonist reveals her true identity. Dias Gomes's *O Bem-Amado* (1973), the first *telenovela* broadcast in color also became one of Globo's first exports abroad.[77]

As with the silver screen, the most powerful image of the *mulata* on the small screen in the early decades of the rise of television was, as with film, in the televised versions of Jorge Amado's works, in particular, in the *telenovela*, *Gabriela* (broadcast in 1975). This role launched Sonia Braga's career into high gear. In 1978, she cemented her role as a *novela* star of the first rank in *Dancin' Days*. Braga followed her success on television on the big screen with *Dama da lotação* (1978), *Dona Flor* (1980) *Eu te amo* (1981), the film version of *Gabriela* (1983), followed by a series of Hollywood productions – *Kiss of the Spider Woman* (1985), the *Milagro Beanfield War* (1988), and *Moon Over Parador* (1988) – alongside some of the most prominent directors and actors of the times (Robert

Redford, Raul Julia, Richard Dreyfuss, Hector Babenco). Daniel Filho, one of the giants of the rise of Globo, personally selected Braga for the role of Gabriela. In his words, "Sonia Braga was Gabriela. Sunbathing, a little cinnamon on that skin and ... Sonia was Gabriela." Completely convinced of the genius of his choice, Filho goes on to say, "Can anyone suggest another Gabriela? No! I think that no one else in the world could suggest another Gabriela."[78]

As in her film roles in *Gabriela* and *Dona Flor*, Braga became the greatest icon of Jorge Amado and Gilberto Freyre's *mestiçagem* as the *mulata* Gabriela. Daniel Filho's comments reveal the irony noted in the previous Chapter – that the iconic *mulata* on both the small and big screen in the 1970s and 1980s was, in fact, a light-skinned woman who had to resort to tanning and makeup to assume the appearance of a light-skinned *mulata* – a *morena*. Once again, Sonia Braga's success and complete identification with the highly sexualized *mulata* highlights the incredible fluidity of *mestiçagem*. While it may be clear who is white and who is black on Brazilian television, and the former dominate in key roles while the latter appear infrequently, the single largest group of Brazilians – those of racially mixed ancestry – largely go unremarked or studied. The literature that condemns the relegation of black Brazilians to minor roles in *telenovelas* and the focus on the lives of the wealthy whites fails to grapple with the more difficult question of the role of the 45 percent of Brazilians who check neither black nor white on the national census.

After *Gabriela*, perhaps the most powerful of the images of *mestiçagem* and the *mulata* was the novela *Escrava Isaura* (1976–1977) based on a nineteenth-century novel by Bernardo Guimarães. In this complex tale of seduction, betrayal, slavery, and manumission, Isaura is the illegitimate child of the white overseer and a slave. Of mixed race, but able to "pass" as white, Isaura is another iconic light-skinned *mulata*, reinforcing Alma Guillermoprieto's assertion about Brazilians perceiving *mestiçagem* as the route to a whiter, more beautiful, and acceptable people. *Escrava Isaura* remains one of the most popular *novelas* in Brazilian television history, and a powerful purveyor of images of *mestiçagem* for Brazilian audiences. The production became a huge success in Cuba, China, and dozens of other countries.[79]

Since 1990, the fragmentation of broadcasting and the proliferation of technologies have produced a much more diverse and more complex programming. The Globo management strategy of broadcasting multiple *telenovelas* at 6, 7, 8, and 10 p.m., with the most important slot for the *"novela das oito,"* in effect, laid down the basic programming schedule

that continues in Brazil to the present. Inserting the *JN* at 8:35 p.m., prior
to the "eight o'clock *novela*," turned out to be a brilliant means both to
promote the national news broadcast, as well as to serve as a lead-in to the
most important *telenovela*. On a regular basis, Globo's "eight o'clock"
telenovela and the *JN* captured 70 percent of all viewers.[80] When television arrived in tiny Gurupá in the eastern Amazon in the 1980s, village life
altered to accommodate viewing of the prime-time *novela* (now associated
with nine o'clock). The locals even began referring to the time as the "*hora
da telenovela.*"[81]

The management team at Globo very consciously gauged their audiences and constructed phenomenally successful programming. The goal of
commercial broadcasting is, of course, to generate revenue, and that
means attracting more and more viewers to make advertising on programs
more appealing to businesses, and to generate even greater revenues. One
of the founding figures of Globo, Homero Sánchez (originally from
Panama), led the network's research department. Sánchez carefully analyzed Brazilian social classes, their habits and consumer patterns, and built
programming aimed primarily at the middle class, but with the clear
objective of attracting viewers from all classes. The very design of the
sequence of nightly *novelas*, and the structure and cast of characters in the
novelas, aimed to "reflect" the demographic and class composition of
Brazilian society in the 1970s and 1980s. The *novela* at six was for
children followed by light fare at seven, then the *JN*. The following
programs carried a harder edge, and then the *novela* at ten was one of
"customs, social criticism, and realism" (*costumes, de crítica social, de
realismo*) for the cathartic moment of the evening.[82] Sánchez also understood the importance of the female viewer and privileged her voice in
focus groups and surveys.[83]

Globo's sophisticated research clearly shows that the *novelas* evoked in
viewers a sense of the national, of Brazil as a whole. Viewers saw in the
characters and plots role models of behavior for the nation. The lead
writers of the *novelas* often sought to create a national conversation
about critical societal issues – racism, gender roles, corruption, and social
justice. In one striking example of the power of the dramas to project
national role models, Globo's research on one of its best-known and most
popular novelas, *A Próxima Vítima* (1995), clearly demonstrated that
viewers saw the principal family in the story as the "ideal family" and
the mother as the ideal of the Brazilian woman. The family in the *novela* is
black and the mother is played by the great black actress Zezé Motta.
Although they were black (and most viewers, obviously, were not), the

viewers saw that the family was the only stable one in the drama, and that its members (father, mother, son, and daughter) were all successful in pursuing their dreams and continuing to hold on to each other in a nuclear family.[84]

Surprisingly, much of the analysis of *telenovelas* has focused on issues of class and wealth, and much less so on race. Most of the commentary on race relations has focused on the absence of black actors in the *novelas*, except in menial roles such as cooks, maids, and hired help. Black actors in lead roles are rare in the *telenovelas* (although there are prominent exceptions) and, for decades, they appeared most frequently as domestic servants, drivers, criminals, and members of the lower class.[85] Clearly, this absence has been long-standing and marked. As has been observed often, Brazilian *telenovelas* have very often created glamorous worlds of wealth and opulence.[86] They have focused more on issues of class than on race relations, reflecting the long-standing and widely diffused belief that the most important divide in Brazilian society is not racial, but rather socio-economic. Given its centrality to Brazilian culture and identity, the absence of analysis of *mestiçagem*, especially cultural *mestiçagem*, in Brazilian television is striking. As with the treatment of class, this "silence" effectively reflects the deeply entrenched belief among those in positions of power (in this case, in the media) that Brazil is a mixed culture and that blacks, in fact, do appear rarely in positions of power and authority in Brazil. What is more striking than the rare appearance of black actors in principal roles is the assumption that everyone else is either white or mixed.

While it is clear that black actors and actresses are clearly in the minority in Brazilian *telenovelas*, and that few black actors and actresses have been written into leading roles until very recently, the focus on a black–white contrast misses the subtlety and power of the role of *mestiçagem*, especially in cultural *mestiçagem*. Joel Zito Araújo's influential study of blacks in Brazilian television is correct in emphasizing the absence of "black" characters in leading roles, but when he notes that black actresses inevitably "end up in the arms of the white race" (*acabaram nos braços da raça branca*) he is, in fact, confirming a central trope of Freyre's vision of *mestiçagem*, the coupling of white men with black women. When he goes on to say that "symbolically, these are stories that highlight the whitening of the black segment [of Brazil] and the dissolution of afro-descendants through mixing with euro-descendants." In effect, he is describing the performance of Freyre's vision repeatedly in the world of *telenovelas*.[87] Contrary to his claims that the Brazilian *telenovela* does not "defend" *mestiçagem*, what he describes confirms the central importance of racial mixing, even if the bias is toward whitening.

Milton Gonçalves, one of the most accomplished and visible black actors over the past forty years, epitomizes these assumptions about the nature of Brazilian society. Gonçalves played a prominent lead role in the legendary *Irmãos Coragem* (1970–1971). The first great success of Globo, Gonçalves directed nearly 100 episodes and developed a close relationship with Janete Clair, one of the greatest scriptwriters of the seventies and eighties. When criticized for not including more black actors in the *novela*, Gonçalves responded:

They said I was racist. Funny that blacks said that I did not employ blacks and whites said I was racist because I only employed blacks. So I just tried to mix. Even today, my vision of Brazil is this, it is just mixed![88]

Ethnographic research by anthropologists and those in communication studies confirms that the "Brazilian on the street" does not need to "see" someone of darker skin to perceive them as "mixed" (*mestiço*). In one of the most detailed examinations of the reception of *novelas*, Thais Machado-Borges, to her own surprise, found that her informants (even those who were dark skinned) perceived white, blonde Brazilian actresses as beautiful, not because of their whiteness, but rather because they were "Brazilian" – "living examples of a racially and culturally hybrid Brazil." Visually, this is confirmation of what Livio Sansone has called Brazil's ability to construct "blackness without ethnicity." *Mestiçagem* is not only about color, it is also about culture. In the words of Machado-Borges, "Actresses such as Vera Fischer and Luisa Tomé represent legitimate, Brazilian beauty: a beauty represented as the result of racial and cultural mixture. A beauty that evokes the idea of attraction and interracial sexual meeting, and that is promoted as producing a kind of national desire."[89] The emphasis of research on television has been on "black" characters rather than *mulato* or *moreno* characters, and the focus of most of this research has been on race rather than on culture.

Here we see the power and appeal of Freyre's vision, that *mestiçagem* is both biological and cultural. From the cultural perspective, the collision of peoples and cultures has produced a rich and shared national culture that draws on indigenous, African, and European cultural practices. One need not be dark skinned to be *mestiço* or *mulato*. The music of Daniela Mercury or Chico Science, the dancing of Carla Perez, or the singing of Maria Bethânia incorporates the influences of Afro-Brazil regardless of the color of their skin. The other side of the coin is the classic Brazilian phrase, "money whitens." Pelé may be phenotypically black, but his success marks him as socially white in Brazilian society. Visually, television offers images predominantly of whites, to a much lesser extent those who are brown, and even less of those who are black. Although *Gabriela* provides Brazilians with potent visual images of biological *mestiçagem*, the cultural heritage of *mestiçagem* is visible and audible throughout *novelas* and contemporary society.[90]

BROADCASTING *CARNAVAL* AND *FUTEBOL*

Telenovelas and the *JN* became national, nearly nightly, rituals for Brazilians in the 1970s and 1980s. In the 1980s and 1990s, the annual broadcasting of *carnaval* (usually in February) and the year-long transmission of football games joined the *JN* and *novelas* as ritual, national performances of national identity. As we saw in Chapter 2, *carnaval* in its current incarnation is largely a creation of the first half of the twentieth century, especially after the rise of Getúlio Vargas and his centralizing regimes in the 1930s. *Carnaval* – as performed in Rio de Janeiro – became the iconic version for public consumption, especially for international eyes. *Carnaval* and *futebol* lagged behind *novelas* in their emergence as televised rituals of Brazilian identity. The strange nature of Brazilian soccer clubs and their management model, ironically, delayed *futebol*'s rise to dominance as the preeminent symbol of national identity. The incredible appeal and commercial success of *novelas* helped to slow the full-scale broadcasting of *carnaval*. By the late 1980s, nevertheless, the three great televised performances of Brazilian identity were in the broadcasting reach of nearly all those living within the country's borders – and for many beyond. While the *novelas* and national news programs fully saturated Brazilian popular culture and broadcasting by the early 1990s, *carnaval* and *futebol* did not achieve a similar status until the 1990s. The most sophisticated social science research on Brazilian television has amply documented this later takeoff.

Conrad Kottak, Richard Pace, and James Hinote have produced the most rigorous long-term data on the entry and impact of television on rural areas and small towns.[91] As television (led by Globo) spread into these areas in the 1980s and 1990s, local viewers were gradually exposed to an array of national symbols, rituals, and beliefs, especially via *telenovelas*. Although *carnaval* eventually received an enormous amount of coverage each year on major networks (especially Globo, Manchete, and SBT), and locals understood and watched this national ritual unfold on their screens each year, they consistently downplayed the importance of *carnaval* for themselves and their communities. In tiny Gurupá in the eastern Amazon, and in the village of Arembepe on the Bahian coast, the local versions of the *festas juninas* (June Festivals, another national ritual) assumed a much larger role in local life and culture. While the *festas* helped define local identity, the onslaught of television broadcasting drew locals into a larger conversation about national identity. While conversant with the national ritual and symbols, this marker of national identity clearly did not play as prominent a role in their lives as the *festas juninas* and local identity. In these layered identities, the *festas* trumped *carnaval*, yet both became part of local people's knowledge about national rituals.

Television made possible the diffusion of this national ritual – in all of its aural and visual splendor – across the national territory by the 1990s, and also allowed all the inhabitants of the nation to experience *carnaval* in real time – even if only via their television sets.[92] Even if each locale did not have its own samba schools, parades, masked balls, or if locals did not dance to the rhythm of samba, virtually all the inhabitants of Brazil now had a regular exposure to the music, dance, and the spectacle of this iconic ritual. The versions of *carnaval* might vary across the country from the staggering opulence of Rio de Janeiro, the street festivals of Salvador, or the small-scale adaptations in towns and villages of the interior. The understanding of these symbols and the meaning of this ritual might vary widely across classes and regions, yet it had become one of those few rituals that could be experienced and shared by everyone in the country. Somewhat like the Christmas holidays in the United States, one does not have to be a Christian to be surrounded by, and bombarded by, the sights and sounds of the holiday events. One need not love and participate in *carnaval* or *futebol* to experience their importance and reach.

Both *carnaval* and *futebol* had to compete with the *novelas* and other programming to break into the select group of genres that dominated Brazilian national broadcasting. The resistance of club management in Brazilian *futebol* made it very difficult until the 1990s to broadcast club games even as the great drain of highly talented players began their exodus out of the country to play for the much more lucrative European leagues.[93] World Cup matches were different. Globo could purchase the broadcasting rights and transmit games across Brazil in real time beginning with the glorious "*tri*" in 1970 as Pelé and his teammates won an unprecedent third Jules Rimet trophy in Mexico. For the first time, Brazilians across the nation could experience their team in real time, in color, and in the glory of the so-called *jogo bonito* (beautiful game) style. Ironically, the growing importance, higher ratings, and appeal of the national team accelerated over the next two decades even as the *seleção* (national team) failed to reproduce the glory and success of the 1958–1970 years. Not until 1994 would Brazil once again win the World Cup, yet in the preceding quarter-century television had helped make *futebol* the most dominant symbol of Brazilian identity, and the most potent image of *mestiçagem*.

The emergence and expansion of television broadcasting, especially Rede Globo, transformed Brazil in the 1970s and 1980s creating a truly national, real-time conversation about Brazilian society and culture. The *JN* and *telenovelas* linked up the inhabitants of Brazil and offered them an increasingly common national vocabulary and set of symbols. As scholars of media studies have shown, national broadcasting has made *telenovelas, carnaval,* and *futebol* "the most reliable cultural unifiers" in Brazil.[94] *Futebol* has probably become the most resonant and potent marker of Brazilian national identity, ironically, in an age of globalization and the decline of the great club teams in Brazil.[95] *Carnaval*, perhaps the most prominent of the "traditional" national rituals is a more complicated marker, one that is very resonant with Brazilians, but not nearly as universal as *futebol* has become. Although a truly national ritual and holiday, *carnaval* is not embraced equally across Brazil's regions, and its appeal is enormous, but not as powerful as *telenovelas* and *futebol*.

NOTES

1. Robert Stam, João Luiz Vieira, and Ismael Xavier, "The Shape of Brazilian Cinema in the Postmodern Age," in *Brazilian Cinema*, eds., Randal Johnson and Robert Stam, Expanded Edition (New York: Columbia University Press, 1995), 391.
2. "Os programas tinham enorme audiência. Pela primeira vez, uma criança de Copacabana podia perceber que o búfalo existente nos campos alagados do Amazonas era parte do seu país; da mesma forma, um índio em Belém do Pará conseguia ver pela televisão os altos edifícios do Rio de Janeiro. A ideia de nação começou a ser entendida." Joe Wallach, *Meu capítulo na TV Globo*, texto original editado por Randal Johnson (Rio de Janeiro:Topbooks, 2011), 193.
3. "eu vi um Brasil na TV" Quote in Kehl (1986), 167. See also www.chicobuar que.com.br/letras/byebyebr_79.htm
4. Staubhaar argues that film, in contrast to the nationalizing effects of television, "tends to be more of a globalizing force and that music, in recordings or on the radio, tends to be a complex force with truly local, national, and global

elements all strongly visible." Joseph D. Straubhaar, *World Television: From Global to Local* (Los Angeles: Sage Publications, 2007), 7.

5. Conrad Phillip Kottak, *Prime-Time Society: An Anthropological Analysis of Television and Culture*, updated edition (Walnut Creek, CA: Left Coast Press, 2009), esp. 36–37 and 189.

6. For a treatment of the role of television in the formation of identities in a global context, see Chris Baker, *Television, Globalization and Cultural Identities* (Buckingham, England: Open University Press, 1999).

7. Thomas Hylland Eriksen, "Nationalism and the Internet," *Nations and Nationalism*, 13:1 (2007), 1–17. Esther Hamburger, *O Brasil antenado: a sociedade da novela* (Rio de Janeiro: Jorge Zahar Editor, 2005), 36–38. In comparison, the major newspapers of Rio de Janeiro and São Paulo in the 1980s had daily publishing runs of 160–240,000 copies. There were less than 4 copies per Brazilian in the 1980s, one-third of the number in the 1950s! Carlos Eduardo Lins da Silva, *Muito além do Jardim Botânico: um estudo sobre aaudiência do Jornal Nacional da Globo entre trabalhadores* (São Paulo: Summus, 1985), 27.

8. In a survey in 2010, 65 percent of Brazilians said that television was their preferred source of information, 12 percent turned to newspapers, and 7 percent radio, and 7 percent to the Internet. Uirá Machado, "TV é a principal fonte de informação dos eleitores," *Folha de São Paulo* (28 de julho de 2010), A7. For an essay that places the rise of consumer culture in Brazil in world perspective, see James P. Woodward, "Consumer Culture, Market Empire, and the Global South," *Journal of World History*, 23:2 (June 2012), 375–98.

9. Richard Pace and Brian P. Hinote, *Amazon Town TV: An Audience Ethnography in Gurupá, Brazil* (Austin: University of Texas Press, 2013), 27. See also Adauto Novaes, ed., *Rede imaginária: televisão e democracia* (São Paulo: Companhia das Letras, 1991), 309.

10. Carlos Eduardo Lins da Silva, "Television in Brazil," in David Ward, ed., *Television and Public Policy: Change and Continuity in an Era of Global Liberalization* (New York: Lawrence Erlbaum Associates, 2008), 28–30; Samantha Nogueira Joyce, *Brazilian Telenovelas and the Myth of Racial Democracy* (Lanham, MD: Lexington Books, 2012), 8.

11. Kottak, *Prime-Time Society*, 16.

12. Joyce, *Brazilian Telenovelas and the Myth of Racial Democracy*, 97.

13. "Brazilian television does more to spread national than international culture patterns. It familiarizes rural people with urban and national norms... For most Brazilians, television is the main gateway to the global village." Kottak, *Prime-Time Society*, 189.

14. Straubhaar, *World Television: From Global to Local*, 208–12.

15. Joseph Straubhaar, "Choosing National TV: Cultural Capital, Language, and Cultural Proximity in Brazil," in Michael G. Elasmar, ed., *The Impact of International Television: A Paradigm Shift* (Mahwah, NJ: Lawrence Erlbaum Associates, Publishers, 2003), 95. Quotes from 98.

16. Kottak, *Prime-Time Society*, 10.

17. For a fine summary of developmental nationalism in these years, see Rafael R. Ioris, *Transforming Brazil: A History of National Development in the Postwar Era* (New York: Routledge, 2014), esp. 38, 118, 127.

18. Hamburger, *O Brasil antenado*, 33.

19. See, for example, Barbara Moore, Marvin R. Bensman, and Jim Van Dyke, *Prime-Time Television: A Concise History* (Westport, CT: Praeger, 2006) and Eric Burns, *Invasion of the Mind Snatcher: Television's Conquest of America in the Fifties* (Philadelphia: Temple University Press, 2010).

20. Among the most important studies of this revolution are: Pace and Hinote, *Amazon Town TV*; Kottak, *Prime-Time Society*; Lins da Silva, *Muito além do Jardim Botânico*; Thomas Tufte, *Living with the Rubbish Queen: Telenovelas, Culture and Modernity in Brazil* (Luton, UK: University of Luton Press, 2000); Antonio La Pastina, "The Telenovela Way of Knowledge: An Ethnographic Reception Study among Rural Viewers in Brazil," Ph.D. diss., University of Texas at Austin, 1999.

21. Lins da Silva, *Muito além do Jardim Botânico*, 26–27. The largest circulations, of course, were in Rio de Janeiro and São Paulo with Roberto Marinho's *O Globo* in Rio at the top of the list with around 240,000.

22. Maria Rita Kehl, "Eu vi um Brasil na TV," in Inimá F. Simões, Alcir Henrique da Costa, Maria Rita Kehl, *Um país no ar: história da TV brasileira em três canais* (São Paulo: Editora Brasiliense S.A., 1986), 167–276; Kottak, *Prime-Time Society*, 20–51.

23. In the mid-1950s there were just a quarter of a million television sets in Rio de Janeiro, São Paulo, and Belo Horizonte combined reaching perhaps a million viewers. (The three state capitals had a combined population of 7–8 million in the 1950s.) In comparison, the city of São Paulo had more than 160 cinema screens and nearly 60 million tickets sold in 1956. Cinema remained a more important form of leisure than television into the 1970s. Simões, Costa, Kehl, *Um país no ar*, 47–48.

24. Simões, Costa, Kehl, *Um país no ar*, 86; Wallach, 86–87; Hamburger, *O Brasil antenado*, 22.

25. Cassiano Ferreira Simões e Fernando Mattos, "Elementos histórico-regulatórios da televisão brasileira," in Brittos e Bolaño, *Rede Globo*, 41, and, Fernando Morais, *Chatô, o rei do Brasil* (São Paulo: Companhia das Letras, 1994).

26. Wallach, 16–17, 27, 86–92; Kehl, "Eu vi um Brasil na TV," 167–276.

27. For the Globo version of the story, see Wallach, esp. 40–45. For a harshly critical analysis, see Daniel Herz, *A história secreta da Rede Globo* (Porto Alegre: tchê, 1987), esp. 123–90.

28. For a detailed and sophisticated analysis of the revolution in telecommunications and the unification of the national territory, especially since the 1960s, see Milton Santos e María Laura Silveira, *O Brasil: território e sociedade no início do século XXI*, 12ª.edn. (Rio de Janeiro: Editora Record, 2008).

29. For a very nuanced and perceptive account of this interplay of talent and power, see Lins da Silva, *Muito além do Jardim Botânico*. For the construction of the network, see Maria Rita Kehl, "Eu vi um Brasil na TV," 191.

30. Kottak and Pace both describe this process of transformation, in the first case in the tiny fishing village of Arembepe, Bahia, and in the second, in the small Amazonian town, Gurupá. Conrad Phillip Kottak, *Assault on Paradise: Social Change in a Brazilian Village*, 2nd edn. (New York: McGraw-Hill, Inc., 1992) and Richard Pace, *The Struggle for Amazon Town: Gurupá Revisited* (Boulder, CO: Lynne Rienner, 1998).

31. Kottak, *Prime-Time Society*, xxvi.

32. Tufte, 80.

33. Kottak, *Prime-Time Society*, 12. By the beginning of the twenty-first century, nearly 90 percent of Brazilian households had a television set. Thais Machado-Borges, *Only for You!: Brazilians and the Telenovela Flow* (Stockholm: Stockholm Studies in Social Anthropology, 2003), 6.

34. Wallach, 131–37 and Marialva Barbosa e Ana Paula Goulart Ribeiro, "Telejornalismo na Globo: vestígios, narrativa e temporalidade," in Valério Cruz Brittos e César Ricardo Siqueira Bolaño, orgs., *Rede Globo:40 anos de poder e hegemonia* (São Paulo: Paulus, 2005), 218–19.

35. Tufte, 80.

36. For an example of the emphatic denunciation of Globo, see Herz, *A história secreta da Rede Globo*. A very positive "official" version is Pedro Bial, *Roberto Marinho* (Rio de Janeiro: Jorge Zahar Editor, 2005).

37. "*The main purpose of commercial television is neither to entertain nor to enlighten, but to sell.*" (emphasis in original) Kottak, *Prime-Time Society*, 23.

    Aguinaldo Silva afirma: "a TV é um negócio explorado por capitais privados, que depende de anunciantes. Para ter anunciantes, ela depende de altos índices de audiência. E para ter audiência, ela tem que ser média, mediana mesmo. Não pode ser de vanguarda, porque a emissora vai à falência. Isso é elementar ... O que uma novela precisa é ser popular. Se é popular é boa."

                                        Ortiz, Borelli, Ramos, *Telenovela*, 159.

38. For works with a similar perspective, see Lins da Silva, *Muito além do Jardim Botânico*; Kottak, *Prime-Time Society*; and, Straubhaar, *World Television*. Straubhaar argues that the creation and dissemination of "preferred televisual messages" takes shape out of at least six key groups: the State, advertisers, networks, writers, producers, and the audience. Straubhaar, 151.

39. Hamburger, *O Brasil antenado*, 35.

40. Silvia Helena Simões Borelli, "Telenovelas: padrão de produção e matrizes populares," in Brittos e Bolaño, *Rede Globo*, 187; and, Lins da Silva, *Muito além do Jardim Botânico*, 29.

41. For a fine, but in-house, history of the first 35 years of the *Jornal Nacional*, see *Jornal Nacional: a notícia faz história/Memória Globo* (Rio de Janeiro: Jorge Zahar Editor, 2004).

42. Brittos e Bolaño, *Rede Globo*, 189.

43. Roberto Marinho "Achava que a América era exemplo a ser seguido pelo Brasil." Wallach, 72.

44. Kottak, *Prime-Time Society*, 37–38.

45. Nahuel Ribke, "Decoding Television Censorship during the Last Brazilian Military Regime," *Media History*, 17:1 (2011), 49–61.

46. Globo spent more than half of its budget producing the highly lucrative *novelas*. Kehl, "Eu vi um Brasil na TV," 243 and 265–66.

47. Lins da Silva, *Muito além do Jardim Botânico*, 38; Hamburger, *O Brasil antenado*, 35.

48. "Sinto-me feliz, todas as noites, quando ligo a televisão para assistir ao jornal. Enquanto as notícias dão conta de greves, agitações, atentados e conflitos em várias partes do mundo, o Brasil marcha em paz, rumo ao desenvolvimento. É como se eu tomasse um tranquilizante, após um dia de trabalho." Quoted in Lins da Silva, *Muito além do Jardim Botânico*, 39.

49. Kottak, *Prime-Time Society*, 36–37 and 91–92.

50. "No trem da abertura, a Rede Globo é o ultimo vagão e o Jornal Nacional é o último banco. Mas, mesmo chegando atrasados, nós também vamos chegar na mesma estação que a locomotiva." Quoted in Lins da Silva, *Muito além do Jardim Botânico*, 40.

51. Eles "não eram alienados nem massa ignara". Lins da Silva, *Muito além do Jardim Botânico*, 141.

52. Straubhaar, *World Television*, 242.

53. Artur da Távola, *A telenovela brasileira: história, análise e conteúdo* (São Paulo: Globo, 1996), 111–17.

54. Straubhaar, *World Television*, 152–57. Quote on 155.

55. "With 30–40 years of telenovelas and with more than 50 years of radio-novelas, most Brazilians have been born with novelas as part of their everyday life." Tufte, 87.

56. "A telenovela, cotidiana e doméstica, transformou-se nesse período na principal forma de produção de imagem ideal do homem brasileiro. Mais especificamente, as novelas das 20h da Globo, as mais abrangentes e mais assistidas da televisão brasileira, cumpriram nos anos 70 – quando começaram a se modernizar e a se afirmar com uma estética realista – o papel de oferecer ao brasileiro desenraizado que perdeu sua identidade cultural um espelho glamurizado, mais próximo da realidade de seu desejo do que da realidade de sua vida, e que por isso mesmo funcionou como elemento conformador de uma nova identidade, identidade brasileira, identidade-de-brasileiros, talvez o mais parecido com uma identidade nacional que este país já teve." Kehl, "Eu vi um Brasil na TV," 289.

57. "A novela da televisão veiculou maciçamente a dramaturgia brasileira. Colocou no vídeo o que o cinema brasileiro já tinha colocado na tela: o coronel, o drama rural. Com isso habituou o povo a se ver, a ter o seu próprio espelho. Até aí o cara que morava em favela só via filmes de lordes, fazendeiros, 'gentefina'. Então, chegou a telenovela e fez o que o cinema já tinha feito, sem nunca ter conseguido chegar ao público por causa do monopólio das salas de exibição. A Globo produz as suas novelas e ele mesma as leva dentro das casas. Não há intermédiarios e essa é a sua grande vantagem." Quoted in Távola, 56.

58. "Sem novela uma estação não vive; porque a novela dá audiência fixa. A base da televisão é a novela." Kehl, "Euvi um Brasilna TV," 243.

59. Tufte, 106.

60. Tufte, 16, quote from 19.

61. "la televisión es **medio** no sólo en el sentido instrumental – medible en los efectos que produce – sino en el más profundamente cultural de **mediación** entre la realidad y el deseo, entre lo que vivimos y lo que soñamos." [emphasis in original] J. Martín-Barbero y Sonia Muñoz, coord., *Televisión y melodrama: géneros y lecturas de la telenovela y Colombia* (Bogotá: Tercer Mundo Editores, 1992), 15.

62. Hamburger argues that, "Programas televisivos de sucesso expressam uma *sintonia* entre produtores e telespectadores. Profissionais de televisão devem *antenar* expectativas do público. *Antenar, sintonizar*, verbos que ganharam novo sentido para expressar um senso de conectividade, o qual combina referência à sensibilidade fisiológica dos animais e à propriedade de transmissão dos aparelhos electrónicos. Um bom profissional de televisão, um pesquisador, um produtor, diretor ou escritor, deve estar antenado, ou seja, deve expressar inquietações do público." Hamburger, *O Brasil antenado*, 60.

63. At times, the *novela* attracted 40 percent of all male viewers. Esther Hamburger, "Telenovelas e Interpretações do Brasil," *Lua Nova*, 82 (2011), 67 and 75.

64. For example, see Távola, 33. See also, Hamburger, *O Brasil antenado*, 19–20.

65. "Fazer novela envolve uma dinâmica complexa de relações entre equipes de profissionais e entre estas e o público, mediados pela imprensa e por jogos de poder." Hamburger, *O Brasil antenado*, 40–45. Quote from 44–45.

66. Jesús Martín-Barbero, *De los medios a las mediaciones: comunicación, cultura y hegemonía* (Barcelona: Gustavo Gili, 1987). "In this way the processes of mediation become infinite processes in which meaning is produced in the constant interaction between the media product and the viewers or listeners as well as the social interaction between people." Tufte, 19. "[T]he telenovela is a site of mediations between production, reception, and culture. There is constant negotiation between the writers, director, production team, actors, audience, and institutions that participate in the social formation." Joyce, *Brazilian Telenovelas and the Myth of Racial Democracy*, 5.

67. Brittos e Bolaño, *Rede Globo*, 197–98. An extensive and sophisticated study of the *novela Rei do Gado* (1996–1997) showed clearly that the episodes provoke serious discussion in the homes of viewers. Neuza Sanches e João Gabriel de Lima, "Entre a tela e a vida real," *Veja* (12 February 1997), 52–56. For a detailed analysis of the interplay between the writers and viewers of *Rei do Gado*, see Straubhaar, *World Television*, 156–57.

68. According to Hamburger, "As novelas da Rede Globo se tornaram espaço privilegiado de atualização de uma comunidade nacional imaginada como 'país do futuro', um tema antigo caro a Stefan Zweig." Hamburger, "Telenovelas e Interpretações do Brasil," 78.

69. Tufte, 101–2; Dias Gomes, *Apenas um subversivo* (Rio de Janeiro: Bertrand Brasil, 1998), 257. For an in-depth analysis of the first decades of national *telenovelas*, see Renato Ortiz, Silvia Helena Simões Borelli, José Mário Ortiz Ramos, *Telenovela: história e produção* (São Paulo: Editora Brasiliense, 1989).

70. "tramas no tempo contemporâneo, sucessivamente atualizado, e em espaços geográficos, urbanos o rurais, facilmente reconhecíveis, assim como um

recurso a convenções do documentário, estruturaram um universo verossímil, reconhecido como o território nacional." Hamburger, *O Brasil antenado*, 149.

71. Esther Hamburger, "Telenovelas e Interpretações do Brasil," *Lua Nova*, 82 (2011), 70–71.

72. Kottak, *Prime-Time Society*, 42.

73. Ortiz, Borelli, Ramos, *Telenovela*, 78–79; Joel Zito Araújo, *A negação do Brasil: o negro na telenovela brasileira* (São Paulo: Editora SENAC, 2000), 105.

74. Straubhaar, *World Television*, 155. Some literary critics have noted the parallel with the "herói sem nenhum carater" of Mário de Andrade's classic, *Macunaíma*.

75. Gomes, *Apenas um subversivo*.

76. José Bonifácio Oliveira Sobrinho, *O livro do Boni* (Rio de Janeiro: Casa da Palavra, 2011), 341–42.

77. Tufte, 105.

78. "Sonia Braga era *a* Gabriela. Banho de sol, um pouco de canela naquele pele e ... Sonia Braga ia ser Gabriela. Alguém pode sugerir outra Gabriela? Não! Acho que ninguém no mundo poderia sugerir outra Gabriela." Daniel Filho, *O circo eletrônico: fazendo TV no Brasil* (Rio de Janeiro: Jorge Zahar Editor, 2001), 303–4.

79. Oliveira Sobrinho, *O livro do Boni*, 338–39; Ortiz, Borelli, Ramos, *Telenovelas*, 185.

80. Kehl, "Eu vi um Brasil na TV," 266.

81. Pace and Hinote, *Amazon Town TV*, 93.

82. In these years, roughly 10 percent of Brazilians were in the upper class (A), another 30 percent in the upper middle class (B), 40 percent in the middle class (C), and 20 percent in the lower classes (D & E). Hamburger, *O Brasil antenado*, 51–55. Quote from 51.

83. Hamburger, *O Brasil antenado*, 50–51. Oliveira Sobrinho, *O livro do Boni*, 421–24.

84. Hamburger, *O Brasil antenado*, 57–58.

85. See, for example, Joel Zito Araújo, *A negação do Brasil: o negro na telenovela brasileira* (São Paulo: Editora SENAC, 2000).

86. In the famous words of Joãozinho Trinta, one of Brazil's most famous *carnaval* designers, "Only intellectuals like misery. The poor prefer luxury." Quoted in Edmonds, *Pretty Modern*, epigraph on frontispiece.

87. "simbolicamente, são histórias que ressaltam o branqueamento do segmento negro e a dissolução dos afro-descendentes na miscegenação com os euro-descendentes." Araújo, *A negação do Brasil*, 183.

88. "Diziam que eu era racista. Engraçado que os negros diziam que eu não escalava negros. e os brancos diziam que eu era racista porque só escalava negros. Então eu procurava misturar. Até hoje, a minha visão de Brasil é essa, é mistura mesmo!" Araújo, *A negação do Brasil*, 117.

89. Machado-Borges, 143; Livio Sansone, *Blackness Without Ethnicity: Constructing Race in Brazil* (New York: Palgrave Macmillan, 2003).

90. "A exclusão racial no Brasil fala em duas vozes: uma, no privado, sobre o valor da branquitude e outra, pronunciada em alto e bom som, sobre a noção de que cor e raça são de importância relativa já que a população é mestiça." Liv Sovik, *Aqui ninguém é branco* (Rio de Janeiro: Aeroplano, 2009), 38.

91. Kottak, *Prime-Time Society*, esp. 167–69 and 174–76; Pace and Hinote, *Amazon TV*, esp. 164–65.

92. Even an elderly Japanese-Brazilian living the life of a hermit deep in the Amazon uses a generator and antenna to watch his favorite team, Flamengo! Simon Romero, "A 'Hermit of the Jungle' Stands Guard in the Amazon," *New York Times* (9 May 2015), A4.

93. Cesar Gordon and Ronaldo Helal, "The Crisis of Brazilian Football: Perspectives for the Twenty-First Century," in J. A. Mangan and Lamartine P. DaCosta, eds., *Sport in Latin American Society: Past and Present* (London: Frank Cass, 2002), 150.

94. Kottak, *Prime-Time Society*, 36–37.

95. In a recent national poll, both men (82%) and women (72%) named *futebol* as the greatest passion of Brazilians. The next closest passion (at 35%) was beer, with *carnaval* coming in third (at 30%). The poll was conducted by the highly regarded research agency, the Instituto Brasileiro de Opinião Pública e Estatística, IBOPE. www.ibope.com.br/pt-br/noticias/Paginas/Futebol-e-a-maior-paixao-dos-brasileiros.aspx[accessed 16 December 2014]

5

The Beautiful Game

Performing the Freyrean Vision

Tell me how you play, and I will tell you who you are.

Traditional football saying

It was football that joined together the national anthem and the people, that married the team jersey and the flag, that popularized the idea of the fatherland and of the nation as something within the reach of the common man and not just the 'doctor' and the boss. The world championships that we conquered compelled us to bring together bourgeois civility and carnival; play and official religious belief; magic and church; capitalist investment and love for Brazil.[1]

Roberto DaMatta

By using a unique body language and inventing an original style for a quasi-universal sport, Brazil's working class have succeeded in making a silent contribution to their relative social ascent while furnishing an important domain for Brazilian national identity, wherein they have contributed to reverse the elite's racist stereotypes – and an ethnocentrism internalized by society as a whole.[2]

José Sergio Leite Lopes

In futebol there is art, dignity, genius, bad luck, gods and demons, freedom and fate, flags, hymns and tears, and above all the discovery that although Brazil is bad at a lot of things, it is good with the ball. It is a football champion, which is very important. After all, it is better to be a champion in samba, carnival and football than in war or the sale of rockets.[3]

David Goldblatt

CREATING THE MYTH OF *FUTEBOL-MULATO*

Radio, film, and television helped create and shape an ongoing conversation about national identity in Brazil from the 1930s to the 1990s. The aural and visual cultures facilitated by these technologies eventually brought a shared set of myths, symbols, and rituals into the *bairros* and homes of all the inhabitants within Brazil's borders – and beyond. Samba emerged as the archetypal Brazilian music, *carnaval* as the iconic cultural ritual, and *mestiçagem* as Brazil's most powerful national myth. These technologies and media helped forge a mélange of popular and elite cultures, at the same time defining and redefining the meaning of "popular." The emergence of Rede Globo in the 1960s and 1970s initiated the final stage in the evolution of Gilberto Freyre's vision of *mestiçagem* as *the* dominant national myth, one that outshone and overwhelmed all other competing narratives of national identity. Televised soccer – *futebol* – provided the final piece in the decades-long construction of this narrative. Beginning in 1970, all Brazilians could watch the Freyrean vision performed before their very eyes, played out on football pitches across Brazil, and around the globe – in real time. For some, "The twentieth century was, for Brazil, the football century."[4]

The phenomenal success and appeal of *futebol*, and Brazil's extraordinary triumphs in the international arena, provided an unprecedented stage for performing this version of Brazilian identity.[5] Many Brazilians (and foreigners) saw in the faces and skills of the players, especially on the national team (*seleção nacional*), the very embodiment of Freyre's vision.[6] The phenomenal success of Brazil – World Cup victories in 1958, 1962, 1970 – and the roles of players such as Garrincha and Pelé, seemed to confirm that Brazil *was* the land of racial and cultural mixture, and that *mestiçagem* produced results that confirmed the nation's exuberance and greatness. These were victories "of art over strength, of intuition and spontaneity over reason, of magic over technology, in short, the victory of a football and a nation which were harmonized by the mixing of their differences." The Brazilians had taken an English game, transformed it into a means of social mobility and success for some poor and dark-skinned Brazilians, and developed a universally recognized style of play (*futebol-arte*) that, seemingly, was the fruit of the very racial and cultural mixture that Freyre located at the core of national culture.[7]

Futebol, especially during the World Cup, became in the last half of the twentieth century "a collective ritual, as a carnivalesque spectacular and as a historical narrative, open to all Brazilians." Incredible "global success

FIGURE 5.1   The Brazilian National Team, 1958, Stockholm, Sweden
Source:AFP/AFP/Getty Images

and poetic acclaim" provided *futebol* with a role in Brazilian society and culture even more encompassing than samba and *carnaval*.[8] It became a sort of civic religion open to all Brazilians regardless of class, color, origin, or gender. "Soccer," says the great Mexican writer Juan Villoro, "has much less to do with sporting triumphs than with the desire to form an emotional community."[9] For the Brazilians, it has been about both sporting triumphs and forming an emotional community. (The legendary soccer broadcaster Galvão Bueno has described himself as "a salesman of emotions.")[10] The power of this narrative of *futebol-mulato* (in the words of Gilberto Freyre) and the myth of *mestiçagem* reinforced each other and gradually came to dominate the way Brazilians envisioned their own national style of play, and the way international observers saw Brazil's style of football – and Brazil.[11] As with the Freyrean vision, the narrative of *futebol-mulato* or *futebol-arte*, as the Brazilian style began to face criticism and skeptics by the 1980s, and by the beginning of the twenty-first century, few experts would argue that Brazil still had a distinctive style, much less one that could be equated with the *futebol-arte* of the glory days of Pelé and the *tri-campeões*. Even more so than its larger national myth of *mestiçagem*, the myth of *futebol-arte* had entered into crisis by the 1990s.[12]

As many Brazilian writers have pointed out, *futebol* became fundamental to national identity both through the efforts of the State (as well as cultural and political elites) and by capturing the hearts and minds of the *povo*. In the words of the sociologist Janet Lever in her classic study *Soccer Madness*, "Sport contributes to national integration by giving people of different social classes, ethnicities, races, and religions something to share as a basis for their ritual solidarity."[13] For the late literary critic and historian Nicolau Sevcenko, "football lends itself marvelously to the consolidation of identity linkages full of affective power." It is a team sport that does not require any specific physical gifts, and it can be played anywhere, with simple rules that are easily understood.[14] Football also plays a key role in the ongoing and complex interaction of regional and national identities. For most of the time, fans devote themselves ardently to their *time* (team), be it Flamengo, Atlético Mineiro, Sport, or one of much less power and importance. Yet, when the national team plays, and when the World Cup takes place every four years, the local and regional rivalries give way to an even more potent emotional attachment to the *seleção*.

Beginning with the Vargas regimes in the 1930s through the military dictatorship in the 1960s and 1970s, Brazil's political leaders have attempted to harness the popularity of the sport for State purposes. Under the Estado Novo (1937–1945), and much like the fascist regimes in Europe, Vargas sought to support this emerging sport as a symbol of national success.[15] In 1942, the Vargas regime brought all football clubs under the *Conselho Nacional de Desportos* (CND) to centralize and harness the growing popularity and appeal of *futebol*. (In 1979, the military regime mandated that all clubs come under the supervision of the newly created *Confederação Brasileira de Futebol* [CBF].)[16] The military regime invested heavily in the national team in 1970 and then fully exploited this crowning moment in Brazilian *futebol* for their vision of nation-building and nationalism. Much as with television, samba, and *carnaval, futebol* became such a vital part of national culture not because it was imposed by the State but rather as a result of the collective support from tens of millions of common people for their players and teams. *Futebol*'s enormous appeal, the efforts of the State, with the power of television (after 1970), all combined to make this sport the most vibrant and potent symbol of Brazilian national identity, and the World Cup competition as one of the key national rituals, even more encompassing than *carnaval*.[17] As *futebol* scholar Édison Gastaldo has argued, no national holiday provokes as intense nationalistic feelings as Brazil's World Cup matches.[18]

The rise of *futebol* in Brazil began in the early twentieth century as it moved from an elite, amateur, club-based pastime to a professional sport increasingly dominated by players from the lower and middle classes, and the preferred sport of the *povo*.[19] The emergence of *futebol* as the national sport of Brazil after the 1930s parallels and intertwines with the development of radio, film, television, and the Freyrean vision of *mestiçagem*. The international failures (and then successes) of Brazilian *futebol* provided an important, ongoing forum for the discussion of race in Brazil – from the disastrous World Cup defeat in the newly inaugurated Maracanã stadium in 1950 to the unparalleled success of the Brazilian team winning three of four World Cup championships between 1958 and 1970 to the humiliating defeat in the 2014 semifinals against Germany in the newly refurbished Mineirão. Across the last six or seven decades, Brazilians have intensely argued about the nature and direction of their *futebol*, if there really existed a Brazilian style, and whether that style and its phenomenal successes in the "golden age" (1958–1970) could be reproduced.

At the very moment that national television emerged in Brazil in the 1970s and 1980s, Brazilian *futebol* had been consecrated on an international stage as the best in the world with its own distinct style based on athleticism, improvisation, and a natural beauty – *futebol-arte*. For Roberto DaMatta, this Brazilian style, of *futebol-mulato*, is one that places high value on "the exceptionally skillful use of the body and the legs which creates a beautiful game to watch."[20] The great English historian Eric Hobsbawm expressed a widespread view when he remarked, "who, having seen the Brazilian team in its days of glory will deny its claim to art?"[21] From Leônidas da Silva in the 1930s and 1940s, to Didi and Garrincha in the 1950s, to Pelé in the 1960s and 1970s, commentators defined Brazilian *futebol* as *mestiço* or *mulato* shaped by the mix of races on the pitch and their style of play.

Just as *Casa-grande e senzala* stands as the manifesto of the role of *mestiçagem* in the formation of Brazilian society, one foundational book has deeply shaped the way Brazilians think about *futebol* and race – Mário Filho's *O negro no futebol brasileiro* (first edition, 1947).[22] The son of one of the early twentieth century's most prominent journalists (Mário Rodrigues), and the brother of Brazil's most notable playwright (Nelson

Rodrigues), Mário Filho was also a personal friend of Gilberto Freyre.[23] In the 1930s and 1940s, Mário Filho became one of Brazil's most important and influential sportswriters and publishers. He played a key role in the organization of Rio's samba schools into the version of *carnaval* that became standardized in the 1930s and 1940s. While bringing the competitive sports model to *carnaval* in Rio, Mário Filho brought the carnivalesque spirit to *futebol*.[24] The vision of Brazilian *futebol* that he constructed in *O negro no futebol brasileiro* became as dominant in Brazilians' vision of their national sport as Freyre's interpretation of Brazilian culture.[25] Building on Freyre's 1938 essay on Brazil's play in the World Cup, Mário Filho took the concept of *futebol-mulato* and provided it with a providential historical narrative.[26] The first edition of the book vividly chronicles the rise of Brazil's distinctive version of football as the story of the triumph of *mestiçagem* and racial democracy on the playing fields of the nation, and by extension, in Brazilian society.

Although about "the *negro*," the book tells the tale of not only blacks but also the racially mixed, from the first *mulato* star in the 1910s and 1920s (Friedenreich) to Leônidas da Silva, the *Diamante Negro*, and Domingos da Guia in the 1930s and 1940s. The second, revised edition (1964), appeared in the aftermath of the World Cup titles in 1958 (Sweden) and 1962 (Chile), featuring Garrincha (of racially mixed parentage) and Edson Arantes do Nascimento – better known as Pelé. Although Mário Filho placed *mestiçagem* and the creativity it produced at the core of Brazilian *futebol* and its success, he seemed to have a strong bias for the rational, controlled creativity of Domingos da Guia over the *malandragem* and undisciplined play of da Silva. In the second edition, he recognized the extraordinary skills of Garrincha, but preferred the more disciplined play of Pelé, who he christened "the King" (*o Rei*).[27] As Denaldo de Souza has emphasized, "The work consolidated the representation of Brazilian football as an ideal of guile and art and against the European style of football that gave greater value to efficiency and strength."[28] Freyre wrote the foreword for the 1947 edition praising the interpretation and helping consecrate the book as the definitive work on the subject. No other book has had more influence in the way Brazilian *futebol* has been interpreted by Brazilians and non-Brazilians.

FROM ENGLISH SPORT TO *JOGO DO POVO*

Even more so than music, football reveals the truly transnational processes at play in the creation of "national" identities. The Brazilians gradually adopted an English game, developed their own version, came to dominate world football, and became the greatest exporter of professional players across the globe. By the 1990s, Brazilian players and fans participated in a truly global sports network with hundreds of Brazilians playing in the European premier leagues (and other leagues around the globe) and many Europeans and Latin Americans playing in Brazilian leagues. Within the country, and around the world, Brazil by the 1970s and 1980s had become known as the soccer or *futebol* nation. This narrative affirms both Brazil's excellence as a global football power and *futebol*'s place at the core of national identity. One much debated corollary of this narrative is the belief that Brazilians somehow experience football more intensely and vividly than other nations.[29] Despite winning their unprecedented fourth World Cup in the United States in 1994, the Brazilian team and coach came under heavy criticism for playing *unlike* Brazilians.[30] Much national soul searching took place around a discussion of whether Brazil had lost its ability to play and win with its distinctive *futebol-arte*, whether that style of football was even viable then in world competitions.

In the first half of the twentieth century, football in both Brazil and the rest of the world moved from the exclusive clubs and schools of the British elite to become the "lay religion of the working class."[31] Eduardo Galeano, the great Uruguayan writer and football enthusiast, has summed up this transition: "Soccer had made a lovely voyage: first organized in the colleges and universities of England, it brought joy to the lives of South Americans who had never set foot in a school."[32] The world, Hobsbawm observes, made soccer its own. Ironically, as football became more globalized in the late twentieth century, the World Cup became a symbolic battleground for nation-states and "styles" of football even as the "local" teams in the European leagues became completely multinational.

Like samba and *carnaval* in Rio, *futebol* was virtually nonexistent in Brazil in the late nineteenth century, and just beginning to come of age when Gilberto Freyre published *Casa-grande e senzala* in the early 1930s. Professional leagues, racially mixed teams, and the first national stars emerged along with radio in the 1930s and 1940s.[33] The medium of film documented and publicized Brazil's early excellence in the international arena, as well as its catastrophic failure against Uruguay in the 1950 World Cup. Film and television helped make *futebol* an increasingly important part of Brazil's visual culture in the 1960s, and television consecrated the country's excellence, broadcasting the record-breaking third title in Mexico in 1970. In the decades after 1970, national television broadcasting helped consolidate *futebol* as a central, if not the central, symbol of Brazilian identity – at home and abroad.[34]

Most historians date the organizational beginnings of football in Brazil to Charles Miller, the Brazilian-born and European-educated son of an Englishman in São Paulo, who was one of the first to pursue serious efforts to teach and promote football in Brazil in the 1890s.[35] In the early decades of the twentieth century, the upper classes created teams, usually connected to social clubs and businesses. For these modernizing Brazilian elites, football represented a physical culture and amateurism based on a set of rules of fair play that represented the best of the "civilized" English society they so admired. For several decades, they tried to impose and maintain this vision on the growing football culture in Brazil, and to exclude the poor and darker skinned from "invading" the game and the football pitch.[36] In the first decades of the twentieth century, "football associations" formed, at times taking on the names and logos of British teams. Corinthians, for example, one of the two most popular teams in contemporary Brazil, was founded in São Paulo in 1910, named after a touring British team (made up of Oxford and Cambridge graduates).[37] The formation of some of these teams also took on a "national" turn, as the Portuguese, German, and Italian communities in Brazil organized their own clubs. A few of the great teams in contemporary Brazilian *futebol* took shape around these "foreign" communities in Brazil. Organized in Rio de Janeiro in 1915, Vasco da Gama arose out of the Portuguese immigrant community, while Palmeiras (originally known as Palestra Itália) in São Paulo emerged out of the Italian community in 1915 (changing its name in 1942 due to anti-Axis sentiments). Gremio (in Porto Alegre) was founded by German and English immigrants in 1930.[38]

Much like baseball, football, and basketball in the United States, *futebol* in Brazil offered a lucky few of the less privileged an opportunity to excel on the playing field and move up in society. By the 1920s, it had become increasingly difficult for teams to ignore these outstanding players whose class and color normally excluded them from the top clubs. Already in the first decade of the twentieth century, the Bangu Athletic Club regularly fielded players of all colors drawn from the workers in a British-operated textile factory on the western edge of the city of Rio de Janeiro.[39] The turning point in professionalization and "breaking the color barrier" was Vasco da Gama's racially mixed championship team in 1923. Despite vigorous efforts by the first division clubs to exclude the lower classes and nonwhites, by the 1930s professional leagues had emerged in Rio and São Paulo, and talent, not socioeconomic status, determined excellence on the pitch.[40] In effect, the 1930s mark the emergence of *futebol* as a professional sport increasingly built on athletic talent, across class and racial barriers, and fully embraced as a sport of the *povo*.[41]

This growing tension between amateur/professional and elitism/merit provided early evidence of the democratic nature of *futebol* and its unusual place within Brazilian society. As Roberto DaMatta has so effectively described it, the football pitch became a strikingly egalitarian arena in a society long characterized by hierarchy, privilege, inequality, and racism. This sport, as he notes, "invented to entertain and discipline," in Brazil, "transformed itself (without wanting or knowing it) into the first and probably the most powerful professor of democracy and equality."[42] At the same time, DaMatta points out, the old local values and the imported new ones may have conflicted, but they also survived alongside each other. The "local cultural values, born of a particularist, hierarchical and traditional view of the world," mixed "with a universalist, individualist, and modern logic."[43]

A dynamic mix of discipline and roguishness (*malandragem*) has also long characterized Brazilian *futebol*. The State (and team owners, I would add) promoted sport as a means of disciplining society while many of the greatest and most popular players have continually flouted rules and norms.[44] From Leônidas da Silva in the 1930s and 1940s to Garrincha in the 1950s and 1960s to Romário in the 1980s and 1990s, the "bad boy" or *malandro* has been a staple of Brazilian football, and all of them have been hugely popular with fans. This duality, some would argue, has been at the core of Brazil's struggle to win and remain at the top of world football. While the creativity and improvisation of the *malandro* may be at the heart of the Brazilian style of *futebol-arte*, many Brazilian coaches have sought to impose enough discipline on the style to forge successful teams. The discipline imposed by Carlos Alberto Parreira on the national team's play in the 1994 World Cup drew widespread criticism even though the *seleção* won the title. For many, Parreira had succeeded not only in winning but in suppressing the very essence of *futebol-arte* making too many concessions to *futebol-força*. The beautiful play of Ronaldo and Neymar in recent years illustrates this valuation of *futebol-arte* and the constant tension with efforts by coaches to harness improvisation and individual skill to create teams that can compete and win against the soccer powers in Europe (and Argentina).[45]

Most historians of *futebol* would date Brazil's debut on the international stage to its success in the South American Championship hosted in

Rio de Janeiro in 1919. Artur Friedenreich, the child of a black woman and a German immigrant, scored the winning goal and quickly became the country's first sports star. In an age when *futebol* made the transition from elitist and amateur to a professional sport followed and played by the *povo*, Friedenreich became its first great *craque* (crack player, in the language of the day). One of the few *mulatos* playing the game, he was its biggest star (inversely, somewhat like the white Larry Bird in the 1980s in a National Basketball Association dominated by black players). Throughout the 1920s and 1930s, the leaders of most of the elite teams in Rio de Janeiro and São Paulo balked at professionalization and resisted allowing skill to determine the composition of national teams instead of hierarchy, class, and color prejudices. As a consequence, the larger national debate over the role of race in Brazilian society spilled over into football. For some, it became increasingly clear that national teams did poorly in international competitions precisely because they were selected based on their skin color and class, not on their skills. The dramatic success of the racially mixed Friedenreich presented an enormous challenge for the elitists. The athletic successes of the *mulatos, mestiços*, and black players presented a direct challenge to the old-style, amateur football, and highlighted practices of racial prejudice and exclusion.[46]

For the great cultural critic José Wisnik, "the mulato becomes, rightly, in football and literature, the best interpreter of this cultural configuration [those who are both included and excluded]. Strictly speaking, he is a metaracial, cultural, and social figure who, because of his complex and hybrid nature, can cover for whites and blacks who are literally not mulatos, but are mediators of hybridism."[47] The *mulato*, in both sport and literature, according to Wisnik, is neither rejected nor accepted as the one who "*guards the unconfessable secret of everything*" – "centuries of slavery *and* miscegenation" (emphasis in original).[48] The *mulato* and miscegenation may produce the dynamism and creativity in Brazilian society, but they also confront Brazilians directly with their sordid past of exclusion, subjugation, and racial domination. In the years after 1930, *futebol* became a nationwide stage for playing out this racial and cultural drama, and an inescapable forum for discussions about the very nature of Brazilian society and culture. *Futebol* over these decades provided vivid and dramatic moments when the entire nation cheered, jeered, celebrated, and bemoaned the legacies of their centuries of experience with slavery and racial mixing.

Brazil's next great moment on the international stage was the 1938 World Cup in France.[49] After terrible performances in the first two

World Cups (1930 in Uruguay and 1934 in Italy), for the first time in a major international competition, the Brazilians demonstrated they could play with the best. By 1938, the transition to a team that reflected Brazil's color spectrum was complete.[50] With Domingos da Guia and Leônidas da Silva as the stars (on defense and offense), and an array of racially mixed players, the Brazilians put on a show of their *futebol-arte*. For the first time, radio became a major factor in the promotion of the sport as broadcasters dramatically conveyed the excitement and success of the team across Brazil's airwaves. Leônidas was the top scorer in the tournament, and Brazil finished in third place, losing to eventual champion Italy in the semifinal match. Feted in the French press, Leônidas came home with a nickname, *o Diamante Negro*. In the aftermath of the Cup, one opinion poll showed that Leônidas had become one of the three most popular and celebrated figures in the country, along with the great popular singer Orlando Silva and President Getúlio Vargas.[51] As players such as Domingos da Guia and Leônidas gradually made this English game their own with a distinct national style, a great Brazilian sportswriter made them iconic figures of not only a national style but Brazil's identity.[52]

FUTEBOL-MESTIÇO, FUTEBOL-MULATO, FUTEBOL-ARTE

Mário Filho's writings, his book and his daily journalism, helped firmly establish the myth of *mestiçagem* as central to the identity of Brazilian *futebol* and national identity in the 1940s and 1950s.[53] He adopted Freyre's use of the terms "dionysian" and "apollonian" to analyze playing styles in Brazilian and international football. According to Freyre, "Brazilian football is a dance full of irrational surprises and Dionysiac variations."[54] For Freyre, *futebol* embodied the essence of *mestiçagem* and Brazilian culture in contrast to the cold, rational, and controlled play of the Europeans, which he described as apollonian. For Mário Filho, these contrasting styles also characterized Leônidas da Silva and Domingos da Guia. Although he recognized the brilliance of Leônidas, he seems to have preferred Domingos. Leônidas allowed his dionysian tendencies to dominate his apollonian virtues, while Domingos reversed this mix. The former symbolized the worst defects in the Brazilian character, the *malandro* without constraints. Domingos da Guia, according to Alchorne de Souza, "was the perfect player, he who could best symbolize the nation: Brazilian, disciplined, rational, hardworking and black."[55]

FIGURE 5.2 Leônidas da Silva, World Cup, 1938, Bordeaux, France
Source: STAFF/AFP/Getty Images

Radio and, to a lesser extent, film helped promote the diffusion and massification of *futebol* throughout Brazil in the 1950s and 1960s, reaching into every corner of the country, making players like Domingos and Leônidas national icons. The 1950s began with the greatest tragedy of Brazilian *futebol*, and concluded with the first glimpses of its greatest glories. Ironically, the great tragedy, "the mother of all defeats," may have done as much to consolidate *futebol* as central to Brazilian identity as the country's later World Cup triumphs.[56] Perhaps no other moment in Brazilian sports history – not even its greatest victories – has received as much attention as the *Maracanazo* of 1950. The selection of Brazil to host the 1950 World Cup was testimony to its emergence in the 1940s as a respected football power. In preparation for the event, the Brazilians constructed the largest stadium in the world, and Mário Filho played a prominent role in the selection of the site and scale of the venue – Maracanã.[57] With the home field advantage and a great *seleção*, Brazil quickly became the favorite to win the Cup.

Lamartine Babo, one of the great popular composers of the period, wrote an inspiring anthem for the team, and games took place across Brazil, from Recife to Porto Alegre. Carmen Miranda performed a wildly popular version of the song.[58] The Brazilian team was barely challenged, outscoring their opponents 21–4 in the first five games. Their final game against Uruguay in Maracanã determined the champion. For most of the Brazilian press, the outcome was a foregone conclusion and the celebrations began early. To the astonishment and dismay of the Brazilians, Uruguay won 2–1, spoiling the victory party and provoking decades of agony and soul searching among Brazilian football fans. The winning goal was captured on film and the nightmare was replayed again and again in the aftermath of this national disaster.[59]

One of the principal effects of this shocking defeat were attacks in the media and in many writers' works in the years and decades since, attacks that blamed the loss on the team's black players, in particular, two of its stars – Bigode and Barbosa.[60] The more sophisticated criticism focused on their perceived faulty playing skills, but most simply attacked their dignity and exhibited outright racism. These players, especially the goalie Barbosa, spent the rest of their lives plagued by the stigma of the great defeat. (At the 1994 World Cup in the United States the Brazilian coaches would not even allow Barbosa to visit the *seleção* for fear of bad luck.)[61] When the second, revised edition of *O negro no futebol brasileiro* appeared in 1964, a sober and chastened Mário Filho had retreated from the optimistic conclusions of the 1947 edition – that *futebol* reflected the democratization of Brazil and testimony to Freyre's racial democracy. The first edition, he now wrote, "had accepted an optimistic vision with respect to racial integration that was still not fully realized in football, without doubt the larger field which would open up for the social ascent of the black man."[62]

In the 1950s and 1960s, three players – Didi, Garrincha, and Pelé – became the iconic figures of black and racially mixed players in Brazilian *futebol*. After the disaster of the *Maracanazo* in 1950, the national team did not excel in the 1954 World Cup in Switzerland. Many continued to attribute the "failures" of Brazilian *futebol* to *pretos* and *mulatos*. In retrospect, Brazil was on the eve of more than a decade of international success – three championship trophies in four World Cup competitions – and it would be teams led by Didi, Garrincha, and Pelé that achieved this unparalleled feat. When Brazil won the World Cup in Sweden in 1958 it was the first championship won by a racially mixed team, and Didi was recognized as the outstanding player of the tournament. As José Sergio

Leite Lopes has observed, these nonwhite players "helped turn physical disadvantages and stigma like skin color into embodiments of excellence in football."[63] The final game was broadcast live on Brazilian radio stations and Osvaldo Sampaio's *Price of Victory* immortalized the team on film.[64] One of the great filmmakers of the era, Joaquim Pedro de Andrade, made an hour-long documentary, *Garrincha: Alegria do Povo* (1963), that portrayed him both as hero and antihero.[65] For many historians of Brazilian *futebol*, the 1958 victory "was the point when football became the national ritual, the barometer of the nation's health, and the crowning achievement of an unambiguously mulatto Brazil."[66]

Although many would see the tragic Garrincha as the truly extraordinary force behind the victories in 1958 and 1962, Mário Filho turned instead to Pelé as the ultimate exemplar of *mestiçagem* and *futebol-arte*, a game that Pelé would make famous as the *jogo bonito*. The second, revised edition of *O negro no futebol brasileiro* (1964) appeared after the glories of 1958 and 1962 with new material consecrating Garrincha and Pelé as the saviors and royalty of Brazilian *futebol* (as the brilliant successors to Domingos da Guia and Leônidas da Silva).[67] Pelé was "*o Rei*" and Garrincha was the "*Alegria do Povo*."[68] For Mário Filho, the 1958 championship was conquered "without a stain. Never was a team so clean, so English, in the English meaning of the ideal, the hidden ideal of all Brazilians." Garrincha, in this version, performed miracles, delighting spectators with his Chaplinesque playfulness, with his "jester's style" provoking laughs – he was "the fool who was not a fool." In contrast, Pelé did not provoke laughter, but rather awe and respect. "With Pelé one felt the grandeur of football as the passion of the people, as drama, as destiny. Pelé was destiny itself. He was destiny dressed in the yellow jersey of the Brazilian team."[69] While lauding Garrincha, Mário Filho placed Pelé on a pedestal as a player unparalleled in his greatness. "Pelé already seemed to walk with a compass in his hand. He knew all the roads. The playing field was his kingdom, the ball, his scepter. It was impossible not to recognize him for what he was – 'the King'."[70] Returning to his Freyrean analysis, Mário Filho concludes his profoundly influential book asserting that "What in Garrincha was instinct, in Pelé was reason. He did not make a play that was not thought out. And thought out with eyes open, those childlike eyes, wide open, discovering the world."[71] In his glory, Pelé liberated blacks with his achievements. He made it possible for "blacks, Brazilians and everyone, openly to be black."[72]

Garrincha's death in 1983 provoked a massive outpouring of grief and eulogizing. In the eyes of some, an even greater player than Pelé and a better example of *futebol-arte*, Garrincha had lived the life of the *malandro* as opposed to Pelé's successes as a businessman, sports icon, and entrepreneur.[73] Each in their own way towered as symbols of the narrative of *mestiçagem*. Pelé's much publicized romance with the blonde, blue-eyed Xuxa – star of television and film – in the 1980s seemed to epitomize Freyre's highly sexualized encounter of whites and blacks in the formation of Brazilian society. (Pelé's first two wives are white and his third wife is Japanese-Brazilian.)[74] A less generous interpretation casts this powerful black athlete as the ultimate example of how "money whitens" in Brazil. For all intents and purposes, Pelé was no longer black; he was simply a Brazilian success story. Garrincha, in contrast, the truly *mestiço malandro*, spent most of the last two decades of his short life (he died at age 49) struggling with physical ailments, alcoholism, and a highly publicized and complicated personal life. In contrast to the Nordic Xuxa, Garrincha loved and (ultimately) lived with the great black samba singer Elza Soares. Their affair and marriage were tempestuous and filled the gossip pages. After the disappointing showing of the *seleção* in the 1982 World Cup, Garrincha's tragic death of cirrhosis of the liver in 1983 seemed to mark the end of the era of *futebol-arte*.[75]

After the glories and national euphoria produced by the back-to-back championships in Sweden and Chile, Brazil's performance in the 1966 World Cup in England proved an enormous disappointment. Preparations for the competition have been described as chaotic, and the coach severely criticized for his choice of a number of players past their prime. Brazil exited in the first round of play, its worst performance in decades. In the aftermath of the disaster, the great Pelé described the experience as an unmitigated disaster, and declared he would never play in another World Cup. Brazil, it seemed, had lost its artistry and ability to play the *jogo bonito*.[76] (This was a recurring conversation each time Brazil performed poorly in the World Cup – in the 1980s and 1990s after the "tri," and in the last decade even after the unprecedented fourth and fifth wins in 1994 and 2002. In the aftermath of the disastrous defeat in the 2014 semifinal, this discussion has intensified once again.)

The quick exit of Brazil in the 1966 World Cup chastened the Brazilians and forced a reevaluation of their style of play, but the unprecedented third championship in Mexico in 1970 seemed to consecrate the finesse and the true greatness of *futebol-arte* and its brightest star. This extraordinary championship, unlike the previous two in 1958 and 1962, and the failure in 1966, was televised live throughout Brazil. For a select few in Brazil, the transmissions were, for the first time, in color. In succeeding

years, color transmissions would become the norm. This was made possible by the policies of the military regime (1964–1985) and their close
partner, the emerging giant of Brazilian telecommunications, Rede Globo
(as seen in Chapter 4). It was the construction of a national television
broadcasting system through the efforts of the military regime and Globo
that provided the final means to transform *futebol* into the truly national
sport of Brazil and the most visible ritual and symbol of the myth of
mestiçagem and national identity. (Roberto Marinho hired Armando
Nogueira, one of the giants of national sportswriting in the 1950s and
1960s, to direct Rede Globo's news division, and he was also one of the
creators of the *Jornal Nacional*.)[77]

Radio and film helped make *futebol* a game of the masses from the
1930s to the 1960s. In the following decades, Globo made it possible for
the vast majority of the people living within Brazil's borders to experience
the thrill of victory and a powerful identification with their team, their
nation, and the symbols of that nation (flag, national anthem, colors).
The World Cup victories in 1958 and 1962 generated a series of songs
across genres and composers, and reached enormous audiences via radio.
Major artists have produced a long line of music since the 1950s that
highlight their own passion for *futebol*, as well as its centrality to Brazilian
culture. Jorge Ben Jor's *Umbabarauma* (1976) samba-rock composition is
but one of the most popular of this genre.[78] Films for mass audiences, such
as *Price of Victory*, and documentaries, such as those about Garrincha
and Pelé, are but a few examples of those devoted exclusively to *futebol*,
not to mention the many, many films that position soccer as central to
daily life.[79] The broadcasts of the final and the qualifying round games
garnered nearly 100 percent ratings on Brazilian television! (This is inconceivable for any sporting event in the United States, even the Super Bowl.)
Everything came "to a halt for these games: the beaches are deserted,
factories and shops close, traffic is reduced to a trickle. Everyone returns
home, goes to a neighbor's, or crowds in front of appliance store windows
to watch television."[80] Television also magnified and reinforced the narratives of Brazil as the *futebol nation* with its own national style of play –
futebol-arte.

By the 1970s, it seemed to all the world, especially football commentators, that Brazil was truly blessed with the most beautiful and the
most effective style of play. The legendary Scottish sportswriter Hugh
McIlvanney wrote that the 1970 team "may have represented the highest
point of beauty and sophistication the game is destined to reach."[81] Tony
Mason adds, "Here was grace under pressure, with individual ball control

of an almost magical kind and passing more like a caress than a kick."[82] For Gilberto Freyre and Mário Filho, it was now an easy step to remind the world that the source of *futebol-arte* was *mestiçagem* – both racial and cultural. "[O]ur manner of playing football appears to me," Freyre observed in the late 1930s, "to contrast with that of the Europeans through a conjunction of qualities of surprise, guile, astuteness, swiftness, and at the same time the brilliance of individual spontaneity which reveals a mulatto quality." He went to argue that the *malandro* was "the true affirmation of Brazil." Brazilian football was a lyrical, "dionysian dance."[83] The style of the Brazilians, one could see, was samba on the soccer pitch.

Brazil's repressive military regime recognized the power and appeal of *futebol* and worked assiduously to create the national team for the 1970 World Cup. The government commissioned Miguel Gustavo's upbeat tune "Para Frente Brasil [Forward Brazil]" for the event, and it became the theme song of the regime. The lyrics proclaimed, "All of a sudden there is a wave of positive energy, it is as if all of Brazil are holding hands. All join together in the same emotion. We are all one heart. All together, let's go, forward Brazil, save our national team."[84] The *seleção* played six games and won all of them. Each victory was celebrated, quite consciously, in the style of *carnaval* with samba schools and *blocos* filling the streets. In effect, two national rituals converged as one.[85] When the team returned to Brazil after its victory in Mexico, they received an official presidential welcome and lunch, as well as a substantial tax-free bonus payment. Needless to say, the regime made sure to inundate the country with photos of the players and coaches with President Emílio Médici. The regime's slogan "ninguem segura mais o Brasil" (no one holds back Brazil) also figured prominently in photos and propaganda with the champions. Not unlike Argentina in 1978, the generals consciously and carefully used the athletes and their success for the nationalistic ambitions of the military regime.[86]

As the previous chapter showed, in the 1970s, Globo eventually connected all of the country's inhabitants through a vast telecommunications system built not only on radio but, more importantly, on television. After a century and a half of efforts to construct a nation and a national identity, all Brazilians could both experience and be exposed to a common set of myths, symbols, and rituals – and they could see this in living color. The convergence of Globo's ambitious plans to conquer Brazil's airwaves and Pelé's conquest of global football in the 1970s consecrated *futebol* as the country's preeminent sport and its most expressive symbol of *mestiçagem* and national identity. In describing the champions the great poet Ferreira Gullar proclaimed in 1970, "it is the *povo* hailing itself, since soccer represents nothing else but, and the stars of the Seleção are nothing less than, the *povo*."[87] Mário Filho's prose, Pelé's feet, the military's ambitions, and Globo's business acumen, all converged to produce the climactic moment for Gilberto Freyre's vision of Brazilian culture and identity.[88]

Strangely enough, the structure of Brazilian *futebol* accelerated the televised coverage of the national team while holding back the broadcasting of domestic clubs. Management of clubs resisted the creation of state and then national championships into the 1970s and 1980s. At the same time, they blocked live transmission of games fearing the effects on ticket sales for games. Consequently, the government granted Globo exclusive rights to broadcast the games of the *seleção*, opening the path for all Brazilians simultaneously to see their national team in real time. When the clubs finally capitulated to television broadcasters (in 1987), the major league clubs had to take a backseat to the enormous fans of the *telenovelas*. Teams played on Sundays (a day without *novelas*) and Wednesdays after 10 p.m. (once the *novelas* ended).[89] For most of four years, Brazilians were devout followers of Flamengo, Corinthians, Atlético Mineiro, Cruzeiro, and other clubs. When the *seleção* played, especially in the Copa, those club differences were set aside and they all became Brazilians. Localism and regionalism receded as nationalism reigned supreme.

By 1970, radio, newspapers, and television virtually saturated the inhabitants of Brazil with news of *futebol* and the World Cup.[90] Although the resonance of *futebol* in the early 1970s was still deeply gendered, the World Cup galvanized the entire country – male and female. Betty Milan, remembering her own youth in the 1950s, has commented on how women could not participate in discussions with men about football, and they were not expected to understand the game.[91] Yet, she also agrees with many male writers who have asserted the fundamental importance of *futebol* for the formation of national identity – for all Brazilians.[92] As Lever shows, up through the 1970s girls were consciously and systematically excluded from playing football, and many Brazilians viewed *futebol* as "a man's game requiring masculine endurance and involving violent contact." In the 1970 World Cup games, women were "caught up in them as patriots more than as soccer fans."[93]

For decades, *futebol* reflected the dominant male vision expressed in Freyre's narrative about Brazilian history and identity. Although by the

1980s there were reportedly more than 3,000 women's teams in Brazil, the women's game has remained undeveloped and hindered by continuing notions that *futebol* is a masculine sport. Female players often have been treated more like sexual objects than athletes. Marta, universally recognized as the greatest female player in the world in the first decade of this century, has played in the United States and Europe because of the lack of support and basic infrastructure for women's football in Brazil.[94] While the *seleção feminina* has been one of the best in the world since the 1990s, the women's World Cup does not receive anywhere close to the attention in Brazil as the men's competition.[95] For males, a connection to *futebol* and the national team was virtually universal – nearly all of Lever's male interview subjects followed professional soccer. Playing *futebol* "is a near universal experience for boys in all regions of Brazil." When Lever interviewed 200 working-class men in the 1970s, all but one had watched the final game in the 1970 World Cup, and he was the only one who did not recognize Pelé's photograph![96]

IDENTITY AND THE END OF *FUTEBOL-ARTE*?

Like Freyre's vision of Brazil and *mestiçagem*, the potent narrative of *futebol-arte* also achieved its broadest influence in the 1970s. In retrospect, the momentous 1970 *tricampeonato* would establish the high-water mark of *futebol-arte* and the so-called Brazilian style and the end of the "golden age" of Brazilian *futebol*. According to the English novelist Nick Hornby, the 1970 team "had revealed a kind of platonic ideal that nobody, not even the Brazilians would ever be able to find again."[97] It would be twenty-four years and six World Cup competitions before Brazil would win another championship. Always one of the giants of international competition, and globally recognized as one of a handful of countries with the best football, the string of successes (three of four championships between 1958 and 1970) would not be repeated. Brazil reached the semi-finals in West Germany in 1974 and Argentina in 1978, but had to settle for third place each time.[98] Generational shifts in players marked the 1970s and 1980s as Pelé retired and new stars appeared. Ironically, the teams in 1982 (Spain) and 1986 (Mexico) were some of the most talented ever, in particular, the 1982 squad. This immensely talented team was knocked out of the competition by Italy and its great shooting star, Paulo Rossi, in a game that pivoted dramatically against Brazil in the second half. Even more notable, two of the greatest stars of the decade were white players – Zico and Sócrates. Some wondered if Brazilian *futebol* had taken a new direction with less *mestiçagem*, less *jogo bonito*, and no *futebol-arte*. As if to drive the point home, Brazil's archrival Argentina eliminated them in the first game of the second round of the 1990 Cup in Italy!

Since the 1970s, Brazilians have debated about the nature and future of their football, between *futebol-arte* and *futebol-força*, between a truly Brazilian style and European influences. This has also been a discussion about *mestiçagem*, Brazilian identity, and Freyre's (and Mário Filho's) version of *futebol-mulato*. For the traditionalists, what has made Brazilian *futebol* exciting and successful – guile, *malandragem*, individual scoring talent, the magical – are the very elements that the advocates for change want to limit or eliminate. The 1980s teams with Zico, Falcão, Roberto Dinamite, and Caju (among others) seemed to revive *futebol-arte* even if these great players were unable to win a World Cup. Ironically, the great *craques* were largely white with Zico and Sócrates as the greatest successors to Garrincha and Pelé. During years of transition from dictatorship to democracy, these teams and players seemed to return Brazil to the style of the golden age. For the critics, these failures were evidence of the need for a more defensive, tougher, controlled – European – style of play.

From 1994 to 2002, Brazil returned to impressive success in the World Cup competitions, but few would argue that the *futebol-arte* of the 1950s and 1960s had returned. Brazil's fourth championship (the *tetra-campeão*) has long been criticized as the opposite of 1970, i.e., a style of *jogo feio*. Coach Carlos Alberto Parreira's strategy and tactics may have led to victory, but those hoping for *futebol-arte* complained bitterly of the stodgy, defensive, low-scoring style of play.[99] The Cup did mark the return of *mestiçagem* to the team with its controversial star, Romário, the epitome of *malandragem* both on and off the field.[100] In many ways, the ongoing struggle between Romário, the 1990s successor to Leônidas and Garrincha, and coaches such as Parreira is one example of the continuing battle since 1970 between those who believe in this magical thing called *futebol-arte* and those who argue that Brazilian football must modernize and become less individualistic and playful. It is the contemporary version of the tension between the apollonian and dionysian styles that Freyre contrasted in the 1930s.[101]

The coverage of the games in Brazil demonstrated how central *futebol* had become to Brazilian culture by the 1990s. More than 400 Brazilian journalists covered the 1994 Copa in the United States, and Globo (with its exclusive television coverage rights) used ten camera crews for each of Brazil's games. Two-thirds of the country watched the early games and close to everyone in Brazil watched the final game as Brazil won dramatically on penalty kicks against Italy.[102] As the 1998 World Cup approached, Brazil appeared on the verge of returning to a dominance and style reminiscent of the 1960s in 1998 when, once again, they fielded an immensely talented team led by Ronaldo, widely viewed as the greatest player in the game, and a true successor to the heritage of Pelé. Coached by Zagallo, one of the key players of the era of the *tri-campeonato*, Brazil made it to the final game against host France only to experience one of the most bizarre episodes in World Cup history. Ronaldo suffered an apparent seizure shortly before the game began, managed to play the game, but the Brazilians seemed to be almost zombie-like as France dismantled them 3–0 in front of a home crowd. At the moment that it appeared *futebol-arte* would be re-consecrated with consecutive World Cup victories, the team collapsed in full view of hundreds of millions of television viewers around the globe.

Brazil and Ronaldo redeemed themselves at the 2002 World Cup in Korea and Japan, as they won six consecutive games and the final against Germany (2–0). Ronaldo surpassed Pelé as the highest scoring player of all time in World Cup competition, and showed flashes of *futebol-arte* brilliance during the tournament. Nevertheless, in 2006 in Italy and 2010 in South Africa, the Brazilian squad was eliminated in the quarterfinals, losing to France in 2006 and the Netherlands in 2010. (It should also be noted that winning in 1994, losing in the 1998 final, and winning in 2002 would be, for almost any other country on the planet, the pinnacle of football success. In Brazil, this stretch and the aftermath are dominated by the complaints over the style of play in 1994, the great fiasco of Ronaldo, and the 1998 final.) The audiences in Brazil for these recent World Cup tournaments have been extraordinary. On average, 95 percent of all viewers (more than 100 million people) simultaneously watch Brazil's games. The highest audience rating ever for Brazilian television (98 per cent) was Brazil's victory over England in the 2002 quarterfinal match in Japan – a game that was televised at 3:30 a.m. in Brazil![103] By the end of the twentieth century, watching the national team had become one of the most important rituals in Brazilian society on a scale even more pronounced and widespread than any other ritual with the possible exception of *carnaval*.

Globo has continued its broadcasting domination, acquiring exclusive rights to transmit the FIFA World Cup matches in Brazil. The *Jornal Nacional* (and its competitors) reinforces the importance of the games and the tournament for the nation through their nightly reporting. As much as 80–90 percent of the newscasts on the night of games were devoted to coverage of the Cup. This intense and extensive media coverage of the *seleção* continually reemphasizes to everyone in Brazil that the team represents the nation, and that they symbolize *brasilidade*.[104] The opening ceremonies for each match with the *seleção* emotionally singing the national anthem, wearing the colors of the nation's flag, and preparing to play for their country all drive home to tens of millions of Brazilians that they are Brazilians, that they share common symbols and rituals. As Eric Hobsbawm so notably observed, "The imagined community of millions seem more real in the form of 11 named people."[105] In Brazil, of course, the names are short and often nicknames!

Brazil hosted the 2014 World Cup and, once again, Maracanã stadium served as the scene of the final game. The differences (and some similarities) between 1950 and 2014 are striking. In 1950 radio was the dominant technological medium for sports in a country with 50 million inhabitants (mostly rural), very little filming of *futebol*, and no television. *Futebol* had just a couple of decades experience with professionalization, and the formation of the national team was a highly political and quirky process that drew largely on a few clubs in Rio and São Paulo. The enormous hype around the tournament, Brazil's impressive play, and the even more exaggerated publicity and expectations for the final game against Uruguay helped consolidate *futebol* as a key component of Brazilian identity. In 2014 Brazil's population has passed 200 million inhabitants (overwhelmingly urban) in a society completely saturated with television broadcasting, a vibrant film industry, and radio. Since 1958 Brazil has won five World Cup tournaments and played in the *finals another*, a record unmatched by any country. *Futebol* has become what one writer has labeled "the greatest popular expression of the country" (*a maior expressão popular do país*) and one that resonates with virtually all 200 million Brazilians.[106] Even more so than in 1950, the pressure on the Brazilian team to win the tournament at home was enormous and, ultimately, fatal. To lose in 1950 was a national disaster for a country with an excellent team with no real history of international success. With the incredible achievements since 1958, and home field advantage, Brazilians expected no less than the championship trophy. The team's catastrophic collapse in the first thirty minutes of the semifinal against Germany was likely more due to psychological pressure than lack of talent or strategy. The "*Mineirazo*" of 2014 will probably now go down into the country's football annals as an embarrassing bookend to the *Maracanazo* of 1950.[107]

The nature of the "national" team has also fundamentally shifted since the 1950s and 1960s. A few Brazilian players played in Europe in those years, but the great stars rarely left Brazil and most did not stay abroad for long. Nearly every starting player of the 1970 champions played in Brazil, most prominently Pelé, long a star for Santos. Only after his retirement, and past his prime, did he move to the United States to play in New York, partly to promote football in the world's largest and most lucrative sports market, and partly to make the transition from star player to successful businessman. In the 1980s, star players such as Zico and Falcão moved to the European leagues at the end of their careers. By the 1990s, great players in their teens and early twenties moved quickly to European teams. Of the immensely talented 1982 team, just two of the starters (Falcão and Edinho) played for European teams, and just two *"estrangeiros"* played in the 1986 team. In the 1990s, more than half of the twenty-two team members were *estrangeiros*, and, by the 2010 World Cup, nearly all the starting players in the "national" team played regularly abroad, principally in Europe.[108]

The 1980s mark the end of an era, for *futebol* and for the Freyrean vision of *futebol-mulato*. Although the national team (and Brazilian clubs) visibly reminds the public of the country's history of racial and cultural *mestiçagem* it has become increasingly difficult and controversial to speak of a national style of play. Clearly, young players may grow up and even come of age playing within Brazil, but the influence of styles of play from all over the globe have a powerful impact on these players as they spend increasingly longer portions of their careers in Europe and around the world. Television has made football a global sport with a power unlike any other. In the twentieth century, the public experienced a tension and dynamic between the local (their club team) and the national (the *seleção* made up of club players). In the twenty-first century the tension is now between the local, national, and international as the best Brazilian players invariably move to the high-paying European clubs.[109] Increasingly, nearly the entire "national" team is composed of *estrangeiros*. Furthermore, the expansion of football on television, especially since the mid-1990s, also provides players in Brazil with visual exposure (if not physical participation) to styles of play from around the globe. Much like the debates over national identity – does it exist? – an intense debate now swells around the notion of national styles of play. The *seleção* may continue to be *mestiço*, but does that mean they share a style of play that one could label *futebol mestiço* or *mulato*?

GILBERTO FREYRE, MÁRIO FILHO, *MESTIÇAGEM*, AND CITIZENSHIP

Gilberto Freyre's vision of *mestiçagem* would reach its greatest influence as the most powerful master narrative of Brazilian identity in the 1970s, and the extraordinary success of a sport embraced by the masses seemed to provide some of the most persuasive and visible evidence of the "truth" of Freyre's (and Mário Filho's) arguments. I want to emphasize how the consecration of this "truth" was not accomplished simply because an authoritarian military regime or powerful corporate interests wanted to impose this vision, but because their efforts converged with decades of development at the grassroots level of *futebol*. The *povo*, quite literally, created *futebol-arte* and the brilliant *mestiço* teams that produced football greatness. The military and corporate powers were smart enough to understand that they needed to recognize this *mestiço* genius and promote the *jogo bonito* as quintessentially Brazilian. This support from corporate capitalism and the military regime helped bring to fruition decades of cultural nationalism that fed into the emergence of a nascent civic nationalism, one that would then play a critical role in propelling a process of re-democratization that brought an end to two decades of military rule and the emergence of a "new" republic. *Futebol* by the 1980s had arguably become the single most expressive symbol of national identity, a symbol that all sought to claim for their own nationalistic projects – authoritarian or democratic. Gilberto Freyre's vision of *mestiçagem* appeared to explain the brilliance and genius of *futebol-arte*, even at the moment that his vision would begin to come under sustained assault as the master narrative of Brazilian identity and *futebol*.

Futebol – *mestiço* or not – had become by the 1980s and 1990s one of the most powerful cultural and social forces in Brazil. Emerging alongside and in conversation with Freyre's vision, even more than samba and *carnaval*, it helped bind together an imagined community of Brazilians. Culturally, "football establishes *malandragem* legitimately and openly as the art of survival and *jogo de cintura* as the national style."[110] Politically, it became a powerful means to establish bonds across class, color, and (more recently) gender. As Brian Owensby has observed, "At the level of the collective subconscious, unity as expressed through soccer may have become so imperative that any threat to it from overt prejudice could be seen and experienced as an affront to the nation."[111] To return to the epigraph at the beginning of this chapter, *futebol* made it possible to bring together the symbols of nationhood (flag, anthem, colors). In the words of

DaMatta, it was through "football that we were able in Brazil to bring together the Nation-State and society."[112]

As television helped make *futebol* a truly national sport the football clubs also helped foster civil society across Brazil. Unlike U.S. sports teams, Brazilian teams are "owned" by the fans, they are clubs with membership open to virtually anyone. Management serves on a pro-bono basis (which clearly favors those already with substantial means at their disposal). The ferocious identification with teams is impressive and, in recent years, has led to serious problems of violence (in stadiums and out) often instigated and led by the *torcidas organizadas* (fan clubs). From the 1950s to the 1970s, "Brazilian football clubs constituted one of the most active elements of urban civil society, drawing social classes together and providing somewhere that popular and high cultures could mix."[113] This truly national social phenomenon became one of the most important breeding grounds in Brazil for civic engagement and cultural creativity. In the early 1980s, the Corinthians Democracy movement led by star players such as Sócrates and Wladimir made their demands as players for more control over their destinies into demands for the return of democracy as the military regime fought to manage the transition back to civilian rule. The legendary Sócrates became one of the iconic sports figures to take to the stage in support of the *diretas já* campaign in 1983–1984.[114]

Janet Lever observed as early as the 1980s that "By providing a structure for human loyalty from grass roots to international levels, soccer reinforces the individual's citizenship in multiple groups at the same time." It forges bonds between strangers and friends.[115] Even in places as remote as Indian reservations in the Amazon, the World Cup and the *seleção* come to serve as symbols of the nation.[116] Success on a world stage, even in sport, "remains unparalleled as a source of patriotic pride and global recognition ... the tri-championship sharpened Brazilians' national consciousness as it underscored their valued world membership."[117] This cultural and social "game" has regularly reinforced Brazilians sense of themselves as Brazilians, and it has helped pave the way for the construction of their identity as citizens of the nation.[118] In the words of Matthew Shirts, *futebol* "has generated an identity that has served as a sort of unofficial citizenship in the country" even as that citizenship has been flawed and incomplete, especially for the masses.[119] Since the 1950s, in those moments in international competition when Brazil has demonstrated its mastery of the game, Brazilians can truly experience their nation and people as exceptional. Conversely, the enormous emotional investment in the national team not only leads to

FIGURE 5.3 Casagrande and Corinthians Democracy
Source: José Pinto/Abril Comunicações S/A

unambiguous joy (at least five times since 1958); the failure to live up to
the enormous expectations of winning also produces national depression
and angst (as in 1950, 1998, and 2014). These momentous highs and
lows, on a truly national scale, demonstrate the centrality of *futebol* to
Brazil's identity as a nation and Brazilians as a people. As one English
critic astutely noted, when the *seleção* has taken the field at the World
Cup, "Brazil existed in a more complete way than at any other
moment."[120] I agree with DaMatta when he argues that it was the success
of Brazilians at this simple yet universal game that transformed the way

Brazilians once saw themselves. This positive view of Brazilian identity was not imposed from outside or above by elites or colonizers, but came from millions of Brazilians taking pride in the accomplishments of athletes who came primarily from the *povo*.[121]

Along with samba and *carnaval, futebol* is a twentieth-century creation, and one that continues to evolve. Over the last two decades, Brazilians have experienced highs (1994, 2002) and lows (1998 final, 2014 semifinal) in the World Cup, as they have grappled with the meaning of *futebol* for Brazil, Brazilian identity, and their image as the *futebol* nation. The emergence of professional football with outstanding racially mixed teams, competitive on a world stage, accompanied the transformation of the country from a rural, agrarian nation to an urban, industrial power from the 1930s to the 1990s. Freyre's vision of *mestiçagem*, translated brilliantly by Mário Filho and others, produced the potent narrative of *futebol-arte* and Brazilian excellence on the soccer pitch. With globalization, and the continuing export of Brazilian players to Europe, this narrative becomes more difficult to sustain. Since its inception, Freyre's version of Brazilian identity has been one rich in the mixture of peoples and cultures and, unlike many nationalisms, it has lacked a strong xenophobic component. Since the Modernists of the early twentieth century, Brazilians have forged a "cosmopolitan nationalism," one that perhaps will be capable of evolving in the face of the forces of globalization.[122] As football continues to grow as perhaps the most important global sports business dominated by brand franchises (Manchester United, Barcelona, Real Madrid) and multinational corporations (Adidas, Nike), how will Brazilians (or any other nation) continue to cling to a narrative of national style? Is there a Brazilian style of *futebol* and, if so, can it be sustained? The *malandragem* of *futebol-arte* has persisted in the play of some of the great stars such as Romário and Ronaldo, Ronaldinho and now Neymar.[123] It is clear, however, that the *futebol-arte* of the golden age is long gone, even if some of its flashes of brilliance reappear in great Brazilian players. Some commentators have even begun to question whether Brazil is still the land of football.[124] In the end, will *futebol-mestiço* become an unsustainable narrative, and *mestiçagem* a fading myth of Brazilian identity?

NOTES

1. "Foi o futebol que juntou hino e povo, que consorciou camisa e bandeira, que popularizou a idéia de pátria e de nação como algo ao alcance do homem comum e não apenas do 'doutor' e do mandão. Os campeonatos mundiais que

conquistamos obrigaram a juntar civismo burguês e carnaval; jogo e crença religiosa oficial; magia e igreja; investimento capitalista e amor pelo Brasil." Roberto DaMatta, *A bola corre mais que os homens: duas Copas, treze crônicas e três ensaios sobre futebol* (Rio de Janeiro: Rocco, 2006), 111.

2. José Sergio Leite Lopes, "Class, Ethnicity, and Color in the Making of Brazilian Football," *Daedalus*, 129:2 (Spring 2000), 265.

3. David Goldblatt, *Futebol Nation: A Footballing History of Brazil* (London: Penguin, 2014), xxi.

4. Gordon and Helal, "The Crisis of Brazilian Football," 139.

5. Football in Brazil, especially *futebol* as central to Brazilian identity, has generated an enormous literature over the past generation. The best, and most recent, introductions to the subject are Lúcia Gaspar e Virgínia Barbosa, *O futebol brasileiro, 1894 a 2013: uma bibliografia* (Recife: Fundação Joaquim Nabuco, 2013), especially the "Apresentação," by Túlio Velho Barreto, and the special issue of *Soccer & Society*, 15:1 (2014) on soccer in Brazil, especially Martin Curi, "Soccer in Brazil: An Introduction," 2–7.

6. One analysis of the 2002 and 2006 World Cup teams "revealed that three-quarters of the players came from poor or rural backgrounds or both, or were sufficiently dark-skinned to be considered non-white in Brazil's complicated but informal system of racial classification." Rohter, *Brazil on the Rise*, 98.

7. "It was believed that this style expressed specific traces of the Brazilian 'character' or 'spirit', particularly the theory of harmony between European and African, white and black. The idea that Brazilian football appeared, on the pitch, as a sort of 'dance', which expressed characteristics such as cunning, art, musicality, *ginga* (swing) and spontaneity followed from this belief." Both quotes are from Gordon and Helal, "The Crisis of Brazilian Football," 146.

8. Goldblatt, *Futebol Nation*, xix.

9. Randal C. Archibold, "Mexican Writer Mines the Soccer Field for Metaphors," *New York Times* (26 October 2013), A5.

10. Galvão Bueno has called all the World Cup tournaments for Brazil on Globo since 1974! "Sou vendedor de emoções," *Veja* (23 de julho 2014), 20.

11. Tiago Fernandes Maranhão and Jorge Knijnik, "Futebol Mulato: Racial Constructs in Brazilian Football," *Cosmopolitan Civil Societies Journal*, 3:2 (2011), 55–71.

12. For an excellent survey of Brazilian football and the long-term tension between *futebol-arte* and *futebol-força*, see Roger Kittleson, *The Country of Football: Soccer and the Making of Modern Brazil* (Berkeley: University of California Press, 2014). For a discussion of Freyre's notion of *futebol-mulato*, see 45–48.

13. Janet Lever, *Soccer Madness* (Chicago: University of Chicago Press, 1983), 19.

14. "[O] futebol se presta maravilhosamente para consolidar vínculos de identidade plenos de carga afetiva." Nicolau Sevcenko, "Futebol, metrópoles e desatinos," *Revista USP*, 22 (Junho-Agosto 1994), 35–36.

15. Vargas clearly recognized the growing appeal and importance of football in Brazil. In his diary he commented on Brazil's loss to Italy in the 1938 World Cup semifinal match, "O jogo monopolizou as atenções. A perda do *team*

brasileiro para o italiano causou uma grande decepção e tristeza no espírito público, com se se tratasse de uma desgraça nacional." Quoted in Velho Barreto, "Apresentação," 2. See also, Kittleson, *The Country of Football*, 35–38.

16. Gordon and Helal, "The Crisis of Brazilian Football," 145–48.

17. For a discussion of the role of State and people, see Denaldo Alchorne de Souza, *O Brasil entra em campo!: construções e reconstruções da identidade nacional (1930–1947)* (São Paulo: Annablume, 2008), especially chapter 1 and Conclusion. See also, Lever, *Soccer Madness*, 59–69. "In a survey taken right after the 1970 victory, 90 percent of the lower-class respondents identified Brazilian soccer with the Brazilian nation." Lever, *Soccer Madness*, 158.

18. Cited in Kittleson, *The Country of Football*, 217.

19. By the 1920s, football had already become so integral to popular culture that the great modernist writer Mário de Andrade included reference to it in his iconic *Macunaíma*. "The first bug fell in Campinas, miles away; it was a caterpillar. The second bug fell thereabouts too, it was a woolly bear; the leather ball fell in a field. It was thus that Mannape introduced the coffee bug, Jiqué the cotton boll weevil and Macunaima the football; three of the main pests in the country today." Quoted in Tony Mason, *Passion of the People?: Football in South America* (London: Verso, 1995), 119.

20. "[O] uso excepcionalmente habilidoso do corpo e das pernas, o que cri um jogo bonito de ver." Roberto DaMatta, "Antropologia do óbvio: notas em torno do significado social do futebol brasileiro," *Revista USP: Dossiê Futebol*, 22 (1994), 16.

21. Hobsbawm, *The Age of Extremes*, 198.

22. Mário L. Rodrigues Filho, *O negro no foot-ball brasileiro* (Rio de Janeiro: Irmãos Pongetti, 1947). In the second edition, "foot-ball" became "futebol." The book has gone through four editions: 1947, 1964, 1994, and 2003. My citations come from the fourth edition, *O negro no futebol brasileiro* (Rio de Janeiro: Mauad, 2003).

23. Nelson Rodrigues was also a brilliant sports journalist. For some of his most memorable columns, see Nelson Rodrigues, *À sombra das chuteiras imortais: crônicas de futebol*, Ruy Castro, ed. (São Paulo: Companhia das Letras, 1993) and *A pátria em chuteiras: novas crônicas de futebol*, Ruy Castro, ed. (São Paulo: Companhia das Letras, 1994).

24. Bernardo Borges Buarque de Holanda, "The Fan as Actor: The Popularization of Soccer and Brazil's Sports Audience," *Soccer & Society*, 15:1 (2014), 15.

25. Túlio Velho Barreto, "Gilberto Freyre e o futebol-arte," *Revista USP*, 62 (junho-agosto 2004), 233–38.

26. Freyre's famous initial statement on the topic is Gilberto Freyre, "Foot-ball mulato," *Diario de Pernambuco*, Recife (17 junho 1938).

27. For a close analysis of the work of Mário Filho, see Souza, *O Brasil entra em campo!*, chapter 8; and, José Miguel Wisnik, *Veneno remédio: o futebol e o Brasil* (São Paulo: Companhia das Letras, 2008), esp. 197, 238–39. Souza has been criticized by some for overstating the contrast in Mário Filho's analysis of Garrincha and Pelé.

28. "A obra consolidou a representação de futebol brasileiro como um ideal de astúcia e arte e contra a representação européia de um futebol que dava mais valor à eficiência e à força." Souza, *O Brasil entra em campo!*, 174.

29. For a discussion of this corollary notion, see Ronaldo Helal and Antonio Jorges Soares, "The Decline of the 'Soccer-Nation': Journalism, Soccer and National Identity in the 2002 World Cup," *Soccer & Society*, 15:1 (2014), 132–46.

30. Mason, *Passion of the People?*, 149. Carlos Alberto Parreira stated during the 1994 World Cup tournament that "We will play in the way today's football demands. Magic and dreams are finished in football. We have to combine technique and efficiency." Mason, *Passion of the People?*, 154.

31. Hobsbawm quoted in Wisnik, *Veneno rémedio*, 43.

32. Eduardo Galeano, *Soccer in Sun and Shadow*, trans. Mark Fried (New York: Nation Books, 2013), 33–34.

33. The first live commentary of a football match was in São Paulo in 1931. Goldblatt, *Futebol Nation*, 46.

34. In 1970, "Popular polls showed near unanimity in the sentiment that it was soccer, not coffee or samba, that put Brazil on the modern map." Lever, *Soccer Madness*, 69.

35. For an account of Miller and the early years of Brazilian football, see Alex Bellos, *Futebol: The Brazilian Way of Life* (London: Bloomsbury, 2002), 27–41. This much discussed and disputed story is also recounted in Lever, *Soccer Madness*, 39–41; and Leonardo Affonso de Miranda Pereira, *Footballmania: uma história social do futebol no Rio de Janeiro – 1902–1938* (Rio de Janeiro: Editora Nova Fronteira, 2000), 22–23.

36. Lopes, "Class, Ethnicity, and Color in the Making of Brazilian Football,", 242–44; Gregg P. Bocketti, "Playing with National Identity: Brazil in International Football, 1900–1925," in Hendrik Kraay, ed., *Negotiating Identities in Modern Latin America* (Calgary: University of Calgary Press, 2007), 74.

37. Bellos, *Futebol*, 141; Lever, *Soccer Madness*, 40–41; Bocketti, "Playing with National Identity," 75.

38. Bellos, *Futebol*, 391–97; Lopes, "Class, Ethnicity, and Color in the Making of Brazilian Football," 257; Greg P. Bocketti, "Italian Immigrants, Brazilian Football, and the Dilemma of National Identity," *Journal of Latin American Studies*, 40:2 (2008), 275–302.

39. "The board of directors at the Bangú factory were quick to discover ... football could be adopted as a pedagogical and disciplinary technique for 'total institutions,' a technique invented by elite English boarding schools but applicable to shaping working-class youth in various types of institutions." Lopes, "Class, Ethnicity, and Color in the Making of Brazilian Football," 245–46. Quote is from page 246.

40. From "1906 to 1922, no team with a black or mulatto player won a championship match [in Rio]." Mason, *Passion of the People?*, 49; Anatol Rosenfeld, *Negro, macumba e futebol* (São Paulo: EDUSP, 1993), 84–85.

41. Bellos, *Futebol*, 31–33; "The 1930s were thus marked by progress in a process of democratization within football, both for the professional definition of players, coaches, and trainers, and the incorporation of a broader, mass

public." Lopes, "Class, Ethnicity, and Color in the Making of Brazilian Football," 256. By 1980, 80 percent of Brazilian footballers were from the lowest social classes. Lever, *Soccer Madness*, 130. For the democratization of the fan base, see Buarque de Holanda, "The Fan as Actor," 8–18.

42. "[I]nventado para diverter e disciplinar ... transformou-se (sem querer ou saber) no primeiro e provavelmente no seu mais contundente professor de democracia e de igualdade." DaMatta, *A bola corre mais que os homens*, 142.

43. "[V]alores culturais locais, nascidos de uma visão de mundo tradicional, hierárquica e particularista ... com uma lógica moderna, individualista e universalista." DaMatta, *A bola corre mais que os homens*, 146.

44. Souza, *O Brasil entra em campo!*, see, for example, chapter 6.

45. Édison Gastaldo, "Soccer and Media in Brazil," *Soccer & Society*, 15:1 (2014), 125. Parreira responded to critics by saying he believed in "futebol de resultados." Kittleson, *The Country of Football*, 168.

46. Mason, *Passion of the People?*, 49.

47. "O mulato vem de ser, justamente, no futebol e a literatura, o melhor intérprete dessa configuração cultural [those who are both included and excluded]. A rigor, ele é uma figura social, cultural e metarracial que pode recobrir às vezes, pela sua natureza híbrida e complexa, brancos e negros que não são literalmente mulatos, mas que são mediadores do hibridismo." Wisnik, *Veneno remédio*, 199.

48. "guarda o segredo inconfessável do todo" – "séculos de escravidão e miscigenação" Wisnik, *Veneno remédio*, 199 and 231. Emphasis in the original.

49. Carlos Eduardo Sarmento, "Futebol e Brasilidade: O Papel do Estado Nacional na Construção do Imaginário acerca da Seleção Brasileira," *Cadernos FGV Projetos*, 5:13 (junho 2010), 57–62.

50. For a brief account, see Maurício Drumond, "O esporte como política de Estado: Vargas," in Del Priore e Andrade de Melo, *História do esporte no Brasil*, 230–33.

51. Bellos, *Futebol*, 38–41; Wisnik, *Veneno remédio*, 193; and, Mason, *Passion of the People?*, 43–44; Rosenfeld, *Negro, macumba e futebol*, 100–1. A candy maker created a new chocolate bar, Diamante Negro, in honor of Leônidas, one that is still marketed.

52. "Since 1938, when Brazil dazzled Europe at the World Cup in France, the European and then the world's media have framed Brazilian football as exotic and other-worldly, musical and terpsichorean, a unique blend of the effective and the aesthetic." Goldblatt, *Futebol Nation*, xii.

53. Another of Freyre's close associates, the great Northeastern novelist José Lins do Rego, also claimed that the national team was "a portrait of our racial democracy." Quoted in Gordon and Helal, "Crisis of Brazilian Football," 146.

54. Quoted in Lever, *Soccer Madness*, 42.

55. "era o jogador perfeito, aquele que melhor poderia simbolizar a nação: brasileiro, disciplinado, racional, trabalhador e negro." Souza, *O Brasil entra em campo!*, 191.

56. "a mãe de todas as derrotas" – The phrase is from Simoni Lahud Guedes, "Futebol e identidade nacional: reflexões sobre o Brasil," in Del Priore e Andrade de Melo, *História do esporte no Brasil*, 465.

57. In homage to the great sports journalist, the stadium was given his name in the aftermath of his death in 1966.

58. Bellos, *Futebol*, chapter 3, "The Fateful Final."

59. For a classic account of this fiasco, see Paulo Perdigão, *Anatomia de uma derrota* (Porto Alegre: L & PM Editores, 1986).

60. Lopes, "Class, Ethnicity, and Color in the Making of Brazilian Football," 259–60.

61. Souza, *O Brasil entra em campo!*, 190; Juan Villoro, *Dios es redondo* (México: Editorial Planeta Mexicana, 2006), 65–69.

62. "teria aceito uma visão otimista a respeto de uma integração racial que não se realizara ainda no futebol, sem dúvida o campo mais vasto que se abrira para a ascensão social do preto" Rodrigues Filho, *O negro no futebol brasileiro*, 16.

63. Lopes, "Class, Ethnicity, and Color in the Making of Brazilian Football," 261.

64. Mason, *Passion of the People?*, 86.

65. Maurício Lissovsky, "Garrincha," in Bayman and Pinazza, *Directory of World Cinema: Brazil*, 197–98.

66. Goldblatt, *Futebol Nation*, 101.

67. The first edition carried the title *O negro no foot-ball do Brasil* (Irmãos Pongetti Editories, 1947), the second edition shifted to *O negro no foot-ball brasileiro* (Editora Civilização Brasileira, 1964), and definitively changing to *O negro no futebol brasileiro* with a third edition (Editora Firmo, 1994).

68. Goldblatt, *Futebol Nation*, 104.

69. "sem uma mancha. Nunca uma equipe foi mais limpa, mais inglesa, no sentido do inglês ideal, ideal recôndito de todo brasileiro." "jeitão de bobo" "O bobo que não era bobo." "Em Pelé se sentia toda a grandeza do futebol como paixão do povo, como drama, como destino. Pelé era o próprio destino. Era o destino que vestia a camisa amarela do escrete brasileiro." Rodrigues Filho, *O negro no futebol brasileiro*, 328–29.

70. "Já Pelé parecia que andava de bússola na mão. Conhecia todos os caminhos. O campo era o reino dele, a bola, o cetro. Era impossível deixar de reconhecer que ele era o 'Rei.'" Rodrigues Filho, *O negro no futebol brasileiro*, 336.

71. "O que em Garrincha é instinto, em Pelé é raciocínio. Não faz uma jogada que não seja pensada. E pensada de olhos abertos, aqueles olhos de criança, escancarados, descrobrindo o mundo." Rodrigues Filho, *O negro no futebol brasileiro*, 340.

72. "os pretos, os brasileiros e de todo o mundo, pudessem livremente ser pretos." Rodrigues Filho, *O negro no futebol brasileiro*, 343.

73. For an unflinching and unflattering portrayal of Pelé's business and professional career, see Franklin Foer, *How Soccer Explains the World: An Unlikely Theory of Globalization* (New York: Harper Perennial, 2004), chapter 5, "How Soccer Explains the Survival of the Top Hats," 115–40.

74. Amelia Simpson, *Xuxa: The Mega-Marketing of Gender, Race, and Modernity* (Philadelphia: Temple University Press, 1993), 34–37; Lever, 141–44; Bellos, *Futebol*, 115.

75. Mason, *Passion of the People?*, 101–2; Goldblatt, *Futebol Nation*, 156–7; Ruy Castro, *Estrela solitária: um brasileiro chamado Garrincha* (São Paulo: Companhia das Letras, 2009), chapters 12–21.

76. Garry Jenkins, *The Beautiful Team: In Search of Pelé and the 1970 Brazilians* (New York: Simon & Schuster, 1998), 9–14.

77. João Máximo, "Armando Nogueira, a poesia em jogo," *O Globo*, 30 de março de 2010, 31.

78. Goldblatt, *Futebol Nation*, 114–15 and 136.

79. Ibid., 115–19.

80. Lever, *Soccer Madness*, 81–82.

81. Quoted in Jenkins, *The Beautiful Team*, xvii.

82. Mason, *Passion of the People?*, 102.

83. Ibid., 122. For the full quote, see Carlos Eduardo Barbosa Sarmento, *A construção da nação canarinho: uma história institucional d seleção brasileira de futebol, 1914–1970* (Rio de Janeiro: Editora FGV, 2013), 70–71.

84. Gordon and Helal, "The Crisis in Brazilian Football," 148.

85. Arno Vogel, "O Momento Feliz, Reflexões sobre o Futebol e o Ethos Nacional," in Roberto DaMatta, Luiz Felipe Baêta Neves Flores, Simoni Lahud Guedes, Arno Vogel, *Universo do futebol: esporte e sociedade brasileira* (Rio de Janeiro: Ediçoes Pinakotheke, 1982), 110–11.

86. Lever, "Sport in a Fractured Society," 93.

87. Quoted in Kittleson, *The Country of Football*, 99.

88. The military regime also created a national sport lottery in 1969 to finance government projects. As Lever points out, "In addition to producing revenue, the soccer lottery has made an intended contribution to territorial unification, for it was designed to stimulate among Brazilians awareness of their own imposing geography. Strict policy dictates that the thirteen games included in the weekly lottery pool must represent all regions of the country, even though the best soccer is played in the southern states." Janet Lever, "Sport in a Fractured Society: Brazil under Military Rule," in Joseph L. Arbena, ed., *Sport and Society in Latin America: Diffusion, Dependency, and the Rise of Mass Culture* (New York: Greenwood Press, 1988), 91.

89. McGrath, "Samba Soccer," *The New Yorker* (13 January 2014), 51 and 54; Gordon and Helal, "The Crisis in Brazilian Football," 150.

90. Lever, *Soccer Madness*, 82–83.

91. Betty Milan, *Brasil: o país da bola* (São Paulo: Best Editora, 1989), 1.

92. "Nós, brasileiros, nos fazemos através do Braaasilll, e é por isso que na Copa do Mundo nos vestimos de verde e amarelo, nos apropriamos da bandeira para agitar no estádio ou no corso e assim, torcendo, no certificamos da unidade nacional. Nossa identidade não se molda através do Estado, da Igreja ou da Universidade. Os nossos heróis são os jogadores os carnavalescos, os homens que desafiam em campo a própria lei da gravidade e os que vemos sambar numa corola iluminada de penas e de plumas, nos carros alegóricos da avenida." Betty Milan, *Brasil: o país da bola* (Rio de Janeiro: Editora Record, 2014), 23.

93. Lever, *Soccer Madness*, 72 and 81.
94. Marta was FIFA World Player of the Year five years running, from 2006–2010. Dave Zirin, *Brazil's Dance with the Devil: The World Cup, the Olympics, and the Fight for Democracy* (Chicago: Haymarket Books, 2014), 111; José Paulo Florenzano, "Dictatorship, Re-Democratization and Brazilian Football in the 1970s and 1980s," in Paulo Fontes and Bernardo Buarque de Hollanda, eds., *The Country of Football: Politics, Popular Culture & the Beautiful Game in Brazil* (London: Hurst & Company, 2014), 162–64.
95. Goldblatt, *Futebol Nation*, 146–47 and Leda Maria da Costa, "Beauty, Effort, and Talent: A Brief History of Brazilian Women's Soccer in Press Discourse," *Soccer & Society*, 15:1 (2014), 81–92.
96. Lever, *Soccer Madness*, 105–107, and 123. The only exception was a recent migrant to Rio de Janeiro from a small town in Northeastern Brazil. Quote is from 111.
97. Quoted in Kittleson, *The Country of Football*, 54.
98. In one of the more controversial championships, Brazil failed to make the final in 1978 in Argentina despite winning or tying all their games.
99. "When Brazil won its fourth World Cup, only a few of the celebrating journalists managed to hide their nostalgia for the marvel days of the past. The team of Romário and Bebeto played an efficent match, but is stingy on poetry ... the style of play imposed by the manager, successful but lacking in magic: Brazil had sold its soul to modern soccer." Galeano, *Soccer in Sun and Shadow*, 240.
100. "Brazilian football – in its best moments – is exactly that which Romário does: pisses on hotel windows, prays in the chapel of São Conrado. But on the pitch, he embodies all the demons of our soul – and wins." Carlos Heitor Cony, quote in Kittleson, *The Country of Football*, 173.
101. Helal and Soares, "The Decline of the Soccer-Nation," 137 and 140.
102. Goldblatt, *Futebol Nation*, 163.
103. Édison Gastaldo, "Soccer and Media in Brazil," *Soccer & Society*, 15:1 (2014), 126.
104. Gastaldo, "Soccer and Media in Brazil," 127–29.
105. Ben Hoyle, "Football and the Old Marxist Who Says That It Explains the New World," *London Times* (6 October 2007).
106. Marcos Guterman, *O futebol explica o Brasil: uma história da maior expressão popular do país* (São Paulo: Contexto, 2009).
107. "A vitória do Brasil na Copa de 1958 iniciou uma revolução copernicana na geopolítica do futebol. A vitória de 1970, a terceira em quatro Copas, consolidou a convicção de que subdesenvolvidos, em futebol, eram os europeus. A Copa de 2014 repõe as coisas em seus lugares." Roberto Pompeu de Toledo, "Rescaldo do rescaldo," *Veja* (23 de julho 2014), 114.
108. Claudia Silva Jacobs, *Futebol exportação* (Rio de Janeiro: Editora Senac Rio, 2006), 11–25. In 1986, 2 of 24 members of the seleção played in Europe; in 2002, the number rose to 8; in 2010, to 21; and in 2014, almost the entire team. Goldblatt, *Futebol Nation*, 166, 202–3.
109. Eric Hobsbawm, *Globalisation, Democracy and Terrorism* (London: Little, Brown, 2007), 90–92.

110. "o futebol institui aberta e legitimamente a malandragem com arte de sobrevivência e o jogo de cintura como estilo nacional." DaMatta, *A bola corre mais que os homens*, 164–66. Quote is from 165. Jogo de cintura translates roughly as flexibility or ability to improvise on the spot.

111. Owensby, "Toward a History of Brazil's 'Cordial Racism,'" 335.

112. "futebol que conseguimos no Brasil somar o Estado nacional e a sociedade." DaMatta, *A bola corre mais que os homens*, 164–66. Quote is from 166.

113. Goldblatt, *Futebol Nation*, 105. For the recent problems with violence and the torcidas organizadas, see 206–7 and Ben McGrath, "Samba Soccer: The Transformation of Brazil's Most Storied Team," *The New Yorker* (13 January 2014), 44–57.

114. McGrath, "Samba Soccer," 50; Simon Romero, "Sócrates, Brazilian Soccer Star and Activist, Dies at 57," *New York Times* (5 December 2011), A21; Kittleson, *The Country of Football*, 134–51; Florenzano, "Dictatorship, Re-Democratization and Brazilian Football in the 1970s and 1980s," 162–65.

115. Lever, *Soccer Madness*, 146, quote is from 109.

116. Bellos, *Futebol*, 86. For a description of the reception of the 2014 World Cup games via television in a remote Amazonian village, see Jeré Longman, "Deep in the Amazon, an Isolated Village Tunes in to the World Cup," *New York Times*, 20 June 2014, www.nytimes.com/2014/06/22/sports/worldcup/deep-in-the-amazon-an-isolated-village-tunes-in-the-world-cup.html?_r=0 [accessed 14 July 2014]

117. Lever, *Soccer Madness*, 147.

118. Lever, "Sport in a Fractured Society: Brazil under Military Rule," 88.

119. Matthew Shirts, "Sócrates, Corinthians, and Questions of Democracy and Citizenship," in Arbena, *Sport and Society in Latin America*, 109.

120. Goldblatt, *Futebol Nation*, xiv.

121. "Paradoxalmente, foi esse jogo estrangeiro, claramente elitista, repleto de nomes desconhecidos e impronunciáveis pelo povo semi-alfabeto e monolíngue do Brasil que, graças à força das redefiniçoes culturais não previstas, provocadas pelo processo aculturativo, se transformava no principal agente de uma radical, porque positiva, redefinição dos modos de perceber as possibilidades e as capacidades do Brasil." DaMatta, *A bola corre mais que os homens*, 144.

122. For a fascinating discussion of the "cosmopolitan nationalism" of FC Barcelona, see Foer, *How Soccer Explains the World*, chapter 8, "How Soccer Explains the Discreet Charm of Bourgeois Nationalism," 193–216.

123. For very recent examples of international writers and their perception of Brazil as the land of the *jogo bonito* and *malandragem*, see Janusz Michallik, "After Humiliation Against Germany, Brazil Must Go Back to Joga [sic] Bonito Roots," (10 July 2014), http://bleacherreport.com/articles/2124332-after-humiliation-against-germany-brazil-must-go-back-to-joga-bonito-roots [accessed 15 July 2014]; "Neymar's cultural significance to Brazil transcends soccer, World Cup," si.com [accessed 16 July 2014].

124. Gordon and Helal, "The Crisis in Brazilian Football," 141.

6

The Sounds of Cultural Citizenship

To a greater degree than cinema, popular literature, or sport, [popular music] emerged as a decisive forum for debate over national identity, and Brazilians began to view the exercise of musical preference in the cultural marketplace as an act with enormous consequences.[1]

Bryan McCann

In Brazil music has been both an instrument through which disenfranchised groups have asserted claims of citizenship, as well as a tool in the formulation of disciplinary or repressive state policies.[2]

Idelber Avelar and Christopher Dunn

CULTURAL CITIZENSHIP AND CULTURAL NATIONALISM

In the early twentieth century, radio and music played a key role in the emergence of a national identity built around the myth of *mestiçagem*. In the 1930s and 1940s, radio served as the most important medium in the national conversation about identity, and popular music reached more of Brazil's inhabitants than any other cultural modality. Although film emerged by the 1940s and 1950s as the crucial visual medium in the conversation, its reach did not extend as far and wide as radio (although film also helped disseminate popular music through sound tracks). From the 1950s to the 1990s, popular music (along with *futebol*) became the most pervasive and potent mode for the communication of the myth of *mestiçagem*.[3] The emergence of a dynamic, mass popular music scene in the 1960s and 1970s (with radio increasingly assisted and then eclipsed by television) paralleled the politics of repression and helped consolidate narratives of national identity both in opposition to the military's vision and, ironically, in convergence with it. In the 1980s, popular music served as one of the most powerful instruments for cultural nationalism, the re-democratization of Brazil, an emerging civic nationalism, and the expansion of citizenship.[4]

As discussed in Chapter 2, popular music plays a fundamental role in the formation of collective identity. The power of music is its ability "to evoke strong, visceral, even visual memories and thus to assure listeners of their own continuity." John Burdick has argued that "As people consider, reflect, and talk about music together, they learn shared ways of thinking about their lives." Music is not simply an expression of identity but also helps shape and constitute identity, both personal and collective. In particular, music can build and reinforce a sense of collective identity through "a shared, emotionally charged narrative of a group's origin, ancestry, glory, rights, endurance, suffering, resistance, and interaction with other groups." For most Brazilians, the dominant shared narrative throughout much of the twentieth century has been the myth of *mestiçagem*. The emergence and spread of samba after the 1920s helped shape the narrative and disseminate it across Brazil. In the decades after 1960, popular music reinforced the narrative, thoroughly permeating and dominating contending narratives of Brazilian culture and identity.[5]

By definition, truly popular music becomes possible only with the emergence of mass culture in an age of mass communications – especially radio and television. Popular music, then, is both an instrument for its formation and consolidation and an important measure of the maturation of the nation in the twentieth century. Samba emerged out of neighborhoods in the urban core of Rio de Janeiro in the early twentieth century to become a truly national – and literally, popular – music in the 1920s and 1930s with the florescence of radio broadcasting and the onset of the mass production of records and phonographs. Other regional forms of music such as frevo, maracatu, and forró also found audiences across the country through radio and the recording business after 1930.[6] (Once again, the regional and the national emerged, cross-fertilized, and developed simultaneously.) In many ways, the rise of the market for popular music in Brazil provides some of the most persuasive empirical evidence of the participation of most Brazilians in the consolidation of (competing) national narratives and the Brazilian nation.

Recent scholarship has shown the importance of music to the formation not only of narratives of national identity but also to the expansion of citizenship in Brazil, especially in the decades after the 1930s.[7] Recent scholarship has shown how popular music has been Brazil's richest form of popular art. Avelar and Dunn have emphasized the role of popular music in the formation of "cultural citizenship," while I emphasize its power in the formation of cultural nationalism in Brazil since the 1930s.[8] Popular music (along with film, television, and *futebol*) fostered and reinforced a sense of cultural belonging, of being part of that imagined community of Brazilians. The struggle for citizenship in Brazil has been fraught with challenges, even after the 1930s. The cultural arena provided Brazilians opportunities for participation and belonging that were not open to them in the political arena, especially during the years of dictatorship (1937–1945 and 1964–1985).[9] Cultural nationalism (and citizenship) helped forge an increasingly cohesive community of Brazilians, and the basis for a sense of belonging to one people and one nation by the 1970s. The rising struggle for full civic and political citizenship in the 1960s and 1970s blossomed in the 1980s and 1990s into one of the most important arenas of Brazilian life. The construction of a potent cultural nationalism paved the way for an unprecedented conversation about civic nationalism that centered on civic and political citizenship by the late 1980s and early 1990s.

MUSIC, REGION, NATION

Much like *futebol*, popular music became increasingly professionalized and nationalized in the 1930s and 1940s, came of age in the 1950s, and entered into full flower in the 1960s and 1970s. The mass communication technologies of the twentieth century – radio, film, television – provided the most important tools in the emergence and florescence of popular music in Brazil (and elsewhere). As we have already seen, the recording industry appeared in Brazil in the late 1920s along with the sales of phonographs. The subsidiaries of European and American companies established offices and manufacturing (initially in Rio de Janeiro and São Paulo) in 1928 and 1929. Their agents quickly signed up local talent – Carmen Miranda, Pixinguinha, and others – to record on their labels. At the same time (as we saw in Chapters 2 and 3), the expansion of radio stations provided outlets across the country, and stations played these records for the masses. By April 1929, cinema with sound (talkies) had appeared in Brazil. Each of these new technologies promoted and produced popular culture through music by the 1930s and made aural and visual cultures even more important as media for the increasing integration of a truly national imagined community.[10] They also reinforced the power and influence of Rio de

Janeiro, and secondarily, São Paulo, in the conversation about region and nation in the decades after World War I.

Not unlike the digital era of the early twenty-first century (although in a much more rudimentary fashion), the new technologies provided the vehicle for the recording and broadcasting of many different local and regional musical genres. Samba may have emerged out of the urban core of Rio de Janeiro, but other forms of local and regional music simultaneously emerged out of the studios and stations of other major cities in Brazil. From the Northeast, baião, forró, frevo, and maracatu emerged and flourished in the 1940s and 1950s. In the 1980s and 1990s, música sertaneja and música caipira exploded across much of Brazil's interior, especially the central south and west.[11] Many other musical genres identified with various regions of Brazil emerged in the mid- to late-twentieth century, yet none would achieve the power of samba as the symbol of Brazilian music and national identity. The fusion of samba and *carnaval* in Rio in the 1930s consolidated the dominance of samba as the principal musical signifier of Brazilian identity. "Thereafter, samba would be considered representative of the nation, while other Brazilian musical genres would be considered merely *regional* styles."[12]

Most writers describe the 1930s and 1940s as the "golden age" of Brazilian radio and music. It is a period of enormous creativity by dozens of artists – musicians, singers, composers – and the consecration of samba as the quintessential Brazilian musical form. As Bryan McCann has so eloquently shown, during this golden age popular music and culture were radically reinterpreted, and by the 1950s "a new set of themes and practices had been consolidated, and it is that set which continues to define popular cultural life in Brazil." The way Brazilians "understand their nation, their racial politics, their conflicts of gender – in short, themselves" comes from the musical transformation of this period.[13] With hundreds of radio stations spread across Brazil by the 1950s, popular music had become the most important national cultural medium. Many creative artists such as Wilson Batista, Noel Rosa, and Geraldo Pereira created and recreated samba in the golden age, making it a truly national music and using it both to exalt the nation and critique it for its failings.

Of all the brilliant composers of this period, Ari Barroso is perhaps the most emblematic. His prolific pen produced dozens of successful recordings, radio provided the most important means of reaching an ever larger audience, and his lyrics glorified the nationalism of the period (both official and unofficial). Barroso epitomizes the "bottom-up" and "top-down" convergence of grassroots production and acceptance of samba, and the efforts of the State to co-opt samba to forge a coherent national identity. White, middle class, and trained as a lawyer, this ambitious and brilliant composer from the interior of Minas Gerais began by composing some of the most infectious *carnaval* songs of the 1930s. As McCann shows, he was an astute manager of his career and the airwaves to further his career. He gradually moved from the simpler songs for *carnaval* "to complex works of intricate but instantly memorable melody and harmony," and from lyrics "on romance and quotidian life to rapturous effusions on the glories of Brazil." His understanding and articulation of popular music and its origins in *mestiçagem* placed him "on the cutting edge of Brazilian social thought." In McCann's words, "for Barroso, samba was a national anthem."[14]

Although not initially a big success, his *Aquarela do Brasil* (Watercolor of Brazil), written and first recorded in 1939, became over the years the most recorded Brazilian song of all time (later only surpassed by the *Girl from Ipanema*). Ironically, the song did not become a huge success and anthem for the nation until after it appeared in Walt Disney's 1942 film *The Three Caballeros*. This "popular national anthem" contains all of the key elements of the Freyrean vision: the sly *mulato* ("*meu mulato inzoneiro*"), the *sensual morena* ("*morena sestrosa*"), the black mammy ("*mãe preta*"), and a Brazil that is beautiful and dark ("*esse Brasil lindo e trigueiro*"). Rádio Nacional, the most influential radio station of the 1940s, and a close ally of the Vargas regime, promoted the song heavily, and openly declared samba and its sentiments as the core of national identity. This variety of samba, samba-exaltação, celebrated the African contributions to Brazilian culture even as the government attempted to tame and domesticate these contributions. Record sales and airplay demonstrate the massive public success of the music and the well-documented efforts of the Vargas regime confirm the convergence of musical popularity and State-directed efforts at nation-building around the Freyrean vision.[15]

Even as samba took shape as the "national" music of Brazil in the golden age of radio, other popular forms of music from across Brazil also gained national audiences, although they remained identified as "regional" musical styles. This ongoing interplay between regional and national in musical styles reflects the similar processes in the constant formation and interaction of regional and national narratives in Brazil since the 1930s, and continues today.[16] While Rio de Janeiro and São Paulo in Southeastern Brazil would dominate national telecommunications and the cultural industry in the country in the twentieth century, the

Northeast would emerge with its own strong narratives of regional identity, and popular musical forms reflected these contending narratives. With the massive migrations of millions of *nordestinos* to Southeastern Brazil after 1930, and especially to São Paulo, it is no surprise that the diffusion and popularity of many of these "Northeastern" musical styles move beyond the territorial confines of the geographical region that the government defines as the Northeast.[17]

The Northeast, in particular, generated many different musical styles from baião to frevo and forró. Dorival Caymmi and Luiz Gonzaga's music, styles, and images came to personify the Northeast, and two of its many regional identities. Gonzaga played the role of the *sertanejo* while Caymmi projected the image of the coastal region, especially Bahia and its Afro-Brazilian culture. These varied styles, on many levels, communicated the rich ethnic and cultural mix that reinforced the Freyrean vision. Freyre's archetypal Brazil, after all, was his romanticized image of Recife, and for his good friend Jorge Amado, it was the rich cultural and ethnic mixture in Salvador. The music of Caymmi and Gonzaga provided the sound track to Freyre and Amado's literary imagery of a Brazil born out of the collision of Indians, Portuguese, and Africans on the northeastern coastal zone of Brazil. The coastal narrative (personified by Caymmi), especially emanating from Salvador, highlighted the African contribution to *mestiçagem* while the narrative of the interior/*sertão* (personified by Gonzaga) had the *caboclo* and the Indian contribution as its core. Through baião and forró Gonzaga evoked for millions of *nordestinos* in the burgeoning urban landscapes of the Southeast a longing (*saudade*) for a lost, rural past in their native Northeast.[18] Ironically, it helped forge a powerful sense of Northeastern identity for multitudes of migrants who had left the region even as a regional identity was taking shape. His music "did not so much reproduce some sort of traditional peasant discourse as help make such an identity plausible and compelling."[19] Although their music experienced a declining audience by the 1960s with the advent of other musical styles, they would be visibly reclaimed and revived by younger artists such as Caetano Veloso in another wave of musical *mestiçagem*.[20]

Bossa nova provides something of a musical bridge between the popular music of radio's golden age and what has become known as *Música Popular Brasileira* (MPB) in the 1960s, 1970s, and 1980s. It bridges musical styles, the shift from radio to television, and from music that was largely national to styles that draw increasingly on global musical cross-currents and, in turn, influences music around the globe.[21] Carmen Miranda and others brought samba to international audiences by the 1940s. *Bossa nova* exploded onto the world music scene in the late 1950s and early 1960s, and diminished in its influence with the rise of rock and roll, the British invasion of North America, and the counterculture in the second half of the 1960s. Although many have criticized *bossa nova* as largely a musical form arising out of the white, affluent suburbs of the Zona Sul in Rio, it is the epitome of Brazilian cultural *mestiçagem*. The creative hands and minds of João Gilberto, Antônio Carlos Jobim, Vinícius de Morais, Baden Powell, and others took the samba created in the previous few decades into a beautiful, melodic, and lyrical counterpoint samba. Initially, seen by some in Brazil as too avant-garde and strange, *bossa nova* quickly conquered an international audience and helped draw jazz musicians and aficionados to Brazil. Jobim and Morais's *Garota de Ipanema* (Girl from Ipanema) quickly became one of the most recorded songs of all time, and the version sung jointly by Gilberto and his (then) wife Astrud won a Grammy for song of the year in 1964. *Bossa nova*, much like umbanda in religion (and rock and roll), transformed a "black" music (samba) into one with a "white" face (*bossa nova*).

The cool and hip style of *bossa nova*, although identified primarily with Rio's Zona Sul and a more elitist form of music, arose out of the confluence of artists from difference regions of Brazil. Gilberto, its most famous icon, came from the interior of Bahia. Jobim was a *carioca*, as was Vinícius de Morais, but the latter had lived all over the world, including a crucial period in Los Angeles in the Brazilian diplomatic corps. Jobim and Gilberto, in particular, had produced a new musical style by drawing on Brazilian popular music as well as classical music. Jobim was deeply influenced by the giant of Brazilian classical music, and great figure of the Modernist Movement, Heitor Villa-Lobos. The brilliant musical experimentation that transformed samba into *bossa nova* followed the experimentation that had given rise to samba in the 1910s and 1920s. A new wave of young musicians emerged in the late 1960s, and though they admired *bossa nova*, they turned to a new musical movement that in many ways also drew on the Modernists of the 1920s who had helped give birth to the cultural nationalism that the myth of *mestiçagem* had come to dominate by the 1930s.[22]

MÚSICA POPULAR BRASILEIRA AND CULTURAL NATIONALISM

Like much of the western world, Brazil experienced tremendous social, political, and cultural upheaval in the 1960s and 1970s. This upheaval was both part of the larger processes disrupting and reshaping the Western world and, at the same time, uniquely Brazilian. In politics, the Cold War profoundly affected Brazil (along with the rest of Latin America). The polarizing ideological battles between capitalism and various forms of socialism played out in Brazil, and deeply shaped the domestic political struggle that culminated in the military coup in April 1964. Over the next two decades, the right-wing, anti-communist, pro-US military dictatorship (1964–1985) sought to promote its own brand of nationalism, and to suppress any contending voices. Brazilian society continued to experience the massive migration from the countryside to the cities as the nation moved from a majority rural population to an urban and industrial society. Brazil's economy grew dramatically in the decades after the 1950s, moving from around fiftieth in the world in GDP to become one of the fifteen largest economies on the planet. The social conflicts over land continued in the countryside and the massive expansion of *favelas* and the demand for services of all types transformed politics and social relations. The growth of Brazil's population – from about 50 million in 1950 to around 125 million by the 1980s – along with massive urbanization contributed immensely to the expansion and deepening of popular culture, the culture industry, and a new dynamism.[23]

In many ways, the most important voices in popular culture in this period harkened back to the Modernist Movement of the 1920s and 1930s. The self-styled bohemian counterculture of the Modernists provided inspiration for the cultural rebels of the 1960s as they drew on their cultural ancestors (their grandparents's generation) to fashion a new counterculture. The "dominant" culture of the 1960s and 1970s was not only seen as bourgeois and inhibited; it was also clearly authoritarian and corporate (both in the traditional sense of corporatism and in the modern sense of the modern business enterprise). As with any counterculture in the West, the rebels lashed out at bourgeois values, hierarchy, "traditional" gender roles, and authority. After April 1964, the military regime saw this rebellion as not only culturally repugnant but also politically subversive. As Dunn notes, "With nearly all avenues of organized political opposition cut off, middle-class urban youth turned to more personal and 'spiritual' quests, often aided by drug consumption, psychoanalysis, macrobiotics, and non-Western religions." They produced their novel notions of fashion, language, hairstyles, and what was hip (*bacana*).[24]

The most prominent example of this countercultural turn, and one that has been written about extensively, is *Tropicalismo*. The "tropicalists" continued the decades-long process of experimentation, creativity, challenging the tradition/modernity binary, and forging new forms of cultural hybridity.[25] Chris Dunn has astutely observed that Tropicália exemplified cultural hybridity and broke down barriers between traditional and modern, national and international, erudite and popular music, between elite and popular audiences.[26] Much like the Modernists they consciously adapted the cannibalist metaphor, consuming and producing music that blended elements from many of Brazil's musical traditions as well as from the international popular music explosion of the 1960s and 1970s.[27] The tropicalists, more so than any other musicians in this period, made "explicit the competing imperatives of civic-minded participation, professional success, and aesthetic experimentalism in an emerging market for pop music."[28]

As Dunn has shown, the tropicalists continued a long intellectual tradition and grappled with the question of cultural nationalism and national identity. They fiercely criticized those (such as Gilberto Freyre) who argued for a homogeneous and unitary vision of national identity even while adopting some of the approaches and terminology of the Modernists and their *mestiço* nationalism. Tropicalists returned to the classic work of Oswald de Andrade and his cannibalist manifesto. Caetano Veloso later declared that "the idea of cannibalism fit us, the tropicalists, like a glove. We were 'eating' the Beatles and Jimi Hendrix."[29] Gilberto Gil, Veloso, and others of a new musical vanguard (Tom Zé, Os Mutantes, Gal Costa, for example) shocked both the conservative supporters of the military regime and their precursors in popular music who saw the introduction of the instruments and styles of rock and roll as morally degenerate, culturally inappropriate, or politically unacceptable (depending on one's position on the ideological spectrum). Tropicalists both drew on previous forms of music (such as samba or *bossa nova*) and critiqued them. They were on the cutting edge of popular music while standing on the shoulders of decades of iconic Brazilian musicians and musical styles. At the same time, they brilliantly utilized the medium of television.[30]

This exceptionally talented group of artists from Bahia also drew on the regional symbols and identity that had emerged in the previous decades and reinforced a sense of *baianidade* (Bahian-ness). They simultaneously reinforced the sense of national identity built around the narrative of *mestiçagem* and the regional identity constructed around the symbols of Bahia's African heritage such as candomblé, capoeira, and a distinctive culinary tradition. In their efforts to critique a repressive military regime, they used music to highlight the region as a space of welcoming cultural difference. These countercultural artists managed to challenge the authoritarianism of the military regime through a musical language that reinforced both a regional identity and a cultural nationalism.[31] The music of the tropicalists from Bahia offered a new version of Freyre's comments dating back to the 1920s that the people of Bahia were "the most harmoniously mestizo of America and the most expressively Brazilian of Brazil."[32]

The music of the tropicalists and MPB both celebrated and critiqued the myth of *mestiçagem*. At the same time, they simultaneously continued the decades-long tradition of highlighting *mestiçagem* as central to Brazilian identity while opening up the conversation about national identity in ways that would make it increasingly impossible for Freyre's vision to continue to exercise such a powerful role in the national psyche. As millions and millions more Brazilians took part in an increasingly vibrant and truly national cultural mix, the reach of the Freyrean vision grew even as its critics multiplied and intensified. Gil, the child of a middle-class family of racially mixed origins, thoughtfully analyzed his *mulato* family history, discrimination in Brazil, and notions of national identity, eventually embracing the black consciousness movement. Veloso, despite his early criticisms of the dominant vision of national identity, gradually moved to an accommodation with Freyre and the myth of *mestiçagem*, saying that "a nation cannot exist without a myth. I think Freyre has been very important to the building of our best myth as a nation, the myth of racial democracy."[33] Gil and Veloso represent the two paths flowing out of popular culture by the 1980s – the continuing power and appeal of the Freyrean vision and the steady growth of opposition to the vision, especially from the black consciousness movement in Brazil.[34]

Television became the principal forum for the contending forces within popular music, and Brazilian culture in the 1960s. The economic boom of the late 1960s and early 1970s (the so-called "miracle") expanded the Brazilian middle class and working class, promoted consumption, including a dramatic rise in records and tapes, making Brazil the sixth-largest market in the world in terms of sales by 1980. The constant usage of popular music, especially MPB, on the sound tracks of the *telenovelas* also helped dramatically expand markets and sales.[35] As new influences, especially international ones, permeated popular music, these struggles took shape in front of the eyes and ears of a rapidly growing television public, especially in Brazil's cities. In retrospect, this was a foreshadowing of the role of television in the 1980s and 1990s, especially in the *diretas já* campaign in 1984 and the mass movement calling for the impeachment of President Fernando Collor in 1992. While the tropicalists represented the daring countercultural and (ultimately) political challenges to the established order, Roberto Carlos and the Jovem Guarda emerged as the most influential and popular performers of the highly commercial Brazilian version of North Atlantic rock 'n' roll.[36] The more politically active musicians accused Roberto Carlos and his romantic music as un-Brazilian, inauthentic, and (for some) as supporting the status quo (i.e., the dictatorship).

Brazilian artists, both those who would become iconic figures (Roberto Carlos, Gal Costa, Caetano Veloso, Gilberto Gil, Chico Buarque, among others) and many other less successful performers competed for air time and popularity on the musical showcases provided by the rapidly emerging television stations. TV Record's *O Fino*, hosted by Elis Regina, and *Jovem Guarda*, hosted by Roberto Carlos, engaged in a ratings battle in the late 1960s that expanded the range and reach of the new forms of popular music. The music on the former came to be known as *Música Popular Brasileira* (MPB) and as more political while the latter was seen as more apolitical.[37] Although many of the artists on both programs went on to become huge stars over the succeeding decades, the *Jovem Guarda* and its form of pop music developed the larger mass audience and appeal. Both programs helped fuel the expansion of television and a mass consumer market for popular music.[38]

Televised music festivals in the late 1960s became another prominent venue for the promotion of popular music and the mobilization of large numbers of Brazilians in a period of intense political suppression and "demobilization." One clear purpose of the organizers of these festivals was to provide "a venue for the mass-mediated promotion of 'authentic' Brazilian music," in particular of the more politically aware MPB artists.[39] Many new, young, and innovative artists came of age in these live, televised carnivalesque shows.[40] Much like *American Idol*-style programs today, the festivals involved a lengthy process of submissions, judging, and then performances before judges and large live audiences. These events became so popular that one journalist asserted that "In no soccer stadium does one see so much enthusiasm and passion, which suggests the immense importance attributed by Brazilians to music, its composers, and its singers." The incredibly lively and contentious crowds, seen live on television, also foreshadowed the protests of the 1980s and early 1990s. The young Chico Buarque and Geraldo Vandré achieved national visibility virtually overnight for their compositions. Vandré's

1968 festival song *Pra não dizer que não falei das flores* (So they don't say that I never spoke of flowers) became the anthem of the student protest movement in the late 1960s and early 1970s. The military regime banned the song, and its reappearance on the radio in 1979 (sung by Simone under the title of *Caminhando* [Walking]) signaled a key shift in politics and culture with the *abertura* in the last years of the regime.[41]

As much as the tropicalists represent a new stage in the national conversation about *mestiçagem*, Chico Buarque de Holanda (b. 1944) epitomizes the move from cultural to civic nationalism through his extraordinarily prolific career.[42] Son of one of the most important Brazilian intellectuals of the twentieth century, Sérgio Buarque de Holanda, Chico's personal networks and his musical production embody "the best of the best of the history of Brazilian music" linking modernists, samba, *bossa nova*, MPB, and its successors. Beginning in the 1960s, his work offers us a brilliant musical, cultural, and political commentary on Brazil. Through his father and the intellectuals and artists who circulated through his home in the 1940s and 1950s (in Brazil and in Europe), Chico Buarque's music and personal history have roots in the Modernists of the 1920s and 1930s and in multiple intellectual and artistic paths leading from those decades to the late twentieth century.[43]

As a child, Chico began to play the guitar and fall in love with music, and he was encouraged by a close family friend, Vinícius de Morais. Although he reluctantly entered the architecture faculty at the Universidade de São Paulo in the early 1960s, he immediately began playing and composing, achieving very quick success. His early works in the 1960s appeared to some of the more politically conscious as light-weight and mere pop music. In one of the iconic moments of the 1960s music festivals, the crowd vociferously booed the announcement that *Sabiá*, a song co-written by Tom Jobim and Chico Buarque, had won first prize. Geraldo Vandré, just before he performed his now famous *Para não dizer que não falei das flores*, responded to the crowd, declaring that *Sabiá* and its composers "merited our respect." He then proceeded to sing the song that became the most famous anthem of those who opposed the dictatorship. Vandré paid a high personal price for his music, facing intense interrogation, exile, and later walking away from his musical career. Despite the criticism of the highly politicized crowd, *Sabiá* is a song of exile and longing that came to epitomize the feelings of many who were already in exile and those who soon joined them.[44] Within months of the festival, the military high command issued AI-5 and the "coup within the coup" in December 1968 initiated the most brutal and repressive phase of the military regime.

Part of the brilliance of Chico Buarque's music in these years was his ability to compose exceptionally appealing music with subtle lyrics that provided incisive social and political commentary. His earliest success *Pedro Pedreiro* (1965) playfully traces the hard life of a typical poor stone mason. As one noted critic has pointed out, the song is in the poetic-musical tradition of Villa-Lobos.[45] As the regime became more repressive and censorship more sweeping and invasive, Chico Buarque's lyrics, like those of many popular artists, became more subtly subversive. *Apesar de você* (In Spite of You, 1970) cleverly criticizes the military for the creation of the repressive regime and takes its title from the phrase "In spite of you, tomorrow will be another day." After he faced interrogation, Buarque and his young family went into exile for a little over a year to Italy.[46]

Perhaps the most emblematic of Chico Buarque's protest songs is *Cálice* (with Gilberto Gil and Milton Nascimento, 1978). A clever play on the word chalice (*cálice*) and shut up (*cale-se*), the song is a thinly veiled critique of the military regime with the refrain "Father, take away from me this chalice/shut up of wine tinted with blood." The song was released in 1978 just before the political amnesty of 1979 and the gradual political opening (*abertura*). Although the regime initially attempted to ban the song, it became an enormous popular success (along with Vandré's song *Caminhando*). Soon thereafter he composed another iconic song, the title theme for the enormously successful film *Bye Bye Brasil* (Cacá Diegues, 1979).[47] Starring some of Brazil's greatest actors (Betty Faria and José Wilker), the film cleverly presents the allegorical story of a roving circus troupe as they move across a Brazil in the process of transformation during the military regime's "economic miracle." In one of the emblematic scenes the troupe arrives in a small town in the interior only to find everyone in town glued to the one television set watching a *telenovela*. In contrast to the regime's nationalistic slogan, "para frente, Brasil" (forward, Brazil), the song invokes a melancholy tone scanning a Brazil trampled by the military's ideal of modernization. Invoking Ary Barroso's iconic *Aquarela do Brasil*, the lyrics note that *aquela aquarela mudou* (that watercolor has changed). In a direct reference to the regime's support for Rede Globo and its efforts to shape a new image of the country, Buarque observes "*Eu vi um Brasil na TV*" (I saw a Brazil on TV).[48]

Chico Buarque emerged in the 1960s and 1970s as one of the most prolific and innovative composers in Brazilian music. With a creativity that places him alongside his brilliant predecessors from earlier generations (Barroso, Jobim), and a social consciousness that eventually brought him directly into the sights of the dictatorship, Chico Buarque became one of the most important musical artists of MPB. He became a sort of combination of Bob Dylan and Paul Simon with the ability to fuse compositional genius with a lyrical brilliance that could subtly and incisively reveal the core features of Brazilian society and politics. In the 1960s and 1970s this placed him at the cutting edge of political commentary on the military regime and artistic innovation. Charles Perrone has called him "viva voce, the *conscience* of an entire generation" (of the middle class, to be more precise).[49] Along with Caetano Veloso and Gilberto Gil he has been one of the most enduring talents of the artists who came of age during the dictatorship.[50]

The enormous popular success of the tropicalistas and the protest music of many other artists such as Vandré and Chico Buarque persuaded the military that MPB was the number one cultural enemy of the regime.[51] The regime interrogated and jailed many of these artists and a steady stream of them (Caetano, Gil, Chico, Vandré) went into exile after 1968. Their enormous creativity and vitality, however, brought them back to Brazil to produce not only incredibly important political commentary but some of the finest music in Brazilian culture in the twentieth century. Their cultural resonance and popularity played an enormously important role in the emergence of a potent civic nationalism in the 1970s and 1980s as Brazilians challenged the dictatorship and then moved the country toward re-democratization.

POPULAR MUSIC, NATIONALISM, CITIZENSHIP

In many ways, the massive expansion of popular music (made possible by the consolidation of radio and television broadcasting across virtually the entire national territory) and the steady (if not entirely successful) protest movements throughout the 1960s and 1970s prepared the way for the emergence of a flourishing civic nationalism and discussion of citizenship in the 1980s and 1990s. The enormously creative and sophisticated protest songs that were also commercially successful fostered an ongoing conversation in both lyrics and among the public about civic and cultural nationalisms. These developments helped pave the way for the two largest public mobilizations of the post-1964 period: the *diretas já* campaign in 1984 and the impeachment of Fernando Collor de Mello in 1992. Nothing on the scale of these mass mobilizations in the streets of Brazil would be seen again for another generation – until 2013.

Yet, the incredible florescence of Brazilian popular music from the 1960s to the 1980s, building on the equally vibrant and creative period from the 1930s to the 1950s, marks a turning point in the cultural life of the country, in the conversation about national identity and nationalism, and in the old binaries – erudite/popular, elites/masses, center/periphery. The 1990s signaled a new era not only in Brazilian culture but also globally, as new digital technologies became available, revolutionizing communications – from the personal to the global village. The rise of cable and satellite television broadcasting, personal computers, cell phones, and the simplification of recording technology have made it possible for virtually anyone to produce and distribute music. Just as the emergence of recording technology in the early twentieth century and the rise of radio broadcasting defined and redefined the very meaning of popular culture, the new digital technologies that have taken shape by the beginning of the twenty-first century force us once again to rethink the very meaning of "popular culture." Aural culture may, in fact, redefine the very nature of how we think of the public sphere and popular culture.[52]

Just as Rede Globo's stranglehold on television broadcasting dramatically shifted with the spread of cable and satellite in the 1990s, so too did the music culture industry begin to experience a revolution that is ongoing. At the end of the twentieth century, the multinational recording conglomerates appeared to be headed toward a global domination of the music business. Today, they grapple with ways to combat constantly declining sales of physical recordings, and to control the sale and distribution of digital downloads and streaming.[53] From the 1930s to the 1980s, Brazilian artists who wanted to reach ever larger audiences desperately needed record contracts, airplay on radio stations, and appearances on television to reach beyond the clubs and venues where they managed to perform. The invention of the World Wide Web, YouTube, and the like has now made it possible for artists to record and distribute their music independent of the traditional pillars of the culture industry – i.e., corporations. As the last "record" stores on the planet become novelty shops for LPs (long play vinyl records), and as the multinational conglomerates see their sales diminished by alternative methods of downloading, the most popular music in Brazil today – "the ones that are sung in the streets of big cities and that really inspire people to dance at the most exciting parties – are not the ones that play most often on radio, appear on TV shows, or are released by big recording companies."[54]

Technobrega, forró, lambadão, funk, pop vaneirão, and other forms of music have surged across Brazil, selling millions of CDs and downloads in a "parallel" market independent of the radio and television broadcasters and record companies. As Hermano Vianna has observed, this music is ignored by music critics in major newspapers, not discussed in the academic seminars and debates about popular culture, and operates outside the aural world of millions of more affluent Brazilians. Vianna sums up this new cultural transformation of the past two decades by noting that "It is as if they were too popular to be authentically popular."[55] Just as Brazilians grappled in the 1920s and 1930s with what was authentically Brazilian, what was popular culture, and whose voices should be heard in these debates, Brazilians in the 2020s and 2030s will be debating the same issues, but under very different technological and cultural conditions.

These new conditions that began to emerge in the 1990s, not just in Brazil but also across wide swaths of the planet, have brought an end to a phase that lasted about three-quarters of a century in Brazil. Just as the technologies of recording, radio, film, and television made possible a national conversation about Brazilian identity, and provided the means for the Freyrean vision of *mestiçagem* to emerge as the dominant narrative of national identity, the digital technologies of the early twentieth century will make it increasingly difficult, if not impossible, for any narrative of national identity to exert the influence and power that the Freyrean vision has held in the decades from the 1930s to the 1990s. Contemporary artists may not seek today to define a single national narrative, yet they continue to define what it means to be Brazilian. Cultural cannibalism and *mestiçagem* remain central to the discourse of popular music even as the sounds of Brazilian music become more complex, global, and diverse. Globalization has not homogenized Brazil even as it has complicated narratives of national identity.[56]

I began this chapter arguing that music has provided the most important forum for the discussion of national identity in Brazil in the twentieth century. I believe this is still true in the early decades of the twenty-first century. One of the challenges of the historian attempting to recover the conversation in this music (and beyond it) in the twentieth century – especially prior to the 1960s – is how to access and evaluate the role of the vast majority of Brazilians (those who do not work for the government or the culture industry) in the conversation. To what extent are government officials and agencies, Rede Globo, and the managers of the cultural industries able to impose their values and views? To what extent do the great masses create and shape the conversation? In this century, the new digital technologies have completely altered the roles and have complicated the evaluation in new ways. The venues for the conversation have multiplied and the access of tens of millions of Brazilians to countless voices has made the conversation more chaotic, diverse, and unmanageable.

Much of the discussion and debate about the formation (or not) of national identity in Brazil has focused on the power of the information flows from the "center" and the lack of power of those on the "periphery" (i.e., most Brazilians for most of the twentieth century). The recent technological shifts make it harder and harder to speak of center and periphery. The new technologies have fundamentally changed the terms of the debate in ways that we will be grappling with for some time to come. In the words of Vianna, "More and more, the periphery takes everything over. It is no longer the center that includes the periphery. The periphery now includes the center. The center, excluded from the party, becomes the periphery of the periphery."[57] The formation, consolidation, and shifting nature of identities have become even more complex and the old notions of top-down, bottom-up, hegemony, and the like appear increasingly outmoded means of analysis.

NOTES

1. McCann, *Hello, Hello Brazil*, 5.
2. "Introduction: Music as Practice of Citizenship in Brazil," in *Brazilian Popular Music and Citizenship*, eds., Idelber Avelar and Christopher Dunn (Durham, NC: Duke University Press, 2011), 1.
3. "Throughout the twentieth century, Brazilian popular music has been the most important vehicle for the affirmation of this *mestiço* national identity both at home and abroad." Dunn, *Brutality Garden*, 13.
4. See, for example, Marcelo Ridenti, *Brasilidade revolucionária: um século de cultura e política* (São Paulo: Editora UNESP, 2010), esp. 85–120.
5. This paragraph and my views here draw heavily on Burdick, *The Color of Sound*, esp. 18–27. Quotes are from 19 and 20.
6. Frevo is "a highly syncopated, fast tempo marcha" that originated in Recife. Maracatu is "an Afro-Brazilian processional dance performed during Carnaval in Recife and other cities in Pernambuco and Ceará." McGowan and Pessanha, *The Brazilian Sound*, 123 and 141.
7. Avelar and Dunn, *Brazilian Popular Music and Citizenship*.
8. Quoting Toby Miller, Avelar and Dunn define cultural citizenship as "the maintenance and development of cultural lineage through education, custom, language, and religion and the positive acknowledgment of difference in and by the mainstream." They also argue that "the construction of citizenship in all of its dimensions takes place primarily within national boundaries even as it is informed by international and postnational discourses and practices." Avelar and Dunn, *Brazilian Popular Music and Citizenship*, 3 and 7.

9. Owensby, "Toward a History of Brazil's 'Cordial Racism'," 339.

10. Jairo Severiano, *Uma história da música popular brasileira: das origens à modernidade* (São Paulo: Editora 34, 2008), 96–103; Mendonça, *Carmen Miranda*, 27–29.

11. Jack Draper III, "Forró's Wars of Maneuver and Position: Popular Northeastern Music, Critical Regionalism, and a Culture of Migration," *Latin American Research Review*, 46:1 (2011), 80–101; John P. Murphy, *Music in Brazil: Experiencing Music, Expressing Culture* (New York: Oxford University Press, 2006); Severiano, *Uma história da música popular brasileira*, 107–326.

12. Vianna, *Mystery of Samba*, 78.

13. McCann, *Hello, Hello Brazil*, 4.

14. *Ibid.*, 68–70.

15. *Ibid.*, 70–78.

16. See, for example, Frederick Moehn, *Contemporary Carioca: Technologies of Mixing in a Brazilian Music Scene* (Durham, NC: Duke University Press, 2012), 57.

17. Campbell, "The Brazilian Northeast, Inside Out."

18. Perrone, *Masters of Contemporary Brazilian Song*, xix.

19. Muniz de Albuquerque, *Invention of the Northeast*, 120. For a brilliant analysis of Gonzaga and the invention of northeastern identity, see 114–24.

20. Draper, "Forró's Wars of Maneuver and Position," 80–101.

21. "By the mid-1960s, television had become the principal site for cultural struggles in Brazilian popular music." Dunn, *Brutality Garden*, 58. Although many forms of Brazilian music had been influenced by international styles for decades (if not centuries), the direct connections with the global influences in this case were clear and explicit.

22. Castro, *Chega de saudade*.

23. "The 1960s also witnessed the consolidation of a national culture industry that sought to tap into consumer markets primarily in urban areas." Dunn, *Brutality Garden*, 37.

24. Dunn, *Brutality Garden*, 170.

25. This section draws heavily on Chris Dunn's excellent study, *Brutality Garden*.

26. *Ibid.*, 3.

27. "Robert Stam has argued that popular music has been more successful than any other area of Brazilian culture in generating syntheses that are simultaneously local and cosmopolitan, popular and experimental, pleasurable and political." *Ibid.*, 10–11.

28. *Ibid.*, 38.

29. Caetano Veloso, *Verdade tropical* (São Paulo: Companhia das Letras, 1997), 247.

30. Jason Borge, "*Panis et Circensis*: The Brazilian Circus Imaginary from Modernism to Tropicalism," *Luso-Brazilian Review*, 51:1 (2014), 199–219.

31. Christopher Dunn, unpublished chapter from book manuscript on the Brazilian counterculture, "The Sweetest Barbarians: Baianidade, Candomblé, and the Brazilian Counterculture of the 1970s."

32. "a mais harmoniosamente mestiça da América e a mais expressivamente brasileira do Brasil." Quote from *Bahia e baianos* (29) in Patricia de Santana

Pinho, "Gilberto Freyre e a Baianidade," in Lund e McNee, *Gilberto Freyre e os estudos latino-americanos*, 238.

33. Dunn, *Brutality Garden*, 214.
34. Dunn, "A retomada freyreana," 35–38. When Gil became Minister of Culture in 2003, however, his *discurso de posse* sounded very Freyrean! He described Brazilian culture as "Uma cultura diversificada, plural mas que é como um verbo conjugado por pessoas diversas, em tempos e modos distintos. Porque, ao mesmo tempo, essa cultura é uma: cultura tropical sincrética tecida ao abrigo e à luz da língua portuguesa." www1.folha.uol.com.br/folha/brasil/ult96u44344.shtml [accessed 15 August 2016] My thanks to Chris Dunn for bringing this speech to my attention.
35. Sean Stroud, *The Defence of Tradition in Brazilian Popular Music: Politics, Culture and the Creation of* Música Popular Brasileira (Aldershot, UK: Ashgate, 2008), 80 and 95.
36. "[K]nown as *iê-iê-iê* (a reference to the refrain from the Beatles' hit song 'She Loves You')." Dunn, *Brutality Garden*, 58.
37. In MPB, "Hybridization was common, as composers mixed and remixed Brazilian parameters – rhythms, patterns of harmony, instruments – with those of rock, blues, soul, funk, some discothèque, Jamaican reggae, and, to a limited degree, African music." Perrone, *Masters of Contemporary Brazilian Song: MPB 1965–1985*, xxxii.
38. Dunn, *Brutality Garden*, 58–61. "By the 1970s MPB had become synonymous with authentic Brazilian popular music." Martha de Ulhôa Carvalho, "Tupi or Not Tupi MPB: Popular Music and Identity in Brazil," in David J. Hess and Roberto A. DaMatta, eds., *The Brazilian Puzzle: Culture on the Borderlands of the Western World* (New York: Columbia University Press, 1995), 172.
39. The material for this section comes from Dunn, *Brutality Garden*, 61–65. See also, Perrone, *Masters of Contemporary Brazilian Song: MPB 1965–1985*, xxix and xxxi.
40. Stroud, *The Defence of Tradition*, 67.
41. Victoria Langland, *Speaking of Flowers: Students Movements and the Making and Remembering of 1968 in Military Brazil* (Durham: Duke University Press, 2013), especially 1–4.
42. An excellent analysis of Buarque and his music is chapter 1, "Chico Buarque: A Unanimous Construction," in Perrone, *Masters of Contemporary Brazilian Song: MPB 1965–1985*, 1–44.
43. Regina Zappa, *Chico Buarque: para todos*, 4ª. edn. (Rio de Janeiro: Relume Dumará, 1999), 49; Fernando de Barros e Silva, *Chico Buarque* (São Paulo: PubliFolha, 2004), 18–23.
44. Zappa, *Chico Buarque*, 66; Severiano, *Uma história da música popular brasileira*, 354–55.
45. Severiano, *Uma história da música popular brasileira*, 355.
46. Zappa, *Chico Buarque*, 104–9.
47. Rafael Leopoldo AS Ferreira, "Bye Bye Brazil," in Bayman and Pinazza, *Directory of World Cinema: Brazil*, 257–58.
48. Silva, *Chico Buarque*, 88–91.

49. Perrone, *Masters of Contemporary Brazilian Song: MPB 1965–1985*, 216.

50. Very early in his career (1977), the eminent music critic José Ramos Tinhorão called him "o maior compositor saído da classe média após o advento da Bossa Nova." Zappa, *Chico Buarque*, 68.

51. Tárik de Souza quoted in Zappa, *Chico Buarque*, 103.

52. Ana María Ochoa Gautier, "Social Transculturation, Epistemologies of Purification and the Aural Public Sphere in Latin America," in Jonathan Sterne, ed. *The Sound Studies Reader* (London: Routledge, 2012), 388–404.

53. Ben Sisario and Karl Russell, "In Shift to Streaming, Music Business Has Lost Billions," *New York Times* (24 March 2016), www.nytimes.com/2016/03/2 5/business/media/music-sales-remain-steady-but-lucrative-cd-sales-decline.h tml?_r=0 [accessed 1 July 2016].

54. Hermano Vianna, "Technobrega, Forró, Lambadão: The Parallel Music of Brazil," in Avelar and Dunn, *Brazilian Music and Citizenship*, 247.

55. Vianna, "Technobrega, Forró, Lambadão," 247.

56. Moehn, *Contemporary Carioca*, esp. 14, 56, 79, 104, 151, and 205.

57. *Ibid.*, 249.

7

Culture, Identity, and Citizenship

People become citizens as they come to feel themselves part of a nation and a State. Citizenship as we know it then involves loyalty to a State and identification with a nation. The two do not always appear together. The identification with the nation might be stronger than the loyalty with the State, and vice versa. In general, national identity comes from factors such as religion, language and, above all, struggles and wars against common enemies. Loyalty to the State depends on the degree of participation in political life.[1]

José Murilo de Carvalho

CIVIC AND CULTURAL NATIONALISMS

For much of the twentieth century Brazilians constructed a vibrant cultural nationalism largely in the absence of a strong civic nationalism.[2] They could feel themselves part of the nation through their deep affective attachments to samba, *carnaval*, and *futebol* as sites for the expression of a cultural citizenship and belonging, in the absence of the rights they should have enjoyed through civic citizenship.[3] From the 1930s to the 1980s, a powerful and coherent narrative of cultural identity took shape around Freyre's vision of *mestiçagem* while Brazilians struggled to create a civic identity in decades dominated by various forms of authoritarianism and limited representative politics. Even while the technological waves of radio, film, and television gradually drew the inhabitants of the country together around shared cultural myths, rituals, and symbols, successive waves of political authoritarianism and exclusion reinforced centuries of hierarchy, inequality, and clientelism, hindering the formation and expansion of full citizenship and civic identity. The creation and florescence of a strong cultural identity and nationalism constructed around the myth of *mestiçagem* by the 1980s facilitated the growth and maturation of civic nationalism, citizenship, and re-democratization as Brazil moved from military rule to mass democratic politics. The myth of *mestiçagem* – the positive belief that Brazilians were *one people* forged from centuries of racial and cultural mixing – emerged in the twentieth century as the dominant narrative of the *nation*. With the full-blown emergence of a civic nationalism at the end of the century, State and nation converged, arguably more fully and completely than at any time in Brazil's history.

The maturation of the dominant narrative of cultural identity and the emergence of an increasingly powerful civic identity in the 1980s and 1990s highlight the contradictions, complexities, and ironies of the formation and development of both nation and State in Brazil. In the aftermath of the declaration of independence in 1822 elites took control of the apparatus of the colony to create their own State independent of Portugal and the Portuguese monarchy. The great challenges in the following century and a half were to impose the power of the State across the vast expanses of "Brazil" – as it appeared on maps – and to create a nation. As Murilo de Carvalho's quote at the beginning of this chapter notes, loyalty to the State requires participation in political life, something the constitutional monarchy dominated by powerful landed elites in the nineteenth century was clearly not fully committed to extending to the majority of the inhabitants of Brazil. Loyalty to the nation – recognition of the *very existence* of the nation – presumes the creation of a sense of common identity, a shared culture. The Brazilian State emerged quickly, if weakly, in the nineteenth century, expanded gradually across the national territory, and has remained potent, but has also faced serious crises (most notably, c. 1840, 1890, 1930, and 1964). This State expanded its "monopoly of violence" across the country in fits and starts for much of the first century after independence. The age of Vargas, in many ways, signaled the turning point in this process. I have argued that the Brazilian nation does not fully emerge until the middle of the twentieth century. The loyalty and participation to sustain both, I believe, finally converged in the 1980s and 1990s – although their relationship remained tenuous and fraught with tensions.

CITIZENSHIPS

In this chapter we come full circle back to where we began in Chapter 1. In the century from the declaration of independence in the 1820s to the

rise of Getúlio Vargas in the 1920s and 1930s, a robust political citizenship remained restricted to a very small portion of the population in
Brazil, and the formation of civic identity (like cultural identity) faced
enormous obstacles. A tiny fragment of the country's inhabitants, primarily the landowning class and merchants, enjoyed the most fundamental
classical liberal political rights – liberty and equality. In the 1820s, a third
of the population consisted of slaves (with very few rights), and in the
1870s, 1.5 million slaves still made up 15 percent of the country's inhabitants. Of the remaining 7–8 million inhabitants, just 13 percent voted.
With new, and more restrictive, voting laws after 1881 the number of
eligible voters declined by 90 percent and less than 1 percent voted (about
100,000) in parliamentary elections. By the 1930 presidential elections,
this percentage had risen to slightly less than 6 percent. One startling
measure of the lack of access to political participation is the first presidential election under the Republic in 1894. In the city of Rio de Janeiro,
with a population of more than a half million, less than 8,000 *cariocas* cast
votes![4]

In 1945 (the first open national election for president since 1930), the
figure reached 13.4 percent (equal to the 1870s), and continued to rise into
the 1960s. In 1962, the percentage of eligible voters reached one-quarter
of the population. Ironically, under the repressive and heavily controlled
politics of the military regime (1964–1985) the vote expanded dramatically, by more than 160 percent. In 1960, less than 20 percent of the
population voted, while in 1986, nearly 50 percent exercised the vote in
municipal and state elections. The 1988 Constitution finally removed the
literacy requirement for voting and extended the vote to all Brazilians over
the age of sixteen. By 1998, Brazil had more than 106 million registered
voters, more than two-thirds of the country's inhabitants.[5] In effect, mass
politics did not take shape in Brazil until the late 1940s, faced stiff
challenges under a repressive military regime, and emerged full blown
only in the 1990s.

Citizenship normally includes both social and political rights. Brazil
has historically moved forward more quickly on the extension of the
former, and much slower on the latter. The Vargas regimes intensified
this "model" of citizenship extending substantial social rights, especially
to urban, industrial (primarily male) workers, in the 1930s and 1940s in
an era of very limited civil and political rights. "Workers," Murilo de
Carvalho notes, "were incorporated into society by virtue of social legislation and not through independent political and union activity."[6]
In many ways, the military regime reproduced the Vargas model,

gradually conceding additional social rights while maintaining restricted political rights. The "post-1930 Brazilian authoritarianism always sought to compensate for the lack of political liberty with social paternalism."[7]

The struggle for the rights of citizenship has been long and arduous in Brazil. Throughout the nineteenth century the Brazilian State exercised its "legitimate" violence frequently in suppressing regional revolts in the 1820s, 1830s, and 1840s, uprisings often characterized by claims to the rights of citizenship.[8] In less dramatic ways, ordinary people all across Brazil over the past two centuries have struggled at the grassroots locally to claim access to what we would today call "social and political rights."[9] Some have done this through organizing themselves in associations, clubs, and resisting the power of the State in small but important ways. More dramatically, the numerous regional revolts against the authority of the central State probably made many of the inhabitants of Brazil conscious, for the first time, of their identity as Brazilians. As they fought to crush the uprisings, whether as members of the army or as antagonists to the rebels, these inhabitants of Brazil must have grappled with their own sympathies and sense of belonging to the young "nation" and the monarchy. The life-and-death choices of military conflict would have forced the participants to take sides and consider their loyalties.

In the nineteenth century, the Paraguayan War (1864–1870) stands out as the first great moment in the formation of a national community in Brazil.[10] As the State mobilized more than 135,000 men from provinces across the country in a long, drawn-out struggle, probably for the first time, most of the inhabitants of the country confronted "national" issues at relatively the same moment. In the age of the telegraph and the newspaper, the battles and bloodshed the war produced were disseminated and discussed across the populated regions of the country over several years. (The impact of Paraguay comes closest to the impact of Benedict Anderson's "print culture" in fostering a sense of an imagined Brazilian community.) Whether voluntarily or through impressment, the war pulled tens of thousands of men (free and slave) into a brutal struggle against a common enemy. The armed forces, especially the army, would be one of the most important, one of the very few truly national institutions that would serve as an ongoing means to assert the power of the State across the country's territory and disseminate the views of the State.[11] Nevertheless, Brazil fought no other major international wars and faced no clear foreign enemies again until the 1940s.[12] From the perspective of the central government the principal enemies from the 1870s until the 1930s were all internal! The Proclamation of the Republic, in fact, moved

Brazil back toward regionalism and decentralization, simultaneously weakening the forces that promote the formation of nationalism and national identity.

Along with the political discussions about the Paraguayan War, the long debate over slavery and abolition provided the other truly national conversation in the nineteenth century.[13] The war also brought the issue of abolition to the forefront of discussion in politics and society by drawing on slaves as soldiers and promising them freedom as the reward for their service to the *patria*. The role of slaves in the conflict also helped push forward the legislative debate that resulted in the Law of the Free Womb in 1871. As in the United States, the abolitionist struggle formed an important part of this battle of millions to achieve basic political rights, a battle that continued for decades in the aftermath of emancipation for millions of poor Brazilians, including those descended from slaves.[14] Yet, while this struggle had the potential to unify millions to free their fellow inhabitants of the country, persuading rich and poor Brazilians that the slaves (many born in Africa) were their equals deserving of the rights of citizenship was just as difficult in Brazil as it was in the United States, before and after emancipation. In the years after abolition in 1888, profound socioeconomic inequalities replaced slavery as the open wound in Brazilian society.[15] José Bonifácio had declared in 1823 that "slavery was a cancer that corroded our civic life and impeded the construction of the nation." Inequality became that cancer after 1888.[16]

In a society shaped for centuries by a corporatist ethos, pronounced hierarchy, inequality, clientelism, and patronage hindered the formation of civil society and civic organizations. The power of the State to repress and co-opt was enormous. A public sphere fitfully struggled to take shape throughout the nineteenth century. Throughout the early twentieth century grassroots struggles took shape against these forces of repression and co-optation as the *povo* fought to establish their rights. Some of these efforts took the form of violent revolts (such as the Contestado Rebellion in southern Brazil); others followed more institutional paths, such as the battles to establish labor unions; while the least documented and understood are the many associations and civic groups across the towns and countryside of Brazil.[17] As James Holston has argued, the very nature of citizenship in Brazil frustrated those who struggled to assert and claim their rights.[18]

The constitutional law that guaranteed equality also constructed privileges and hierarchies that denied rights to many poor Brazilians. Much like the histories of the United States and Western Europe, Brazil has experienced an ongoing struggle across the nineteenth and twentieth centuries as more and more Brazilians have fought tenaciously to gain access to the rights enjoyed by a minority of their compatriots. Both Holston and Brodwyn Fischer have brilliantly dissected this struggle in São Paulo and Rio de Janeiro.[19] Land tenure and ownership have long been the key to this struggle, in the countryside in the nineteenth century, and in the rapidly growing cities in the twentieth century. As Fischer has shown for Rio de Janeiro after 1930, the poor in the *favelas* managed "to claim some degree of urban permanence... to build a legal existence, establishing a critical foothold in the city of laws," but the citizenship of poor people remained "incomplete and fragmented." The poor "often used laws, but few have come to believe in them, and without that belief the rule of law has never become a dominant praxis."[20]

Fischer also highlights the ongoing contradiction of the expansion of social rights after 1930 while political rights remain restricted. For poor Brazilians, even access to social rights remained restricted given their inability to access legal rights and their employment overwhelmingly outside the formal sector. Consequently, the loyalty of the poor to nation was less pronounced in the 1930s and 1940s than their commitment to family. As Fischer observes, "alternate incarnations of Vargas's core values did not generate rights, only vague claims to charity. Social and economic citizenship was a privilege, not an entitlement; thus, oddly, it often came to reinforce, not ameliorate, long entrenched inequities of power and opportunity." The benefits Vargas offered Brazilians "became less a variant of citizenship than a sophisticated form of patronage, an uncertain basket of perks distributed to the skilled, the lucky, the well connected, and the bureaucratically agile. Poor people's citizenship remained a partial and uncertain enterprise, defined by scarcity rather than security of rights."[21] In the decades after the 1930s, the poor in Rio (and by extension, in much of Brazil) became increasingly embedded in a system that both provided increasing social and political rights to those in the formal sector and made it difficult (but not impossible) for those in the informal sector to access those rights fully.

Holston persuasively argues that Brazilian legal regimes across the past two centuries have both created the parameters of citizenship (theoretically) for all, while legitimating privileges and inequalities. Poor people on the peripheries (*periferia*) of cities such as São Paulo and Rio de Janeiro have challenged this "entrenched" citizenship, especially over the past thirty years, with an "insurgent" citizenship. The former has long been a "formal membership, based on principles of incorporation into the nation-state; the other is the substantive distribution of the rights, meanings, institutions, and practices that membership entails to those deemed citizens." Paradoxically, Brazilian national citizenship has been both universal and inclusive while simultaneously "massively inegalitarian in distribution." This form of citizenship, therefore, is "a mechanism to distribute inequality."[22]

In the 1970s and 1980s movements began to emerge in Brazil as those who have not enjoyed the privileges of citizenship increasingly organized and fought for their rights as "insurgents." The very language of "citizenship" emerged at the forefront of social and political movements.[23] As social movements took shape in the 1980s and 1990s during the process of re-democratization, new and sometimes conflicting views of citizenship emerged in Brazil (and elsewhere).[24] Evelina Dagnino has argued that these movements redefined citizenship and "placed a strong emphasis on the cultural dimensions of citizenship, incorporating contemporary concerns with subjectivities, identities, and the right to difference." More than just legal and political rights, this new vision of citizenship called "for a radical transformation of cultural practices that reproduce social inequality and exclusion." This broader vision of citizenship "represented a project for a new sociability" that envisions citizenship as more than a relationship between the individual and the State, but as "a parameter for all social relations," a *"project for a new sociability"* (emphasis in original).[25]

The half-century of cultural nationalism constructed around the myth of *mestiçagem* laid much of the groundwork for the full-blown emergence of these citizenship movements. By the 1980s the work of constructing the nation – of creating a sense of loyalty and belonging to something called Brazil – had matured. This notion of belonging to the nation – to a national cultural community – and the repression of political rights under the military regime combined to produce movements across all of Brazil involving tens of millions of people demanding their rights *as Brazilians*.[26] In many ways, the decades of cultural nationalism, of identity construction, paved the way and made possible the rise of movements dedicated to democratization and citizenship. Tens of millions now saw themselves as Brazilians, with loyalties to the nation, and they now demanded the rights promised to them by the State. They could see themselves as included in an imagined cultural community of Brazilians, but saw themselves as excluded from the political community of Brazil. They struggled to integrate the nation and the State, to convert their cultural belonging into political inclusion.[27]

The most spectacular and visible convergence of Brazil's cultural and civic nationalisms can be seen in two moments of massive popular mobilization: the *diretas já* campaign in 1984 and the impeachment of President Fernando Collor de Mello in 1992. In each of these two movements, millions of people took to the streets in the largest public demonstrations (*manifestações*) in the country's history. The first movement failed to achieve its specific political objective – to compel congress to pass legislation calling for the first direct election of a president since 1960. Despite this failure, the movement sounded the death knell of the authoritarian regime, began the final stage in the transition to civilian rule, and marked the massive emergence of national movements seeking the full rights of citizenship for all Brazilians. The second movement built on the first and helped make possible a specific political objective – the impeachment of President Collor de Mello. Both movements consolidated and solidified cultural nationalism as Brazilians quite literally wrapped themselves in some of the most visible symbols of national loyalty and belonging – the flag and its colors – drawing on the powerful rituals, symbols, and personalities of popular culture. Ironically, at the very moment that nearly all those in Brazil finally saw themselves as Brazilians with common myths, rituals, and symbols, the most powerful myth of national identity had already entered into relative decline, facing sustained challenges made possible by a more open, democratic society and the emergence of a dynamic civil society.

THE *DIRETAS JÁ* CAMPAIGN

Brazil's transition from repressive dictatorship to fulsome democracy in the late twentieth century may have been the longest of any nation in Latin America. After the phenomenal economic expansion of the Brazilian "miracle" and the intense repression of the late 1960s and early 1970s, the military regime began a long, slow process of *distensão* (decompression) and *abertura* (opening) that clearly gained traction with the presidency of Ernesto Geisel (1974–1979) counseled by his key advisor, General Golbery do Couto e Silva.[28] The economic crises of the 1970s – most notably the oil shocks in 1973 and 1979 – and the debt crisis and massive inflation of the 1980s steadily discredited the regime even as the "threat" of leftist subversion gradually disappeared. In 1980, inflation surpassed 100 percent per annum and rose to more than 200 percent by 1984–1985. The regime's twin objectives in taking power in 1964 – crushing the threat of leftist revolution and building a strong national economy ("security and development") – had been achieved in the first case, and failed miserably in the second. Geisel's personal choice as his successor, General João Baptista Figueiredo, became the final military president (1979–1985) and the key transitional figure between dictatorship and democracy.

The regime eventually settled on a plan for a "controlled" transition to civilian rule through the election of Figueiredo's successor in an electoral college, an institution the military regime had created and stacked with a majority from the government party. In 1979, the government promulgated a law that ended the official two-party system – the Aliança Renovadora Nacional (ARENA) and the Movimento Democrático Brasileiro (MDB) – allowing the formation of new parties under tightly regulated rules. The regime clearly hoped that ARENA would remain the majority party and the MDB would lose its strength as the opposition fragmented into multiple parties. Initially, this strategy appeared to work as the ARENA became (ironically) the Partido Democrático Social (PDS) and the MDB split into the Partido do Movimento Democrático Brasileiro (PMBD) and four additional, smaller parties.[29] As maneuvering began for the proposed indirect election (scheduled for January 1985) a movement took shape in congress to pass a law to elect the next president in a direct national election – the first since 1960. What began as congressional deal-making in 1983 around the Dante de Oliveira amendment gradually and dramatically in early 1984 emerged as a national movement that eventually brought millions of Brazilians into the streets to demonstrate their support for immediate direct elections for president (*diretas já*).[30]

Although the Dante de Oliveira amendment to the constitution drew little attention and support initially, the momentum for direct elections built throughout 1983, receiving the public support of major figures in the Catholic Church (the charismatic Cardinal Paulo Evaristo Arns of São Paulo and Dom Ivo Lorscheiter, General-Secretary of the National Conference of Brazilian Bishops) and some of the most visible opposition politicians – Teotônio Villela, Ulysses Guimarães, Luis Inácia Lula da Silva, and many others. The first public rallies in 1983 drew a few thousand participants. As the congressional vote on the amendment drew close in April 1984, rallies in Goiânia, Porto Alegre, and Rio de Janeiro drew crowds in the hundreds of thousands, and the April 16 rally in São Paulo may have attracted *a million* participants.[31]

The campaign represented a turning point not only for civil society and civic nationalism in Brazil but also for the media. After years of working

FIGURE 7.1 *Diretas já* Demonstrations
Source: Reprodução Veja/Edição 815/Abril Comunicações S/A

closely with the military regime in a tense relationship of government censorship and self-censorship, Globo and other major networks did not provide much coverage of the early stages of the movement. Eventually, the media could no longer ignore this massive public movement and provided full and dramatic coverage, fully breaking for the first time with government censorship guidelines. Globo, in fact, shifted from its long (sometimes qualified) support for the regime and made the rallies major media events. Some of the most notable figures of Brazilian popular culture eagerly joined the rallies and became their icons. Chico Buarque, Elba Ramalho, and Fafá de Belém became the movement's musical voices.

The great *futebol* star Sócrates demonstrated his support not only at the rallies but on the pitch. Perhaps most symbolic, the voice of Brazilian *futebol* broadcasting, Osmar Santos, became the "vocal trademark" of the rallies.[32] Cultural and civic nationalism, civil society, and popular culture converged in the *diretas já* campaign in ways and on a scale that had never been seen in Brazil.

Ricardo Kotscho, a reporter for the *Folha de São Paulo*, covered the campaign from its inception and has left us with an eyewitness account by an astute journalist writing for what was then the country's largest daily newspaper, and one widely renowned for its oppositionist stance. As Kotscho moves from the small rallies of a few thousand to the growing crowds as the opposition politicians take their "caravan" from city to city and state to state, he records not only an eruption of civic participation but also deeply intertwined roles of civic and cultural nationalism. From rally to rally, Kotscho describes the *carnaval*-like atmosphere heightened by the presence of some of the most beloved figures in Brazilian popular music. Chico Buarque sings his famous songs that had bedeviled the military regime for nearly twenty years. *Apesar de você*, in particular, became one of the frequently repeated songs. In the campaign rallies, the previously censored song became an anthem both criticizing the regime and promising "tomorrow will be a different day." During *carnaval* in March 1983, the electoral question dominated in the lyrics of the parades and music.

Fafá de Belém was the singer who became most profoundly associated with the campaigns with her version of the national anthem and a composition by the legendary Milton Nascimento, *Menestrel de Alagoas* (Minstrel from Alagoas). Nascimento composed the song to honor Teotônio Villela, a politician from Alagoas who had served as a senator affiliated with ARENA, but who increasingly criticized the lack of democracy and by the late 1970s had moved to the MDB. This powerful voice for re-democratization died on the day of the first rally in São Paulo on November 27, 1983. For many observers, Fafá de Belém (then in her late twenties) became the muse of the *diretas já* campaign, producing a powerful blend of civic nationalism with popular music and culture.

Repeatedly, Kotscho describes the rallies with a "climate of Carnaval mixed with the World Cup," and the multitudes "looking like soccer fans on championship game day." In early March on the eve of *carnaval* in Belo Horizonte, with a crowd of several hundred thousand, Reinaldo, a star for Atlético Mineiro and the national team (1978), appeared on the stage.[33] The crowd loved it and, according to Kotscho, "carnaval began yesterday, with the climate of victory of the National Team in a World

Cup." For Kotscho, that year became the "carnaval of the direct elections." At the massive rally in São Paulo on March 4, the participants dressed in green and yellow and sang the national anthem "as if it were a samba-exaltação of Ary Barroso." During *carnaval*, Brazilians refashioned classic songs to address the campaign. Carmen Miranda's classic *Mamãe eu quero* (Mommy I Want) became a call for the vote: "Mommy I want/give me a ballot box/give me a ballot box/give me a ballot box."[34] In these enormous civic rallies, millions of Brazilians clamored for their right to vote as citizens of the nation, dressed in the colors of the flag, sang their national anthem to the tune of samba, turned the gatherings into *carnaval*-like festivities, and bonded as Brazilians on a scale perhaps not seen in the country in anything short of a World Cup victory celebration.[35]

The campaign became a pivotal moment not only for the Brazilian people but also for Rede Globo.[36] Initially, Globo ignored the campaign and relegated information about the rallies to minor notices. As the rallies became ever larger, and as more and more media outlets covered the campaign, Globo found itself caught between two powerful contending forces: the military regime that had helped make the network so successful and a truly mass mobilization of Brazilians demanding a full-scale return to democracy. Globo devoted just forty-five seconds of coverage to the rally in São Paulo on January 25, 1984. Not until the Rio de Janeiro rally in early April did the network finally cross the line to provide full coverage. In effect, Roberto Marinho and the network realized the time had come to abandon its comfortable alliance with the military regime to join the bandwagon of re-democratization. The response confirmed their decision. More people watched the coverage of the Rio rally than the World Cup games (a few months later). Brazil's most important weekly, *Veja*, summarized Globo's move, noting that it recognized "the journalistic importance of the events and simultaneously recognized that to remain outside the movement could be highly prejudicial to its larger strategic interests."[37]

IMPEACHMENT, CITIZENSHIP, AND NATIONALISM

The *diretas já* campaign in 1983–1984 provided the first dramatic act in the full-blown emergence of a new civic nationalism in Brazil. In the words of Leonardo Avritzer, the campaign sounded "the death knell for authoritarianism in Brazil."[38] The impeachment of President Fernando Collor de Mello offered even more powerful evidence of this emergent civic nationalism, and its convergence with Brazil's long-standing cultural nationalism.[39] The meteoric rise and fall of Fernando Collor also highlight both the power and limitations of Rede Globo as his impeachment quite literally evolved into a *telenovela* watched by the entire nation.[40] Although these two national political acts did not mark the emergence of full citizenship for all Brazilians, both helped move Brazil into a new era of cultural and civic nationalism at the end of the twentieth century.

With the failure of the *diretas já* campaign, the military regime's plans to choose a successor to President João Figueiredo moved forward, although in a direction the military had not expected. Had the process gone forward as planned, the electoral college would have approved a successor chosen by Figueiredo and his military colleagues. The PDS made up a solid majority (356) of the 686 electors. Two unanticipated political shifts derailed the official plans for this indirect election. *Paulista* politician Paulo Maluf gradually emerged as the most powerful contender in the government party and he alienated many of his colleagues in the PDS, dividing the party. Known for his hard charging and tough tactics, promising patronage for votes, and tarred with charges of corruption, Maluf managed to outmaneuver the other major PDS candidates, in particular, Aureliano Chaves, former governor of Minas Gerais and Figueiredo's vice-president. A powerful rift emerged among the majority electors from the PDS.[41]

Equally unexpected, the opposition to the PDS managed to rally behind a single candidate, Tancredo Neves, the elderly (74) and highly respected governor of Minas Gerais. Unable to stomach a Maluf presidency, a significant portion of the PDS broke ranks to join the opposition support for Neves. In exchange for their defection, Senator José Sarney, former head of the PDS, was offered the vice-presidential nomination with Neves. In January 1985, this pact produced a smashing victory for the Neves–Sarney ticket and a resounding and embarrassing defeat for the government in its own electoral college. The generals may have turned aside the constitutional amendment for direct elections, but they ineptly failed to control their own indirect election for president. Tragically, Neves fell ill on the eve of his inauguration and died after an excruciating month of unsuccessful surgeries and treatments for a perforated intestine.[42] His death prompted a massive outpouring of emotion that evoked many of the symbols of Brazilian nationalism – from the colors of the flag, to the national anthem, to comparisons of Neves with the icon of the eighteenth-century *Inconfidência Mineira*, Tiradentes, long one of the most famous symbols of *mineiro* identity and Brazilian nationalism.

Several million mourners lined the route as his coffin moved through São Paulo and then Belo Horizonte, ultimately to his burial in a mausoleum/ shrine in São João del Rei. In the eyes of millions of Brazilians he became a martyr for the new democracy and a secular saint of the nation.[43]

At the very moment the opposition seemed poised to take power from the military regime, the former president of the government party (Sarney) suddenly and unexpectedly became president. Sarney spent the next five years employing the vast patronage of the State to stay in power.[44] After several economic shock plans failed to tame runaway inflation (reaching 50 percent per month), and corruption scandals, disillusionment with Sarney and the "transition" to democracy ran rampant. One of the most popular *telenovelas* in the history of Brazilian television, Globo's *Roque Santeiro* (1985–1986) provided Brazilians with a thinly veiled critique of the flawed transition from dictatorship to democracy and a cast of some of the biggest stars in Brazilian film and television. Set in the fictional small town of Asa Branca, it told the story of Luís Roque Dalton (José Wilker), a local maker of the images of saints (*santeiro*) who, legend had it, married Porcina (Regina Duarte) the shop attendant, and then died defending the town against a gang of thugs. The town prospered due to the legend of the "virtuous" Roque and miracles attributed to him, a narrative promoted by Porcina and the local political boss, Sinhozinho Malta (Lima Duarte). Roque suddenly reappears after seventeen years and his presence threatens to destroy the legend and the town's claim to fame. In the final episodes the "widow" Porcina must choose between Roque and Malta, and she finally chose the latter, a way for the principal authors (the legendary *novela* writers Dias Gomes and Aguinaldo Silva) to signal disillusionment with the transition and the unexpected presidency of Sarney. Nearly 100 percent of television sets in Brazil were turned to Globo during these final episodes.[45] Once again, a *telenovela* (and Globo) provided Brazilians with one of the most powerful vehicles for a national forum about politics, culture, and identity.

The focus of those Brazilians seeking full re-democratization in the late 1980s became the writing of a new constitution. The congress elected in 1986 simultaneously became a constitutional assembly, and after much negotiation and deal-making, it produced the country's seventh constitution. Among other things, the 1988 Constitution redefined citizenship for all Brazilians and called for direct national elections for president in 1989.[46] The greatest surprise of the 1989 campaign was the emergence of Fernando Collor de Mello and his victory in the second round of the presidential election.[47] Just forty years old when he assumed the presidency in March 1990, Collor comes from a wealthy and well-connected family in the tiny (and notoriously corrupt) northeastern state of Alagoas. Although a member of the most elite of elite Brazilians – his maternal grandfather was one of Getúlio Vargas's labor ministers and his father was a powerful sugar planter and politician – Collor was able to forge a campaign that presented him as the anti-candidate and a force for change – seeming to rise above partisan politics and the traditionally corrupt system of patronage politics. Following in a long tradition in Brazilian political history, he offered himself as the messianic figure that would save Brazil from the chaos of the debt crisis, runaway inflation, and political corruption. Key to the spectacular rise of Fernando Collor, by nearly all accounts, was Roberto Marinho and Rede Globo.[48]

Collor's rise and fall illustrate the power and limitations of Rede Globo, the changing role of television in Brazilian society and politics, and the maturation of civic nationalism in the 1980s and 1990s. Globo had become the dominant media corporation via Marinho's very close relationship with the military regime, and as the country moved slowly and fitfully toward re-democratization, Marinho faced difficult choices over how he chose to use his media power. The emergence of the *diretas já* campaign as a national grassroots movement epitomized these choices. Public opinion polls clearly demonstrated that more than 85 percent of the eligible voters surveyed wanted direct presidential elections, yet the military regime opposed the Dante de Oliveira amendment.[49] As nearly 75 million Brazilians prepared to vote for president in 1989 (many for the first time), Marinho used the power of Globo and its coverage of candidates to influence the election. As Luis Inácio "Lula" da Silva and Leonel Brizola, both firebrand leftists, emerged as early favorites, Globo's coverage clearly favored their more moderate opponents, in particular, Senator Mário Covas from São Paulo and Ulysses Guimarães, also from São Paulo (and the president of the Brazilian congress). Although both had been key opponents of the military regime in the MDB, and Guimarães had been one of the most visible leaders of the *diretas já* movement, they appeared to Marinho as viable and safe alternatives to Brizola and Lula. Brizola was the brother-in-law of João Goulart (deposed by the military coup in 1964), and one of the most charismatic orators on the Left. The Right feared Brizola's electoral pull perhaps more than that of any other leftist. Lula, a poor immigrant from northeastern Brazil to São Paulo, had emerged in the 1980s as a national political figure, as the best-known labor leader in the country. He was one of the principal founders of the Partido dos Trabalhadores (PT) and the Right also feared this bearded, Marxist *nordestino*. Nearly all of the more than twenty candidates ran campaigns attacking the wildly unpopular Sarney administration.[50]

Despite Globo's favorable coverage, neither Covas nor Guimarães garnered much electoral support, and they finished fourth and seventh (respectively) with a combined 15 percent of the vote in the election on November 15, 1989.[51] Collor captured nearly 30 percent of the vote (22 million) and Lula finished a distant second with 16 percent (11 million), less than 500,000 votes ahead of Brizola. The runoff election on December 17, 1989, shaped up as a clear choice between Collor (on the Right) and Lula (on the Left). Globo's support for Collor became clear in the weeks leading up to the final vote, which Collor won handily with 53 percent of the valid vote and 35 million votes. In one infamous moment, a craftily edited version of the final debate between Lula and Collor that substantially skewed in Collor's favor appeared on the *Jornal Nacional*.[52] Although Marinho and Globo did not single-handedly create and elect Collor, they played a critical role in his rise to prominence and election.

Much like a Greek tragedy, Fernando Collor's meteoric rise in 1989 was followed by an equally dramatic fall from power in 1992.[53] Collor had run as an outsider and he (like Jânio Quadros three decades earlier) suffered from his election outside the traditional networks of political parties and power brokers. His campaign against the corruption of the "system" (and what Brazilians cleverly called "maharajas") and his promises to bring the rights and benefits of citizenship to all Brazilians, especially the downtrodden, came back to haunt him. Along with his campaign manager, the shady P.C. Farias, Collor had built an enormous campaign contributions scheme that funneled tens of millions of dollars into a personal slush fund that provided everything from landscaping for his luxurious home to extravagant purchases of jewelry and clothing for his wife (in effect, living like a maharaja). In mid-1992, when his disgruntled and disaffected brother went public with details of the massive kickback scheme, the wrath of the traditional power brokers, press, and public rained down on the president.[54]

Collor's impeachment and trial in the Brazilian Congress and Senate became a lightning rod for mass mobilization as Brazilians invoked their rights as citizens to voice their disgust with presidential corruption and as they pressed for his removal from office. The mobilization around

FIGURE 7.2 Fernando Collor Impeachment Demonstrations
Source: ANTONIO SCORZA/AFP/Getty Images

a civic nationalism that had accelerated in the early 1980s with re-
democratization, and coalesced so dramatically around the failed *diretas
já* movement, now succeeded. As with the *diretas já* campaign, millions of
Brazilians poured into the streets across the nation to call for his impeachment. The political transition across the "long" 1980s had empowered
Brazilians to claim their rights as citizens, and to demand an end to
corruption. When the embattled president called for his supporters to
take to the streets in the national colors (green and yellow), millions of
his opponents showed their antagonism by appearing in black singing
sambas and calling for *impeachment já* (a direct reference to the *diretas já*
movement).[55] For the second time in less than a decade, millions of
Brazilians across the country mobilized, demonstrated, and invoked the
symbols of nationalism to invoke their rights as citizens to shape the
nation's destiny. In late December 1992, the Chamber of Deputies voted
to impeach Collor by a lopsided margin of 441 to 38, and the Senate voted
to convict him 76 to 5.[56] Parallel to the political events in 1992–1993,
Globo televised another very popular *novela, Deus nos Acuda*, that parodied the real-life tales of corruption, scandal, and payoffs with a fictional
story of Celestina (the great comedian Dercy Gonçalves), a guardian angel
unsure whether she wanted to save Brazil or not. Once again, Brazilian life
and art intermingled.[57]

CHALLENGES TO THE FREYREAN VISION

In the half-century from the publication of *Casa-grande e senzala* in the early 1930s to the re-democratization of the 1980s, cultural nationalism grew and matured in Brazil, and its dominant narrative was Freyre's vision of *mestiçagem*. The creation and expansion of an imagined community of Brazilians in that half-century gradually integrated the national territory culturally, bringing the nation fully to life. As the inhabitants of Brazil increasingly saw themselves as Brazilians (as one people and one nation), they embraced in ever larger numbers the myths, symbols, and rituals of the dominant narrative of national culture – from the myth of *mestiçagem* to *carnaval*, samba, *futebol*, a national anthem, and a flag.[58] Ironically, at the very moment that this cultural nationalism reached full maturity in the 1980s, and helped foster an emerging civic nationalism, its power and influence peaked and began to erode substantially. Two influential (sometimes converging) movements – and a new technological wave – emerged to challenge Freyre's vision of Brazilian identity, and they would continue to weaken its influence over the next generation, but not completely push it from its role as the dominant narrative of cultural nationalism and identity in Brazil.

In one of ironies of Brazilian history, at the very moment that this modernizing project to create a sense of national identity finally experienced its greatest success in the 1970s and 1980s, intellectuals and activists had already begun to deconstruct the meaning of identity, nation, nationalism, and modernity, and they began to proclaim the very *impossibility* of the modernizing project and the very notion of this version of "a" national identity. In the early 1980s, the study of nationalism and national identity experienced a moment of resurgence marked by the publication of the influential works of Benedict Anderson, Eric Hobsbawm, Anthony Smith, Ernest Gellner, and others.[59] By the 1990s, a new wave of scholars had begun to question and deconstruct the very notion of national identity and its viability.[60] (This scholarly turn has been more pronounced outside of the Brazilian academy than inside it.)

In theoretical terms, some Brazilian intellectuals and academics rejected the very notion of such a thing called national identity. Concretely, they ferociously attacked Gilberto Freyre's version of *brasilidade* – more specifically his ideas on racial democracy. As Antônio Sérgio Guimarães has pointed out, Freyre was likely not the first to use the term "racial democracy," although he quickly adopted the terminology in the late 1940s. As his formulation and defense of racial democracy became more emphatic and pronounced after 1950, a new generation of Brazilian and Brazilianist social scientists began to demonstrate with sophisticated quantitative and qualitative data that Brazil was not free of racial prejudice and discrimination, and that racial democracy was not a reality in Brazil.[61] The UNESCO studies of the 1950s mobilizing such luminaries of Brazilian social science as Florestan Fernandes, Octávio Ianni, and Fernando Henrique Cardoso began the careful, empirical dissection of prejudice and discrimination in Brazilian society. The military regime, however, would have none of this research (especially by leftist scholars) and enshrined Freyre and his vision of *mestiçagem* as one of the key pillars of their right-wing nationalism. Ironically, the repressive intransigence of the regime (intellectually and politically) re-energized the black movement in Brazil – helping the movement become truly national. As Freyre became increasingly allied to the right-wing, authoritarian Salazar regime in Portugal, and the military regime in Brazil, in his later years he became an ardent and intransigent defender of his views on racial democracy, and the principal lightning rod for those challenging the view that Brazil was a *mestiço* people and a racial democracy.[62]

Much more important than this intellectual movement, in the 1970s and 1980s, a new black consciousness movement took shape in Brazil – one that condemned Freyre and his vision as racist and completely wrong.[63] This movement has sought not only to alter intellectuals' and academics' views of national identity but also to produce a transformation in Brazilian popular culture. As Paulina Alberto has so deftly demonstrated, black intellectuals in twentieth-century Brazil initially embraced and then eventually denounced Freyre's vision of *mestiçagem*. Organizations such as the *Frente Negra Brasileira* and *Teatro Experimental Negro* in the first half of the twentieth century had mobilized to raise awareness of racism and discrimination in Brazil. Prior to the 1960s, however, influential black thinkers generally turned to *mestiçagem* and racial democracy as a means to include Brazil's African heritage as a foundation of national culture, and "to assert their own belonging as African-descended Brazilians within" the nation. The most famous black intellectual and militant in twentieth-century Brazil, Abdias do Nascimento declared in 1950 that *mestiçagem* in Brazil was producing "a well-delineated doctrine of racial democracy, that will serve as a lesson and model to other nations of complex ethnic formation."[64]

In the two decades following the end of Vargas's Estado Novo (1937–1945) and the military coup of 1964, black intellectuals "remained committed to turning the dominant idea of racial democracy to their advantage, refining and contesting its meanings in a democratic public sphere." The military dictatorship seized on Freyre, *mestiçagem*, and racial democracy as tools of a repressive State, closing all discussion and negotiation, and suppressing race-based organizing. In the words of Alberto, "regime ideologues proclaimed racial and cultural *mestiçagem* to be a pillar of national order, strength, and security." To challenge the Freyrean vision became tantamount to subversion under a regime that brutally repressed all opposition. Rather than a path toward racial inclusion, the experience of black intellectuals under military rule convinced them that racial democracy was "an insidious mirage disguising a bleak and violent landscape of racism."[65] In exile in the United States during the military regime, by the 1970s and 1980s, Nascimento shifted his views and stridently condemned Freyre's work, and notions of *mestiçagem* and racial democracy.[66]

Brazilian black activists (*militantes negros*) consciously and very publicly assumed their identity as *negros* and created organizations that encouraged all Brazilians classified in the census as *pardos* or *pretos* to see themselves as black (*negro*). The long-standing view that Brazil was a three-tiered/trinary society (whites, mixed, blacks) came under intense assault by both political activists and engaged social scientists who increasingly mounted a powerful argument that Brazil was, in fact, a two-tiered/binary society divided between those who are white and those who are not.[67] Black activists not only rejected the Freyrean notion that Brazil was a *mestiço* nation; they countered that the population of *pardos* and *pretos* combined made Brazil a nation with a black majority, ruled by a repressive white minority.[68] Black consciousness organizations such as the Sociedade de Intercâmbio Brasil-África (SINBA) and the Instituto de Pesquisas das Culturas Negras (IPCN) in Rio de Janeiro and the Movimento Negro Unificado (MNU) in São Paulo emerged in the mid-1970s as focal points of black activism.[69]

At the core of this debate is how to define racial groups, especially those categories used in official statistics. Melissa Nobles's wonderful book on race and censuses in Brazil and the United States expertly shows the changing nature of categories on the official censuses in both countries over the last two centuries. Just as census categories across decades in the United States reflect and shape changing racial attitudes, the Brazilian censuses have largely been constructed in the twentieth century to convey notions of whitening and racial democracy. "Brazil's intelligentsia, political elite, and census officials," she argues, "have emphasized racial 'mixture' with the same vigilance their U.S. counterparts have emphasized racial 'purity.'" When the Brazilian military removed the "color question" from the 1970 census and then attempted to keep it out of the 1980 census, social scientists protested loudly. Writing in response to these protests in the *Folha de São Paulo*, the elderly Gilberto Freyre argued that the color question was unnecessary because Brazilians had moved beyond racial origins to become members of a Brazilian "meta-race." The correct color choice for all Brazilians, he believed, was *moreno*.[70]

Nearly all recent social science research shows clear differences in wages, income, education, and opportunity by race. Yet, the most cutting-edge research has demonstrated how problematic this discussion becomes when one looks closely at racial categories, how they are constructed, and used in comparisons. The tendency of much of the most-cited research on racial inequalities over the past thirty years has widely accepted a dichotomous format (white/non-white), the very "binary racial lense" that has been the objective of the black movement, and more recently, the Brazilian government. In a very recent analysis of the ways researchers use categories, "Brazil's population oscillates between 40.7% and 70.4% white, between 0% and 40.1% brown, and between 10.8% and 59.3% black/nonwhite, depending on means of classification." Nearly everyone in Brazil recognizes that profound socioeconomic inequalities exist, and have some relationship to color/race. How closely the two are related is sharply contested.[71] For the black activists, the path to addressing these inequalities is clear – affirmative action. Those who seek to move beyond racialism argue for socioeconomic programs, that is, an emphasis on class over race. As Mala Htun has so cogently put it, "there is a tension between trying to get beyond race on the one hand and forming practical strategies to combat racism on the other. Negotiating this tension – affirming the living practice of race while simultaneously denying its essence – is the challenge Brazil faces."[72]

The challenges to the Freyrean vision intensified in the 1990s with the rise of a national discussion about affirmative action, in large part driven by the activism of black consciousness organizations. At its core, this debate is about differing visions of Brazilian identity and Freyre's vision of *mestiçagem*. In the age of identity politics, numerous groups have called for a more pluralistic and multicultural vision of ethnicity in Brazil and they have criticized the homogenizing impact of the Freyrean declaration of a single, unified Brazilian ethnicity.[73] For those who believe that Brazilian society and culture have been forged out of centuries of racial and cultural mixing – essentially Freyre's vision – affirmative action makes no sense and is, in fact, divisive. If mixing has produced a color spectrum with many shades from black to white, then who is black, and therefore deserving of affirmative action? If, on the other hand, Brazil is a nation of two peoples – one white, one nonwhite – divided by a history of racism by one group against the other, then the deserving recipients of affirmative action are clear and the resources of the State must be mobilized to assist them.[74]

The intense debate over affirmative action has divided and polarized Brazilian intellectuals who hold these differing visions of Brazilian history and identity, and it brings to light the linkages and the differences between Freyrean visions of racial democracy and *mestiçagem*. By the 1980s, few Brazilian intellectuals still clung to Freyre's claim that Brazil is a racial democracy, yet many continue to see Brazil as a *mestiço* nation. They understand that *mestiçagem* does not automatically produce racial equality. For these intellectuals, these are two visions that Freyre pioneered and conjoined, but they do not logically lead from one to the other. The proponents of affirmative action, and those promoting black consciousness, reject both visions. For many of them, Freyre's vision of *mestiçagem* is nothing short of a veiled white supremacist ideology that over decades absorbs, tames, and eradicates the African contribution to Brazilian civilization (commits genocide in the words of Nascimento). It is a progressive view of whitening that replaces the openly racist theories of whitening before the 1930s. For them, nevertheless, the result is the same as the racist, scientific theories of the late nineteenth and early twentieth centuries – eradicating blacks and black culture in Brazil.[75] Incensed by the movement's efforts to lump all *pardos* and *pretos* in the census, José Murilo de Carvalho has countered, commits "an attempt at racial genocide perpetuated with the weapon of statistics."[76] Black activists argue that the decades of efforts to forge a single, national "ethnicity" a la Freyre has suppressed alternative identities and ethnicities in a form of cultural erasure. The proponents of a unified national identity, they argue, have pursued national solidarity at the cost of cultural pluralism.[77]

The turning point for both black consciousness movements and those who condemn the myths of racial democracy and *mestiçagem* was the military dictatorship. The regime, in effect, represented an escalation of both the nationalistic rhetoric and authoritarianism of the Estado Novo. Vargas adopted the Freyrean vision. The military enshrined it as truth. As Paulina Alberto has argued, "Representatives of the authoritarian state used the idea that Brazil was a racial democracy to shut down public discussion about racial discrimination and to justify state suppression of race-based organizing."[78] The emerging civic activism of the black consciousness movement in the 1970s and 1980s marked a watershed for the national conversation on race, identity, and nation. Black leaders criticized Freyre and his vision as manipulating the African heritage of Brazil to elite advantage to justify a racist society through the alienation of the masses. In their view, Brazil was not a mestizo nation with a majority of blacks and browns, but rather a majority black nation dominated by a white minority. Freyre had provided the white elites with a narrative that justified whitening and racial domination of a black majority.[79]

The emergence of a potent civic nationalism in the 1980s generated a fractious debate about cultural identity, in particular, the dominant narrative of national identity – Freyre's vision of *mestiçagem*. The maturing cultural nationalism that had been developing since the 1930s simultaneously helped foster the civic nationalism that grew out of re-democratization in the 1970s and 1980s, and then generated clashes as the newly democratic Brazil grappled with how to define and implement citizenship for all. As Dagnino has pointed out, citizenship had become more than a relationship between the individual and the State; it was also about redefining social and cultural practices and places.[80] The cultural nationalism of previous decades had provided the groundwork for claims to a full citizenship, one that was cultural, social, and political. The 1988 Constitution enshrined the principle of equal rights for all Brazilians and under Presidents Fernando Henrique Cardoso (1994–2003) and Luis Inácio Lula da Silva (2003–2011), the government began to promote initiatives that responded to the emerging black activism. President Cardoso made the first tentative efforts to address racism and provide government support to prevent and redress racist practices. In 2003, Lula created a Special Office for the Promotion of Racial Equality (SEPPIR) with cabinet-level status.[81]

While these moves encouraged black consciousness activists, the efforts to construct a legal apparatus for affirmative action seemed to others a path to greater social divisions, special treatment, and the unnecessary racialization of Brazil.[82] Two pieces of legislation, in particular, were at the center of this debate – the Lei de Cotas Raciais (1999) and the Estatuto da Igualdade Racial (2000). In 2006, both these bills became the focal point of contentious debates in the Brazilian congress, media, and among academics. Many intellectuals and social scientists who believe Brazil is a *mestiço* nation wrote a *Carta pública ao Congresso Nacional*: "Todos têm Direitos Iguais na República Democrática" (Public Letter to the National Congress: "Everyone has Equal Rights in the Democratic Republic") and delivered it to the President of the Brazilian Senate in July 2006. While the supporters of quotas and affirmative action argue for the need to redress past discrimination, and that Brazil is a binary society of blacks and whites, these prominent intellectuals see this legislation as antithetical to the very fabric of Brazilian society – one that is racially and culturally mixed. They wholeheartedly agree that discrimination and prejudice have long existed in Brazilian society, but they do not believe the solution is what they call the "racialization" of Brazil.[83] This public letter generated a second "Manifesto em favor da Lei de Cotas e do Estatuto da Igualdade Racial" ("Manifesto in favor of the Law of Quotas and the Statute of Racial Equality") signed by an equally illustrious group of intellectuals and academics, criticizing the first letter and calling for support of the legislation.[84]

Despite several decades of increasing criticism of Freyre, the work of Edward Telles and Stanley Bailey has clearly shown, "a belief in the positive value of miscegenation remains relatively uncontested, a sort of commonsense truth that continues to represent beliefs about Brazilian race relations. Ideas about racial hybridity and syncretism continue to predominate in popular culture."[85] Yet, Gilberto Freyre's narrative of Brazilian identity faces stronger and more strident challenges today than at any time since it began to emerge as the dominant narrative in the mid-twentieth century. More than a just a debate about social policy, at the heart of this heated conversation is "the country's understanding and portrayal of itself."[86] Is Brazil a multiethnic, multicultural nation or is it a *mestiço* one?[87]

The voices that have emerged over the last few decades to challenge the Freyrean vision have also been accompanied by a new technological wave that makes the creation, maintenance, and dominance of any narrative of national identity increasingly unlikely. The Internet and the incredible access it has given to millions of voices in Brazil since the mid-1990s have not only produced many challenges to the dominant narratives; they have also created many, many more complex contributions to any conversation about hybridity and *mestiçagem*. While the greatest focus of the attacks on Freyre over the past generation (or more) has been his notion of racial democracy, the rise of black consciousness movements has also mounted a sustained assault over the last three decades on Freyre's more fundamental contribution to national identity, his writings about *mestiçagem*. Most public opinion polls, and most intellectuals, have buried the argument that Brazil is a racial democracy, and that Brazilians believe Brazil is a racial democracy. The central question for those who believe in the myth of *mestiçagem*, and for those who believe there is such a thing as a dominant narrative of national identity, is the ability of the Freyrean vision of *mestiçagem* to survive these attacks and critiques. If, as I have argued, this narrative of *mestiçagem* has been at the core of the dominant narrative of Brazilian identity in the second half of the twentieth century, and if its hold on the Brazilian collective psyche declines, what will that mean for Brazilian identity in the twenty-first century?

NOTES

1. "As pessoas se tornavam cidadãs à medida que passavam a se sentir parte de uma nação e de um Estado. Da cidadania como a conhecemos fazem parte então a lealdade a um Estado e a identificação com uma nação. As duas coisas também nem sempre aparecem juntas. A identificação à nação pode ser mais forte do que a lealdade ao Estado, e vice-versa. Em geral, a identidade nacional se deve a fatores como religião, língua e, sobretudo, lutas e guerras contra inimigos comuns. A lealdade ao Estado depende do grau de participação na vida política." José Murilo de Carvalho, *Cidadania no Brasil: o longo caminho*, 7ª. ed. (Rio de Janeiro: Civilização Brasileira, 2005), 12.

2. "Excluído da comunidade política, não tendo reconhecida a dignidade de seu trabalho, o povo brasileiro refez-se por meio da cultura." Leonardo Avritzer, org., *Experiências nacionais de participação social* (São Paulo: Cortez, 2009), 23.

3. "To be Brazilian, from this perspective, is to rise to a moral plane above the pettiness, corruptions, and exclusions of politics. Perhaps more precisely, it is to build a firewall between a positive sense of national identity, experienced as an always yearned-for unity, and the uncertainties of official citizenship, experienced in many different ways, including racially, as fragmentation and exclusion from political participation." Owensby, "Toward a History of Brazil's 'Cordial Racism,'" 339.

4. Murilo de Carvalho, *Cidadania no Brasil*, 31, 39–40.

5. *Ibid.*, 40, 146, 201. For the dramatic rise in voters during the military regime, see Kurt von Mettenheim, *The Brazilian Voter: Mass Politics in Democratic Transition, 1974–1986* (Pittsburgh: University of Pittsburgh Press, 1995). Leslie Bethell, "Política no Brasil: De eleições sem democracia a democracia sem cidadania," in *Brasil: Fardo do passado, promessa do futuro*, ed. Leslie Bethell (Rio de Janeiro: Civilização Brasileira, 2002), esp. 17–18; Bolívar Lamounier y Judith Muszynski, "Brasil," in *Enciclopedia electoral latinoamericana y del Caribe*, ed. Dieter Nohlen (San José, Costa Rica: Instituto Interamericano de Derechos Humanos, 1993), 93; and Potencial Pesquisas, *Evolução do eleitorado brasileiro, Brasil em dados* (Salvador, Brazil: Potencial Pesquisa e Informação, 2010), www.potencialpesquisas.com/brasil-em-dados/

6. "Os trabalhadores foram incorporados à sociedade por virtude das leis sociais e não de sua ação sindical e política independente." Murilo de Carvalho, *Cidadania no Brasil*, 124.

7. "o autoritarismo brasileiro pós-30 sempre procurou compensar a falta de liberdade política com o paternalismo social." *Ibid.*, 190.

8. See, for example, Mark Harris, *Rebellion on the Amazon: The Cabanagem, Race, and Popular Culture in the North of Brazil, 1798–1840* (New York: Cambridge University Press, 2010) and, Jeffrey Mosher, *Political Struggle, Ideology, and State Building: Pernambuco and the Construction of Brazil, 1817–1850* (Lincoln: University of Nebraska Press, 2008).

9. For a classic analysis of similar struggles and processes in Mexico, see Joseph and Nugent, eds., *Everyday Forms of State Formation.*

10. Thomas E. Skidmore, "The Paraguayan War: A Constitutional, Political, and Economic Turning Point for Brazil," in Jessé Souza and Valter Sinder, eds., *Imagining Brazil* (Plymouth, UK: Lexington Books, 2005), 91–101; Murilo de Carvalho, *Cidadania no Brasil*, 38.

11. Peter M. Beattie, *The Tribute of Blood: Army, Honor, Race, and Nation in Brazil, 1864–1945* (Durham, NC: Duke University Press, 2001).

12. Murilo de Carvalho, *Cidadania no Brasil*, 78–79.

13. "[T]he interconnection and scale of abolitionist activism in the 1880s marked a distinct era in the history of Brazilian political mobilizations." Celso Thomas Castilho, "Performing Abolitionism, Enacting Citizenship: The Social Construction of Political Rights in 1880s Recife, Brazil," *Hispanic American Historical Review*, 93:3 (August 2013), 380.

14. Eric Foner, *Reconstruction: America's Unfinished Revolution, 1863–1877* (New York: Harper, 2002).

15. Castilho, *Slave Emancipation and Transformations in Brazilian Political Citizenship.*

16. "a escravidão era um câncer que corroía nossa vida cívica e impedia a construção da nação." Murilo de Carvalho, *Cidadania no Brasil*, 229.

17. See, for example, Todd Diacon, *Millenarian Vision, Capitalist Reality: Brazil's Contestado Rebellion, 1912–1916* (Durham, NC: Duke University Press, 1991); Francis Foot Hardman e Victor Leonardi, *História da indústria e do trabalho no Brasil (das origens aos anos 20)*, 2ª. edn. rev. (São Paulo: Editora Ática S.A., 1991).

18. Holston, *Insurgent Citizenship.*

19. Fischer has an incisive review of Holston's book: Brodwyn Fischer, "Histories and Anthropologies of Citizenship," *American Anthropologist*, 112:1 (March 2010), 154–56.

20. Fischer, *A Poverty of Rights*, 7–8.

21. Fischer, *A Poverty of Rights*, esp. 63 and 90. Quotes are from 126 and 147.

22. Holston, *Insurgent Citizenship*, 7.

23. Holston observes that "When I first went to Brazil in 1980, I barely heard the words citizen or citizenship in everyday conversation." Holston, *Insurgent Citizenship*, 4. Two more recent studies of the everyday struggle for rights are: Bryan McCann, *Hard Times in the Marvelous City: From Dictatorship to Democracy in the Favelas of Rio de Janeiro* (Durham, NC: Duke University Press, 2014); and, Brodwyn Fischer, Bryan McCann, and Javier Auyero, *Cities from Scratch: Poverty and Informality in Urban Latin America* (Durham, NC: Duke University Press, 2014).

24. Leonardo Avritzer, "Sociedade Civil e Participação no Brasil Democrático," in Carlos Ranulfo Melo, Manuel Alcántara Sáez, orgs., *A democracia brasileira: balanço e perspectivas para o século 21* (Belo Horizonte: Editora UFMG, 2007), 405–20.
25. Evelina Dagnino, "Citizenship: A Perverse Confluence," *Development in Practice*, 17:4–5 (August 2007), 549 and 552.
26. Holston says of the residents of the periphery of the city of São Paulo, "residents made clear to me that without a doubt they considered themselves fully Brazilian, no less so than any other member of the nation-state." Holston, *Insurgent Citizenship*, 40.
27. T. H. Marshall, the great theorist of citizenship, described citizenship as "a direct sense of community membership based on loyalty to a civilization which is a common possession." Cited in Holston, *Insurgent Citizenship*, 24.
28. The classic volume in English on the military regime is Thomas E. Skidmore, *The Politics of Military Rule in Brazil, 1964–85* (New York: Oxford University Press, 1988). In Portuguese, the multivolume work by Elio Gaspari, *A ditadura envergonhada; A ditadura escancarada; A ditadura derrotada; A ditadura encurralada;* and, *A ditadura acabada* (São Paulo: Companhia das Letras, 2002–2016), is fundamental for understanding the nature of the regime.
29. The other parties were the Partido dos Trabalhadores Brasileiros (PTB), the Partido Democrático Trabalhista (PDT), the Partido dos Trabalhadores (PT), and the Partido Popular (PP). Skidmore, *Politics of Military Rule*, 219–20.
30. For a concise description of the *diretas já* movement, see Skidmore, *Politics of Military Rule*, 240–44; and, Alberto Tosi Rodrigues, *Diretas Já: o grito preso na garganta* (São Paulo: Editora Fundação Perseu Abramo, 2003). A more detailed analysis is Edison Bertoncelo, *A Campanha das Diretas e a democratização* (São Paulo: Associação Editorial Humanitas, FAPESP, 2007). For a deeply personal journalistic account, see Ricardo Kotscho, *Explode um novo Brasil: diário da Campanha das Diretas* (São Paulo: Brasiliense, 1984). Polls in 1983 showed that more than three-quarters of Brazilians wanted direct elections for president. Bertoncelo, *A Campanha das Diretas*, 105.
31. Bertoncelo estimates that more than 5 million people participated in nearly 100 mass meetings and parades. *A Campanha das Diretas*, 180. Bryan Pitts, "The Inadvertent Opposition: The São Paulo Political Class and the Demise of Brazil's Military Regime, 1968–1985," Ph.D. Diss., Duke University, 2013, 460–62.
32. Skidmore, *Politics of Military Rule*, 242; Kotscho, *Explode um novo Brasil*, 9.
33. For more on Reinaldo's political actions during this period, see Euclides de Freitas Couto, *Da ditadura à ditadura: uma história política do futebol brasileiro (1930–1978)* (Niterói: Editora da UFF, 2014), 222–49.
34. Bertoncelo, *A Campanha das Diretas*, 160.
35. "clima de Carnaval misturado com Copa de Mundo"; "parecendo torcida de futebol em dia de final de campeonato"; "o carnaval começou ontem, em clima de vitória da Seleção Brasileira numa Copa do Mundo"; "carnaval das

diretas"; "como se fosse um samba-exaltação de Ary Barroso"; "Mamãe eu quero/me dá uma urna/me dá uma urna/me dá uma urna". For some examples of comparisons to *carnaval* and *futebol*, Kotscho, *Explode um novo Brasil*, 81, 82, 88, 110. Quotes are from 17, 36, 86, and 89. See also Shirts, "Sócrates, Corinthians, and Questions of Democracy and Citizenship."

36. For the perspectives of some of the key figures at Globo during this moment, see *Jornal Nacional: a notícia faz história/Memória Globo*, 154–71.

37. Joseph D. Straubhaar, "Television and Video in the Transition from Military to Civilian Rule in Brazil," *Latin American Research Review*, 24:1 (1989), 150–54. Quote is from page 147 citing "Diretas no Video," *Veja*, 18 April 1984, 93–94.

38. Leonardo Avritzer, "The Conflict Between Civil Society and Political Society in Post-authoritarian Brazil: An Analysis of the Impeachment of Fernando Collor de Mello," in Keith S. Rosenn and Richard Downes, eds., *Corruption and Political Reform in Brazil: The Impact of Collor's Impeachment* (Miami, FL: North-South Center Press at the University of Miami, 1999), 131.

39. For an excellent survey of the literature of the impeachment, see Brasilio Sallum Jr. e Guilherme Stolle Paixão e Casarões, "O Impeachment do Presidente Collor: A Literatura e o Processo," *Lua Nova*, 82 (2011), 163–200.

40. *Jornal Nacional*, 270–76.

41. For a succinct survey of the indirect election in 1985, see Skidmore, *Politics of Military Rule*, 244–55. For an excellent recent synthesis of the process leading up to the election see Pitts, "The Inadvertent Opposition," 460–73.

42. Gilberto Dimenstein, et al., *O complô que elegeu Tancredo* (Rio de Janeiro: Editorial JB, 1985).

43. Skidmore, *The Politics of Military Rule in Brazil*, 260–61.

44. Avritzer, "The Conflict Between Civil Society and Political Society in Post-authoritarian Brazil," 132–34.

45. Mauro P. Porto, *Media Power and Democratization in Brazil: TV Globo and the Dilemmas of Political Accountability* (New York: Routledge, 2012), 130–31.

46. Timothy J. Power, "Political Institutions in Brazil: Politics as a Permanent Constitutional Convention," in Peter R. Kingstone and Timothy J. Power, eds., *Democratic Brazil: Actors, Institutions, and Processes* (Pittsburgh: University of Pittsburgh Press, 2000), 17–35.

47. Thomas E. Skidmore, "Collor's Downfall in Historical Perspective," in Rosenn and Downes, *Corruption and Political Reform in Brazil*, 1–19.

48. Skidmore, "Collor's Downfall in Historical Perspective". Collor is the youngest president in Brazilian history.

49. Gontijo, *A voz do povo*, 139.

50. Porto, *Media Power and Democratization in* Brazil, 80–86.

51. The election fell on the one hundredth anniversary of the military coup that overthrew Pedro II and proclaimed the republic.

52. In the last direct presidential election in 1960, fewer than 13 million voted, an 80 percent turnout of registered voters. Potencial Pesquisas, *Evolução do eleitorado brasileiro, Brasil em dados* (Salvador, Brazil, 2010), www.poten cialpesquisas.com/brasil-em-dados/

53. For an excellent synthesis and analysis, see Kurt Weyland, "The Rise and Fall of President Collor and Its Impact on Brazilian Democracy," *Journal of Interamerican Studies and World Affairs*, 35:1 (1993), 1–37.

54. Rosenn and Downes, eds., *Corruption and Political Reform in Brazil*. For a highly literary description of the corruption and the role of P.C. Farias, see Peter Robb, *A Death in Brazil: A Book of Omissions* (New York: Henry Holt and Company, 2004).

55. Alberto Tosi Rodrigues, *O Brasil de Fernando a Fernando: neoliberalismo, corrupção e protesto na política brasileira de 1989 a 1994* (Ijuí, Rio Grande do Sul: Editora UNIJUÍ, 2000), esp. 201–52.

56. Skidmore, "Collor's Downfall in Historical Perspective," esp. 12 and 14; Stéphane Monclaire, "Le quasi-impeachment du président Collor. Questions sur la 'consolidation de la démocratie' brésilienne," *Revue française de science politique*, 44:1 (1994), 41–43.

57. Porto, *Media Power and Democratization in Brazil*, 133–34.

58. No doubt with the help of the design of the uniforms of the *seleção*, the Brazilian flag has become in recent years one of the most important universal symbols of national identity. While often scorned under the military dictatorship, the flag was reappropriated in the demonstrations for re-democratization in the 1980s and 1990s. Nearly everyone, of all parties and persuasions, claims the flag in demonstrations these days. "Dando Bandeira," *Revista O Globo* (14 July 2013), 26–29.

59. Benedict Anderson, *Imagined Communities: Reflections on the Origin and Spread of Nationalism*, rev. edn. (New York: Verson, 2006) [originally published in 1983]; E. J. Hobsbawm, *Nations and Nationalism since 1780: Programme, Myth, Reality*, 2nd edn. (Cambridge: Cambridge University Press, 1992); Gellner, *Nations and Nationalism*; Smith *The Nation in History: Historiographical Debates about Ethnicity and Nationalism*.

60. For a very recent argument against the notion of national identities, see Seigel, *Uneven Encounters*, esp. the Preface and Introduction.

61. The now-classic work on quantifying inequalities based on color categories is that of Carlos Hasenbalg and Nelson do Valle Silva. For an overview of the debate on race and inequalities, see Telles, *Race in Another America*, chapter 2 and Bailey, *Legacies of Race*, chapters 2 and 3.

62. Alberto, *Terms of Inclusion*, Chapter 6, "Decolonization," 245–96; Dante Moreira Leite, *O caráter nacional brasileiro*, 2ª. ed. (São Paulo: Pioneira, 1969), 271.

63. See, for example, Jeferson Bacelar & Carlos Caroso, orgs., *Brasil, um país de negros?* (Rio de Janeiro: Pallas, 1999); Michael Hanchard, *Party/Politics: Horizons in Black Political Thought* (New York: Oxford University Press, 2006); Michael George Hanchard, *Orpheus and Power: The Movimento Negro of Rio de Janeiro and São Paulo, Brazil, 1945–1988* (Princeton, NJ: Princeton University Press, 1994); Howard Winant, "Rethinking Race in Brazil," *Journal of Latin American Studies*, 24:1 (February 1992), 173–92.

64. Alberto, *Terms of Inclusion*. Quotes are from 17 and 12, respectively.

65. *Ibid.*, 245–46 and 249.

66. See, for example, Abdias do Nascimento, *O genocídio do negro brasileiro: processo de um racismo mascarado* (Rio de Janeiro: Paz e Terra, 1978) and its English language edition, *Brazil: Mixture or Massacre?: Essays on the Genocide of a Black People*, 2nd. edn. rev., trans. Elisa Larkin Nascimento (Dover, MA: Majority Press, 1989).

67. Mala Htun adeptly shows how the emergence of this policy and civic debate emerges out of grassroots activism from below and presidential politics from above in the midst of a changing international environment around race. Htun, "From 'Racial Democracy' to Affirmative Action: Changing State Policy on Race in Brazil," 60–98.

68. Alberto, *Terms of Inclusion*, 266 and 295.

69. Verena Alberti e Amilcar Araujo Pereira, orgs., *Histórias do movimento negro no Brasil: depoimentos ao CPDOC* (Rio de Janeiro: Fundação Getúlio Vargas, CPDOC: Pallas, 2007); Alberto, *Terms of Inclusion*, 260–69; and, Hanchard, *Orpheus and Power*, esp. chapter 6.

70. Nobles, *Shades of Citizenship*, esp. 86–87 and 117–18. Quote is from 87.

71. Stanley R. Bailey, Mara Loveman, Jeronimo O. Muniz, "Measures of 'Race' and the Analysis of Racial Inequality in Brazil," *Social Science Research*, 42 (2013), 106–19. Quote is from 112. See, for example, "Notes on Racial and Political Inequality in Brazil," in Michael Hanchard, ed., *Racial Politics in Contemporary Brazil* (Durham, NC: Duke University Press, 1999), 154–78.

72. Htun, "From 'Racial Democracy' to Affirmative Action," 85.

73. "In much of Latin America since about 1990, there have been important shifts toward official multiculturalism, manifest in political and other legal reforms, which have given recognition and rights to indigenous and Afro-descendant minorities." Wade, et al., *Mestizo Genomics*, "Introduction," 15.

74. For a concise summary, see Edward Telles and Marcelo Paixão, "Affirmative Action in Brazil," *LASA Forum*, 44:2 (Spring 2013), 10–12.

75. See, for example, Peter Fry, Yvonne Maggie, Marcos Chor Maio, Simone Monteiro, Ricardo Ventura Santos, orgs., *Divisões perigosas: políticas raciais no Brasil contemporâneo* (Rio de Janeiro: Civilização Brasileira, 2007).

76. José Murilo de Carvalho, "Genocídio racial estatístico," in Fry, Maggie, Maio, Monteiro, Santos, orgs., *Divisões perigosas*, 111–15.

77. Kabengele Munanga, *Rediscutindo a mestiçagem no Brasil: identidade nacional versus identidade negra* (Petrópolis: Editora Vozes, 1999), esp. 108 and 110.

78. Alberto, *Terms of Inclusion*, 245.

79. Alberto, *Terms of Inclusion*, 261–66 and 294–95. "In the Brazilian context, use of essentialist discourses and practices offers a means of challenging hegemonic nationalist discourses which are premised on racial anti-essentialism." Caldwell, *Negras in Brazil*, 179.

80. Dagnino, "Citizenship: A Perverse Confluence," 552.

81. Ollie A. Johnson III, "Afro-Brazilian Politics: White Supremacy, Black Struggle, and Affirmative Action," in Kingstone and Power, *Democratic Brazil Revisited*, 209–30; Telles, "Chapter Three: From Racial Democracy to Affirmative Action," *Race in Another America*, 47–77.

82. For an emphatic rejection of the efforts to describe Brazil as a binary racial structure, see Ali Kamel, *Não somos racistas: uma reação aos que querem nos transformar numa nação bicolor* (Rio de Janeiro: Nova Fronteira, 2006).

83. Fry, et al., *Divisões perigosas.* "Genocídio racial estatístico," *Globo* (27 December 2004), 7.

84. Johnson, "Afro-Brazilian Politics," 227–28.

85. Telles, *Race in Another America*, 77. See also, Bailey, *Legacies of Race.*

86. Htun, "From 'Racial Democracy' to Affirmative Action," 61.

87. "We are either multi-ethnic or we are mixed." Yvonne Maggie, "Does Mário Andrade Live On?: Debating the Brazilian Modernist Ideological Repertory," *Vibrant*, 5:1 (2008), 54.

EPILOGUE

Nation and Identity in the Twentieth and the Twenty-First Centuries

The difficulties of black movements [in Brazil] in mobilizing all blacks and mestizos around a single "black" identity are because, up to the present, they have not been able to destroy the ideal of whitening. Some national voices are trying, at the moment, to move forward the discussion around a "mestizo" identity capable of bringing together all Brazilians (whites, blacks, mestizos). I see in this proposal a new ideological subtlety to recuperate the idea of national unity never achieved by the failed physical whitening [of Brazil]. This proposal of a new, unique mestizo identity goes against the black movements and other so-called minorities who fight for the construction of a pluralistic society and one of multiple identities.[1]

Kabengele Munanga

THE RETURN OF GILBERTO FREYRE

In 1987, at the very moment of re-democratization and the emergence of social movements predictating a new racial politics, Gilberto Freyre passed away. Born at the dawn of the twentieth century when the dominant narrative about *mestiçagem* was overwhelmingly negative, as a young man Freyre stood the narrative on its head and helped cast it as positive for Brazilians. At the end of the twentieth century, as he passed from this world and fully into the Brazilian cultural imaginary, the myth of *mestiçagem* once again took on a negative connotation, but in very different ways than a century earlier. Two seemingly contradictory and parallel processes have taken shape over the past four decades. A new generation of activists emerged attacking the Freyrean vision of racial democracy *and* the myth of *mestiçagem*. At the same time, Gilberto Freyre's work inspired a new generation of seminars, symposia, and publications – what some

251

have called a *retomada* (rediscovery) of Freyre's work.[2] Even as social activists amplified their critiques and rejection of Freyre, scholars reevaluated his work largely agreeing that racial democracy was clearly an unrealized ideal while providing a new appreciation for the myth of *mestiçagem* as central to Brazilian culture and identity. By the early 2000s, the two processes had become deeply intertwined with both taking up the work of Freyre as central to the future of Brazil – the one definitively to denounce Freyre, the other to appreciate the meaning of the Freyrean myth of *mestiçagem* for Brazilian identity. Both sides of this debate recognize and acknowledge the power of the Freyrean vision – the former to diminish its hold on the popular imaginary and to redefine national identity, the latter to explain why it does indeed define Brazilian identity.

Kabengele Munanga sums up the anti-Freyre view emphasizing that the myth of *mestiçagem* may have made a positive contribution in recognizing the contribution of Indians and Africans to the formation of Brazilian culture, but he condemns the myth as simply another means to obliterate difference, create one monolithic racial and cultural identity, and move Brazil in the direction of cultural and racial whitening. The myth promotes a form of ethnocide or genocide. In short, Freyre may have put a positive spin on what had once been a negative view of mixing, but in the end, for Munanga, Freyre became another powerful proponent of whitening. As with other black movements in Latin America, for Munanga, the myth of *mestiçagem* promotes the view that Afrodescendants are simply an "ingredient" in the drive to forge a monochromatic, unitary national identity. In contrast, these movements argue for a multiculturalism that recognizes "the cultural, ethnic, and racial diversity of national populations, making visible Afrodescendant populations."[3]

The rise of a new identity politics in Brazil, the increasing visibility of black movements, and legislation over the past thirty years demonstrate the decline of the Freyrean vision of *mestiçagem*, but not its demise. The great challenge for the opponents of Freyre is to reduce the myth's persistence and power in popular culture. Daniela Mercury's phenomenally popular song, *Umbigo do mundo*, is but one of the most visible and compelling examples of the power and reach of Gilberto Freyre's positive vision of *mestiçagem* and its place at the core of the dominant narrative of Brazilian identity in the twentieth century, and into the twenty-first.

Right here is the navel of the world/where beauty has many faces/colors and races, strange mixtures/ebony skins, of indigenous blood/eyes that shine like emeralds/ mestizo faces of a new race/with a future that is arriving/under the sun in the navel of the world/and everyone is dancing samba.[4]

This irresistible samba-reggae song with a driving beat that could almost bring the dead dancing out of their graves conveys the essence of Freyre's vision through popular music across the airwaves via radio and YouTube to the eyes and ears of all Brazilians – in Brazil and beyond. The charismatic and immensely popular Mercury, and the contingent of artists who perform on stage with her, vividly convey Freyre's vision to millions of people – in Brazil and around the world – the fundamentals of the dominant narrative of Brazilian identity over the past three-quarters of a century.

Mercury's invocation of mestizo faces, the coming of a new age where the sun is shining on a people dancing samba, is perhaps a more powerful testimony to the reach of the Freyrean vision than any scholarly argument or scientific poll. As one of Brazil's most popular and dynamic artists, she both channels this Freyrean vision and reflects how profoundly it permeates the worldview of the vast majority of Brazilians at the beginning of the twenty-first century. The power of this idea continues in both popular culture and high politics. On several occasions in the past two decades, Freyre's work has inspired samba school themes during *carnaval* in Rio. What other Brazilian intellectual could make that claim?[5] President Luis Inácio Lula da Silva declared in 2009, "We are not only a mixed people, but a people who like very much to be mixed; it is our identity."[6] Sophisticated polling clearly demonstrates that "ethnic and racial boundaries appeared blurred in the popular mindset in favor of a more inclusive nationalist category of Brazilianness." The Freyrean shift from a negative emphasis on race and biology in the early twentieth century is now reflected in a widespread and positive view across society that cultural mixture defines Brazilians as Brazilians. Biology matters, but culture matters more.[7]

TECHNOLOGY: FORGING AND ERODING NARRATIVES

Throughout this essay, I have argued that new waves of technology have been the keys to the rise and successful diffusion of the vision of a provincial northeastern intellectual to create a national conversation about race and identity dominated by that vision. These technological waves helped forge an imagined community, an *imaginário nacional*, beginning in the 1930s with the expansion of radio broadcasting, continuing with the spread of cinema across the vast terrain of Brazil, and climaxing with the construction of a truly national television broadcasting after the mid-1960s. By the 1980s, it became possible to reach almost all those living within the political boundaries of the Brazilian nation-state and to communicate with them nearly simultaneously. Just as the military regime had dreamed, the State finally had the ability to transmit its views to the nation on an unprecedented scale and scope. In retrospect, the military regime, and many others, overestimated the power they imagined this technology would provide them. At the same time, at the very moment they managed to achieve this technological feat, new voices in Brazil began to challenge the "official" narrative, and a new wave of technology began to undermine and subvert the technological hegemony the military mistakenly believed they had constructed.

Although the challenges to the Freyrean myth from intellectuals and Afro-Brazilian groups have, no doubt, weakened its dominance in the national imaginary, the greatest threat to the cohesion of any national community on the planet in the early twenty-first century is the Internet and the expansion of its reach and access. While nation-builders once dreamed of implementing new technologies to reach all within their borders to disseminate an official vision of nationhood, now they grapple with ways to limit and control the flows of information on the seemingly ubiquitous highways and byways of the global electronic village. Beginning in the 1990s, the rise of the latest technological wave (the Internet, global broadcasting, social media) has both increased and intensified the reach of mass communications and the ability of governments to disseminate their messages while also providing more and more people with access to a nearly unlimited supply of challenges and alternatives to any official story.[8] The digital communication technologies of this century have now made possible, and likely, the creation of national communities in which every member is connected to every other member. This technocratic dream of nation-builders, however, now becomes a nightmare of patrolling the national "borders" and the ability of the State to disseminate, dominate, and define a single narrative of national identity. At the very moment that the technological ability to simultaneously reach all the potential participants in the imagined community of the nation has become a reality, the State's ability to shape and control a single narrative of national identity becomes illusory.

Just as the technology of radio transformed Brazil and nation-building in the 1920s and 1930s, the arrival of the Internet in the 1990s has likely brought an end to the technological cycles that helped create a Brazilian nation built around the myth of *mestiçagem*. Although there is clearly a digital divide in Brazil as in other parts of the world, access has been rapidly expanding (not unlike radio in the early twentieth century).[9] By 2012, half of the population in Brazil over the age of ten had accessed the Internet and the percentage of homes with Internet access had reached 40 percent. Fixed broadband lines connected nearly all of the country's nearly 6,000 municipalities. As with radio in an earlier era, many of those without direct access relatively easily gain access through public means such as schools, libraries, and Internet cafes. Brazil is now the second-largest market in the world of Facebook, with nearly 60 million accounts, and more than 40 million Brazilians use Twitter. Cell phones have become universal even among the poorest Brazilians, and wireless broadband technology via phones encompasses more than 90 percent of the population. Sales of smartphone technology make Brazil the fifth-largest market in the world.[10]

Like much of the world, Brazil is experiencing a profound technological transition that is ongoing. Despite the rapid expansion of the Internet and social media, television, newspapers, and radio continue to serve as the most important sources of information for Brazilians of all social classes. When questioned about sources of information on the eve of the 2010 presidential election, more than two-thirds of voters relied on television, only 12 percent turned to newspapers, just 7 percent to radio, and another 7 percent to the Internet. When asked about the three most important sources, the percentages rose to nearly 90 percent for television, 54 percent for newspapers, and 52 percent for radio (and just 27 percent for the Internet). Television remains dominant, but a dramatic shift is clearly taking shape.[11]

All the mass media – radio, film, television, Internet – will continue to provide the principal sites for the ongoing conversation about identities in Brazil. Whether through popular music on the radio (also now streamed via the Internet), the preoccupation of filmmakers with national identity and its symbols, *telenovelas* and televised *futebol*, or social media, the constant fashioning and refashioning of popular culture will continue.[12] Culture in Brazil (and elsewhere) is never static. Cultures are in a process of constant change, adapting and discarding, renewing and rejecting.[13] The new technologies have made possible previously unimaginable musical mixtures and productions by virtually anyone helping create a new musical commons that includes those in *favelas*, wealthy urban neighborhoods, and rural areas. Styles from tecnobrega to pop vaneirão and funk carioca have thrived and gained enormous audiences across Brazil and especially among those of less economic means. This new version of *mestiçagem* has attracted international attention and led one prominent filmmaker to call Brazil the remix nation.[14] Some would even argue that the aurality of media in the late twentieth century has recast culture and the public sphere in Latin America. Participation and belonging are reshaped more and more by the sonic in an "aural region."[15]

In the late 1990s, Gilberto Gil reworked the landmark samba *Pelo Telefone* using new technologies and with references to global cities using Internet jargon and made the song easily accessible on the World Wide Web. The name of this refashioned samba by one of the most important tropicalistas (and future Minister of Culture): *Pelo Internet!*[16] At the same time, *telenovelas* continue as one of the most important sites for the conversation about *brasilidade*. Globo's *Avenida Brasil* became the most commercially successful *novela* of all time in 2012 attracting an average audience of more than 45 million viewers per episode over 180 episodes. The success of this *novela* derived in large part from its constant emphasis on the emerging new middle class, some 30–40 million people rising out of "Class D" into "Class C."[17] The Internet has not ended the influence of radio, film, and television; rather, it has added a new medium and intensified interaction with the others.

This new technological wave that began in the 1990s has fundamentally altered the conversation about identities, especially national identity. It has intensified the long-standing interaction of the local, regional, national, and global to produce new and more complicated cultural configurations. Nevertheless, as Megwen Loveless's study of forró shows, Brazilians continue a conversation that maintains "a tightly-knit sense of place" while participating in a global marketplace.[18] Even if there is less of a consensus about *brasilidade* in popular music than in the age of Carmen Miranda and Dorival Caymmi, and even if composers may not be as concerned with seeing Brazil as an organic whole, they continue to grapple with what it means to be Brazilian.[19] Even with the glorification of multiple identities and multiculturalism, "the desire," as Frederick Moehn's recent study shows, to define what it means "to be Brazilian in the contemporary world – and musically to perform Brazilianness" is as strong as ever. "The very notion that miscegenation defines Brazilian identity is daily reinscribed in musical sound and talk about music."[20] Even as the power of the myth of *mestiçagem* wanes, it remains an enormously powerful force in Brazilian popular music and culture.

MODERNITY, POST MODERNITY, AND THE CREATION OF IDENTITIES

In many ways, the great dream of the nineteenth-century founding fathers and nation-builders has now eluded their descendants *twice* – even though, for a few decades in this century, it seemed within their grasp. The efforts of the Liberals and Conservatives in the nineteenth century to create new nations out of former Iberian colonies centered on an impossible ideal for their century – to make all of the inhabitants of their imagined territories into neo-Europeans.[21] From the plains of North America to the deserts of Patagonia non-European peoples (culturally and biologically) formed the majority or near majority of the newly proclaimed nations of Latin America. Sarmiento dreamed of fertilizing the pampas with the blood of the "barbaric" gauchos and Rodó implored the youth of Latin America to emulate modern France, as well as ancient Rome and Greece. Yet, at the dawn of the twentieth century, probably only Sarmiento's Argentina and Rodó's Uruguay were firmly on their way to realizing something akin to their dream of remaking Latin American nations in their imagined ideal of what for them was a "modern" Europe (especially England and France). In countries like Mexico and Brazil – home to more than half of all the inhabitants of Latin America – the vast majority of the population were of African or Indian descent, or racially and culturally mixed heritage. In 1900, to the continuing despair of the intellectual great-grandchildren of the first wave of nation-builders in the 1820s, remaking the region to fit the ideals of Sarmiento and Rodó remained perplexing, daunting, and (for most) impossible.

The Brazilian Modernists of the 1920s revived the dream of the nation-builders of the 1820s while consciously rejecting the purely Europeanist vision of the founders with a *mestiço* message of "primitive modernity." They were the inheritors both of the nation-building projects of the nineteenth century and of the modernist vision of nationalism and national identity. Yet, they reoriented that vision to Brazilianize it and replace the pessimism and fears of "mongrelization" in the previous century with an exuberant and positive view of *mestiçagem* and Brazilian identity. In retrospect, Freyre and the Modernists initiated a cycle that lasted about three-quarters of a century when one dominant narrative of national identity emerged, flourished, and eventually permeated many sectors of Brazilian society. The Freyrean vision achieved a dominance and resonance, creating an imagined community, a nation constituted by a people with a cohesion unlike that ever experienced in Brazil before, and probably in the future.

The maturation of the State, new technologies, and the emergence of mass, popular culture created the conditions in the decades from the 1930s to the 1980s for most Brazilians to share a common set of rituals and symbols held together by the myth of *mestiçagem*. The great modernist project of the nineteenth century, reformulated by the Brazilian Modernists of the 1920s, finally appeared to have become reality by the 1970s and 1980s. By the beginning of the twenty-first century, however, it has become increasingly evident that the conditions that made possible the dominance of the Freyrean narrative coalesced for a few decades and will now likely unravel. The postmodern scenario of decentered, multiple voices has become the reality of global communications in the twenty-first century. The State remains enormously powerful (witness the repressive powers of various States from China to Russia to Guantanamo), yet its ability to fashion a cohesive cultural nationalism and identity on the scale of 200 million people now seems unlikely and impossible. Ironically, at the very moment that new technologies have intensified the surveillance powers of the State, they have also fragmented and decentered the production and mediation of popular culture within the boundaries of nations, especially large ones.[22]

I am not among those who would declare the death of the nation-state. Globalization is transforming the planet and has produced fundamental challenges to the now outmoded notions of nation. The culture industries that helped forge such a powerful and coherent national narrative in the twentieth century have themselves become globalized and devalue the nation, as a political, economic, or cultural entity.[23] Nations will continue to exist (and some will remain very powerful) but global culture industries will also continue to fragment, differentiate, and deterritorialize.[24] Globalization, despite the fears of some, will not create one homogeneous world culture.[25] The supposed causality and hegemony of the State that occupied the work of so many authors in the last decades of the past century have given way to a recognition of the limits of State power, multicausality, and the incredible complexities of identity formation in this century. The technologies of culture industries can reinforce and strengthen nationalism, facilitate transnational and global identities, and at the same time give new vigor and dynamism to the local.[26] In the words of Doris Sommer, "culture enables agency," even for the less powerful, and culture can become a weapon for the weak, even if power is inordinately and unequally distributed around the globe.[27] Popular culture becomes an alternative means of expression and participation often outside of official institutions, even as the State remains perhaps the principal site of national identity formation.[28]

I have emphasized in this interpretation that while the efforts of the State are fundamental they are also sometimes ineffectual and, at other times, reshaped by unanticipated movements "from below."[29] The State is not simply an autonomous apparatus of power controlled by the elites to subject the masses. In the twentieth century, the State and popular culture are interpenetrating, interconnected, and inseparable. While those with great power may hold more cards than those large numbers of peoples with little power, their lives and destinies affect each other and the influence does not flow one way. The shaping of Brazilian identity is a multidimensional and multifoci process that cannot be simplified (as it was so often in the past) to State or cultural hegemony.[30] To apply to the nation Muniz de Albuquerque's analysis of the Northeast, Brazilian identity was created "by many hands often working independently and unconsciously."[31]

The ideal of the modern nation to integrate all its inhabitants into a single, homogeneous national culture with shared myths, rituals, and symbols may have had its greatest moment in the mid-twentieth century in most of Latin America. In the more technologically advanced countries such as Argentina, Mexico, and Brazil (to name a few), this maturation of State, technology, and popular culture made it possible to integrate national populations to a greater extent than ever before, yet this integration and cohesion now seem the fruit of a historical moment that may have passed. In this sense, the postmodern critique of nationalism and national identity – that they are illusions and illusory – may have greater explanatory power for this century than the last. For the radicals, "Latin America is losing its national projects."[32] I am still not persuaded that the power of nationalism, nation-building, and national projects is disappearing in Latin America. Clearly, the lessons of Brazil's experience with nationalism and nation-building in the last three-quarters of the twentieth century do not apply to all of Latin America, much less all countries around the globe. Nevertheless, this historical experience raises important questions for all those studying nationalism and nation-building – be they scholars, politicians, technocrats, or anyone else.

Cultural identities, as Stuart Hall noted many years ago, are always in transformation and in the process of both being and becoming, and I would add, fading.[33] They have histories, and this book has attempted to trace the history of one immensely potent form of Brazilian cultural identity. My focus here has not been to isolate and capture some essence of Brazilian identity, but rather to show the process of identity formation – and dissolution. Brazilian identity and other identities are always unfinished works in progress. After all, history is about change over time. Cultural identities, however, are not just about the past; they also have futures and what it means to be Brazilian in 2080 will look very different than 1980 or 1880. In that latter year, samba did not yet exist, *carnaval* bore very little resemblance to its late twentieth-century version, and football had not yet arrived in Brazil. *Mestiçagem* played a large role in Brazilian life and intellectual debates, but nearly all major observers viewed it in an overwhelmingly negative light. In 1880, then, the most important myth, symbols, and rituals of Brazilian identity in the late twentieth century had yet to appear, much less form crucial parts of a meta-narrative. It would be foolish and naïve to believe that somehow those signifiers associated with Freyre's myth of *mestiçagem* in 1980 will still define *brasilidade* in 2080. Too often those who have fervently appealed to this grand narrative as Brazil's past, and its present, also assume that it is Brazil's future.[34] This is a flawed assumption. The pace of change with the new technologies of the digital era has accelerated beyond those of previous technologies, even those of the mid-twentieth century. Constructed over decades, the dominant narrative of Brazilian identity could fade even more rapidly, and the construction of newer narratives will, no doubt, move at a much faster pace than in the past. These momentous technologies, as Arjun Appadurai has pointed out, have created for billions of people across the planet many new opportunities to imagine themselves and their groups. The *imaginário* (national, regional, local, or otherwise) has expanded, allowing more "persons in more parts of the world" to "consider a wider set of possible lives than they ever did before." It has increased "the plurality of imagined worlds."[35]

BACK TO RACE AND IDENTITY

Race has been central to many forms of nationalism over the last two centuries. For the primordialists, ethnicity (Armenians, Aryans, Slavs, and many others) has long been central to defining national identities. Nationalism in the Americas has not been built on imagined primordial ethnicities. The closest example to primordialism in the Americas is Mexico with its official emphasis on the Aztec past, but even Mexican nationalism has been constructed not on that "primordial ethnicity" but rather on the forging of a "cosmic race" with the collision of Indians and Spaniards – a people formed out of the colonial crucible.[36] The nationalisms of the Americas have largely been constructed on new identities forged after 1492. Unlike the truly primordial identity claims in the Old World, the new ethnicities of the Americas have an identifiable moment of conception and formation in the conquest and colonization of all of the Americas. In the United States, a powerful civic nationalism based on a "civic religion" – the principles of equality and liberty – has taken shape over more than two centuries in a dangerous dance with various strands of racial nationalism.[37] In countries with significant indigenous populations (Mexico, Guatemala, Ecuador, Peru, Bolivia) the struggle to construct nationalism and national identity has been complicated by ethnic and racial divisions and centuries of oppression. In Brazil and Cuba, two of the countries with the largest populations of African descent in the Americas, the forging of national identity has been shaped by debates over the role of race in their histories. Brazilians and Cubans have argued for more than a century over the impact of their African heritage in the formation of national identity. In Cuba, one of the most forceful narratives has been one of a "raceless" identity, denying a long history of prejudice and discrimination. Yet, few scholars would accept that Cuba has been a raceless society.[38] In some ways, Gilberto Freyre's "racial democracy" has been the Brazilian parallel to this discourse of racelessness in Cuba.

As I have repeatedly pointed out in this book, my focus here has not been Freyre's racial democracy but rather his vision of *mestiçagem* – that all Brazilians share a common history of racial *and* cultural mixing of Native Americans, Africans, and Europeans. A growing literature in the social sciences, primarily of sociologists and anthropologists, has convincingly demonstrated that Brazilians do not believe they live in a racial democracy, although nearly all Brazilians aspire to the ideal.[39] Racial democracy is, like *mestiçagem*, a myth, not because it is untrue, but because it is an ideal that resonates with most Brazilians. I agree with Peter Fry that it is a noble ideal for any society in a world so often ripped apart by racial and ethnic conflict.[40] The more important debate in Brazil today is not about Freyre's vision of racial democracy but about his views on *mestiçagem*. The emergence of a significant, if small, *Movimento Negro* over the last few decades has produced the most sustained challenge to Freyre's views and the myth of *mestiçagem*. As Kabengele Munanga's words at the beginning of this chapter demonstrate, Brazil (and other Latin American countries) has vigorously challenged the myth of *mestiçagem/mestizaje*. These social movements seek to replace the unitary vision of *mestiçagem* with a pluralistic and multicultural narrative for the nations of Latin America.[41]

The genius of the myth of *mestiçagem*, this notion of hybridity and mixture, is its incredible flexibility and versatility. In *Casa-grande & senzala*, Gilberto Freyre radically reformulated Brazilian culture through his interpretation of *mestiçagem*, one that rejected racial and cultural purity for heterogeneity, ambiguity, and polyphony.[42] This version of hybridity encapsulates processes of biological and cultural mixing that have been taking place for centuries, and continue. At the center of this myth of origin is a potent narrative of sexuality and nation – of the power of the libidinous white male over the emasculated black man, and the creation of the eroticized *mulata*.[43] The foundational moment of the Brazilian people is profoundly gendered: the white European male taking as his sexual partner the African female to produce the *mulata* (and the *mulato*). As Idelber Avelar has argued, the emphasis and visibility of this sexual fable are paralleled by the invisibility of the unspeakable – any relationship between the black male and the white female.[44] This foundational sexual moment of racial encounter, for Freyre, both "whitens" Brazilians phenotypically and recognizes the contributions of Africans and Indians to the formation of Brazilian culture.

Most of the great intellectual figures who grappled with the nature of Brazilian identity since the late nineteenth century have offered an interpretation of this narrative of desire and sexuality – this origin myth.[45] Yet, this myth of *mestiçagem* allows for a variety of interpretations, from the virulent racism of the late nineteenth century that condemned Brazil to backwardness to the Freyrean vision in the twentieth century that has produced such cultural optimism. In one version of this myth, Brazilians recognize and honor the African and Indian and their cultural contributions to the formation of a Brazil that is *moreno* both phenotypically and culturally. In another, more sinister version, those contributions are acknowledged, but as a means to the creation of a racially and culturally whiter Brazil. Munanga's words in the epigraph for this chapter sum up the darker interpretation. I believe that the protean nature of the myth of *mestiçagem* has been critical to its success in the twentieth century as the dominant narrative of Brazilian national identity.

The protean myth also has a chameleon face, one which allows Brazilians to change colors – seemingly at will.[46] At its simplest, individuals choose their color for the census or surveys or official forms. On a social level, someone can change skin tones through the presentation of self and the perceptions of others. On a legal level, legislation in recent years has made it possible for communities to assume their black or indigenous identity even when those identities were absent in the past or when families from the same community make very different choices.[47] *Mestiçagem* has cannibalized all comers, to use the language of the Modernists, giving Brazilians enormous flexibility in assembling their identity, culture, race, and color. This allows Ruy Castro to claim that "Brazilians are black people of every possible color," or Liv Sovik to claim that in Brazil "no one is white."[48] This fluidity confounds black activists and creates obstacles in their stuggle to persuade mixed-race Brazilians to assume a black identity.[49] There are some indications, in fact, that growing numbers of Brazilians prefer the category *moreno*, an attitude that would please Gilberto Freyre.[50] Robin Sheriff's ethnographic work in the *favelas* of Rio indicates that *favelados* do not use a binary, two race discourse in everyday speech.[51] The myth of *mestiçagem* accommodates many colors and voices, making it difficult to dislodge.

The move from race and color to culture as the means of defining groups in Brazil complicates "racial" categories and produces very fluid and flexible identities that are continually contested and challenged.[52] In a sense, nearly everyone in Brazil agrees with the origin myth – that Brazilians emerge out of the mixing of Europeans, Indians, and Africans. The fundamental disagreement is over how to categorize the people who are the descendants of this biological and cultural mixing. Indians have historically been the most overshadowed of the three peoples and the most paradoxical. In the words of Tracy Devine Guzmán, while the Indian has been seen as one of the three pillars of *mestiçagem*, indigenism "has often served as a counter discourse to both the concept and the programmatic endorsement of nation-based homogeneity."[53] As we have seen, who is black is at the core of the national debate today. For the black movement, at a minimum, all who check off *preto* and *pardo* on the census should be classified as black, a crude self-described color category that ignores culture. Those assuming a *negro* identity could range across the entire color spectrum if they choose to identify with significant markers of black identity.[54] As one anthropologist has put it, black identity is not defined by phenotype but rather by consciousness of an ethnic category that includes "an array of cultural practices, religious beliefs, and contested ideas about the importance of Africa in the construction of Black identity."[55] Finally, this long history of mixing means, in the words of R. L. Segato, that "Whiteness in Brazil is impregnated by blackness." Whiteness, therefore, "is never fully achieved, never certain."[56]

The conversation about race and national identity in Brazil has been going on for two centuries and has not, and will not, come to a definitive conclusion. As Prasenjit Duara has argued, a polyphony of contradictory, contending voices characterizes nationalism as contested terrain where complete agreement is never reached.[57] What makes nationalism powerful is not the ability to achieve complete consensus among every single individual in a nation; rather, it is the ability to resonate with a substantial segment. In the more successful examples of nationalism, that segment may reach a very high percentage of the population. The ties that bind encompass the vast mass of the inhabitants of the nation. The myth of *mestiçagem* never resonated with every single inhabitant of Brazil, but, by the 1970s and 1980s, it formed an important part of the mental landscape of the vast majority of Brazilians, and still does. Its power and reach may have declined over the past generation, but it remains the dominant narrative of Brazilian identity, even if under more sustained challenges than at any time since its emergence in the 1930s and 1940s.

The debate over affirmative action and racism has focused Brazilians on the myth of *mestiçagem* and the very core of what it means to be Brazilian.[58] The debate has split Brazilians into two camps clearly at odds with each other. On the one hand, the proponents of affirmative action claim that Brazil is a bipolar society (like the United States was historically) with just two kinds of people – those who are white and those who are not – that Freyre was wrong, and the racial and cultural mixture he glorified does not define Brazilians. On the other hand, there are those who believe that *mestiçagem* defines Brazilians and their identity, and that it is impossible to divide Brazilians into white and nonwhite. Brazil, for these two contending narratives, is either a continuum of colors or it is racially bipolar. For the supporters of the continuum view, to support affirmative action with arguments for binary racial categories is misguided and heavy-handed. More importantly, it misses the cultural *mestiçagem* that is at the heart of the Freyrean narrative, and ultimately more important than biological *mestiçagem*. For the opponents of the Freyrean vision, the only way to redress discrimination and prejudice is to recognize what they see as a binary system of whites and nonwhites. Over the last two decades, the debate over affirmative action based on race has focused Brazilians directly and openly on Freyre's vision and the very meaning of *brasilidade*.[59]

Recent genomic studies have begun to show that Freyre was clearly right about biological mixing.[60] Across all regions of Brazil and across all colors (white, brown, and black), European genetic ancestry is predominant.[61] One only has to listen and observe to see that cultural mixing continues to be fundamental to the vibrancy and effervescence of Brazilian culture. To acknowledge this racial and cultural *mestiçagem* does not require the denial of a long history of prejudice and discrimination in Brazil. More subtle color lines than the once rigid categories of race in the United States or South Africa may have produced a Brazilian society and culture that are complex and rich, but not devoid of prejudice and discrimination. The key question for those seeking to fight prejudice and discrimination is this: is it really necessary to have a binary system of *racial* classification to acknowledge and root out the injustice or can this be done while accepting the historical fluidity of color categories in Brazil? This is the heart of the great divide over the myth of *mestiçagem*, the Freyrean vision, and Brazilian identity today.

Ironically, at the very moment that the United States appears to be slowly moving toward what was long seen as the Brazilian pattern – of a society divided along color/class rather than on race/class – many activists want to move Brazil toward the old U.S. racial model built on hypodescent and the one-drop rule.[62] Both societies have entered a period of flux with the once dominant narratives. In the past fifty years the United States has put into place the legal mechanisms to eliminate segregation and discrimination. With the rise of interracial marriage, substantial immigration from Latin America and the Caribbean, and the increasing recognition of racially mixed identities, race relations in the United States have been increasingly "Brazilianized."[63] This momentous shift in American society has produced an ironic backlash among some African Americans who now attempt to cling on to the old essentialism that whites imposed on them to reinforce segregation.[64] As numerous observers have pointed out, the civil rights movement in the United States gained enormous power from the solidarity of African Americans who all experienced prejudice, discrimination, and segregation regardless of their socioeconomic class. They saw themselves as a distinct racial group, and this provided them with the power to make a social movement. This lesson has been a powerful motivating force in the *Movimento Negro* in Brazil as activists seek to create the solidarity that a sordid legal history helped forge among blacks in the United States. The persistence of the myth of *mestiçagem* in Brazil, however, has made it very difficult for the black movement to persuade large number of Brazilians to accept the narrative of bipolarity, racial differences, and multiculturalism. This narrative seems to many to be "un-Brazilian." This has created a potent paradox: How can Brazil "ensure appropriate citizen rights for millions of persons that are victims of racism but that, for a series of reasons, will not mobilize against it?" How can the black movement "organize persons under a category that is both highly stigmatized and can be escaped from?"[65]

At the same time, the old solidarity of the black community in the United States erodes with the recognition of new racial categories and class stratification among people of color. Intense discussions about a "post-racial" America and "color blindness" are ongoing in the United States, especially since the election of Barack Obama, a man who historically would have been considered a *mulato* in Brazil. Ironically, at the very same time as U.S. racial relations become seemingly more Brazilian, black activists in Brazil have emerged as vocal advocates of moving toward the old U.S. model.[66] For black activists in both the United States and Brazil, Obama is black even though his mother was white. For those who recognize a history of *mestiçagem* in both societies, Obama is racially mixed, a *mulato*. These two very different perceptions crystalize the two dominant patterns that both societies are grappling with today.[67]

NATION, REGIONS, NATIONALISM, AND NATIONAL IDENTITY

Much like race, nations are constructed, and both have powerful and enduring effects on the lives of the millions within national borders even if they are "fictions." The nationalism of the Third Reich – and the German nation – may have been socially and culturally constructed, they may have been "fictions," but both were very real and profoundly affected hundreds of millions of people in the mid-twentieth century, and beyond. As the renowned anthropologist Claude Lévi-Strauss pointed out long ago, identity may be abstract with no real existence, but it is an "indispensable point of reference."[68] Race and national identity may be culturally constructed and constantly shifting, but they have very real and meaningful resonance for tens of millions of Brazilians. When Brazilians experience prejudice, discrimination, and repression, whether due to the color of their skin, their accent, or their social class, these actions often stem from the cultural constructs of racial, regional, or class identities. These identities may be "discourses," but they have concrete and direct impact on lives even as these actions reinforce the discourses. At certain moments, such as during the World Cup, these discourses might bind millions together as Brazilians, while at others they divide them as *paulistas, nordestinos, gaúchos,* or *mineiros*. Brazilians, like other peoples, live multiple identities simultaneously, and identifying with the nation is one of the most powerful and encompassing of these identities.[69]

Part of the genius and creativity of Brazilians is (to steal a phrase from F. Scott Fitzgerald) "the ability to hold two opposed ideas in mind at the same time and still retain the ability to function."[70] The myth of *mestiçagem* includes forms of regionalism ranging from the glorification of African heritage in Bahia to the promotion of whiteness as modernity in São Paulo. The nationalization of *mestiçagem* has diffused "African-derived elements" throughout Brazilian culture instead of forging "a robustly distinct *negro* 'community of culture.'" In the words of the anthropologist R. L. Segato, the lack of "discrete cultural niches" in Brazil "is not the outcome of a process of expropriation and cannibalization of black symbols by Brazilian society at large but is, much to the contrary, the result of a strong African presence that has invaded and conquered the white cultural space in an irreversible process."[71] Bahia has forged a strong sense of regional identity with claims to the cradle of Brazilian culture and identity built around an African heritage and the role of the black mother of Brazil. At the same time, São Paulo has constructed a whitened narrative that, despite the Freyrean vision, equates "modernity and progress with whiteness or Europeanness."[72] Brazilians might add to Fitzgerald's definition the ability to hold multiple opposed ideas at the same time![73]

Nation, as I have used it in this book, is a people within a defined set of political borders bound together by their attachment to a common set of myths, rituals, and symbols. I agree with Craig Calhoun that nationalism is a discourse, a project, and an "ethical imperative." The dominant discourse in Brazil for most of the twentieth century has been constructed around Gilberto Freyre's vision of *mestiçagem*; the project has been to create an integrated nation-state; and the imperative has been to heighten the sense of *brasilidade*. The creation of the nation has taken shape across the last three-quarters of the twentieth century simultaneously, and in interaction with significant regional identities. In many ways, Brazil was a symbolic battleground as the regions within the country attempted to assert their own myths, symbols, and rituals as the most Brazilian.[74] "Regionalism and nationalism emerge together," says Muniz de Albuquerque, "like twins in a fraternal but competitive relationship from the moment of birth, each offering new potentialities for the other and lending special forms of credence to the other."[75] Even as the Brazilian nation emerged in the twentieth century, regional identities in Brazil's South, Southeast, North, and Northeast also took shape: *gaúchos, mineiros, paulistas, cariocas, baianos*, and *nordestinos* (to cite the most prominent examples). These identities, despite their strength and influence, have always been unstable and shifting.

Symbols and rituals associated with these regional identities entered into the national conversation about *brasilidade* and some of them eventually came to be seen as quintessentially Brazilian even when they initially arose out of very specific locales or regions. Brazilians might recognize and understand *gaúchos'* fascination with cowboy culture and maté, but they would not come to see it as defining all Brazilians. Samba, however, burst out of the *bairros* of Rio in the early twentieth century and became widely recognized as central to Brazilian identity. The myth of *mestiçagem* stands out as the most important intersection of these regional identities with *brasilidade*. Each region of Brazil developed its own version of *mestiçagem*, in a sense, the regional variation on the national narrative. In Rio, Bahia, and Recife, the Northeastern narrative highlighted the African heritage and the *mulato/a*; in the backlands of the Northeast, the tough *sertanejo*; in Amazonia, the *caboclo*. Even in the Far South and São Paulo, two regions that so often contrast their whiteness to the rest of Brazil (especially the Northeast), the narratives begin with Portuguese and Indians mixing, to produce the legendary *bandeirante* in the *paulista* narrative. The *paulistas* acknowledge the master narrative of *mestiçagem* even if it is one that emphasizes whitening. At the other end of the spectrum, *baianos* readily embraced the narrative and constructed what was probably the most racially and culturally inclusive vision of *mestiçagem*. Ultimately, Freyre's vision of *mestiçagem* provided the most inclusive version, one capable of recognizing the great diversity of Brazil (regional, racial, cultural) while still offering a unitary identity.[76]

The Freyrean vision of *mestiçagem* has also been impressively inclusive of immigrants and emigrants. Freyre's origin myth of "lubricious" races from Europe, Africa, and the Americas mixing to produce a meta-race has been expansive enough to include the many different kinds of Europeans entering Brazil since independence, waves of Japanese, Syrians, and Lebanese, and more recently, Koreans and Chinese. Although these latter groups may have something akin to ethnic identities, those identities (anymore than regional identities) do not prevent them from being Brazilians in the Freyrean sense. When Brazilians of any "ethnic" background leave Brazil to live abroad, they learn to "perform" *brasilidade* as they celebrate *carnaval*, seek out *feijoada*, and cheer for their *seleção*. Japanese Brazilians, to take one prominent example, have been rudely made aware of their *brasilidade* as tens of thousands of them have returned to work and live in Japan. The discourse of cultural *mestiçagem* has made it possible for this immigrant nation to absorb new waves of peoples beyond the three founding races, to become Brazilians. It has given those who live abroad a narrative to emulate.[77]

As with the formation of all kinds of identities, Brazilians seek to define themselves as distinct from "others." With regional identities, the Other becomes Brazilians not from one's region. For most nations, nationalism emerges with the creation of an external enemy or enemies, a process that helps consolidate and define national identity. One of the most striking features of Brazilian identity is the lack of xenophobia. Perhaps more than any other large nation, Brazil and Brazilians have forged their identity less out of a sense of fear or hatred of foreigners than out of a sense of distinctiveness.[78] Freyre's vision of the Other was societies like the United States and South Africa that openly discriminated against people of color. His emphasis on *mestiçagem* and racial democracy aimed to differentiate Brazil from the United States and South Africa as a positive example for the rest of the world. This optimism and positive orientation characterize Brazilian identity. In two widely cited national surveys in the mid-1990s Brazilians overwhelmingly described themselves as more cheerful, hospitable, loving, and religious than other peoples. Despite the widespread acknowledgement of racial prejudice and discrimination in Brazilian society, Brazilians have what some have called a "prejudice against prejudice."[79] This is a nationalism built on optimism and love rather than fear and hatred. Brazilian nationalism, clearly, is at the other end of the xenophobia spectrum from Nazi Germany or even contemporary France.[80] At the same time, the flip side of Brazilians' impressive optimism and joy is the long-standing fear and lack of confidence in their ability to realize their potential. The joy and affirmation of samba and *carnaval* are counterbalanced by the misery and sorrow flowing from the profound inequalities, injustices, and violence in Brazilian society. This lingering pessimism in the Brazilian psyche has long been epitomized by the often-repeated saying that "Brazil is the country of the future ... and always will be."[81]

BRAZILIAN EXCEPTIONALISM?

One of the most enduring debates in U.S. history revolves around the idea of "American exceptionalism."[82] Is there something special and exceptional about the historical path of the United States that sets it apart from other countries? Has the United States forged a path, be it in pursuit of capitalist innovation or political freedoms that sets it apart from all nations? The processes the United States has experienced over the past two hundred years in building a nation clearly do not look very different than those of many other countries. Just as in the case of Brazil, the United States has constructed a dominant narrative of national identity, an imagined community, and a national imaginary through the interactions of the State, mass media, and popular culture. One might argue that some of the results are unique or exceptional, but certainly not the processes. Brazil, despite the long-standing misgivings of its people and a historical strain of pessimism that continues to permeate Brazilian culture, has produced some exceptional results out of processes of nation-building shared with other countries in the modern world.

Detailed and rigorous social science research since the 1950s has demonstrated (and continues to demonstrate) that Brazil has not been free of prejudice and discrimination based on skin color.[83] That is clear. Although Brazil does not have a long history of State-sanctioned discrimination as in the United States and South Africa, the complex mixing in Brazil has produced a much more subtle and nuanced system of prejudice and discrimination than those State-supported systems in the United States and South Africa in the twentieth century.[84] Brazil may have become profoundly culturally and racially mixed, but racial prejudice and discrimination have not disappeared.[85] Edward Telles's sophisticated research has shown that "Brazil's miscegenation is real and indicates relatively widespread interracial sociability." Nevertheless, "Brazil's racism and racial inequality are peacefully reproduced, for the most part, largely because of miscegenation."[86] Paradoxically, Brazil is both incredibly mixed, but staggeringly unequal, and the mixing has contributed to the inequality. Both sides in the debate over the path to the future have built their arguments on ample empirical evidence. Those who believe that *mestiçagem* defines Brazil and those who see a country divided by race and racial inequalities each are right in their own way. Ironically, *mestiçagem* has been fundamental to Brazil, it turns out, but it has not produced racial democracy, by any stretch of the imagination. The great contemporary debate in Brazil, as we have seen, hinges on what policies to adopt to redress inequalities. Should Brazilians do this by dismantling the myth of *mestiçagem*, highlighting racial identities, pluralism, and differences, or by building on the myth, de-emphasizing race, and appealing to unity through diversity?

Very recent survey data from the Project on Ethnicity and Race in Latin America (PERLA) offer sophisticated evidence on how the Brazilian narrative of national identity and Brazilian nationalism have been exceptional when compared to the rest of Latin America. More than

80 percent of respondents across racial groups "believed that Brazil is a mixed country" and nearly as many (78.8 percent) saw this as positive. At the same time, Brazil differs strikingly from the other three cases in PERLA's study: Mexico, Peru, and Colombia. The convergence between skin color and racial categories (both as self-identified and by the interviewer) was much stronger than in the other countries. Race in Brazil clearly matters, yet identity and appearance were more important in the survey data than color in predicting racial inequalities (again in contrast to the other three countries). When it comes to color, Brazil has less racial ambiguity than the other countries, yet, paradoxically, there is more ambiguity about who is Afrodescendant because of the fluidity of culture and appearance. Finally, when asked to choose between racial and national identity, Brazilians overwhelmingly (90 percent and higher across racial categories) chose national identity.[87]

Clearly, at the beginning of the twenty-first century, the myth of *mestiçagem* retains enormous power, but several decades of sustained criticism has heightened racial awareness in Brazil while at the same time failing to raise the percentage of Brazilians identifying with the *Movimento Negro* beyond a tenth of the population. This conversation about race, identity, and inequality has put Brazil in a position unlike its Latin American counterparts. Brazil has moved quickly over the past few decades from widespread denial of racism to government and public recognition, by blacks and whites, "to endorse structural accounts of racial inequality." Contrastingly, in Mexico, PERLA survey respondents "seemed unfamiliar with the notion of race" and the defense of the ideology of *mestizaje* remains a pillar of official discourse.[88] Studies of other Latin American countries have shown ways that national ideologies of *mestizaje* have contributed to the marginalization or silencing of the role of Afrodescendant populations in contrast to official recognition of indigenous peoples in the formation of national identities. While Mexico and Peru (and other nations with large indigenous populations) may have had success in promoting a national narrative of *mestizo* identity, this has been to the exclusion of the role of Afrodescendants. In contrast, the myth of *mestiçagem* has allowed the recognition of all groups, and at the same time, its critics have heightened official and public awareness of racial identities.

The great shift across Latin America, including Brazil, since the last two decades of the twentieth century has been a growing movement to contest the power of myths of *mestiçagem/mestizaje* and to replace them with an emphasis on a new multiculturalism.[89] Once seen as progressive and inclusive, *mestiçagem/mestizaje* is now attacked for erasing difference, promoting homogeneity, and (for some) providing a disguised path to whitening. Multiculturalism, in contrast, promotes an identity politics that celebrates differences, pluralism, and heterogeneity. Again, Brazil stands out over the past generation for the striking support of the State for multiculturalism and the widespread recognition of the need to combat the structures of racism. In Brazil, the myth of *mestiçagem* remains dominant even as multiculturalism has become official government policy. Multiculturalism is, in effect, the insurgent narrative of national identity, but one with State support.[90]

In comparing Brazil to other countries I am struck by one of the great advantages it has over other large nations. Perhaps no other country of continental dimensions has such a cohesive and integrated national culture. This is not to say that all Brazilians share exactly the same symbols, rituals, and beliefs, or that they all agree with each other, but that the vast majority of them do share fundamental cultural patterns. Where else among the large nations of the world today – China, India, the United States, Canada, Russia, Iran, Indonesia, Pakistan – can one find such linguistic, religious, and cultural cohesion? In each of these enormous countries linguistic, sectarian, or ethnic differences (in some cases all three) profoundly fracture their efforts to be cohesive nations. Nearly all of these large nations consist of very substantial populations speaking different languages, with religious traditions that (in some cases) are at war with each other, and with ethnic groups that are bitterly divided and (at times) in bitter conflict. Brazil is perhaps the best example of any large country of the hybrid, creole nation with a national culture that at once fuses popular and erudite culture.[91]

With the exception of a small percentage of the population (primarily several hundred thousand Native Americans and some immigrants), Brazil today has just one language. In none of the other large nations is the linguistic homogeneity even close to that found in Brazil. The long-standing religious intolerance of the colonial period (and to some extent, the Empire) ironically has given Brazil a spiritual unity rare in large nations. Religious prejudice has always existed in Brazil, and continues, but the sectarian divisions and conflicts in Brazil are minimal compared to these other nations. Although Afro-Brazilian religious groups were periodically repressed under the Empire and after the formation of the Republic, by the mid-twentieth century they had become officially recognized and accepted as a foundational feature of Brazilian culture. Until the 1980s, nearly all Brazilians shared a culture with roots in Christianity and the Judeo-Christian tradition. By the second half of the century, those who did not explicitly share these traditions were small in numbers, and their religious and spiritual practices were tolerated and respected by most Brazilians. Perhaps the greatest religious shift in Brazilian culture over the last five centuries has been the profound and relatively rapid shift of large numbers of people from Catholicism to evangelical Protestantism. As recently as 1970, more than 90 percent of Brazilians described themselves as Catholics (even if nominally). By 2010, this percentage had dropped to 65 percent, and continues to decline. The greatest religious tensions in Brazilian society over the next generations may be between the growing adherents of evangelical Protestantism (who grew from 5 to 22 percent between 1970 and 2010) and Catholics and practitioners of Afro-Brazilian religions.[92]

In contrast to this impressive cultural cohesion, Brazil remains a country severely hobbled by long-standing socioeconomic inequities, discrimination, and political exclusion. The battles over affirmative action and race draw together all of these issues and the need to address them now. Many of the social movements that emerged in Brazil (and Latin America) in the 1970s and 1980s have sought to address social and political injustices through the creation of new forms of association and citizenship. The *Movimento Negro*, women's organizations, the LGBT movement, and others (whatever their differences or disagreements) fight for all Brazilians to become full members, full participants, in their society. Over the past generation this struggle has made it possible for all Brazilians to see themselves as citizens, but also to recognize that not all citizenship in Brazil is equal. The rhetoric of citizenship is now at the forefront of the national conversation as millions of Brazilians seek to make the rhetoric a reality. As I have argued, the formation of a national cultural community, an imagined community in the words of Anderson, created a cultural citizenship in Brazil that preceded the emergence of a full-blown national struggle for political, social, and economic citizenship in the late twentieth century. This cultural participation through avenues provided by music, dance, *carnaval*, and *futebol* created a kind of "unofficial" citizenship. Through the creation and participation in this national cultural community, the inhabitants of the country have become Brazilians and continually offered their own interpretations of what it means to be Brazilian.[93]

In an age of the expansion of neo-liberalism, an emphasis on the market and the individual, the cultural and political trajectory of Brazil has long been one that is more communitarian and organic than the liberalism of the United States. Brazilian nationalism has been more about the nation as "an organic whole, a moral, political and economic entity whose ends would be realized in the State" than the nation as a collection of individuals.[94] Leonardo Avritzer has astutely pointed out the ironies of the social movements of the past four decades in Latin America. In their efforts to promote their vision of a more pluralistic social space, they strongly contested the homogeneity and unity historically promoted by national identity narratives constructed through popular culture. In their efforts to create a new public sphere, one antagonistic to the State, they challenged the very notion of the nation. They rejected the State and deconstructed the nation.[95]

Decades of developing cultural nationalism helped pave the way for the eruption of a vibrant civic nationalism in Brazil after 1970. Ironically, this new civic nationalism has critiqued and condemned the efforts to construct a homogeneous, unitary cultural nationalism. The arguments for a new kind of democracy – one with multiple citizenships based on gender, race, ethnicity, or other traits – stress pluralism and diversity. The proponents of this identity politics reject the national projects and citizenship of "the moderns." Theirs is a profound and emphatic rejection not only of Freyre and his vision but of the modernist project of the 1920s and 1930s. All of us, in this age of the Internet and social media, may be global and citizens in multiple ways, but our citizenship is also ultimately local.[96] Brazil is not alone in these processes taking place in what Daniel T. Rodgers has described as "an era of disaggregation, a great age of fracture," a time when "Imagined collectivities shrank" and "Identities became intersectional and elective. Concepts of society fragmented."[97]

This fracturing has enormously complicated the narratives of nationalism in Latin America in the twentieth century. The region has moved from nationalisms in much of the region that glorified *mestiçagem/mestizaje* (Mexico, Peru, Brazil, for example) with a rhetoric of inclusion (of all racial and ethnic groups) to a sustained critique that condemns these narratives as exclusionary and racist. The emergence of multiculturalism has shifted the conversation from national identity to a focus on selfhood and otherness. National identity in the twentieth century, in Brazil and elsewhere, was always a work in progress. I fully agree with the eminent historian of France David Bell, who has written that attempting to write about national identity can be "akin to trying to chain down the sea." He goes on to observe that the nation may survive in the future, but in ways very different than the last two centuries. Rather than homogeneity, the nation will serve as "a site of exchange where different cultures meet and mix, in constant movement."[98]

The challenge for Brazil, and all nations, in the twenty-first century is how to construct or preserve an imagined community or collective imaginary while recognizing the diversity and pluralism that characterize so many nations today. Brazil's dominant narrative in the twentieth century glorified the mixing and meeting of cultures. In many ways, Gilberto Freyre has remained a vital figure in Brazilian culture because of the optimism and confidence of his version of *mestiçagem*. The cleverness (*jeito*) of the Brazilians has been to build an imagined community around an incredibly plastic myth of *mestiçagem*.[99] More so than probably most countries in the second half of the twentieth century, one narrative of national identity prevailed. The question is whether this narrative, or any narrative, will exert such power in Brazil in this century.

NOTES

1. "As dificuldades dos movimentos negros em mobilizar todos os negros e mestiços em torno de uma única identidade 'negra' viriam do fato de que não conseguiram destruir até hoje o ideal do branqueamento. Algumas vozes nacionais estão tentando, atualmente, encaminhar a discussão em torno da identidade 'mestiça', capaz de reunir todos os brasileiros (brancos, negros, mestiços). Vejo nessa proposta uma nova sutileza ideológica para recuperar a idéia da unidade nacional não alcançada pelo fracassado branqueamento físico. Essa proposta de uma nova identidade, única, vai na contramão dos movimentos negros e outras chamadas minorias, que lutam para a construção de uma sociedade plural e de identidades múltiplas." Munanga, *Rediscutindo a mestiçagem no Brasil*, 16.
2. See, for example, Joshua Lund e Malcolm McNee, eds., *Gilberto Freyre e os estudos latino-americanos*; Burke and Pallares-Burke, *Gilberto Freyre*; Enrique Rodríguez Larreta e Guillermo Giucci, *Gilberto Freyre, uma biografia cultural*; Ricardo Benzaquen de Araújo, *Guerra e paz*; Skidmore, "Raízes de Gilberto Freyre,"; and, Joaquim Falcão e Rosa Maria Barboza de Araújo, orgs., *O imperador das idéias*.
3. Jean Muteba Rahier, *Black Social Movements in Latin America: From Monocultural Mestizaje to Multiculturalism* (New York: Palgrave Macmillan, 2012), 2.
4. "Isso aqui é umbigo do mundo/onde a beleza tem muitas caras/côres e raças, misturas raras/peles de ébano, de sangue indígena/olhos que brilham como esmeraldas/caras mestiças de uma nova raça/com um futuro que está chegando/sobre o sol no umbigo do mundo/e todo o mundo está sambando." Daniela Mercury, *Umbigo do mundo* (2003), www.youtube.com/watch?v=V WEzPmXiSkQ [accessed 27 July 2016].

5. David Cleary, "Race, Nationalism and Social Theory in Brazil: Rethinking Gilberto Freyre," WPTC-99–09 (Cambridge, MA: David Rockefeller Center for Latin American Studies, Harvard University, n.d.), 21.

6. "Não só somos um povo misturado, mas um povo que gosta muito de ser misturado; é o que faz a nossa identidade." Quoted in Maria Lúcia Garcia Pallares-Burke, *O triunfo do fracasso*, 347.

7. "If asked about origin or ancestry, the majority of Brazilians simply reply 'Brazilian,' which suggests a very murky situation for the categorization of Brazilians by ancestry or into ethnic groups." Bailey, *Legacies of Race*, 82–83.

8. "Assim com há enfraquecimento do poder do Estado, há fragmentação da identidade nacional. O Estado-Nação se vê desafiado dos dois lados." Murilo de Carvalho, *Cidadania no Brasil*, 226.

9. Access reproduces long-standing inequalities in Brazil. The South and Southeast have the best access to broadband; the North the worst. More than 80 percent of those with incomes above twenty minimum salaries have access while only about 20 percent of those with less than five minimum salaries do. Vivian Oswald, "Ipea: Serviço de Internet em Banda Larga no País é Caro, Lento e Desigual," *O Globo* (27 abril 2010), Economia, 27.

10. Peter T. Knight, "The Internet in Brazil," *Braudel Papers*, 47 (2013), 4–6.

11. Uirá Machado, "TV É a Principal Fonte de Informação dos Eleitores," A7. Newspapers continue to thrive and enjoy the greatest credibility among the different media. "Circulação de Jornais no País Cresce 4,7%," *Folha de São Paulo* (2 dezembro 2005), B8.

12. For the continuing fascination of Brazilian directors and their constant referencing of symbols of national identity in their films, see Heise, *Remaking Brazil*, 168.

13. "[A]ll culture is the result of a selection and a combination – constantly renewed – of its sources." "[T]oday all cultures are border cultures." García-Canclini, *Hybrid Cultures*, 141 and 261. Following Stuart Hall, "Instead of thinking of a national culture as unified, we should think of them as constituting a discursive device which represents difference as unity or identity." Quoted in Heise, *Remaking Brazil*, 18.

14. *RiP!: A Remix Manifesto*, Brett Gaylor, dir. (2008).

15. Ochoa Gautier, "Social Transculturation, Epistemologies of Purification and the Aural Public Sphere in Latin America."

16. www.youtube.com/watch?v=628zOWAy64g. See also, Charles A. Perrone and Christopher Dunn, eds., *Brazilian Popular Music and Globalization* (Gainesville: University Press of Florida, 2001), chapter 1. "[A]lthough samba's popularity has varied over the years it has never gone out of fashion completely, and due to its capacity to periodically reinvent itself remains among the most popular styles of Brazilian music with the public." Stroud, *The Defence of Tradition*, 102.

17. Anderson Antunes, "Brazilian Telenovela 'Avenida Brasil' Makes Billions by Mirroring Its Viewers' Lives," Forbes.com, 19 October 2012, http://www.forbes.com/sites/andersonantunes/2012/10/19/brazilian-telenovela-makes-billions-by-mirroring-its-viewers-lives/ [accessed 12 June 2015].

18. Megwen May Loveless, "The Invented Tradition of Forró: A 'Routes' Ethnography of Brazilian Musical 'Roots,'" Ph.D. Dissertation, Harvard University, 2010, 52–53.

19. Hermano Vianna, "Música en plural: nuevas identidades brasileñas," *Revista de Cultura Brasileña*, no. 1 (marzo 1998), 163–64; Cristina Magaldi, "Adopting Imports: New Images and Alliances in Brazilian Popular Music of the 1990s," *Popular Music*, 18:3 (October 1999), 311.

20. Moehn, *Contemporary Carioca*, 14 and 205.

21. "The liberal oligarchies of the late nineteenth and early twentieth centuries acted as if they constituted states, but they only ordered some areas of society in order to promote a subordinate and inconsistent development; they acted as if they formed national cultures, and they barely constructed elite cultures, leaving out enormous indigenous and peasant populations, who manifest their exclusion in a thousand revolts and in the migration that is bringing 'upheaval' to the cities." García Canclini, *Hybrid Cultures*, 7.

22. "[I]n Brazil there has not been, as postmodern reasoning would suppose, a modern stage, in which the world of the arts dictates the norms of cultural production, that is later substituted by another, postmodern stage, in which, because of the mixture of arts with cultural industries, the former's authority is weakened. If we accept such reasoning, Latin American societies and, in particular, Brazil were always postmodern." Ortiz, "Culture and Society," 123.

23. "The very concept of homogenous national cultures, the consensual or continguous transmission of historical traditions, or 'organic' ethnic communities – *as the grounds of cultural comparativism* – are in a profound process of redefinition." Bhabha, *The Location of Culture*, 7.

24. Jorge Larrain, *Identity and Modernity in Latin America* (Cambridge: Polity Press, 2000), 170.

25. "[G]lobalization is not the story of cultural homogenization." Appadurai, *Modernity at Large*, 11.

26. "In a 'global era' of movement and deterritorialization, the Internet is used to strengthen, rather than weaken, national identities." Eriksen, "Nationalism and the Internet," 1.

27. My thinking here has been influenced by the essays of Jesús Martín-Barbero and Doris Sommer in Doris Sommer, ed., *Cultural Agency in the Americas* (Durham, NC: Duke University Press, 2006); García Canclini, *Hybrid Cultures*, esp. 189; and, Appadurai, *Modernity at Large*. "There is growing evidence that the consumption of the mass media throughout the world often provokes resistance, irony, selectivity, and, in general, *agency*." Emphasis in original, 7.

28. In 1970s, the eminent literary critic Roberto Schwarz calculated that "a chamada 'cultura brasileira' não chegaria a atingir, com regularidade e amplitude, 50 mil pessoas, num país de 90 milhões de habitantes." Mota, Carlos Guilherme. *Ideologia da cultura brasileira (1933–1974): pontos de partida para uma revisão histórica* (São Paulo: Editora 34, 2008). Given the argument I have been making in this book, Schwarz's estimate clearly does not recognize popular participation in the formation of Brazilian culture.

29. Most of the "constructivist" theorists of nationalism emphasize a top-down, imposed identity driven by the rise of the modern State and industrial society. "The one persistent feature of this style of nationalism was, and is, that it is *official* – i.e. something emanating from the state, and serving the interests of the state first and foremost." Anderson, *Imagined Communities*, 159.

30. For an example of a pioneering effort to develop a more sophisticated and nuanced approach to State and popular culture, see Joseph and Nugent, *Everyday Forms of State Formation*.

31. Muniz de Albuquerque Jr., *The Invention of the Brazilian Northeast*, 225.

32. García Canclini, *Hybrid Cultures*, xxxvii.

33. Identity "is a matter of 'becoming' as well as of 'being'. It belongs to the future as much as to the past. It is not something which already exists, transcending place, time, history and culture. Cultural identities come from somewhere, have histories. But like everything which is historical, they undergo constant transformation. Far from being eternally fixed in some essentialized past, they are subject to the continuous 'play' of history, culture, and power." Stuart Hall, "Cultural Identity and Diaspora," in J. Rutherford, ed., *Identity: Community, Culture, Difference* (London: Lawrence and Wishart, 1990), 225.

34. "[T]hese authors emphasize the idea that in order to accept this cultural mestizaje one has to look into the past, as if this mestizo identity was constituted in the past once and for all. There is little sense of openness to the future, of the fact that identities, even mestizo ones, historically change." Larrain, *Identity and Modernity*, 158.

35. "[T]he sort of transgenerational stability of knowledge that was pre-supposed in most theories of enculturation (or, in slightly broader terms, of socialization) can no longer be assumed." Appadurai, *Modernity at Large*, 43. Quotes in text are from 53 and 5.

36. José Vasconcelos, *The Cosmic Race: A Bilingual Edition*, Trans. Didier T. Jaén (Baltimore: The Johns Hopkins University Press, 1997); Rick López, *Crafting Mexico: Intellectuals, Artisans, and the State After the Revolution* (Durham, NC: Duke University Press, 2010); Paul Gillingham, *Cuauhtémoc's Bones: Forging National Identity in Modern Mexico* (Albuquerque: University of New Mexico Press, 2011); Jo Tuckman, *Mexico: Democracy Interrupted* (New Haven, CT: Yale University Press, 2012); Roger Bartra, *The Cage of Melancholy: Identity and Metamorphosis in the Mexican Character*, trans. Christopher J. Hall (New Brunswick, NJ: Rutgers University Press, 1992); Claudio Lomnitz, *Deep Mexico, Silent Mexico: An Anthropology of Nationalism* (Minneapolis: University of Minnesota Press, 2001); Enrique Florescano, *National Narratives in Mexico: A History*, trans. Nancy T. Hancock (Norman: University of Oklahoma Press, 2006).

37. Gary Gerstle, *American Crucible: Race and Nation in the Twentieth Century* (Princeton, NJ: Princeton University Press, 2001).

38. Aline Helg, *Our Rightful Share: The Afro-Cuban Struggle for Equality, 1886–1912* (Chapel Hill: University of North Carolina Press, 1996); Ada Ferrer, *Insurgent Cuba: Race, Nation, and Revolution, 1868–98* (Chapel Hill: University of North Carolina Press, 1999); Alejandro de la Fuente, *A*

Nation for All: Race, Inequality, and Politics in Twentieth-Century Cuba (Chapel Hill: University of North Carolina Press, 2001).

39. Bailey, *Legacies of Race*. For poor people of color, racial democracy "is a dream that is about them, about their citizenship and their humanity, their contribution to their country, first as slaves and then as wage laborers. Democracia racial is, as I have noted, their moral high ground, perhaps the only one they have that is recognized, however incompletely and hypocritically by their nation." Sheriff, *Dreaming Inequality*, 221.

40. "Os ideais de não-racialismo e da libertação do indivíduo de qualquer determinação 'racial', que no Brasil se tornaram a ideologia oficial por muitos anos e que formam a visão de mundo de muitos brasileiros até hoje, são valores cada vez mais raros no mundo contemporâneo. Contra as obsessões étnicas e raciais que têm produzido os mais terríveis conflitos e a maior mortandade humana na história recente, vale a pena levar estes ideais a sério." Fry, *A persistência da raça*, 165.

41. See, for example, Rahier, *Black Social Movements in Latin America*.

42. Owensby, "Toward a History of Brazil's 'Cordial Racism,'" 328.

43. A fascinating anthropological examination of this myth of origin in Brazil, and to some extent in South Africa is Moutinho, *Razão, "cor" e desejo*, esp. 424–35. As she points out, in Brazil the story is of the white male and the *mulata*, and the outcome is seen as positive. In South Africa, the story is about the threat of the black male to the white female (similar to the United States), and the result is apartheid.

44. Idelber Avelar, "Cenas dizíveis e indizíveis: raça e sexualidade em Gilberto Freyre," *Luso-Brazilian Review*, 49:1 (2012), 168–86.

45. "Because the mulata is so much a product of national ideology about both race and sexuality, it forms a particular set of images that is much more protected and even exalted as a positive reading of national identity, and not one that is criticized as an overly exoticized or overly sexualized image of black women." Goldstein, *Laughter Out of Place*, 112.

46. For a fascinating study of how racial categories, and *mestiçagem*, play out within families, see Elizabeth Hordge-Freeman, *The Color of Love: Racial Features, Stigma and Socialization in Black Brazilian Families* (Stanford, CA: Stanford University Press, 2015).

47. French, *Legalizing Identities*.

48. Sovik, *Aqui ninguém é branco*; Castro, *Rio de Janeiro*, 82.

49. In a 1986 survey in São Paulo, "When asked what blacks and mulattos should do to defend their rights, 75.3 percent of the black and mulatto respondents and 83.1 percent of whites replied that they would prefer to see the formulation of a movement composed of whites, mulattos, and blacks. Less than 10 percent of each category thought that the problem should be addressed either individually or by an exclusively black movement." Fry, *Persistência de raça*, 178. The original English quote is in "Why Brazil Is Different," *Times Literary Supplement* (8 December 1995), 7.

50. Nobles, *Shades of Citizenship*, 126–28. For a fascinating look at the conversation about color and race, especially among those lower on the socioeconomic scale, see Edmonds, *Pretty Modern*, esp. 133.

51. Robin E. Sheriff, "Embracing Race: Deconstructing Mestiçagem in Rio de Janeiro," *Journal of Latin American Anthropology*, 8:1 (2003), 104.
52. For a discussion of some of the complications of "racial formations" in Brazil, see Winant, "Rethinking Race in Brazil."
53. Tracy L. Devine Guzmán, " 'Diacuí Killed Iracema': Indigenism, Nationalism and the Struggle for Brazilianness," *Bulletin of Latin American Research*, 24:1 (2005), 93.
54. For an example of the problems of setting out a clear definition of black identity, consider the following. "O que chamamos, então, de negro neste livro? O conjunto de pessoas escuras, pobres, descendentes históricos de trabalhadores escravos, afro-brasileiros, identificados por uma cultura festiva (digamos assim), que se vê a si e é vista pelos outros como tal. Negro é para nós, uma configuração histórico-social." Joel Rufino dos Santos, *A história do negro no teatro brasileiro* (Rio de Janeiro: Novas Direções, 2014), 24.
55. Allan Charles Dawson, *In Light of Africa: Globalizing Blackness in Northeast Brazil* (Toronto: University of Toronto Press, 2014), 11.
56. R. L. Segato, "The Color-Blind Subject of Myth; Or, Where to Find Africa in the Nation," *Annual Review of Anthropology*, 27 (1998), 148–49.
57. Duara, *Rescuing History from the Nation*, 8 and 10.
58. For a fascinating analysis of racial perceptions of Brazilians who have lived in the United States, and returned to Brazil, versus those Brazilians who have never lived in the United States, see Tiffany D. Joseph, *Race on the Move: Brazilian Migrants and the Global Reconstruction of Race* (Stanford, CA: Stanford University Press, 2015).
59. "Many intellectuals ... share a belief that our country is divided into distinct 'races' and 'ethnicities,' each with its own 'culture.' *Negra* culture, for example, is spoken of as if it were something practiced only by *negros* in *negro* spaces. However, others, probably including the majority of Brazilians, follow a more modernist tradition, believing that were are all mixed ... For these people 'cultural diversity' is in each Brazilian. They affirm that many whites know how to samba and that not all *negros* can do it very well, that all Brazilians eat *feijoada*, speak the same language and can at some point worship African-religion deities. For them, the notion of ethnicity, race, and separate cultures in Brazil is an out-of-place idea." Peter Fry and Yvonne Maggie quoted in Bailey, *Legacies of Race*, 84. For a contrasting view, see Guimarães, *Classes, raças e democracia*, 124.
60. S. D. J. Pena, L. Bastos-Rodrigues, J. R. Pimenta, "DNA Tests Probe the Genomic Ancestry of Brazilians," *Brazilian Journal of Medical and Biological Research*, 42:10 (2009), 870–76; Sérgio D. J. Pena, Denise R. Carvalho-Silva, Juliana Alves-Silva, et al., "Retrato Molecular do Brasil," *Ciência Hoje*, 159 (2000), 16–25. For reactions to these genetic studies among Brazilians, see Ricardo Ventura Santos e Marcos Chor Maio, "Antropologia, raça e os dilemas das identidades na era da genômica," in Marcos Chor Maio e Ricardo Ventura Santos, orgs. *Raça como questão: história, ciência e identidades no Brasil* (Rio de Janeiro: Editora FIOCRUZ, 2010), 171–96.

61. Santos, Kent, and Gaspar Neto, "From Degeneration to Meeting Point," *Mestizo Genomics*, 47; Peter Wade, "Blackness, Indigeneity, Multiculturalism and Genomics in Brazil, Colombia and Mexico," *Journal of Latin American Studies*, 45:2 (May 2013), 205–33.

62. Htun, "From 'Racial Democracy' to Affirmative Action," 74.

63. For a study that long ago anticipated these debates, see Joel Williamson, *New People: Miscegenation and Mulattoes in the United States* (New York: The Free Press, 1980).

64. For a recent comparative study, see G. Reginald Daniel, *Race and Multiraciality in Brazil and the United State: Converging Paths?* (University Park: The Pennsylvania State University Press, 2006), esp. 185, 216, 237, and 245.

65. Telles, *Race in Another America*, 235–36.

66. Fry, *A persistência da raça*, 177–78 and 209–10.

67. For examples of these debates, see Eduardo Bonilla-Silva, *Racism without Racists: Color-Blind Racism and the Persistence of Racial Inequality in America*, 4th edn. (Lanham, MD: Rowman & Littlefield Publishers, Inc., 2014); Touré, *Whose Afraid of Post-Blackness?: What It Means to Be Black Now* (New York: Free Press, 2011).

68. "[C]e serait en considérant que l'identité est une sorte de foyer virtuel auquel il nous est indispensable de nous référer pour expliquer un certain nombre de choses, mais sans qu'il ait jamais d'existence réele." Claude Lévi-Strauss, et al., *L'identité* (Paris: Editions Grasset et Fasquelle, 1977), 332.

69. For an example study that shows this at the local level, see French, *Legalizing Identities: Becoming Black or Indian in Brazil's Northeast*. "I propose that assuming a black identity in rural Brazil does not preclude multiple identifications on local, national, and international discourses." (155)

70. The original quote is: "The test of a first rate intelligence is the ability to hold two opposed ideas in mind at the same time and still retain the ability to function." F. Scott Fitzgerald, "The Crack-up," *Esquire* (26 February 2008) [first published in the magazine in February, March, and April 1936], www .esquire.com/news-politics/a4310/the-crack-up/ [accessed 9 August 2016]

71. Bailey, *Legacies of Race*, 85; Segato, "The Color-Blind Subject of Myth; Or, Where to Find Africa in the Nation," 148–49.

72. Weinstein, *Color of Modernity*, 282–83 and 343.

73. For a fascinating analysis of what she calls Brazil's "comfortable racial contradiction," and the ways this appears in language, especially about bodies, see Jennifer Roth-Gordon, *Race and the Brazilian Body: Blackness, Whiteness, and Everyday Language in Rio de Janeiro* (Oakland: University of California Press, 2017).

74. For an excellent analysis of this process, see Oliven, *Tradition Matters*, esp. chapter 1. "For each country to cease being 'a country of countries,' it was decisive that radio take up, in a solidary way, the oral cultures of diverse regions and reclaim the proliferating 'vulgarities' in urban centers." García Canclini, *Hybrid Cultures*, 185.

75. Muniz de Albuquerque, *Invention of the Northeast*, 221.

76. For a brilliant analysis of the *paulista* narrative and the slippery nature of *mestiçagem*, see Weinstein, *Color of Modernity*, esp. 216, 293–95, and 337–43. For an excellent study of Bahia, see Ickes, *African-Brazilian Culture*, esp. 230–42.

77. The best synthesis on immigration (and becoming Brazilian) is Lesser, *Immigration, Ethnicity, and National Identity in Brazil*; and on the struggles between ethnicity and Brazilian identity, Lesser, *Negotiating National Identities: Immigrants, Minorities, and the Struggle for Ethnicity in Brazil* (Durham, NC: Duke University Press, 1999). For Japanese Brazilians, see Jeffrey Lesser, ed., *Searching for Home Abroad: Japanese Brazilians and Transnationalism* (Durham, NC: Duke University Press, 2003); Daniel Touro Linger, *No One Home: Brazilian Selves Remade in Japan* (Stanford, CA: Stanford University Press, 2001) and Takeyuki Tsuda, *Strangers in the Ethnic Homeland: Japanese Brazilian Return Migration in Transnational Perspective* (New York: Columbia University Press, 2003), esp. 169–71 and 283–87. For Brazilians abroad, see Margolis, *Goodbye Brazil*, esp. 198–99. For a thoughtful and sensitive personal story of one Brazilian's identity quest, see Cavalcanti, *Almost Home*. See also, Nicola Foote and Michael Goebel, eds., *Immigration and National Identities in Latin America* (Gainesville: University Press of Florida, 2014).

78. Canada is perhaps the closest equivalent to Brazil in this regard.

79. For the Vox Populi poll, see "O Brasileiro Segundo Ele Mesmo," *Veja* (1 janeiro 1996), 48–57; *Lei, justiça e cidadania* (Rio de Janeiro: CPDOC-IFGV/ISER, 1997). Peter Fry, "Politics, Nationality and the Meanings of 'Race' in Brazil," *Daedalus*, 129:2 (Spring 2000), 94.

80. The great Brazilian actress Fernanda Montenegro once observed that "A diferença entre o europeu e o brasileiro é que o brasileiro não se envergonha de dizer que é feliz. Já o europeu, sim." Ancelmo Gois, "No mais," *O Globo* (17 outubro 2009), 20.

81. Although I recognize the power and reach of this "dark side" to the Brazilian psyche, I do not share it. In particular, I disagree with Murilo de Carvalho's pessimism when he asserts that Brazil's myths have "been an instrument of self-delusion" and that "Brazil remains a country of the future, a country of many dreams come untrue." "Dreams Come Untrue," *Daedalus*, 78.

82. Thomas Bender, *A Nation Among Nations: America's Place in World History* (New York: Hill and Wang, 2006), esp. 11 and 296–97; Daniel T. Rogers, "Exceptionalism," in Anthony Molho and Gordon Woods, eds., *Imagined Histories: American Historians Interpret the Past* (Princeton, NJ: Princeton University Press, 1998), 21–40.

83. For a very sophisticated, recent survey and analysis of racial prejudice in Brazil, see Lucio R. Rennó, Amy E. Smith, Matthew L. Layton, and Federico Batista Pereira, *Legitimidade e qualidade da democracia no Brasil: uma visão da cidadania* (São Paulo: Intermeios, 2011), 119–27.

84. In a 1995 survey, nearly 90 percent of those polled acknowledged that there is a system of color prejudice in Brazil, but only 10 percent admitted to

having color prejudice. Another poll in 2011 produced similar results leading some to call this "um preconceito do outro"! Schwarcz, *Nem preto nem branco*, 30–31. See, for example, Anthony W. Marx, *Making Race and Nation: A Comparison of the United States, South Africa, and Brazil* (New York: Cambridge University Press, 1997).

85. "No Brasil convivem duas realidades diversas: de um lado, a descoberta de um país profundamente mestiçado em suas crenças e costumes; de outro, o local de um racismo invisível e de uma hierarquia arraigada na intimidade." Schwarcz, *Nem preto nem branco*, 116.

86. Telles, *Race in Another America*, 192 and 232.

87. Edward Telles and the Project on Ethnicity and Race in Latin America (PERLA), *Pigmentocracies: Ethnicity, Race, and Color in Latin America* (Chapel Hill: The University of North Carolina Press, 2014), esp. 194–96 and 214–17.

88. *Pigmentocracies*, 209 and 222.

89. See, for example, Tianna S. Paschel, *Becoming Black Political Subjects: Movements and Ethno-Racial Rights in Colombia and Brazil* (Princeton, NJ: Princeton University Press, 2016).

90. See, for example, Rahier, *Black Social Movements in Latin America*; Julier Hooker, "Indigenous Inclusion/Black Exclusion: Race, Ethnicity and Multicultural Citizenship in Latin America," *Journal of Latin American Studies*, 37:2 (May 2005), 285–310.

91. Cleary, "Race, Nationalism and Social Theory in Brazil: Rethinking Gilberto Freyre," 4.

92. Pew Research Center, "Brazil's Changing Religious Landscape," www.pew forum.org/2013/07/18/brazils-changing-religious-landscape/ [accessed 11 June 2015].

93. Frances Hagopian, "Paradoxes of Democracy and Citizenship in Brazil," *Latin American Research Review*, 46:3 (2011), 216–27; Shirts, "Sócrates, Corinthians, and Questions of Democracy and Citizenship," 109; Owensby, "Toward a History of Brazil's 'Cordial Racism,'" esp. 338.

94. "Na verdade, o modelo do nacionalismo brasileiro – ao contrário do liberal, que entendia a nação como uma coleção de indivíduos – buscava transformar a nação em um todo orgânico, uma entidade moral, política e econômica cujos fins se realizariam no Estado." Quote is from Schwartzman, Bomeny, Costa, *Tempos de Capanema*, 183. See Evelina Dagnino, "Citizenship: A Perverse Confluence," *Development in Practice*, 17:4–5 (August 2007), 549–56; Avritzer, *Experiências nacionais de participação social*, 24.

95. Leonardo Avritzer, *Democracy and the Public Space in Latin America* (Princeton, NJ: Princeton University Press, 2002), 82–83.

96. George Yúdice, *The Expediency of Culture: Uses of Culture in the Global Era* (Durham, NC: Duke University Press, 2003), 113–15; Martín-Barbero, "Intervening *from* and *through* Research Practices: Meditations on the Cuzco Workshop," *Cultural Agency in the Americas*, 31–32.

97. Daniel T. Rodgers, *Age of Fracture* (Cambridge, MA: The Belknap Press of Harvard University Press, 2011), 5 and 12.

98. Nicola Miller, "The Historiography of Nationalism and National Identity in Latin America," *Nations and Nationalism*, 12:2 (2006), 201–21; Louis A. Pérez, Jr., *On Becoming Cuban: Identity, Nationality, and Culture* (Chapel Hill: University of North Carolina Press, 1999), 8–9; Bell, *The Cult of the Nation in France*, 19 and 217; Claudio Lomnitz has described nationality as a "moving horizon." Lomnitz, *Deep Mexico, Silent Mexico*, xiv.

99. Skidmore, "Raizes de Gilberto Freyre," 20.

Bibliography

Abreu, Martha. *O império do divino: festas religiosas e cultura popular no Rio de Janeiro, 1830–1900*. Rio de Janeiro: Nova Fronteira, 1999.

———. "Mulatas, Crioulos and Morenas: Racial Hierarchy, Gender Relations, and National Identity in Postabolition Popular Song: Southeastern Brazil, 1890–1920," in Pamela Scully and Diana Paton, eds. *Gender and Slave Emancipation in the Atlantic World*. Durham, NC: Duke University Press, 2005. 267–88.

Abreu, Regina. *O enigma de* Os sertões. Rio de Janeiro: Funarte/Rocco, 1998.

"AHR Roundtable: Historians and the Question of 'Modernity,'" *American Historical Review*, 116:3 (June 2011), 631–751.

Alberti, Verena e Amilcar Araujo Pereira, eds. *Histórias do movimento negro no Brasil: depoimentos ao CPDOC*. Rio de Janeiro: Pallas; CPDOC-FGV, 2007.

Alberto, Paulina L. "El Negro Raúl: Lives and Afterlives of an Afro-Argentine Celebrity, 1886 to the Present," *Hispanic American Historical Review*, 96:4 (November 2016), 669–710.

———. "Of Sentiment, Science and Myth: Shifting Metaphors of Racial Inclusion in Twentieth-Century Brazil," *Social History*, 37:3 (August 2012), 261–96.

———. *Terms of Inclusion: Black Intellectuals in Twentieth-Century Brazil*. Chapel Hill, NC: University of North Carolina Press, 2011.

Albuquerque, Jr., Durval Muniz de. *A invenção do nordeste e outras artes*. Recife: Fundação Joaquim Nabuco, Editora Massangana, 1999.

———. *The Invention of the Brazilian Northeast*. trans. Jerry Dennis Metz. Durham, NC: Duke University Press, 2014.

Albuquerque, Roberto Cavalcanti de. *Gilberto Freyre e a invenção do Brasil*. Rio de Janeiro: Editora José Olympio, 2000.

Alencar, José de. *Iracema*. Rio de Janeiro: F. Alves, 1975.

Almeida, Alberto Costa. *A cabeça do brasileiro*. Rio de Janeiro: Editora Record, 2007.

Amado, Jorge. *Dona Flor e seus dois maridos: história de moral e amor: romance*. São Paulo: Martins, 1966.

———. *Dona Flor and Her Two Husbands: A Moral and Amorous Tale*. trans. Harriet de Onís. New York: Avon Books, 1969.

————. *Gabriela, Clove and Cinnamon.* trans. James L. Taylor and William L. Grossman. New York: Knopf, 1962.

————. *Gabriela, cravo e canela.* São Paulo: Martins, 1958.

————. *Tenda dos Milagres; romance.* São Paulo: Martins, 1969.

————. *Tent of Miracles.* trans. Barbara Shelby. New York: A. A. Knopf, 1971.

Amador, José. *Medicine and Nation Building in the Americas, 1890–1940.* Nashville, TN: Vanderbilt University Press, 2015.

Anderson, Benedict. *Imagined Communities: Reflections on the Origin and Spread of Nationalism,* rev. edn. New York: Verso, 2006 [originally published in 1983].

Andrews, George Reid. *The Afro-Argentines of Buenos Aires, 1800–1900.* Madison: University of Wisconsin Press, 1980.

————. *Blackness in the White Nation: A History of Afro-Uruguay.* Chapel Hill: University of North Carolina Press, 2010.

————. "Brazilian Racial Democracy, 1900–90: An American Counterpoint," *Journal of Contemporary History,* 31:3 (July 1996), 483–507.

Antunes, Anderson. "Brazilian Telenovela 'Avenida Brasil' Makes Billions by Mirroring Its Viewers' Lives," *Forbes.com* (19 October 2012), www.forbes.com /sites/andersonantunes/2012/10/19/brazilian-telenovela-makes-billions-by-mir roring-its-viewers-lives/. [accessed 12 June 2015].

Appadurai, Arjun. *Modernity at Large: Cultural Dimensions of Globalization.* Minneapolis: University of Minnesota Press, 1996.

Applegate, Celia. "A Europe of Regions: Reflections on the Historiography of Sub-national Places in Modern Times," *American Historical Review,* 104:4 (October 1999), 1157–82.

Araújo, Joel Zito. *A negação do Brasil: o negro na telenovela brasileira.* São Paulo: Editora SENAC, 2000.

Araújo, Ricardo Benzaquen de. *Guerra e paz:* Casa-Grande & Senzala *e a obra de Gilberto Freyre nos anos 30.* Rio de Janeiro: Editora 34, 1994.

Archetti, Eduardo P. *Masculinities: Football, Polo and the Tango in Argentina.* New York: Berg, 1999.

Archibold, Randal C. "Mexican Writer Mines the Soccer Field for Metaphors," *New York Times* (26 October 2013), A5.

Armani, Carlos Henrique. *Discursos da nação: historicidade e identidade nacional no Brasil en fins do século XIX.* Porto Alegre: EDIPUCRS, 2010.

Avelar, Idelber. "Cenas dizíveis e indizíveis: raça e sexualidade em Gilberto Freyre," *Luso-Brazilian Review,* 49:1 (2012), 168–86.

Avelar, Idelber and Christopher Dunn, eds. *Brazilian Popular Music and Citizenship.* Durham, NC: Duke University Press, 2011.

Avritzer, Leonardo. *Democracy and the Public Space in Latin America.* Princeton, NJ: Princeton University Press, 2002.

————. ed. *Experiências nacionais de participação social.* São Paulo: Cortez, 2009.

————. "Sociedade Civil e Participação no Brasil Democrático," in Carlos Ranulfo Melo, Manuel Alcántara Sáez. orgs. *A democracia brasileira: balanço e perspectivas para o século 21.* Belo Horizonte: Editora UFMG, 2007. 405–20.

Bacelar, Jeferson e Carlos Caroso, eds. *Brasil, um país de negros?* Rio de Janeiro: Pallas; Salvador, BA: CEAO, 1999.

Bailey, Stanley R. *Legacies of Race: Identities, Attitudes, and Politics in Brazil.* Stanford, CA: Stanford University Press, 2009.

Bailey, Stanley R., Mara Loveman, and Jeronimo O. Muniz. "Measures of 'Race' and the Analysis of Racial Inequality in Brazil," *Social Science Research*, 42 (2013), 106–19.

Baker, Chris. *Television, Globalization and Cultural Identities.* Buckingham, England: Open University Press, 1999.

Bandeira, Luiz Alberto Moniz. *Conflito e integração na América do Sul: Brasil, Argentina e Estados Unidos: da Tríplice Aliança ao Mercosul, 1870–2003.* 2ª. edn. rev. Rio de Janeiro: Editora Revan, 2003.

Barbosa, Lívia. *O jeitinho brasileiro.* Rio de Janeiro: Campus, 1992.

Barman, Roderick J. *Brazil: The Forging of a Nation, 1798–1852.* Stanford, CA: Stanford University Press, 1988.

Barreto, Bruno. dir. *Dona Flor e seus dois maridos.* Embrafilme, 1976.

Barreto, Túlio Velho. "Gilberto Freyre e o futebol-arte," *Revista USP*, 62 (junho–agosto 2004), 233–38.

Barth, Fredrik. *Ethnic Groups and Boundaries: The Social Organization of Culture Difference.* Boston: Little, Brown and Company, 1969.

Bartra, Roger. *The Cage of Melancholy: Identity and Metamorphosis in the Mexican Character.* trans. Christopher J. Hall. New Brunswick, NJ: Rutgers University Press, 1992.

Basualdo, Carlos. org. *Tropicália: uma revolução na cultura brasileira [1967–1972].* São Paulo: Cosac Naify, 2007.

Baud, Michiel. "Beyond Benedict Anderson: Nation-Building and Popular Democracy in Latin America," *International Review of Social History*, 50 (2005), 485–98.

Bayman, Louis and Natália Pinazza, eds. *Directory of World Cinema: Brazil,* v. 21. Bristol, UK: Intellect Books, 2013.

Beattie, Peter M. *The Tribute of Blood: Army, Honor, Race, and Nation in Brazil, 1864–1945.* Durham, NC: Duke University Press, 2001.

Bell, David A. *The Cult of the Nation in France: Inventing Nationalism, 1680–1800.* Cambridge, MA: Harvard University, 2001.

Bellos, Alex. *Futebol: The Brazilian Way of Life.* London: Bloomsbury, 2002.

Benamou, Catherine. *It's All True: Orson Welles's Pan-American Odyssey.* Berkeley: University of California Press, 2007.

Bender, Thomas. *A Nation Among Nations: America's Place in World History.* New York: Hill and Wang, 2006.

Berthold, Victor M. *History of the Telephone and Telegraph in Brazil, 1851–1921.* New York: n.p., 1922.

Bertoncelo, Edison. *A Campanha das Diretas e a democratização.* São Paulo: Associação Editorial Humanitas, FAPESP, 2007.

Bertrand, Michael T. *Race, Rock, and Elvis.* Urbana: University of Illinois Press, 2000.

Bethell, Leslie. org. *Brasil: fardo do passado, promessa do future.* trad. Maria Beatriz de Medina. Rio de Janeiro: Civilização Brasileira, 2002.

Bethell, Leslie. ed. *Brazil since 1930, v. IX, Cambridge History of Latin America.* Cambridge: Cambridge University Press, 2008.

Bhabha, Homi K. *The Location of Culture.* London: Routledge, 1994.

Bial, Pedro. *Roberto Marinho.* Rio de Janeiro: Jorge Zahar Editor, 2005.

Bishop-Sanchez, Kathryn. *Creating Carmen Miranda: Race, Camp, and Transnational Stardom.* Nashville, TN: Vanderbilt University Press, 2016.

Blake, Stanley E. *The Vigorous Core of Our Nationality: Race and Regional Identity in Northeastern Brazil.* Pittsburgh, PA: University of Pittsburgh Press, 2011.

Bocayuva, Helena. *Erotismo à brasileira.* Rio de Janeiro: Garamond, 2001.

Bocketti, Gregg P. "Italian Immigrants, Brazilian Football, and the Dilemma of National Identity," *Journal of Latin American Studies,* 40:2 (2008), 275–302.

———. "Playing with National Identity: Brazil in International Football, 1900–1925," in Hendrik Kraay, ed. *Negotiating Identities in Modern Latin America.* Calgary: University of Calgary Press, 2007. 71–89.

Bonfim, Manoel. *A América Latina: males de origem, o parasitismo social e evolução.* 4ª. edn. Rio de Janeiro: Topbooks, 1993 [1905].

Bonilla-Silva, Eduardo. *Racism without Racists: Color-Blind Racism and the Persistence of Racial Inequality in America.* 4th edn. Lanham, MD: Rowman & Littlefield Publishers, Inc., 2014.

Borge, Jason. "*Panis et Circensis*: The Brazilian Circus Imaginery from Modernism to Tropicalism," *Luso-Brazilian Review,* 51:1 (2014), 199–219.

Borgerth, Luiz Eduardo. *Quem e como fizemos a TV Globo.* São Paulo: A Girafa Editora, 2003.

Borges, Dain. "The Recognition of Afro-Brazilian Symbols and Ideas, 1890–1940," *Luso-Brazilian Review,* 32:2 (Winter 1995), 59–78.

Bosco, Francisco. *Dorival Caymmi.* São Paulo: PubliFolha, 2006.

Bosi, Alfredo. *História concisa da literatura brasileira.* 43a edn. São Paulo: Editora Cultrix, 1994.

Botelho, André e Lilia Moritz Schwarcz. orgs. *Um enigma chamado Brasil: 29 intérpretes e um país.* São Paulo: Companhia das Letras, 2009.

Bourdieu, Pierre. "The Field of Cultural Production, or: The Economic World Reversed," in Randal Johnson, ed. *The Field of Cultural Production: Essays on Art and Literature.* New York: Columbia University Press, 1993. 29–73.

Bresser-Pereira, Luiz Carlos. *Developing Brazil: Overcoming the Failure of the Washington Consensus.* Boulder, CO: Lynne Rienner Publishers, 2009.

Breuilly, John. *Nationalism and the State.* 2nd edn. Chicago: University of Chicago Press, 1993.

Britton, John M. *Cables, Crises, and the Press: The Geopolitics of the New International Information System in the Americas, 1866–1903.* Albuquerque: University of New Mexico Press, 2013.

Brittos, Valério Cruz e César Ricardo Siqueira Bolaño. orgs. *Rede Globo: 40 anos de poder e hegemonia.* São Paulo: Paulus, 2005.

Brower, Keith H., Earl E. Fitz, and Enrique Martínez-Vidal. *Jorge Amado: New Critical Essays.* New York: Routledge, 2001.

Brubaker, Rogers. *Nationalism Reframed: Nationhood and the National Question in the New Europe.* Cambridge: Cambridge University Press, 1996.

Bryan, Guilherme. *Quem tem um sonho não dança: cultura jovem brasileira nos anos 80.* Rio de Janeiro: Record, 2004.

Burdick, John. *Blessed Anastácia: Women, Race, and Popular Christianity in Brazil.* New York: Routledge, 1998.

———. *The Color of Sound: Race, Religion, and Music in Brazil.* New York: New York University Press, 2013.

Burke, Peter. "Nationalizing Knowledge," *Study Platform on Interlocking Nationalisms* [SPIN], www.spinnet.eu.

Burke, Peter and Maria Lúcia G. Pallares-Burke. *Gilberto Freyre: Social Theory in the Tropics.* Oxford: Peter Lang, 2008.

Burns, E. Bradford. *The Poverty of Progress: Latin America in the Nineteenth Century.* Berkeley: University of California Press, 1980.

Burns, Eric. *Invasion of the Mind Snatcher: Television's Conquest of America in the Fifties.* Philadelphia: Temple University Press, 2010.

Butler, Kim. *Freedoms Given, Freedoms Won: Afro-Brazilians in Post-Abolition, São Paulo and Salvador.* New Brunswick, NJ: Rutgers University Press, 1998.

Cadena, Marisol de la. *Indigenous Mestizos: The Politics of Race and Culture in Cuzco, Peru, 1919–1991.* Durham, NC: Duke University Press, 2000.

Caldas, Ricardo Wahrendorff e Tânia Montoro. coord. *A evolução do cinema brasileiro no século XX.* Brasília: Casa das Musas, 2006.

Caldwell, Kia Lilly. *Negras in Brazil: Re-envisioning Black Women, Citizenship, and the Politics of Identity.* New Brunswick, NJ: Rutgers University Press, 2007.

Calhoun, Craig. *Nationalism.* Minneapolis: University of Minnesota Press, 1997.

Campbell, Courtney Jeanette. "The Brazilian Northeast, Inside Out: Region, Nation, and Globalization (1926–1968)", Ph.D. Dissertation, Vanderbilt University, 2014.

Capone, Stefania. *A busca da África no candomblé: tradição e poder no Brasil.* Rio de Janeiro: Pallas, 2005.

Carone, Edgard. *O tenentismo: acontecimentos, personagens, programas.* São Paulo: Difel, 1975.

Carvalho, José Murilo de. *Cidadania no Brasil: o longo caminho.* 7ª. edn. Rio de Janeiro: Civilização Brasileira, 2005.

———. "Dreams Come Untrue," *Daedalus,* 129:2 (Spring 2000), 57–82.

———. "Genocídio racial estatístico," *Globo* (27 December 2004), 7.

———. *Pontos e bordados: escritos de história e política.* 2ª. edn. Belo Horizonte: Editora UFMG, 2005.

———. *Teatro de sombras: a política imperial.* Rio de Janeiro: UPERJ/São Paulo: Vértice, 1988.

Carvalho, Martha de Ulhôa, "Tupi or Not Tupi MPB: Popular Music and Identity in Brazil," in David J. Hess and Roberto A. DaMatta, eds. *The Brazilian Puzzle: Culture on the Borderlands of the Western World.* New York: Columbia University Press, 1995. 159–79.

Castello, José. *Vinícius de Moraes: o poeta da paixão, uma biografia.* São Paulo: Companhia das Letras, 1994.

Castilho, Celso Thomas. *Slave Emancipation and Transformations in Brazilian Political Citizenship.* Pittsburgh, PA: University of Pittsburgh Press, 2016.

———. "Performing Abolitionism, Enacting Citizenship: The Social Construction of Political Rights in 1880s Recife, Brazil," *Hispanic American Historical Review*, 93:3 (August 2013), 377–410.

Castro, Ruy. *Carmen: uma biografia*. São Paulo: Companhia das Letras, 2005.

———. *Chega de saudade: a história e as histórias da bossa nova*. São Paulo: Companhia das Letras, 1990.

———. *Estrela solitária: um brasileiro chamado Garrincha*. São Paulo: Companhia das Letras, 2009.

———. *Rio de Janeiro: Carnival Under Fire*. trans. John Gledson. London: Bloomsbury, 2004.

Castro-Klarén, Sara and John Charles Chasteen, eds. *Beyond Imagined Communities: Reading and Writing the Nation in Nineteenth-Century Latin America*. Washington, DC: Woodrow Wilson Center Press; Baltimore, MD: Johns Hopkins University Press, 2003.

Caulfield, Sueann. *In Defense of Honor: Sexual Morality, Modernity, and Nation in Early-Twentieth-Century Brazil*. Durham, NC: Duke University Press, 2000.

Cavalcanti, H. B. *Almost Home: A Brazilian American's Reflections on Faith, Culture, and Immigration*. Madison: University of Wisconsin Press, 2012.

Centeno, Miguel Angel. *Blood and Debt: War and the Nation-State in Latin America*. University Park, PA: The Pennsylvania State University Press, 2002.

Centeno, Miguel Angel and Fernando López-Alves, eds. *The Other Mirror: Grand Theory Through the Lens of Latin America*. Princeton, NJ: Princeton University Press, 2001.

Centro de Pesquisa e Documentação de História Contemporânea do Brasil. *Lei, justiça e cidadania*. Rio de Janeiro: CPDOC-IFGV/ISER, 1997.

Chacon, Vamireh. *A construção da brasilidade (Gilberto Freyre e sua geração)*. Brasília: Paralelo 15 Editores, 2001.

Chamberlain, Bobby J. *Jorge Amado*. Boston: Twayne Publishers, 1990.

Chambers, Sarah C. *From Subjects to Citizens: Honor, Gender, and Politics in Arequipa, Peru, 1780–1854*. University Park: Pennsylvania State University Press, 1999.

Chasteen, John Charles. *National Rhythms, African Roots: The Deep History of Latin American Popular Dance*. Albuquerque: University of New Mexico Press, 2004.

Chatterjee, Partha. *The Nation and Its Fragments: Colonial and Postcolonial Histories*. Princeton, NJ: Princeton University Press, 1993.

Chaui, Marilena. *Brasil: mito fundador e sociedade autoritária*. São Paulo: Editora Fundação Perseu Abramo, 2000.

Chilcote, Ronald H. *Intellectuals and the Search for National Identity in Twentieth-Century Brazil*. New York: Cambridge University Press, 2014.

Cicalo, André. *Urban Encounters: Affirmative Action and Black Identities in Brazil*. New York: Palgrave Macmillan, 2012.

"Circulação de Jornais no País Cresce 4,7%," *Folha de São Paulo* (2 dezembro 2005), B8.

Cleary, David. "Race, Nationalism and Social Theory in Brazil: Rethinking Gilberto Freyre," WPTC-99–09. Cambridge, MA: David Rockefeller Center for Latin American Studies, Harvard University, n.d.

Collier, Simon. *Chile, the Making of a Republic, 1830–1865: Politics and Ideas.* New York: Cambridge University Press, 2003.

Conde, Maite. *Consuming Visions: Cinema, Writing, and Modernity in Rio de Janeiro.* Charlottesville: University of Virginia Press, 2012.

Conrad, Robert Edgar. ed. *Children of God's Fire: A Documentary History of Black Slavery in Brazil.* 2ª. edn. University Park: Penn State Press, 1994.

Constantino, Rodrigo. "Segregação racial," *O Globo,* 7.

Cooper, Frederick. *Colonialism in Question: Theory, Knowledge, History.* Berkeley: University of California Press, 2005.

———. "Conflict and Connection: Rethinking Colonial African History," *American Historical Review,* 99:5 (December 1994), 1516–45.

Costa, Emilia Viotti da. *The Brazilian Empire: Myths and Histories.* rev. edn. Chapel Hill: University of North Carolina Press, 2000.

Costa, Haroldo. *Fala, crioulo.* Rio de Janeiro: Record, 1982.

Costa, Leda Maria da. "Beauty, Effort, and Talent: A Brief History of Brazilian Women's Soccer in Press Discourse," *Soccer & Society,* 15:1 (2014), 81–92.

Couto, Euclides de Freitas. *Da ditadura à ditadura: uma história política do futebol brasileiro (1930–1978).* Niterói: Editora da UFF, 2014.

Crook, Larry and Randal Johnson. eds. *Black Brazil: Culture, Identity, and Social Mobilization.* Los Angeles, CA: UCLA Latin American Center Publications, 1999.

Cunha, Euclides da. *Os sertões (campanha de Canudos).* Leopoldo Bernucci, ed. 2ª. edn. São Paulo: Ateliê Editorial, 2001.

Cunha, Maria Clementina Pereira. *Ecos da folia: uma história do carnaval carioca entre 1880 e 1920.* São Paulo: Companhia das Letras, 2001.

Curran, Mark J. *La literature de cordel: antología bilingüe.* Madrid: Orígenes, 1991.

Dagnino, Evelina. "Citizenship: A Perverse Confluence," *Development in Practice,* 17:4–5 (August 2007), 549–56.

Dagnino, Evelina. coord. *Sociedad civil, esfera pública y democratización en América Latina: Brasil.* trad. Fabiana Davyt, Cristina Larrobla, Amílcar Davyt. Campinas, SP: Editora Unicamp, 2002.

Dale, Joana. "Dando Bandeira," *Revista O Globo,* 9:468 (14 July 2013), 26–29.

DaMatta, Roberto. "Antropologia do óbvio: notas em torno do significado social do futebol brasileiro," *Revista USP: Dossiê Futebol,* 22 (1994), 10–17.

———. *A bola corre mais que os homens: duas Copas, treze crônicas e três ensaios sobre futebol.* Rio de Janeiro: Rocco, 2006.

———. *Carnavais, malandros e heróis: para uma sociologia do dilema brasileiro.* 4ª. edn. Rio de Janeiro: Zahar Editores, 1983.

———. *Relativizando, introdução à antropologia social.* Rio de Janeiro: Rocco, 1990.

DaMatta, Roberto, Luiz Felipe Baêta Neves Flores, Simoni Lahud Guedes, Arno Vogel. *Universo do futebol: esporte e sociedade brasileira.* Rio de Janeiro: Edições Pinakotheke, 1982.

Daniel, G. Reginald. *Race and Multiraciality in Brazil and the United State: Converging Paths?* University Park: The Pennsylvania State University Press, 2006.

Dantas, Carolina Vianna. *O Brasil café com leite: mestiçagem e identidade nacional em periódicos: Rio de Janeiro, 1903–1914*. Rio de Janeiro: Edições Casa de Rui Barbosa, 2010.

D'Araujo, Maria Celina. ed. *As instituições brasileiras da Era Vargas*. Rio de Janeiro: Ed. UERJ/FGV, 1999.

Dávila, Jerry. *Diploma of Whiteness: Race and Social Policy in Brazil, 1917–1945*. Durham, NC: Duke University Press, 2003.

Davis, Darién J. *White Face, Black Mask: Africaneity and the Early Social History of Popular Music in Brazil*. East Lansing: Michigan State University Press, 2009.

Dawson, Allan Charles. *In Light of Africa: Globalizing Blackness in Northeast Brazil*. Toronto: University of Toronto Press, 2014.

De Luca, Tania Regina. *Leituras, projetos e (Re)vista(s) do Brasil (1916–1944)*. São Paulo: Editora Unesp, 2011.

———. *A Revista do Brasil: um diagnóstico para a (n)ação*. São Paulo: Fundação Editora da UNESP, 1999.

Dennison, Stephanie and Lisa Shaw. *Popular Cinema in Brazil*. Manchester: Manchester University Press, 2004.

Diacon, Todd A. *Millenarian Vision, Capitalist Reality: Brazil's Contestado Rebellion, 1912–1916*. Durham, NC: Duke University Press, 1991.

———. *Stringing Together a Nation: Cândido Mariano da Silva Rondon and the Construction of a Modern Brazil, 1906–1930*. Durham, NC: Duke University Press, 2004.

Dimas, Antonio, Jacques Leenhardt e Sandra Jatahy Pesavento. orgs. *Reinventar o Brasil: Gilberto Freyre entre história e ficção*. Porto Alegre: Editora da UFRGS/Editora da USP, 2006.

Dimenstein, Gilberto. et al. *O complô que elegeu Tancredo*. Rio de Janeiro: Editorial JB, 1985.

"Diretas no Video," *Veja*, 815 (18 April 1984), 93–94.

Draper III, Jack. "Forró's Wars of Maneuver and Position: Popular Northeastern Music, Critical Regionalism, and a Culture of Migration," *Latin American Research Review*, 46:1 (2011), 80–101.

Drumond, Maurício. "O esporte como política de Estado: Vargas," in Mary Del Priore e Andrade de Melo, eds. *História do esporte no Brasil*, 213–44.

Duara, Prasenjit. *Rescuing History from the Nation: Questioning Narratives of Modern China*. Chicago: University of Chicago Press, 1995.

Dunn, Christopher. *Brutality Garden: Tropicália and the Emergence of a Brazilian Counterculture*. Chapel Hill: University of North Carolina Press, 2001.

———. "*Desbunde* and Its Discontents: Counterculture and Authoritarian Modernization in Brazil, 1968–1974," *The Americas*, 70:3 (January 2014), 429–58.

Eakin, Marshall C. "Race and Identity: Sílvio Romero, Science, and Social Thought in Late 19th Century Brazil," *Luso-Brazilian Review*, 22:2 (Winter 1985), 151–74.

Earle, Rebecca. *The Return of the Native: Indians and Myth-Making in Spanish America, 1810–1930*. Durham, NC: Duke University Press, 2007.

Echeverria, Regina. *Gonzaguinha e Gonzagão: uma história brasileira*. São Paulo: Leya, 2012.

Edmonds, Alexander. *Pretty Modern: Beauty, Sex, and Plastic Surgery in Brazil.* Durham, NC: Duke University Press, 2010.

Eriksen, Thomas Hylland. "Nationalism and the Internet," *Nations and Nationalism*, 13:1 (2007), 1–17.

Falcão, Joaquim e Rosa Maria Barboza de Araújo. orgs. *O imperador das idéias: Gilberto Freyre em questão.* Rio de Janeiro: Fundação Roberto Marinho/ Topbooks, 2001.

Faoro, Raymundo. *Os donos do poder: formação do patronato politico brasileiro.* 3ª. edn. Porto Alegre: Editora Globo, 1976.

Faria, Luis de Castro. *A contribuição de E. Roquette-Pinto para a antropologia brasileira.* Rio de Janeiro: Universidade do Brasil, Museu Nacional, 1959.

Fausto, Boris e Fernando J. Devoto. *Brasil e Argentina: um ensaio de história comparada (1850–2002).* trad. Sérgio Molina. São Paulo: Editora 34, 2004.

Ferreira, Felipe. *O livro de ouro do carnaval brasileiro.* Rio de Janeiro: Ediouro, 2004.

Ferrer, Ada. *Insurgent Cuba: Race, Nation, and Revolution, 1868–98.* Chapel Hill: University of North Carolina Press, 1999.

Fico, Carlos. *Reinventando o otimismo: ditadura, propaganda e imaginário social no Brasil.* Rio de Janeiro: Editora Fundação Getúlio Vargas, 1997.

Filho, Daniel and João Carlos. *O circo eletrônico: fazendo TV no Brasil.* Rio de Janeiro: Jorge Zahar Editor, 2001.

Fischer, Brodwyn. "Histories and Anthropologies of Citizenship," *American Anthropologist*, 112:1 (March 2010), 154–56.

———. *A Poverty of Rights: Citizenship and Inequality in Twentieth-Century Rio de Janeiro.* Stanford, CA: Stanford University Press, 2008.

Fischer, Brodwyn, Bryan McCann, and Javier Auyero. *Cities from Scratch: Poverty and Informality in Urban Latin America.* Durham, NC: Duke University Press, 2014.

Florescano, Enrique. *National Narratives in Mexico: A History.* trans. Nancy T. Hancock. Norman: University of Oklahoma Press, 2006.

Foer, Franklin. *How Soccer Explains the World: An Unlikely Theory of Globalization.* New York: Harper Perennial, 2005.

Foner, Eric. *Reconstruction: America's Unfinished Revolution, 1863–1877.* New York: Harper, 2002.

Fonseca, Edson Nery da. *Em torno de Gilberto Freyre: ensaios e conferências.* Recife: Fundação Joaquim Nabuco, Ed. Massangana, 2007.

———. *Gilberto Freyre de A a Z: referências essenciais à sua vida e obra.* Rio de Janeiro: Zé Mario Editor, 2002.

Fontes, Paulo. *Um nordeste em São Paulo: trabalhadores migrantes em São Miguel Paulista (1945–66).* Rio de Janeiro: Editora FGV, 2008.

———. "'With a cardboard suitcase in my hand and a pannier on my back': Workers and Northeastern Migrations in the 1950s in São Paulo, Brazil," *Social History*, 36:1 (February 2011), 1–21.

Fontes, Paulo and Bernardo Buarque de Hollanda, eds. *The Country of Football: Politics, Popular Culture & the Beautiful Game in Brazil.* London: Hurst & Company, 2014.

Foote, Nicola and Michael Goebel, eds. *Immigration and National Identities in Latin America*. Gainesville: University Press of Florida, 2014.

Forjaz, Maria Cecília Spina. *Tenentismo e Forças Armadas na Revolução de 30*. Rio de Janeiro: Forense Universitária, 1989.

Frank, Waldo. *South American Journey*. New York: Duell, Sloan and Pearce, 1943.

Frankenberg, Ruth. ed. *Displacing Whiteness: Essays in Social and Cultural Criticism*. Durham, NC: Duke University Press, 1997.

Freire, Juliana Luna. "Whitening, Mixing, Darkening, and Developing: Everything but Indigenous," *Latin American Research Review*, 51:3 (2016), 142–60.

Freire-Medeiros, Bianca. "Hollywood Musicals and the Invention of Rio de Janeiro, 1933–1953," *Cinema Journal*, 41:4 (Summer 2002), 52–67.

Freyre, Gilberto. *Casa-grande & senzala, edição crítica*, Guillermo Giucci, Enrique Rodríguez Larreta e Edson Nery da Fonseca. coords. Madri: ALLCA XX, 2002.

———. *Casa-grande & senzala: introdução à história da sociedade patriarcal no Brasil – 1*, 40ª. edn. Rio de Janeiro: Editora Record, 2000.

———. *Como e porque sou e não sou sociólogo*. Brasília: Editora da Universidade de Brasília, 1968.

———. "Foot-ball mulato," *Diario de Pernambuco*, Recife (17 junho 1938).

———. *Manifesto Regionalista de 1926*. Rio de Janeiro: Departamento de Imprensa Nacional, Os Cadernos da Cultura, 1955.

———. *The Masters and the Slaves [Casa-grande e senzala]: A Study in the Development of Brazilian Civilization*, trans. Samuel Putnam. 2nd edn. rev. New York: Alfred A. Knopf, 1970.

———. *Pessoas, coisas & animais, 1a. série*. Porto Alegre: Editora Globo, 1981.

———. "Social Life in Brazil in the Middle of the 19th Century," *Hispanic American Historical Review*, 5:4 (November 1922), 597–630.

Friendly, Abigail. "The Changing Landscape of Civil Society in Niterói, Brazil," *Latin American Research Review*, 51:1 (2016), 218–41.

Fry, Peter. *A persistência da raça: ensaios antropológicos sobre o Brasil e a África austral*. Rio de Janeiro: Civilização Brasileira, 2005.

Fry, Peter, Yvonne Maggie, Marcos Chor Maio, Simone Monteiro, Ricardo Ventura Santos. orgs. *Divisões perigosas: políticas raciais no Brasil contemporâneo*. Rio de Janeiro: Civilização Brasileira, 2007.

Fryer, Peter. *Rhythms of Resistance: African Musical Heritage in Brazil*. Hanover, NH: Wesleyan University Press/University Press of New England, 2000.

Fuente, Alejandro de la. *A Nation for All: Race, Inequality, and Politics in Twentieth-Century Cuba*. Chapel Hill: University of North Carolina Press, 2001.

Gaffney, Christopher Thomas. *Temples of the Earthbound Gods: Stadiums in the Cultural Landscapes of Rio de Janeiro and Buenos Aires*. Austin: University of Texas Press, 2008.

Galeano, Eduardo. *Soccer in Sun and Shadow*. trans. Mark Fried. New York: Nation Books, 2013.

Gama, Rinaldo. "Biblioteca Nacional," *Veja*, 27:47 (23 novembro 1994), 108–12.

Garcia, Tânia da Costa. *O "it verde" de Carmen Miranda (1930–1946)*. São Paulo: Annablume; Fapesp, 2004.

García Canclini, Néstor. *Consumers and Citizens: Globalization and Multicultural Conflicts*. trans. George Yúdice. Minneapolis: University of Minnesota Press, 2001.

———. *Hybrid Cultures: Strategies for Entering and Leaving Modernity*. trans. Christopher L. Chiappari and Silvia L. López. Minneapolis: University of Minnesota Press, 1995.

Garfield, Seth. *In Search of the Amazon: Brazil, the United States, and the Nature of a Region*. Durham, NC: Duke University Press, 2013.

Garramuño, Florencia. *Primitive Modernities: Tango, Samba, and Nation*. trans. Anna Kazumi Stahl. Stanford, CA: Stanford University Press, 2011.

Gaspar, Lúcia e Virgínia Barbosa. *O futebol brasileiro, 1894 a 2013: uma bibliografia*. Recife: Fundação Joaquim Nabuco, 2013.

Gaspari, Elio. *A ditadura envergonhada; A ditadura escancarada; A ditadura derrotada; and, A ditadura encurralada; A ditadura acabada*. São Paulo: Companhia das Letras, 2002–2016.

Gastaldo, Édison. "Soccer and Media in Brazil," *Soccer & Society*, 15:1 (2014), 123–31.

Gaylor, Brett. dir. *RiP!: A Remix Manifesto*, 2008.

Gellner, Ernest. *Nations and Nationalism*. Ithaca, NY: Cornell University Press, 1983.

Gentile, Emilio. *La Grande Italia: The Myth of the Nation in the Twentieth Century*. trans. Suzanne Dingee and Jennifer Pudney. Madison: University of Wisconsin Press, 2009.

Gerstle, Gary. *American Crucible: Race and Nation in the Twentieth Century*. Princeton, NJ: Princeton University Press, 2001.

Geschiere, Peter. *The Perils of Belonging: Autochthony, Citizenship, and Exclusion in Africa and Europe*. Chicago: University of Chicago Press, 2009.

Giddens, Anthony. *Modernity and Self-Identity: Self and Society in the Late Modern Age*. Stanford, CA: Stanford University Press, 1991.

Gillingham, Paul. *Cuauhtémoc's Bones: Forging National Identity in Modern Mexico*. Albuquerque: University of New Mexico Press, 2011.

Gil-Montero, Martha. *Brazilian Bombshell: The Biography of Carmen Miranda*. New York: Dutton, 1989.

Gois, Ancelmo. "No mais," *O Globo* (17 outubro 2009), 20.

Goldblatt, David. *Futebol Nation: A Footballing History of Brazil*. London: Penguin, 2014.

Goldenberg, Mirian. *Ser homem, ser mulher: dentro e fora do casamento. estudos antropológicos*. Rio de Janeiro: Revan, 1991.

Goldstein, Donna M. *Laughter Out of Place: Race, Class, Violence, and Sexuality in a Rio Shantytown*. Berkeley: University of California Press, 2003.

Gomes, Angela de Castro. *Essa gente do Rio...: modernism e nacionalismo*. Rio de Janeiro: Editora Fundação Getúlio Vargas, 1999.

Gomes, Angela Maria de Castro. coord. *Regionalismo e centralização política: partidos e Constituente no anos 30*. Rio de Janeiro: Editora Nova Fronteira, 1980.

Gomes, Dias. *Apenas um subversivo*. Rio de Janeiro: Bertrand Brasil, 1998.

Gomes, Flávio dos Santos e Olívia Maria Gomes da Cunha. *Quase-cidadão: histórias e antropologias da pós-emancipação no Brasil*. Rio de Janeiro: Editora FGV, 2007.

Gomes, Flávio dos Santos e Petrônio Domingues. *Da nitidez e invisibilidade: legados do pós-emancipação no Brasil*. Belo Horizonte: Fino Traço Editora, 2013.

Gomes, Laura Graziela, Lívia Barbosa, José Augusto Drummond, orgs. *O Brasil não é para principiantes: Carnavais, malandros e heróis, 20 anos depois*. Rio de Janeiro: Fundação Getúlio Vargas, 2000.

Gontijo, Silvana. *A voz do povo: IBOPE do Brasil*. Rio de Janeiro: Editora Objetiva, 1996.

Gordon, Cesar and Ronaldo Helal, "The Crisis of Brazilian Football: Perspectives for the Twenty-First Century," in J. A. Mangan and Lamartine P. DaCosta, eds. *Sport in Latin American Society: Past and Present*. London: Frank Cass, 2002. 139–58.

Gotkowitz, Laura. ed. *Histories of Race and Racism: The Andes and Mesoamerica from Colonial Times to the Present*. Durham, NC: Duke University Press, 2011.

Gouveia, Saulo. *The Triumph of Brazilian Modernism: The Metanarrative of Emancipation and Counter-Narratives*. Chapel Hill: University of North Press, 2013.

Graham, Jessica Lynn. "Representations of Racial Democracy: Race, National Identity, and State Cultural Policy in the United States and Brazil, 1930–1945," Ph.D. diss., The University of Chicago, 2010.

Graham, Richard. "Constructing a Nation in Nineteenth-Century Brazil: Old and New Views on Class, Culture, and the State," *The Journal of the Historical Society*, 1:2–3 (Winter 2000), 17–56.

———. *Patronage and Politics in Nineteenth-Century Brazil*. Stanford, CA: Stanford University Press, 1990.

Grandin, Greg. *The Blood of Guatemala: A History of Race and Nation*. Durham, NC: Duke University Press, 2000.

Greenfeld, Liah. *Nationalism: Five Roads to Modernity*. Cambridge, MA: Harvard University Press, 1992.

Grinbaum, Ricardo. "O Brasileiro Segundo Ele Mesmo," *Veja* (1 janeiro 1996), 48–57.

Gruzinski, Serge. *The Mestizo Mind: The Intellectual Dynamics of Colonization and Globalization*. trans. Deke Dusinberre. New York: Routledge, 2002.

Guardino, Peter. *Peasants, Politics and the Formation of Mexico's National State, Guerrero, 1800–1857*. Stanford, CA: Stanford University Press, 1996.

Guillermoprieto, Alma. *Samba*. New York: Knopf, 1990.

Guimarães, Antonio Sérgio. *Classes, raças e democracia*. São Paulo: Editora 34, 2002.

———. "Preconceito de cor e racismo no Brasil," *Revista de Antropologia*, 47:1 (2004), 9–43.

Guss, David M. *The Festive State: Race, Ethnicity, and Nationalism as Cultural Performance*. Berkeley: University of California Press, 2000.

Guterman, Marcos. *O futebol explica o Brasil: uma história da maior expressão popular do país*. São Paulo: Contexto, 2009.

Guzmán, Tracy Devine. "'Diacuí Killed Iracema': Indigenism, Nationalism and the Struggle for Brazilianness," *Bulletin of Latin American Research*, 24:1 (2005), 92–122.

———. *Native and National in Brazil: Indigeneity after Independence*. Chapel Hill: University of North Carolina Press, 2013.

Hagopian, Frances. "Paradoxes of Democracy and Citizenship in Brazil," *Latin American Research Review*, 46:3 (2011), 216–27.

Hall, Bruce S. *A History of Race in Muslim West Africa, 1600–1960*. New York: Cambridge University Press, 2011.

Hall, Stuart. "Cultural Identity and Diaspora," in J. Rutherford. ed. *Identity: Community, Culture, Difference*. London: Lawrence and Wishart, 1990. 222–37.

———. "The Local and the Global: Globalization and Ethnicity," in Anthony D. King. ed. *Culture, Globalization and the World-System: Contemporary Conditions for the Representation of Identity*. Binghamton, NY: Department of Art and Art History, State University of New York at Binghamton, 1991. 19–39.

Hamburger, Esther. *O Brasil antenado: a sociedade da novela*. Rio de Janeiro: Jorge Zahar Editor, 2005.

———. "Telenovelas e Interpretações do Brasil," *Lua Nova*, 82 (2011), 61–86.

Hamilton, Russell G. "Gabriela Meets Olodum: Paradoxes of Hybridity, Racial Identity, and Black Consciousness in Contemporary Brazil," *Research in African Literatures*, 38:1 (Spring 2007), 181–93.

Hanchard, Michael George. *Orpheus and Power: The Movimento Negro of Rio de Janeiro and São Paulo, Brazil, 1945–1988*. Princeton, NJ: Princeton University Press, 1994.

———. *Party/Politics: New Horizons in Black Political Thought*. New York: Oxford University Press, 2006.

Hardman, Francisco Foot e Victor Leonardi. *História da indústria e do trabalho no Brasil (das origens aos anos 20)*. 2ª. edn. rev. São Paulo: Editora Ática S.A., 1991.

Harris, Mark. *Rebellion on the Amazon: The Cabanagem, Race, and Popular Culture in the North of Brazil, 1798–1840*. New York: Cambridge University Press, 2010.

Hasenbalg, Carlos and Nelson do Valle Silva. "Notes on Racial and Political Inequality in Brazil," in Michael Hanchard. ed. *Racial Politics in Contemporary Brazil*. Durham, NC: Duke University Press, 1999. 154–78.

Heise, T. S. *Remaking Brazil: Contested National Identities in Contemporary Brazilian Cinema*. Cardiff: University of Wales Press, 2012.

Helal, Ronaldo. *Passes e impasses: futebol e cultura de massa no Brasil*. Petrópolis: Vozes, 1997.

Helal, Ronaldo and Antonio Jorge Soares. "The Decline of the 'Soccer-Nation': Journalism, Soccer and National Identity in the 2002 World Cup," *Soccer & Society*, 15:1 (2014), 132–46.

Helg, Aline. *Our Rightful Share: The Afro-Cuban Struggle for Equality,*
1886–1912. Chapel Hill: University of North Carolina Press, 1996.

Hertzman, Marc A. "A Brazilian Counterweight: Music, Intellectual Property and
the African Diaspora in Rio de Janeiro (1910s–1930s)," *Journal of Latin*
American Studies, 41 (2009), 695–722.

———. *Making Samba: A New History of Race and Music in Brazil.* Durham,
NC: Duke University Press, 2013.

———. "Samba." *Encyclopedia of African-American Culture and History.* in
Colin A. Palmer. ed. 2nd edn. Detroit, MI: Macmillan Reference USA, 2006.
1998–2003.

Herz, Daniel. *A história secreta da Rede Globo.* Porto Alegre: tchê, 1987.

Hobsbawm, Eric. *The Age of Extremes: A History of the World, 1914–1991.*
New York: Vintage Books, 1996.

———. *Globalisation, Democracy and Terrorism.* London: Little, Brown, 2007.

———. *Nations and Nationalism since 1780: Programme, Myth, Reality.* 2nd
edn. Cambridge: Cambridge University Press, 1992.

Hobsbawm, Eric and Terence Ranger, eds. *The Invention of Tradition.*
New York: Cambridge University Press, 1992.

Holanda, Bernardo Borges Buarque de. "The Fan as Actor: The Popularization of
Soccer and Brazil's Sports Audience," *Soccer & Society,* 15:1 (2014), 8–18.

Holanda, Sérgio Buarque de. *Raízes do Brasil.* Rio de Janeiro: Editora José
Olympio, 1936.

———. *Roots of Brazil.* trans. G. Harvey Summ. South Bend, IN: University of
Notre Dame Press, 2012.

Holston, James. *Insurgent Citizenship: Disjunctions of Democracy and*
Modernity in Brazil. Princeton, NJ: Princeton University Press, 2008.

Hooker, Juliet. "Indigenous Inclusion/Black Exclusion: Race, Ethnicity and
Multicultural Citizenship in Latin America," *Journal of Latin American*
Studies, 37:2 (May 2005), 285–310.

Hordge-Freeman, Elizabeth. *The Color of Love: Racial Features, Stigma and*
Socialization in Black Brazilian Families. Austin: University of Texas Press,
2015.

Hoyle, Ben. "Football and the Old Marxist Who Says that It Explains the New
World," *London Times* (6 October 2007), www.thetimes.co.uk/tto/sport/foot
ball/article2272866.ece. [accessed 10 June 2015].

Htun, Mala. "From 'Racial Democracy' to Affirmative Action: Changing State
Policy on Race in Brazil," *Latin American Research Review,* 39:1 (February
2004), 60–98.

Hughes, Charles L. *Country Soul: Making Music and Making Race.* Chapel Hill:
University of North Carolina Press, 2015.

Humphreys, James S. *Francis Butler Simkins: A Life.* Gainesville: University Press
of Florida, 2008.

Ianni, Octavio. *A idéia de Brasil moderno.* São Paulo: Editora Brasiliense, 1992.

Ickes, Scott. *African-Brazilian Culture and Regional Identity in Bahia, Brazil.*
Gainesville: University of Florida Press, 2013.

Iglésias, Francisco. *Historiadores do Brasil: capítulos de historiografia brasileira.*
Rio de Janeiro: Nova Fronteira, 2000.

Ignatieff, Michael. *Blood and Belonging: Journeys into the New Nationalism.* New York: Farrar, Straus, and Giroux, 1994.

I'll Take My Stand: The South and the Agrarian Tradition, by Twelve Southerners. New York: Harper and Brothers, 1930.

Ioris, Rafael R. *Transforming Brazil: A History of National Development in the Postwar Era.* New York: Routledge, 2014.

Itzigsohn, José and Matthias vom Hau. "Unfinished Imagined Communities: States, Social Movements, and Nationalism in Latin America," *Theory and Society,* 35:2 (April 2006), 193–212.

Jacobs, Claudia Silva. *Futebol exportação.* Rio de Janeiro: Editora Senac Rio, 2006.

Jenkins, Garry. *The Beautiful Team: In Search of Pelé and the 1970 Brazilians.* New York: Simon & Schuster, 1998.

Johnson, Randal. "The Dynamics of the Brazilian Literary Field, 1930–1945," *Luso-Brazilian Review,* 31:2 (1994), 5–22.

———. *The Film Industry in Brazil: Culture and the State.* Pittsburgh: University of Pittsburgh Press, 1987.

Johnson, Randal and Robert Stam, eds. *Brazilian Cinema.* Expanded Edition. New York: Columbia University Press, 1995.

Jornal Nacional: a notícia faz história/Memória Globo. Rio de Janeiro: Jorge Zahar Editor, 2004.

Joseph, Gilbert M. and Daniel Nugent, "Popular Culture and State Formation in Revolutionary Mexico," in Gilbert M. Joseph and Daniel Nugent, eds. *Everyday Forms of State Formation: Revolution and the Negotiation of Rule in Modern Mexico.* Durham, NC: Duke University Press, 1994.

Joseph, Tiffany D. *Race on the Move: Brazilian Migrants and the Global Reconstruction of Race.* Stanford, CA: Stanford University Press, 2015.

Joyce, Samantha Nogueira. *Brazilian Telenovelas and the Myth of Racial Democracy.* Lanham, MD: Lexington Books, 2012.

Kamel, Ali. *Não somos racistas: uma reação aos que querem nos transformar numa nação bicolor.* Rio de Janeiro: Nova Fronteira, 2006.

Kaufmann, Roberta Fragoso M. "A farsa do país 'racista,'" *O Globo,* 25 de outubro de 2009, 7.

Kingstone, Peter R. and Timothy J. Power, eds. *Democratic Brazil: Actors, Institutions, and Processes.* Pittsburgh, PA: University of Pittsburgh Press, 2000.

———. *Democratic Brazil Revisited.* Pittsburgh, PA: University of Pittsburgh Press, 2008.

Kittleson, Roger. *The Country of Football: Soccer and the Making of Modern Brazil.* Berkeley: University of California Press, 2014.

Knight, Peter T. "The Internet in Brazil," *Braudel Papers,* 47 (2013), 1–8.

Kotscho, Ricardo. *Explode um novo Brasil: diário da Campanha das Diretas.* São Paulo: Brasiliense, 1984.

Kottak, Conrad Phillip. *Assault on Paradise: Social Change in a Brazilian Village.* 2nd edn. New York: McGraw-Hill, Inc., 1992.

———. *Prime-Time Society: An Anthropological Analysis of Television and Culture.* Updated edition. Walnut Creek, CA: Left Coast Press, 2009.

Kraay, Hendrik. *Days of National Festivity in Rio de Janeiro Brazil, 1823–1889.* Stanford, CA: Stanford University Press, 2013.

Kramer, Lloyd. *Nationalism: Political Cultures in Europe and the Americas, 1775–1865.* New York: Twayne Publishers, 1998.

Kroeber, A. L. *Culture Patterns and Processes.* New York: Harcourt Brace and World, 1963.

Lamounier, Bolívar y Judith Muszynski. "Brasil," in Dieter Nohlen, ed. *Enciclopedia electoral latinoamericana y del Caribe.* San José, Costa Rica: Instituto Interamericano de Derechos Humanos, 1993. 93–134.

Langland, Victoria. *Speaking of Flowers: Student Movements and the Making and Remembering of 1968 in Military Brazil.* Durham: Duke University Press, 2013.

La Pastina, Antonio. "The Telenovela Way of Knowledge: An Ethnographic Reception Study among Rural Viewers in Brazil," Ph.D. diss., University of Texas at Austin, 1999.

Larraín, Jorge. *Identidad chilena.* Santiago de Chile: Editorial LOM, 2001.

———. *Identity and Modernity in Latin America.* Cambridge: Polity Press, 2000.

———. *Ideology and Cultural Identity: Modernity and the Third World Presence.* Cambridge: Polity Press, 1994.

Leal, Victor Nunes. *Coronelismo: The Municipality and Representative Government in Brazil.* trans. June Henfrey. New York: Cambridge University Press, 1977.

Legg, Benjamin. "The Bicultural Sex Symbol: Sônia Braga in Brazilian and North American Popular Culture," in Kathryn Bishop-Sanchez and Severino João Medeiros Albuquerque, eds. *Performing Brazil: Essays on Culture, Identity, and the Performing Arts.* Madison: University of Wisconsin Press, 2015. 202–23.

Leite, Dante Moreira. *O caráter nacional brasileiro.* 2ª. edn. São Paulo: Pioneira, 1969.

Leite, Pedro Dias e Bela Megale, "Entrevista Galvão Bueno: Sou vendedor de emoções," *Veja* (23 de julho 2014), 17–21.

Lemos, André e Francisco Paulo Jamil Almeida Marques. "O plano nacional de banda larga brasileira: um estudo de seus limites e efeitos sociais e políticos," *Revista da Associação Nacional dos Programas de Pós-graduação em Comunicação, E-compos,* 15: 1 (jan.–abr. 2012), 1–36.

Lesser, Jeffrey. *Immigration, Ethnicity, and National Identity in Brazil, 1808 to the Present.* New York: Cambridge University Press, 2013.

———. *Negotiating National Identities: Immigrants, Minorities, and the Struggle for Ethnicity in Brazil.* Durham, NC: Duke University Press, 1999.

———. ed. *Searching for Home Abroad: Japanese Brazilians and Transnationalism.* Durham, NC: Duke University Press, 2003.

Lever, Janet. *Soccer Madness.* Chicago: University of Chicago Press, 1983.

———. "Sport in a Fractured Society: Brazil under Military Rule," in Joseph L. Arbena. ed. *Sport and Society in Latin America: Diffusion, Dependency, and the Rise of Mass Culture.* New York: Greenwood Press, 1988. 85–96.

Levine, Robert M. "Elite Intervention in Urban Popular Culture in Modern Brazil," *Luso-Brazilian Review,* 21:2 (Winter 1984), 9–22.

Lévi-Strauss, Claude. *Tristes Tropiques*. trans. John and Doreen Weightman. New York: Penguin, 1992 [originally published in French in 1953].
————. et al. *L'identité*. Paris: Editions Grasset et Fasquelle, 1977.
Lewis, David Levering. *W. E. B. DuBois, 1868–1919: Biography of a Race*. New York: Macmillan, 1994.
Lewis, John. "Why Bossa Nova Is 'The Highest Flowering of Brazilian Culture'", *The Guardian*, 1 (October 2013), www.theguardian.com/music/2013/oct/01/bossa-nova-highest-culture-brazil. [accessed 27 November 2013].
Lima, Nísia Trindade. *Um sertão chamado Brasil: intelectuais e representação geográfica da identidade nacional*. Rio de Janeiro: Revan/IUPERJ, UCAM, 1999.
Linger, Daniel Touro. *No One Home: Brazilian Selves Remade in Japan*. Stanford, CA: Stanford University Press, 2001.
Lomnitz, Claudio. *Deep Mexico, Silent Mexico: An Anthropology of Nationalism*. Minneapolis: University of Minnesota Press, 2001.
Longman, Jeré. "Deep in the Amazon, an Isolated Village Tunes in to the World Cup," *New York Times* (20 June 2014), www.nytimes.com/2014/06/22/sports/worldcup/deep-in-the-amazon-an-isolated-village-tunes-in-the-world-cup.html?_r=0. [accessed 14 July 2014].
Lopes, Antonio Herculano. "Inventing a Mestizo Identity: Musical Theater in Rio de Janeiro 1900–1922," Ph.D. diss., New York University, 2008.
Lopes, José Sergio Leite. "Class, Ethnicity, and Color in the Making of Brazilian Football," *Daedalus*, 129:2 (Spring 2000), 239–70.
Lopes, Reinaldo José. "Quilombola é 40% europeu, mostra DNA," *Folha de São Paulo*, 18 (setembro 2013).
López, Rick. *Crafting Mexico: Intellectuals, Artisans, and the State After the Revolution*. Durham, NC: Duke University Press, 2010.
Loveless, Megwen May. "The Invented Tradition of Forró: A 'Routes' Ethnography of Brazilian Musical 'Roots,'" Ph.D. Dissertation, Harvard University, 2010.
Loveman, Mara. *National Colors: Racial Classification and the State in Latin America*. New York: Oxford University Press, 2014.
————. "The Race to Progress: Census Taking and Nation Making in Brazil (1870–1920)," *Hispanic American Historical Review*, 89:3 (2009), 435–70.
Lund, Joshua e Malcolm McNee, eds. *Gilberto Freyre e os estudos latinoamericanos*. Pittsburgh, PA: University of Pittsburgh, Instituto Internacional de Literatura Iberoamericana, 2006.
Machado, Uirá. "TV É a Principal Fonte de Informação dos Eleitores," *Folha de São Paulo* (28 julho 2010), A7.
Machado-Borges, Thais. *Only for You!: Brazilians and the Telenovela Flow*. Stockholm: Stockholm Studies in Social Anthropology, 2003.
Magaldi, Cristina. "Adopting Imports: New Images and Alliances in Brazilian Popular Music of the 1990s," *Popular Music*, 18:3 (October 1999), 309–29.
Maggie, Yvonne. "Does Mário Andrade Live On?: Debating the Brazilian Modernist Ideological Repertory," *Vibrant*, 5:1 (2008), 34–64.
Maier, Charles S. "'Being There': Place, Territory, and Identity," in Seyla Benhabib, Ian Shapiro, and Danilo Petranovic, eds. *Identities, Affiliations, and Allegiances*. New York: Cambridge University Press, 2007, 67–84.

Maio, Marcos Chor e Ricardo Ventura Santos. orgs. *Raça como questão: história, ciência e identidades no Brasil.* Rio de Janeiro: Editora FIOCRUZ, 2010.

Malerba, Jurandir. *A corte no exílio: civilização e poder no Brasil às vésperas da Independência (1808 a 1821).* São Paulo: Companhia das Letras, 2000.

Mallon, Florencia. *Peasant and Nation: The Making of Postcolonial Mexico and Peru.* Berkeley: University of California Press, 1995.

Manthei, Jennifer J. "The Brazilian *Mulata*: A Wood for All Works," in Hendrik Kraay, ed. *Negotiating Identities in Modern Latin America.* Calgary: University of Calgary Press, 2007, 189–211.

Maranhão, Tiago Fernandes and Jorge Knijnik. "Futebol Mulato: Racial Constructs in Brazilian Football," *Cosmopolitan Civil Societies Journal,* 3:2 (2011), 55–71.

Margolis, Maxine. *Goodbye Brazil: Emigres from the Land of Soccer and Samba.* Madison, WI: University of Wisconsin Press, 2013.

———. *Invisible Minority: Brazilians in New York City,* rev. edn. Gainesville: University of Florida Press, 2009.

Marotti, Giorgio. *Black Characters in the Brazilian Novel.* trans. Maria O. Marotti and Harry Lawton. Los Angeles: Center for Afro-American Studies, University of California, Los Angeles, 1987.

Marquese, Rafael de Bivar. *Administração & escravidão: idéias sobre a gestão da agricultura escravista brasileira.* São Paulo: Editora Hucitec, 1999.

Marras, Sergio. *América Latina: marca registrada.* Buenos Aires: Grupo Editorial Zeta, 1992.

Martín-Barbero, Jesús. *De los medios a las mediaciones: comunicación, cultura y hegemonía.* Barcelona: Gustavo Gili, 1987.

———. *Oficio de cartógrafo: travesías latinoamericanas de la comunicación en la cultura.* México: Fondo de Cultura Económica, 2002.

Martín-Barbero, J. y Sonia Muñoz. coord. *Televisión y melodrama: géneros y lecturas de la telenovela y Colombia.* Bogotá: Tercer Mundo Editores, 1992.

Martins, Luciano. "A Genese de uma Intelligentsia: Os Intelectuais e a Política no Brasil, 1920–1940," *Revista Brasileira de Ciências Sociais,* 2:4 (1987), 65–87.

Martius, Carl Friedrich Philipe von. "Como se deve escrever a história do Brasil," *Revista do Instituto Histórico e Geográfico Brasileiro,* 6:24 (jan. 1845), 381–403.

Marx, Anthony W. *Making Race and Nation: A Comparison of the United States, South Africa, and Brazil.* New York: Cambridge University Press, 1997.

Mason, Bobbie Ann. *Elvis Presley.* New York: Penguin, 2003.

Mason, Tony. *Passion of the People?: Football in South America.* London: Verso, 1995.

Máximo, João. "Armando Nogueira, a poesia em jogo," *O Globo,* 30 (de março de 2010), 31.

McCann, Bryan. *Hard Times in the Marvelous City: From Dictatorship to Democracy in the Favelas of Rio de Janeiro.* Durham, NC: Duke University Press, 2014.

———. *Hello, Hello Brazil: Popular Music in the Making of Modern Brazil.* Durham, NC: Duke University Press, 2004.

McGowan, Chris and Ricardo Pessanha. *The Brazilian Sound: Samba, Bossa Nova, and the Popular Music of Brazil.* New York: Billboard Books, 1991.

McGrath, Ben. "Samba Soccer: The Transformation of Brazil's Most Storied Team," *The New Yorker,* (13 January 2014), 44–57.

Meihy, José Carlos Sebe Bom. *Brasil fora de si: experiências de brasileiros em Nova York.* São Paulo: Parábola Editorial, 2004.

Mendonça, Ana Rita. *Carmen Miranda foi a Washington.* Rio de Janeiro: Editora Record, 1999.

Mettenheim, Kurt von. *The Brazilian Voter: Mass Politics in Democratic Transition, 1974–1986.* Pittsburgh: University of Pittsburgh Press, 1995.

Miceli, Sergio. *Intelectuais à brasileira.* São Paulo: Companhia das Letras, 2001.

Michallik, Janusz. "After Humiliation Against Germany, Brazil Must Go Back to Joga [sic] Bonito Roots," (10 July 2014), http://bleacherreport.com/articles/21 24332-after-humiliation-against-germany-brazil-must-go-back-to-joga-bonito -roots. [accessed 15 July 2014].

Mignolo, Walter D. *The Idea of Latin America.* Oxford: Blackwell, 2005.

Milan, Betty. *O país da bola.* Rio de Janeiro: Editora Record, 2014.

Miller, Marilyn Grace. *Rise and Fall of the Cosmic Race: The Cult of Mestizaje in Latin America.* Austin: University of Texas Press, 2004.

Miller, Nicola. "The Historiography of Nationalism and National Identity in Latin America," *Nations and Nationalism,* 12:2 (2006), 201–21.

———. *In the Shadow of the State: Intellectuals and the Quest for National Identity in Twentieth-Century Spanish America.* London: Verso, 1999.

———. *Reinventing Modernity in Latin America: Intellectuals Imagine the Future, 1900–1930.* New York: Palgrave Macmillan, 2008.

Miller, Nicola and Stephen Hart, eds. *When Was Latin America Modern?* New York: Palgrave Macmillan, 2007.

Moehn, Frederick. *Contemporary Carioca: Technologies of Mixing in a Brazilian Music Scene.* Durham, NC: Duke University Press, 2012.

Monclaire, Stéphane. "Le quasi-impeachment du président Collor. Questions sur la 'consolidation de la démocratie' brésilienne," *Revue française de science politique,* 44:1 (1994), 41–43.

Moore, Barbara, Marvin R. Bensman, and Jim Van Dyke. *Prime-Time Television: A Concise History.* Westport, CT: Praeger, 2006.

Morgan, Edmund S. *Inventing the People.* New York: W. W. Norton, 1988.

Morning, Ann. *The Nature of Race: How Scientists Think and Teach about Human Difference.* Berkeley: University of California Press, 2011.

Morse, Richard M. "Balancing Myth and Evidence: Freyre and Sérgio Buarque," *Luso-Brazilian Review,* 32:2 (Winter 1995), 47–57.

Moser, Benjamin. *Why This World: A Biography of Clarice Lispector.* New York: Oxford University Press, 2009.

Mosher, Jeffrey. *Political Struggle, Ideology, and State Building: Pernambuco and the Construction of Brazil, 1817–1850.* Lincoln: University of Nebraska Press, 2008.

Mota, Carlos Guilherme. *Ideologia da cultura brasileira (1933–1974): pontos de partida para uma revisão histórica* São Paulo: Editora 34, 2008.

Motta, Nelson. *Vale tudo: o som e a fúria de Tim Maia*. Rio de Janeiro: Objetiva, 2007.

Moutinho, Laura. *Razão, "cor" e desejo: uma análise comparativa sobre relacionamentos afetivo-sexuais "inter-raciais" no Brasil e na África do Sul*. São Paulo: Unesp, 2004.

Munanga, Kabengele. *Rediscutindo a mestiçagem no Brasil: identidade nacional versus identidade negra*. Petrópolis: Editora Vozes, 1999.

Murphy, John P. *Music in Brazil: Experiencing Music, Expressing Culture*. New York: Oxford University Press, 2006.

Nadel, Joshua H. *Fútbol: Why Soccer Matters in Latin America*. Gainesville: University Press of Florida, 2014.

Nagib, Lúcia. *Brazil on Screen: Cinema Novo, New Cinema, Utopia*. London: Palgrave Macmillan, 2007.

Nairn, Tom. *Faces of Nationalism: Janus Revisited*. London: Verso, 1997.

Nascimento, Abdias do. *Brazil: Mixture or Massacre?: Essays on the Genocide of a Black People*. 2nd edn. rev. trans. Elisa Larkin Nascimento. Dover, MA: Majority Press, 1989.

———. *O genocídio do negro brasileiro: processo de um racismo mascarado*. Rio de Janeiro: Paz e Terra, 1978.

Needell, Jeffrey D. "The Domestic Civilizing Mission: The Cultural Role of the State in Brazil, 1808–1030," *Luso-Brazilian Review*, 36:1 (Summer 1999), 1–18.

———. "The Foundations of Freyre's Work: Engagement and Disengagement in the Brazil of 1923–1933," *Portuguese Studies*, 27:1 (2011), 8–19.

———. "History, Race, and the State in the Thought of Oliveira Viana," *Hispanic American Historical Review*, 75:1 (February 1995), 1–30.

———. "Identity, Race, Gender and Modernity in the Origins of Gilberto Freyre's Oeuvre," *American Historical Review*, 100:1 (February 1995), 51–77.

———. *The Party of Order: The Conservatives, the State, and Slavery in the Brazilian Monarchy, 1831–1871*. Stanford, CA: Stanford University Press, 2006.

Nobles, Melissa. *Shades of Citizenship: Race and Census in Modern Politics*. New York: Cambridge University Press, 2000.

Novaes, Adauto. ed. *Rede imaginária: televisão e democracia*. São Paulo: Companhia das Letras, 1991.

Nunes, Benedito. *Oswald Canibal*. São Paulo: Perspectiva, 1979.

Ochoa Gautier, Ana María. "Social Transculturation, Epistemologies of Purification and the Aural Public Sphere in Latin America," in Jonathan Sterne, ed. *The Sound Studies Reader*. London: Routledge, 2012. 388–404.

Oliveira, Aloysio de. *De Banda pra lua*. Rio de Janeiro: Record, 1982.

Oliveira, Lúcia Lippi. *Cultura é patrimônio: um guia*. Rio de Janeiro: Editora da FGV, 2008.

———. *A questão nacional na Primeira República*. São Paulo: Editora Brasiliense, 1990.

Oliveira, Lúcia Lippi, Mônica Pimenta Velloso e Ângela Maria Castro Gomes, *Estado Novo: ideologia e poder*. Rio de Janeiro: Zahar Editores, 1982.

Oliveira-Monte, Emanuelle. "Blacks versus Whites: Self-denomination, Soccer, and Race Representations in Brazil," *Luso-Brazilian Review*, 50:2 (2013), 76–92.

Oliveira Sobrinho, José Bonifácio. *O livro do Boni*. Rio de Janeiro: Casa da Palavra, 2011.

Oliven, Ruben George. "National and Regional Identities in Brazil: Rio Grande do Sul and its Peculiarities," *Nations and Nationalism*, 12:2 (2006), 303–20.

———. "Singing Money: Money in Brazilian and North American Popular Music," in David F. Ruccio, ed. *Economic Representations: Academic and Everyday*. New York: Routledge, 2008. 211–32.

———. *Tradition Matters: Modern Gaúcho Identity in Brazil*. trans. Carmen Chaves Tesser. New York: Columbia University Press, 1996.

———. *Violência e cultura no Brasil*. 2ª. edn. Petrópolis: Vozes, 1983.

Omi, Michael and Howard Winant. *Racial Formation in the United States*. 3rd edn. New York: Routledge, 2015

Ortiz, Renato. *Cultura brasileira e identidade nacional*. São Paulo: Brasiliense, 2006.

———. *A moderna tradição brasileira: cultura brasileira e indústria cultural*. São Paulo: Editora Brasiliense, 1988.

Ortiz, Renato, Silvia Helena Simões Borelli, José Mário Ortiz Ramos. *Telenovela: história e produção*. São Paulo: Editora Brasiliense, 1989.

Oswald, Vivian. "IPEA: Serviço de Internet em Banda Larga no País é Caro, Lento e Desigual," *O Globo* (27 abril 2010), Economia, 27.

Owensby, Brian. "Toward a History of Brazil's 'Cordial Racism': Race beyond Liberalism," *Comparative Studies in Society and History*, 47:2 (April 2005), 318–47.

Pace, Richard. *The Struggle for Amazon Town: Gurupá Revisited*. Boulder, CO: Lynne Rienner, 1998.

Pace, Richard and Brian P. Hinote. *Amazon Town TV: An Audience Ethnography in Gurupá, Brazil*. Austin: University of Texas Press, 2013.

Paixão, Marcelo. *A lenda da modernidade encantada: por uma crítica ao pensamento social brasileiro sobre relações raciais e projeto de Estado-Nação*. Curitiba: Editora CRV, 2014.

Pallares-Burke, Maria Lúcia G. *Gilberto Freyre: um vitoriano dos trópicos*. São Paulo: Editora UNESP, 2005.

———. *O triunfo do fracasso: Rudiger Bilden, o amigo esquecido de Gilberto Freyre*. São Paulo: Editora UNESP, 2012.

Parada, Maurício. *Educando corpos e criando a nação: cerimônias cívicas e práticas disciplinares no Estado Novo*. Rio de Janeiro: Editora PUC-Rio, 2009.

Parker, Holt N. "Toward a Definition of Popular Culture," *History and Theory*, 50 (May 2011), 147–70.

Parker, Richard G. *Bodies, Pleasures, and Passions: Sexual Culture in Contemporary Brazil*. Nashville, TN: Vanderbilt University Press, 2009.

Paschel, Tianna S. *Becoming Black Political Subjects: Movements and Ethno-Racial Rights in Colombia and Brazil*. Princeton, NJ: Princeton University Press, 2016.

Peard, Julyan. *Race, Place and Medicine: The Idea of the Tropics in 19th Century Brazilian Medicine.* Durham, NC: Duke University Press, 2000.

Pécaut, Daniel. *Os intelectuais e a política no Brasil: entre o povo e a nação.* trad. Maria Júlia Goldwasser. São Paulo: Editora Ática, 1990.

Pedrosa, Adriano e Lilia Moritz Schwarcz. org. *Histórias mestiças: antologia de textos.* Rio de Janeiro: Cobogó, 2014.

Pena, S. D. J., L. Bastos-Rodrigues, J. R. Pimenta. "DNA Tests Probe the Genomic Ancestry of Brazilians," *Brazilian Journal of Medical and Biological Research,* 42:10 (2009), 870–76.

Pena, Sérgio D. J. e Maria Cátira Bortolini, "Pode a genética definir quem deve se beneficiar das cotas universitárias e demais ações afirmativas?" *Estudos Avançados,* 18:50 (January–April 2004), 31–50.

Pena, Sérgio D. J., Denise R. Carvalho-Silva, Juliana Alves-Silva, et al. "Retrato Molecular do Brasil," *Ciência Hoje,* 159 (2000), 16–25.

Perdigão, Paulo. *Anatomia de uma derrota.* Porto Alegre: L & PM Editores, 1986.

Pereira, Aldo. *Breve história da aviação comercial brasileira.* Rio de Janeiro: Europa, 1987.

Pereira, José Maria. org. *José Olympio: o editor e sua Casa.* Rio de Janeiro: Sextante, 2008.

Pereira, Leonardo Affonso de Miranda. *Footballmania: uma história social do futebol no Rio de Janeiro – 1902–1938.* Rio de Janeiro: Editora Nova Fronteira, 2000.

Pérez, Louis A., Jr. *On Becoming Cuban: Identity, Nationality, and Culture.* Chapel Hill: University of North Carolina Press, 1999.

Perrone, Charles A. *Masters of Contemporary Brazilian Song: MPB 1965–1985.* Austin: University of Texas Press, 1989.

Perrone, Charles A. and Christopher Dunn, eds. *Brazilian Popular Music and Globalization.* Gainesville: University Press of Florida, 2001.

Pew Research Center, "Brazil's Changing Religious Landscape," www.pewforum .org/2013/07/18/brazils-changing-religious-landscape/. [accessed 11 June 2015].

Pinho, Patricia de Santana. *Mama Africa: Reinventing Blackness in Brazil.* Durham, NC: Duke University Press, 2010.

Pitts, Bryan. "The Inadvertent Opposition: The São Paulo Political Class and the Demise of Brazil's Military Regime, 1968–1985," Ph.D. Diss., Duke University, 2013.

Porto, Mauro P. *Media Power and Democratization in Brazil: TV Globo and the Dilemmas of Political Accountability.* New York: Routledge, 2012.

Portocarrero, Gonzalo. *Racismo y mestizaje y otros ensayos.* Lima: Fondo Editorial del Congreso del Perú, 2007.

Potencial Pesquisas. *Evolução do eleitorado brasileiro, Brasil em dados.* Salvador, Brazil, 2010. www.potencialpesquisas.com/brasil-em-dados/.

Pravaz, Natasha. "Brazilian *Mulatice*: Performing Race, Gender, and the Nation," *Journal of Latin American Anthropology,* 8:1 (2003), 116–47.

Preuss, Ori. *Bridging the Island: Brazilians' Views of Spanish America and Themselves, 1865–1912.* Madrid: Iberoamericana – Vervuert, 2011.

Queiroz, Maria Isaura Pereira de. *Carnaval brasileiro: o vivido e o mito.* São Paulo: Editora Brasiliense, 1992.

Querino, Manuel Raimundo. *The African Contribution to Brazilian Civilization.* E. Bradford Burns. trans. and ed. Tempe: Arizona State University, Center for Latin American Studies, Special Studies, No. 18, 1978.

Rahier, Jean Muteba. *Black Social Movements in Latin America: From Monocultural Mestizaje to Multiculturalism.* New York: Palgrave Macmillan, 2012.

Reiter, Bernd. *Negotiating Democracy in Brazil: The Politics of Exclusion.* Boulder, CO: FirstForumPress, 2009.

Reiter, Bernd and Gladys L. Mitchell, eds. *Brazil's New Racial Politics.* Boulder, CO: Lynne Rienner Publishers, 2010.

Rennó, Lucio R., Amy E. Smith, Matthew L. Layton, and Frederico Batista Pereira. *Legitimidade e qualidade da democracia no Brasil: uma visão da cidadania.* São Paulo: Intermeios, 2011.

Revista de Cultura Brasileña, no. 1 (marzo 1998).

Ribeiro, Darcy. *O povo brasileiro: a formação e o sentido do Brasil.* 2ª. edn. São Paulo: Companhia das Letras, 1995.

Ribke, Nahuel. "Decoding Television Censorship during the Last Brazilian Military Regime," *Media History,* 17:1 (2011), 49–61.

Ricupero, Bernardo. *O romantismo e a idéia de nação no Brasil (1830–1870).* São Paulo: Martins Fontes, 2004.

———. *Sete lições sobre as intepretações do Brasil.* 2ª. edn. São Paulo: Alameda, 2008.

Ridenti, Marcelo. *Brasilidade revolucionária: um século de cultura e política.* São Paulo: Editora UNESP, 2010.

Ridenti, Marcelo, Elide Rugai Bastos e Denis Rolland. orgs. *Intelectuais e Estado.* Belo Horizonte: Editora UFMG, 2006.

Robb, Peter. *A Death in Brazil: A Book of Omissions.* New York: Henry Holt and Company, 2004.

Rodgers, Daniel T. *Age of Fracture.* Cambridge, MA: The Belknap Press of Harvard University Press, 2011.

———. "Exceptionalism," in Anthony Molho and Gordon Woods, eds. *Imagined Histories: American Historians Interpret the Past.* Princeton, NJ: Princeton University Press, 1998. 21–40.

Rodó, José Enrique. *Ariel.* Madrid: Cáthedra, 2000 [originally published in 1900].

Rodrigues, Alberto Tosi. *O Brasil de Fernando a Fernando: neoliberalismo, corrupção e protesto na política brasileira de 1989 a 1994.* Ijuí, Rio Grande do Sul: Editora UNIJUÍ, 2000.

———. *Diretas Já: o grito preso na garganta.* São Paulo: Editora Fundação Perseu Abramo, 2003.

Rodrigues, João Carlos. *O negro brasileiro no cinema.* Rio de Janeiro: Pallas, 2001.

Rodrigues, José Honório. *Conciliação e reforma no Brasil; um desafio histórico-cultural.* Rio de Janeiro: Editôra Civilização Brasileira, 1965.

Rodrigues Filho, Mário L. *O negro no foot-ball brasileiro.* Rio de Janeiro: Irmãos Pongetti, 1947.

———. *O negro no futebol brasileiro.* Rio de Janeiro: Mauad, 2003.

Rodrigues, Nelson. *A pátria em chuteiras: novas crônicas de futebol*. Ruy Castro, ed. São Paulo: Companhia das Letras, 1994.

———. *À sombra das chuteiras imortais: crônicas de futebol*. Ruy Castro, ed. São Paulo: Companhia das Letras, 1993.

Rodríguez Larreta, Enrique e Guillermo Giucci. *Gilberto Freyre: uma biografia cultural: a formação de um intelectual brasileiro: 1900–1936*. trad. Josely Vianna Baptista. Rio de Janeiro: Civilização Brasileira, 2007.

Rohter, Larry. *Brazil on the Rise: The Story of a Country Transformed*. New York: Palgrave Macmillan, 2010.

Romero, Sílvio. *História da literatura brasileira*. 7ª. edn. 5 v. Rio de Janeiro/Brasília: José Olympio/INL, 1980.

Romero, Simon. "A 'Hermit of the Jungle' Stands Guard in the Amazon," *New York Times* (9 May 2015), A4.

———. "Sócrates, Brazilian Soccer Star and Activist, Dies at 57," *New York Times* (5 December 2011), A21.

Romo, Anadelia A. *Brazil's Living Museum: Race, Reform, and Tradition in Bahia*. Chapel Hill: University of North Carolina Press, 2010.

———. "Rethinking Race and Culture in Brazil's First Afro-Brazilian Congress of 1934," *Journal of Latin American Studies*, 39 (2007), 31–54.

Rosenfeld, Anatol. *Negro, macumba e futebol*. São Paulo: EDUSP, 1993.

Rosenn, Keith S. and Richard Downes, eds. *Corruption and Political Reform in Brazil: The Impact of Collor's Impeachment*. Miami, FL: North-South Center Press at the University of Miami, 1999.

Roth-Gordon, Jennifer. *Race and the Brazilian Body: Blackness, Whiteness, and Everyday Language in Rio de Janeiro*. Oakland: University of California Press, 2017.

Sá, Simone Pereira de. *Baiana internacional: as mediações culturais de Carmen Miranda*. Rio de Janeiro: MIS Editorial, 2002.

Sachs, Ignacy, Jorge Wilheim, and Sérgio Paulo Pinheiro, eds. *Brazil: A Century of Change*. trans. Robert N. Anderson. Chapel Hill: University of North Carolina Press, 2009.

Sadlier, Darlene. *Brazil Imagined: 1500 to the Present*. Austin: University of Texas Press, 2008.

Sahlins, Peter. *Boundaries: The Making of France and Spain in the Pyrenees*. Berkeley: University of California Press, 1989.

Sallum Jr., Brasilio e Guilherme Stolle Paixão e Casarões, "O Impeachment do Presidente Collor: A Literatura e o Processo," *Lua Nova*, 82 (2011), 163–200.

Sanches, Neuza e João Gabriel de Lima. "Entre a tela e a vida real," *Veja* (12 February 1997), 52–56.

Sanders, James E. *The Vanguard of the Atlantic World: Creating Modernity, Nation, and Democracy in Nineteenth-century Latin America*. Durham, NC: Duke University Press, 2014.

Sandroni, Carlos. *Feitiço decente: transformações do samba no Rio de Janeiro, 1917–1933*. Rio de Janeiro: Jorge Zahar Editor, 2001.

Sansone, Livio. *Blackness Without Ethnicity: Constructing Race in Brazil*. New York: Palgrave Macmillan, 2003.

Sant'Anna, Affonso Romano. *O canibalismo amoroso.* São Paulo: Editora Brasiliense, 1984.

Santos, Jocélio Teles dos. "Nação Mestiça: Discursos e Práticas Oficiais sobre os Afro-brasileiros," *Luso-Brazilian Review*, 36:1 (Summer 1999), 19–31.

Santos, Joel Rufino dos. *A história do negro no teatro brasileiro.* Rio de Janeiro: Novas Direções, 2014.

Santos, Milton e María Laura Silveira. *O Brasil: território e sociedade no início do século XXI*, 12ª. edn. Rio de Janeiro: Editora Record, 2008.

Santos, Sales Augusto de and Obianuju C. Anya. "Who Is Black in Brazil?: A Timely or False Question in Brazilian Race Relations in the Era of Affirmative Action?" *Latin American Perspectives*, 33:4 (July 2006), 30–48.

Sarmento, Carlos Eduardo Barbosa. *A construção da nação canarinho: uma história institucional da seleção brasileira de futebol, 1914–1970.* Rio de Janeiro: Editora FGV, 2013.

———. "Futebol e Brasilidade: O Papel do Estado Nacional na Construção do Imaginário acerca da Seleção Brasileira," *Cadernos FGV Projetos*, 5:13 (junho 2010), 57–62.

Sarmiento, Domingo Faustino. *Facundo: civilización y barbarie, vida de Juan Facundo Quiroga.* 7ª. edn. México: Editorial Porrúa, 1989 [first published 1845].

Sayers, Raymond S. *The Negro in Brazilian Literature.* New York: Hispanic Institute in the United States, 1956.

Schelling, Vivian. ed. *Through the Kaleidoscope: The Experience of Modernity in Latin America.* London: Verso, 2007.

Schwarcz, Lilia Moritz. *As barbas do imperador: D. Pedro II, um monarco nos trópicos.* 3ª. edn. São Paulo: Companhia das Letras, 1999.

———. *O espetáculo das raças: cientistas, instituições e questão racial no Brasil, 1870–1930.* São Paulo: Companhia das Letras, 1993.

———. *Nem preto nem branco, muito pelo contrário: cor e raça na sociabilidade brasileira.* São Paulo: Claro Enigma, 2012.

Schwarcz, Lilia Moritz e Letícia Vidor de Souza Reis. orgs. *Negras imagens.* São Paulo: Editora da Universidade de São Paulo: Estação Ciência, 1996.

Schwartzman, Simon. *Bases do autoritarismo brasileiro.* Rio de Janeiro: Campus, 1982.

Schwartzman, Simon, Helena Maria Bosquet Bomeny, Vanda Maria Ribeiro Costa. *Tempos de Capanema.* 2ª. edn. São Paulo: Paz e Terra/Fundação Getúlio Vargas, 2000.

Scott, James C. *Seeing Like a State: How Certain Schemes to Improve the Human Condition Have Failed.* New Haven, CT: Yale University Press, 1998.

Segato, R. L. "The Color-Blind Subject of Myth; Or, Where to Find Africa in the Nation," *Annual Review of Anthropology*, 27 (1998), 129–51.

Seigel, Micol. *Uneven Encounters: Making Race and Nation in Brazil and the United States.* Durham, NC: Duke University Press, 2009.

Sen, Amartya. *Identity and Violence: The Illusions of Destiny.* New York: W. W. Norton, 2006.

Sevcenko, Nicolau. "Futebol, metrópoles e desatinos," *Revista USP*, 22 (Junho–Agosto 1994), 30–37.

————. *Orfeu extático na metrópole: São Paulo, sociedade e cultura nos frementes anos 20*. São Paulo: Companhia das Letras, 1992.

Severiano, Jairo. *Uma história da música popular brasileira: das origens à modernidade*. São Paulo: Editora 34, 2008.

Sexto, Fabio e Joana Dale, "Em Progresso," *Revista O Globo* (14 July 2013), 24–29.

Shaw, Lisa. *Carmen Miranda*. London: Palgrave Macmillan, 2013.

————. "Vargas on Film: From the Newsreel to the *chanchada*," in Jens R. Hentschke. ed. *Vargas and Brazil: New Perspectives*. New York: Palgrave Macmillan, 2006. 207–26.

Shaw, Lisa and Stephanie Dennison. *Brazilian National Cinema*. London: Routledge, 2007.

Sheriff, Robin E. *Dreaming Equality: Color, Race, and Racism in Urban Brazil*. New Brunswick, NJ: Rutgers University Press, 2001.

————. "Embracing Race: Deconstructing Mestiçagem in Rio de Janeiro," *Journal of Latin American Anthropology*, 8:1 (2003), 86–115.

Shirts, Matthew. "Sócrates, Corinthians, and Questions of Democracy and Citizenship," in Joseph L. Arbena, ed. *Sport and Society in Latin America: Diffusion, Dependency, and the Rise of Mass Culture*. New York: Greenwood Press, 1988. 97–112.

Silva, Carlos Eduardo Lins da. *Muito além do Jardim Botânico: um estudo sobre a audiência do Jornal Nacional da Globo entre trabalhadores*. São Paulo: Summus, 1985.

————. "Television in Brazil," in David Ward, ed. *Television and Public Policy: Change and Continuity in an Era of Global Liberalization*. New York: Lawrence Erlbaum Associates, 2008. 27–43.

Silva, Eduardo. "Integração, Globalização e Festa: A Abolição da Escravatura como História Cultural," in Marco Pamplona. org. *Escravidão, exclusão e cidadania*. Rio de Janeiro: Access, 2001. 107–18.

Silva, Fernando de Barros e. *Chico Buarque*. São Paulo: PubliFolha, 2004.

Silva, Nil Castro da. "Culinária e alimentação em Gilberto Freyre: Raça, identidade e modernidade," *Latin American Research Review*, 49:3 (2014), 3–22.

Simis, Anita. *Estado e cinema no Brasil*. São Paulo: Annablume/FAPESP, 1996.

Simões, Inimá F., Alcir Henrique da Costa, Maria Rita Kehl. *Um país no ar: história da TV brasileira em três canais*. São Paulo: Editora Brasiliense S.A., 1986.

Simpson, Amelia. *Xuxa: The Mega-Marketing of Gender, Race, and Modernity*. Philadelphia: Temple University Press, 1993.

Sisario, Ben and Karl Russell. "In Shift to Streaming, Music Business Has Lost Billions," *New York Times* (24 March 2016), www.nytimes.com/2016/03/25/business/media/music-sales-remain-steady-but-lucrative-cd-sales-decline.html?_r=0. [accessed 1 July 2016].

Skidmore, Thomas E. *Black into White: Race and Nationality in Brazilian Thought*. New York: Oxford University Press, 1974.

———. "The Paraguayan War: A Constitutional, Political, and Economic Turning Point for Brazil," in Jessé Souza and Valter Sinder, eds. *Imagining Brazil*. Plymouth, UK: Lexington Books, 2005. 91–101.

———. *The Politics of Military Rule in Brazil, 1964–85*. New York: Oxford University Press, 1988.

———. "Raízes de Gilberto Freyre," *Journal of Latin American Studies*, 34:1 (2002), 1–20.

Skidmore, Thomas E. ed. *Television, Politics, and the Transition to Democracy in Latin America*. Washington, DC: The Woodrow Wilson Center Press/ Baltimore: The Johns Hopkins University Press, 1993.

Slater, Candice. *Stories on a String: The Brazilian Literatura de cordel*. Berkeley: University of California Press, 1982.

Smith, Anthony D. *The Nation in History: Historiographical Debates about Ethnicity and Nationalism*. Hanover, NH: University Press of New England, 2000.

Sodré, Muniz. *Claros e escuros: identidade, povo e mídia no Brasil*. Petrópolis: Editora Vozes, 1999.

Solberg, Helena. dir. *Carmen Miranda: Bananas Is My Business*. Fox, 1995.

Sommer, Doris. *Foundational Fictions: The National Romances of Latin America*. Berkeley: University of California Press, 1991.

Sommer, Doris. ed. *Cultural Agency in the Americas*. Durham, NC: Duke University Press, 2006.

Sorá, Gustavo. *Brasilianas: José Olympio e a gênese do mercado editorial brasileiro*. São Paulo: Editora da Universidade de São Paulo, 2010.

Souza, Denaldo Alchorne de. *O Brasil entra em campo!: construções e reconstruções da identidade nacional (1930–1947)*. São Paulo: Annablume, 2008.

Souza, Ricardo Luiz de. *Identidade nacional e modernidade brasileira: o diálogo entre Sílvio Romero, Euclides da Cunha, Câmara Cascudo e Gilberto Freyre*. Belo Horizonte: Autêntica, 2007.

———. *Identidade nacional, raça e autoritarismo: a Revolução de 1930 e a interpretação do Brasil*. São Paulo: LCTE Editora, 2008.

Sovik, Liv Rebecca. *Aqui ninguém é branco*. Rio de Janeiro: Aeroplano, 2009.

Stam, Robert. *Tropical Multiculturalism: A Comparative History of Race in Brazilian Cinema and Culture*. Durham, NC: Duke University Press, 1997.

Stepan, Nancy Leys. *The Hour of Eugenics: Race, Gender, and Nation in Latin America*. Ithaca, NY: Cornell University Press, 1991.

Straubhaar, Joseph D. "Choosing National TV: Cultural Capital, Language, and Cultural Proximity in Brazil," in Michael G. Elasmar, ed. *The Impact of International Television: A Paradigm Shift*. Mahwah, NJ: Lawrence Erlbaum Associates, Publishers, 2003. 77–110.

———. "Television and Video in the Transition from Military to Civilian Rule in Brazil," *Latin American Research Review*, 24:1 (1989), 150–54.

———. *World Television: From Global to Local*. Los Angeles: Sage Publications, 2007.

Stroud, Sean. *The Defence of Tradition in Brazilian Popular Music: Politics, Culture and the Creation of Música Popular Brasileira.* Aldershot, UK: Ashgate, 2008.

Summerhill, William Roderick. *Order without Progress: Government, Foreign Investment, and Railroads in Brazil, 1854–1913.* Stanford, CA: Stanford University Press, 2003.

Sussman, Robert Wald. *The Myth of Race: The Troubling Persistence of an Unscientific Idea.* Cambridge, MA: Harvard University Press, 2014.

Távola, Artur da. *A telenovela brasileira: história, análise e conteúdo.* São Paulo: Globo, 1996.

Telles, Edward E. *Race in Another America: The Significance of Skin Color in Brazil.* Princeton: Princeton University Press, 2004.

Telles, Edward and Denia Garcia. "*Mestizaje* and Public Opinion in Latin America," *Latin American Research Review*, 48:3 (2013), 130–52.

Telles, Edward and Marcelo Paixão. "Affirmative Action in Brazil," *LASA Forum*, 44:2 (Spring 2013), 10–12.

Telles, Edward and the Project on Ethnicity and Race in Latin America (PERLA). *Pigmentocracies: Ethnicity, Race, and Color in Latin America.* Chapel Hill: The University of North Carolina Press, 2014.

Thelen, David. "Making History and Making the United States," *Journal of American Studies*, 32:3 (1998), 373–97.

Thurner, Mark. *From Two Republics to One Divided: Contradictions of Postcolonial Nationmaking in Andean Peru.* Durham, NC: Duke University Press, 1997.

Tinhorão, José Ramos. *Música popular de índios, negros e mestiços*, 2ª. edn. Petrópolis: Editora Vozes Ltda., 1975.

———. *Pequena história da música popular da modinha à canção de protesto.* Petrópolis: Editora Vozes Ltda., 1974.

Toledo, Roberto Pompeu de. "Rescaldo do rescaldo," *Veja* (23 de julho 2014), 114.

Torres, Alberto. *O problema nacional brasileiro.* São Paulo: Companhia Editora Nacional, 1914.

Touré. *Who's Afraid of Post-Blackness?: What It Means to Be Black Now.* New York: Free Press, 2011.

Treece, David. "Guns and Roses: Bossa Nova and Brazil's Music of Popular Protest, 1958–1968," *Popular Music*, 16:1 (January 1997), 1–29.

Tsuda, Takeyuki. *Strangers in the Ethnic Homeland: Japanese Brazilian Return Migration in Transnational Perspective.* New York: Columbia University Press, 2003.

Tuckman, Jo. *Mexico: Democracy Interrupted.* New Haven, CT: Yale University Press, 2012.

Tufte, Thomas. *Living with the Rubbish Queen: Telenovelas, Culture and Modernity in Brazil.* Luton, UK: University of Luton Press, 2000.

Turino, Thomas. *Nationalists, Cosmopolitans, and Popular Music in Zimbabwe.* Chicago: University of Chicago Press, 2000.

Turra, Cleusa e Gustavo Venturi, orgs. Folha de São Paulo/Datafolha. *Racismo cordial: a mais complete análise sobre o preconceito de cor no Brasil*. São Paulo: Editora Ática, 1995.

Twine, France Winddance. *Racism in a Racial Democracy: The Maintenance of White Supremacy in Brazil*. New Brunswick, NJ: Rutgers University Press, 1997.

Uricoechea, Fernando. *O minotauro imperial: a burocratização do estado patrimonial brasileiro no século XIX*. Rio de Janeiro: Difel, 1978.

Vargas, João H. Costa. "Hyperconsciousness of Race and Its Negation: The Dialectic of White Supremacy in Brazil," *Identities: Global Studies in Culture and Power*, 11:4 (2004), 443–70.

Vasconcelos, José. *The Cosmic Race: A Bilingual Edition*, trans. Didier T. Jaén. Baltimore: The Johns Hopkins University Press, 1997.

———. *La raza cósmica: misión de la raza iberoamericana, notas de viajes a la América del Sur*. Barcelona: Agencia Mundial de Librería, 192-.

Veloso, Caetano. *Verdade tropical*. São Paulo: Companhia das Letras, 1997.

Ventura, Roberto. *Estilo tropical: história cultural e polêmicas literárias no Brasil, 1870–1914*. São Paulo: Companhia das Letras, 1991.

Viana, Francisco José de Oliveira. *Populações meridionais do Brasil: história, organização, psycologia*. São Paulo: Monteiro Lobato, 1921.

———. *Problemas de política objetiva*. São Paulo: Companhia Editora Nacional, 1930.

Vianna, Hermano. *O mistério do samba*. Rio de Janeiro: Zahar, 1995.

———. *The Mystery of Samba: Popular Music and National Identity in Brazil*. ed. and trans. John Charles Chasteen. Chapel Hill: University of North Carolina Press, 1999.

Villoro, Juan. *Dios es redondo*. México: Editorial Planeta Mexicana, 2006.

Wade, Peter. "Blackness, Indigeneity, Multiculturalism and Genomics in Brazil, Colombia, and Mexico," *Journal of Latin American Studies*, 45:2 (May 2013), 205–33.

———. *Race and Ethnicity in Latin America*. London: Pluto Press, 1997.

———. *Race: An Introduction*. Cambridge: Cambridge University Press, 2015.

Wade, Peter, Carlos López Beltrán, Eduardo Restrepo, and Ricardo Ventura Santos, eds. *Mestizo Genomics: Race Mixture, Nation, and Science in Latin America*. Durham, NC: Duke University Press, 2014.

Walker, Sheila S. "Africanity vs. Blackness: Race, Class and Culture in Brazil," *NACLA Report on the Americas*, 35:6 (2002), 16–20.

Wallach, Joe. *Meu capítulo na TV Globo*. texto original editado por Randal Johnson. Rio de Janeiro: Topbooks, 2011.

Walzer, Michael. "On the Role of Symbolism in Political Thought," *Political Science Quarterly*, 82:2 (June 1967), 191–204.

Weber, Eugen. *Peasants into Frenchmen: The Modernization of Rural France, 1870–1914*. Stanford, CA: Stanford University Press, 1976.

Weinstein, Barbara. *The Color of Modernity: São Paulo and the Making of Race and Nation in Brazil*. Durham, NC: Duke University Press, 2015.

———. "Racializing Regional Difference: São Paulo versus Brazil, 1932," in Nancy P. Appelbaum, Anne S. Macpherson, and Karin Alejandra Rosemblatt, eds. *Race and Nation in Modern Latin America*. Chapel Hill: University of North Carolina Press, 2003. 237–62.

Weyland, Kurt. "The Rise and Fall of President Collor and Its Impact on Brazilian Democracy," *Journal of Interamerican Studies and World Affairs*, 35:1 (1993), 1–37.

Whitten, Norman E. *Histories of the Present: People and Power in Ecuador*. Urbana, IL: University of Illinois Press, 2011.

Wiebe, Robert H. "Humanizing Nationalism," *World Policy Journal*, 13:4 (Winter 1996/1997), 81–88.

———. *Who We Are: A History of Popular Nationalism*. Princeton, NJ: Princeton University Press, 2011.

Williams, Daryle. *Culture Wars: The First Vargas Regime, 1930–1945*. Durham, NC: Duke University Press, 2001.

Williamson, Joel. *New People: Miscegenation and Mulattoes in the United States*. New York: The Free Press, 1980.

Wimmer, Andreas. *Ethnic Boundary Making: Institutions, Power, Networks*. New York: Oxford University Press, 2013.

Winant, Howard. "Rethinking Race in Brazil," *Journal of Latin American Studies*, 24:1 (February 1992), 173–92.

Wisnik, José Miguel. "Entre o erudito e o popular," *Revista de História*, 157:2 (2007), 55–72.

———. *Veneno remédio: o futebol e o Brasil*. São Paulo: Companhia das Letras, 2008.

Wolfe, Joel. *Autos and Progress: The Brazilian Search for Modernity*. New York: Oxford University Press, 2010.

Woodward, James P. "Consumer Culture, Market Empire, and the Global South," *Journal of World History*, 23:2 (June 2012), 375–98.

Young, James. "Neymar's Cultural Significance to Brazil Transcends Soccer, World Cup," si.com [accessed 16 July 2014].

Yúdice, George. *The Expediency of Culture: Uses of Culture in the Global Era*. Durham, NC: Duke University Press, 2003.

Zappa, Regina. *Chico Buarque: para todos*. 4ª. edn. Rio de Janeiro: Relume Dumará, 1999.

Zirin, Dave. *Brazil's Dance with the Devil: The World Cup, the Olympics, and the Fight for Democracy*. Chicago: Haymarket Books, 2014.

Index